THE TRAGEDY OF HUNGARIAN JEWRY

Essays, Documents, Depositions

Edited by

RANDOLPH L. BRAHAM

SOCIAL SCIENCE MONOGRAPHS, BOULDER
and
INSTITUTE FOR HOLOCAUST STUDIES OF
THE CITY UNIVERSITY OF NEW YORK
DISTRIBUTED BY COLUMBIA UNIVERSITY PRESS, NEW YORK

1986

EAST EUROPEAN MONOGRAPHS, NO. CCVIII

Holocaust Studies Series

Randolph L. Braham, Editor
The Institute for Holocaust Studies
The Graduate School and University Center
The City University of New York

Previously published books in the Series:
Perspectives on the Holocaust, 1982
Contemporary Views on the Holocaust, 1983
Genocide and Retribution, 1983
The Hungarian Jewish Catastrophe.
A Selected and Annotated
Bibliography, 1984
Jewish Leadership During the Nazi
Era: Patterns of Behavior in the
Free World, 1985
The Holocaust in Hungary, Forty
Years Later, 1985
The Origins of the Holocaust:
Christian Anti-Semitism, 1986
The Halutz Resistance in
Hungary, 1942-1944, 1986

The Holocaust Series is published in cooperation with
the Institute for Holocaust Studies. These books are
outgrowths of lectures, conferences, and research
projects sponsored by the Institute. It is the purpose
of the series to subject the events and circumstances of
the Holocaust to scrutiny by a variety of academics
who bring different scholarly disciplines to the study.
The first three books in the Series were published by
Kluwer-Nijhoff Publishing of Boston.

CONTENTS

DEPOSITIONS

PREFACE

The history of Hungarian Jewry constitutes one of the most fascinating chapters in the history of world Jewry. It is a chapter full of contradictions and replete with paradoxes. In the 1920s, for example, Nahum Sokolov, the head of the World Zionist Organization, referred to Hungarian Jewry as the dried out branch of world Jewry. Yet it was this Jewish community that provided the founder and first leaders of Zionism: Theodor Herzl and Max Nordau. It was also this community that gave the world many of the towering figures of science, arts, and letters of the twentieth century. Among these were the pioneers of atomic physics, of the jet aircraft, and of the computer. The many musicians—composers, conductors, and performing artists—playwrights and writers of Hungarian-Jewish origin enriched not only their homeland but also the world at large.

The burgeoning of this talent was to a large extent made possible by the Hungarian "liberal" regime that emancipated the Jews in 1867. Ironically, it came to fruition only after the First World War, when Hungary adopted an anti-Jewish law—the first country in Europe to do so. It was partially in the wake of this *Numerus Clausus* Law of 1920, which limited the admission of Jews to institutions of higher learning, that many of the talented Jewish students went to Germany and elsewhere in Western Europe to complete their studies. Following the rise of Nazism in Germany, many of these found haven in the Western democracies, especially in the United States.

During the interwar period, when the tide of Nazism was sweeping Europe, Hungary also was preoccupied with the Jewish question and aimed to redress what it called the injustices of Trianon by a chauvinistic revisionist foreign policy pursued in conjunction with the Third Reich. Domestically, it adopted a series of major anti-Jewish laws, depriving

v

the Jews of their basic civil rights and severely curtailing their economic opportunities.

After Hungary joined the war against the Soviet Union on June 27, 1941, its Jewish community suffered thousands of casualties as a result of drives directed against it. Approximately, 63,000 Jews lost their lives before the German occupation of Hungary on March 19, 1944. Of these, close to 42,000 were labor servicemen who had been deployed along the Ukrainian front, close to 20,000 "alien" Jews who were deported in August 1941 and subsequently slaughtered near Kamenets-Podolsk, and about 1,000 Jews who fell victim to "anti-partisan raids" by the Hungarian military in the so-called Délvidék area in January-February 1942. Yet the close to 800,000 Jews (including converts) of Hungary continued to live a relatively normal life while the Jewish communities in the other parts of Nazi-dominated Europe were being systematically eliminated. Although allied to the Axis, the conservative aristocratic regime of Miklós Kállay consistently rejected the ever recurring German demands for the implementation of the Final Solution program. However, when Hungary lost her *de facto* independence in the wake of the German occupation, it was this community that was subjected, through the wholehearted involvement of Hungarian accomplices, to the most ruthless and speediest extermination program of the Nazis.

In retrospect, this tragic phase of the Holocaust ought not to have taken place, for by that date the leaders of the world—both Jewish and non Jewish—were fully acquainted with the details of Auschwitz, and the victory of the Allies was already clearly visible on the horizon. It is not an accident that the most controversial chapters of the Holocaust are intertwined with the tragedy of Hungarian Jewry: the Allies' failure to bomb Auschwitz and of the rail lines leading to the camps; the refusal of the British to open the gates to Palestine; the "blood for trucks" offer proposed by Eichmann with the backing of Himmler; the Zionist negotiations with the SS; the alleged shortsightedness of the Jewish leaders, and the by now legendary activities of Raoul Wallenberg—to cite but a few.

This volume—the ninth in the Holocaust Studies Series of the Institute for Holocaust Studies of The City University of New York—is devoted to this unique chapter of the Holocaust, its antecedents, and its aftermath. It opens with a well-documented overview of the controversies surrounding it by John S. Conway of the University of British Columbia. Yehuda Don of Bar Ilan University provides an economic analysis of the impact of the anti-Jewish laws on the Jews of Budapest. The next two pieces deal with related aspects of the postwar era in Hungary. Victor Kárády, an associate of the École des Hautes Études en Sciences Sociales of Paris, devotes his attention to the social aspects of assimilation, and Péter Várdy, on the faculty of Technische Hogeschool Twente, Enschede, The Netherlands, focuses on the "Jewish realities" in Socialist Hungary.

The "Documents" section contains important contributions by *dramatis personae*. Dr. Denis Silagi, a Revisionist Zionist who settled in Munich after the war, provides an enlightening overview of the background and operations of the Jewish Work Collective (*Zsidó Munkaközösség*), the shortlived anti-establishment organization that tried to offer the Jews an alternative to the course pursued by the conservative, anti-Zionist leadership. Fülöp Freudiger, the former leader of the Orthodox Jewish Community of Budapest, prepared his memoir—*Five Months*—at the request of this editor in 1972. It provides a valuable insight into the workings of the Central Jewish Council (*Központi Zsidó Tanács*) between March 20 and August 9, 1944, and into the dealings between the Jewish leaders and the SS. His recollections of the Council members and of the Zionist leaders associated with the Relief and Rescue Committee of Budapest (*Va'ad Ezra ve'Hazalah be'Budapest*—Vaada) are particularly valuable. In his August 20, 1944, letter addressed to Rudolph (Rezső) Kasztner, the *de facto* head of the *Vaada,* Freudiger expands on the circumstances that surrounded his controversial escape from Hungary earlier in the month. Ottó Roboz, the former director of the Jewish Orphans' Home for Boys of Budapest (*Zsidó Fiuárvaház*), reviews a dramatic chapter of the Holocaust: his personal involvement in the rescue of Jewish children during the murderous Arrow Cross (*Nyilas*) era.

The "Depositions" section includes three testimonies: One by László Ferenczy, the Lieutenant-Colonel of the Hungarian Gendarmerie, who was in charge of the ghettoization-deportation program in April-July, 1944; one by Shulem Offenbach, a leading figure of the *Vaada;* and one by Lajos Stöckler, a member and later head of the Jewish Council of Budapest. These depositions were prepared for the Political Police Division of the Budapest Police Headquarters of the Hungarian State Police

(*Magyar Államrendőrség Budapest Főkapitányságának Politikai Rendészeti Osztálya*) in April-July, 1946 when the Hungarian authorities were considering the possible indictment of the Council and *Vaada* leaders for collaboration.

The views expressed by the authors are theirs alone and do not necessarily reflect those of the editor or of the Institute for Holocaust Studies.

This volume could not have been completed without the wholehearted cooperation of many people. I am indebted to the contributors for the readiness with which they prepared and revised their valuable studies. I am grateful to Dr. Aladár Schöpflin for his skillful translation of the articles which Karády and Várdy submitted in Hungarian. Special thanks are due to President Harold M. Proshansky and Dean Solomon Goldstein of the Graduate School and University Center of The City University of New York for their consistent support of the Institute for Holocaust Studies. I would also like to express my thanks to the Holocaust Survivors Memorial Foundation, the major supporter of the Institute. I am grateful to the leaders of the World Federation of Hungarian Jews for their special contribution toward the publication of this volume. I am particularly grateful to the many contributors to the Special Holocaust Studies Research and Publication Fund, without whom the publication of the Holocaust Studies Series would not be possible. I am particularly grateful to Valerie and Frank Furth and Susan and Marcel Sand for their understanding of the value of Holocaust Studies and for their consistent support of the Institute's work.

Randolph L. Braham
November 1986

ESSAYS

THE HOLOCAUST IN HUNGARY:
RECENT CONTROVERSIES AND RECONSIDERATIONS*

John S. Conway

On March 19, 1944, Hitler ordered German troops to invade Hungary, largely to prevent any defection by the Hungarian authorities from the Axis to the Allied side. This seizure of power was to have fateful and tragic results for the last surviving groups of Jews—around 800,000—in Nazi-occupied Europe. The implications were quickly realized. As early as March 24, in Washington, D.C., President Roosevelt publicly declared:

As a result of the last few days, hundreds of thousands of Jews, who while living under persecution have at least found a haven from

* I am grateful for the advice and assistance in the preparation of this article of Dr. Rudolf Vrba, Associate Professor, Department of Pharmacology, Faculty of Medicine, University of British Columbia. An earlier version, which has since been revised and up-dated, appeared in *Vierteljahrshefte für Zeitgeschichte,* Munich, vol. 32, no. 2, April 1984, pp. 179-212.

1

death in Hungary and the Balkans, are now threatened with annihilation as Hitler's forces descend more heavily on these lands. That these innocent peoples who have already survived a decade of Hitler's fury should perish on the very eve of triumph over the barbarism which their persecution symbolizes, would be a major tragedy.[1]

Yet this tragedy occurred. Within three months of the invasion, more than half of Hungarian Jewry had been mercilessly rounded up and taken to extermination centres in Poland. Between May 15 and July 8, 1944, no fewer than 437,000 Jews were deported from Hungary. The majority were murdered in the gas chambers of Auschwitz-Birkenau or shot in front of hastily-dug cremation pits. The rest of the deportees were used for slave labor, of whom only some 20,000 returned to Budapest after the defeat of Nazi Germany. Only a belated change of mind by Hungary's rulers, the intervention of foreign powers, and the exigencies of the military situation brought the process to a temporary halt in July 1944. By the time the Russian army liberated Budapest in February 1945 less than a quarter of the Jewish population survived.

In the aftermath, rigorous controversies arose, and still continue about how it was possible that the Nazis could successfully organize the killing of so many victims at a time when the German military power was clearly heading for defeat. No less puzzling was the question as to how it was possible for hundreds of thousands of men, women and children to be herded on to trains bound for "resettlement" without offering any signs of active or passive resistance. One key factor was the secrecy which enveloped the whole procedure of the mass murder of Europe's Jews, and especially the eventual fate of those deportation trains sent to unknown destinations in the east. Without the factor of secrecy, the whole Final Solution and the extent and speed of its execution would have been rendered much more difficult and hardly possible. The particular tragedy of the Hungarian Jews was that their deportation and murder took place when this secrecy was already broken. For, by the end of April 1944, the first authentic reports on the mass murders proceeding at Auschwitz, and the plans afoot to destroy the Jews of Hungary, were known, and had been made available to leading representatives of Hungarian Jewry. Al-

though this fact has been recognized before, its significance has not yet
been properly evaluated. The purpose of this article is to point to the cen-
trality of this crucial issue.

A number of recently published studies has already given rise to renewed controversy about these events, especially about the speed and ruthlessness of the German measures, about the collaboration of the Hungarian
authorities, about the complicity of Jewish leaders, and about the inef-
fectiveness of resistance and rescue efforts.[2] In particular, Randolph L.
Braham's monumental two-volume study, *The Politics of Genocide: The
Holocaust in Hungary*[3] gives a masterly survey of the many problems
involved. The availability of new sources for further documentation, for
example from the British and American archives, has brought to light new
perspectives and revealed additional details, which supplement the record
of the appalling barbarity perpetrated by the Germans, as already shown
in the trials of the German war criminals involved, or in the writings of
survivors. These studies have once again raised vital questions. Why had
the facts of the previous Nazi extermination programs in other parts of
Europe not been broadcast? Why were the Jewish masses not warned of
their imminent fate? Why were the Jews of Budapest able to survive while
their less fortunate compatriots in the provinces were daily deported to
Auschwitz by the thousands? What was the response of the Hungarian
people and especially of the Christian churches? Why did the Western
Powers react so hesitatingly and indifferently to the rescue proposals
made? And to what extent was the tragedy of Hungarian Jewry affected
by the actions and inactions of the Jewish leaders themselves?

Many writers have sought to discover the cause of what they consider
to be this preventable tragedy in the failures of one or more of the participants. Such failures, it is held, are all the more culpable because inaction
could no longer be ascribed to ignorance or skepticism about the Nazi's
goals, but must be due to graver causes. In reviewing these controversies,
my objective has been to show that a special feature of the historiography
of the Hungarian Holocaust has been the continuing belief that such
destruction could have been averted if timely steps had been taken in
1944, after so much was already known about the Nazi cold-blooded
genocide in other parts of Europe, and with the end of the war in sight.
Various proposals put forward at the time, such as alerting the victims of

their likely fate, the mobilization of Hungary's Christian population on their behalf, the organization of greater rescue efforts, the opening of the gates of Palestine to refugees, the sabotaging of the railway lines en route to the death camps in Poland, or the bombing of these camps themselves, have each found their advocates, and the failure to adopt one or the other of such schemes has been consistently criticized. But at the same time, the key element of the suppression of knowledge about the Nazi's extermination intentions and procedures in such camps as Auschwitz has not been treated as fully as it deserves. By contrast, the criticisms made of the various actors in this tragedy are frequently linked with the further purpose of the rehabilitation or justification of the motives and policies, by no means all of them creditable, of other actors in this grim story, or alternatively the vindication of more current political, i.e., post-Holocaust, concerns. The result has been the subtle but systematic distortion of the past in order to support the interests of the present. The conclusion is inescapable that the story of the Holocaust in Hungary is not immune to what can only be described as the deliberate forging of alibis.

The Indifference of the Allies

The policies of the Allied Governments, particularly of Great Britain and the United States—though not of the Soviet Union—toward the plight of the Jews of Europe, and especially of Hungarian Jewry, have been extensively criticized in recent years. This forms part of a larger attempt made by several prominent scholars to show that British and Allied policy on the European Jewish question was often deliberately blind to the unfolding catastrophe, and heartless in its feeble efforts to relieve the situation. The inadequate reactions of the British politicians, it is claimed, were compounded by the bureaucratic thinking of the civil servants who advised them whereby British interests, particularly the safeguarding of the British position in Palestine, was given priority over the fate of the Jews of Europe. Britain and the rest of the free world are thereby indicted as sharing the responsibility for the destruction of European Jewry with Nazi Germany and its accomplices.

Walter Laqueur's book, *The Terrible Secret*,[4] covering the initial years of the war, sought to dispel the notion that the persecutions of the Jews in Europe remained unknown to the Allied authorities. He exposed as untrue the comforting alibi of ignorance, which was so frequently adduced after the war, and which tried to explain away the lack of effective action to counteract the impact of the Nazi Holocaust. At first, this ignorance could be attributed to the disruption of all regular sources of information, both public and private, about events in Eastern Europe, by the lack of specialists in the area, or by the preoccupation with military events in Western Europe. But, as Laqueur convincingly shows, by 1941, and especially after the Nazi invasion of the Soviet Union, these deficiencies had been overcome, and lines of communication had been re-established. The second significant factor was the tight security imposed by the Germans on the eventual fate of the Jews. The evidence is clear that the reports of the deportations from all over Europe, beginning in March 1942 from territories outside of Poland, were silent on this point. All that was known was that they were sent "to an unknown destination in the east." The subsequent Nazi decision to annihilate all of European Jewry was an even more closely-guarded secret, so much so that even today its origin is disputed.[5] But by 1942, the mass murder of the Jews in Eastern Europe was being regularly reported to the British and Allied Governments through leading Jewish circles in neutral countries, who in turn had obtained this information from Jewish sources in the occupied areas. Despite the obstacles placed in their way, such reports were frequently reported in the press.[6] For example, the New York journal, *The Jewish Frontier,* as early as September 1942, revealed both the politics and the technology of genocide of Jews as conducted by the Nazis, with a detailed description of the operation of gas chambers in Chelmno provided by three escapees, who had been employed as gravediggers.[7] Two months later, the same journal clearly spelled out all the stages of the Nazi policy:

Nazi savagery climbs inexorably from step to step in a well-defined pattern:

1. to deprive the Jews of civil rights;
2. to drive the Jews out of the economic life and so make it impossible for Jews to sustain themselves;
3. to segregate them in ghettos where they perish of famine and disease;

4. to exterminate those Jews who have not been killed off in fulfillment of the previous stages.

The documents we bring as testimony in this issue reflect various stages
of the master plan, but it is clear from the latest reports that Hitler has
now mounted the final step of the process. The deportation of the Jews
from France and Poland to unknown destinations allows of only the
most sinister explanation.[8]

By the end of that year, the weight of evidence was sufficient to show that
the mass murder of the Jews was taking place on a terrifying and unprecedented scale. Descriptions of these mass murders of Jews in the concentration camps of Belzec, Chelmno, Sobibor and Treblinka—but significantly
not of Auschwitz, the largest extermination centre of all—were now being
provided by Jewish circles in the occupied countries, and made available to
Jewish organizations, such as the American Jewish Congress, the World
Jewish Congress, and the Jewish Agency for Palestine. Their success in
bringing this news to the western public led to the political pressure for
some response, which produced the Allied Declaration of December 1942,
threatening reprisals against all the perpetrators of these awful atrocities.
The evidence of the Holocaust in progress was no longer unknown.

A second characteristic about the Allied response to these events was
the evident skepticism demonstrated by leading circles in Britain and the
U.S.A. about such reports from Eastern Europe. The memories of atro-
city stories from the First World War, which had been given rapid and
uncritical acceptance, now disposed these men to an extreme caution
when faced with what might be only exaggerated rumors, certainly unverifiable by any regular means. As Arthur Koestler noted in 1944, atro-
city stories which went beyond the limits of previous historical experience
could not be linked with the realities of daily life and were consequently
discounted as fictional fabrications.[9] Laqueur seeks to show that, during
the Second World War, this justified doubt about the authenticity of reports of extermination and murder on an unprecedented scale was compounded by the lack of any realization abroad that anti-Semitism was a
central feature of Nazi thinking, or that plans for the genocide of the Jews
were being implemented systematically throughout all of Nazi-occupied
Europe. This was the "terrible secret" which Laqueur believes was sup-

pressed until the end of 1942 for explicable, if not very creditable, psychological reasons, or for more deliberate political grounds.

Two such grounds are extensively analyzed by Bernard Wasserstein in
his book, *Britain and the Jews of Europe, 1939-1945.*[10] The first was the
reluctance of the British government to give the Jewish factor any pre-
eminent position in their declarations about the war. In part this arose
from the legalistic position that the European Jews were technically citizens of their respective homelands. The British war aim was to achieve
total victory as soon as possible in order to rescue all the victims of Nazi
aggression. To have singled out the Jews as deserving of special treatment
or emphasis would not only have offended Britain's European allies, but
would have played directly into Goebbels' hands, with his oft-repeated
claim that the Allies were waging war to protect the interests of the Jews.
A second factor was the recurrent fear of arousing anti-Semitism in Britain
itself. In the panic of 1940, Jewish and anti-Nazi refugees from Germany
and Austria were interned *en masse* as "enemy aliens." Even after most
were released, the Home Office refused to relax its regulations about
letting more Jewish refugees into Britain, partly on grounds of security,
and partly lest they appear to be treated more favorably than the non-
Jewish victims of Nazism. Wasserstein discounts the view that this policy
was the result of deliberate anti-Semitic prejudice, but believes that

> in the government departments concerned no general effort of sym-
> pathetic imagination appears to have been made to understand the
> peculiar predicament of the Jews as a distinct persecuted group.
> . . . Both at home and abroad it helped to prevent Britain from
> giving effective succour to the Jews of Europe.[11]

Wasserstein, however, goes further in his criticisms of British government policy by linking the Holocaust in Europe with the deliberate refusal by Britain to allow increased immigration to Palestine. The adamant
maintenance of the policy of the 1939 White Paper, limiting Jewish immigration to a total of 75,000, and its heartless implementation which
sealed the escape routes, meant that

> during the early part of the war, when the German government tried
> to dispatch large numbers of Jews beyond the borders of the Reich,
> every practicable tactic was employed by the British Government to
> prevent significant numbers of Jews reaching Palestine (or, indeed,
> anywhere else in the Empire). . . . [12]

Hence the British responsibility for the eventual Holocaust is directly related to the disastrous clash of priorities which placed Jewish survival as
only of secondary importance in Britain's wartime policy.

Very much the same criticisms have been advanced about the United
States' policies toward Jewish refugees. Arthur Morse's scathing attack on
the American policy makers, *While Six Million Died*[13] was strengthened by
the more scholarly treatments of Henry Feingold in his book *The Politics
of Rescue,*[14] and by David Wyman's two books, *Paper Walls* and *The
Abandonment of the Jews.*[15] All three strongly criticize Roosevelt for
capitulating to the pressures of the State Department, whose paranoid
obsessions with the danger of "foreign infiltration" successfully blocked
any open door policy toward the acceptance of Jewish refugees throughout the war. Not until 1944 with the creation of the autonomous War
Refugee Board, did the United States begin to take a more active part in
rescue attempts, which were to be particularly significant in the case of
the Hungarian Jews. But by this time, the majority of Jewish victims had
already been murdered. Even though the United States had no direct responsibility for Palestine, the refusal to challenge the British restrictions,
and the pusillanimous treatment of the refugee issue at the abortive
Bermuda Conference of 1943, amounted to a callous insensitivity to the
Jewish catastrophe and hence to a severe indictment by these authors.

By spring of 1944, when the German plans for the elimination of Hungarian Jewry were being implemented, the British government's dilemma
grew more acute. It was no longer possible to ignore the accumulated reports of genocide. At the end of June, the first eyewitness account of the
extermination machinery in Auschwitz, sent through Switzerland, reached
London and was immediately forwarded to the War Cabinet. At the same
time, the Prime Minister was personally informed that Hungarian Jews
were being deported to Auschwitz at the rate of 10,000 to 12,000 a day.
The British government's perplexity was expressed in Churchill's minute

on this telegram: "Foreign Secretary: What can be done? What can be said?"[16]

The subsequent failure of the Allies to take any significant remedial action has been the subject of recent intense criticism, largely drawn from the newly-available records of the British government. The refusal to make the saving of Hungarian Jewish lives in 1944 a primary war aim is seen as the apogee of the British authorities' negative response throughout the war. In an earlier article, I characterized the British government's attitude as lying between apprehension and indifference.[17] More recently, Yehuda Bauer,[18] Bernard Wasserstein, David Wyman, and Martin Gilbert, the offical biographer of Churchill,[19] as well as others in their reviews of these books,[20] have sharpened their attack on the failures of Allied policy. Summarizing the argument, Martin Gilbert commented:

> But above all the story is one of many failures. The failures, shared by all the Allies, were those of imagination, of response, of intelligence, as piecing together and evaluating what was known, of coordination of initiative, and even at times of sympathy. Success lay elsewhere, with the Nazis, in the killings themselves.[21]

The "Blood for Trucks" Proposal and
The Problem of Bombing Auschwitz

Two particular episodes have become the focus points of debate over the fate of the Hungarian Jews, namely the failure to take up the Nazi offer to exchange a million of these Jews for ten thousand trucks, and the failure to bomb Auschwitz and its gas chambers. The notorious "blood for trucks" scheme was a proposal made by Eichmann whereby the Jewish leaders in Hungary would act as intermediaries between the Nazis and the Allies in order to secure trucks for the German war effort in return for the release of Hungarian Jews. In early May 1944 Eichmann arranged for a Hungarian Jewish representative, Joel Brand, to be sent out of Hungary to Istanbul in order to contact the British in the Middle East. This scheme first became publicly known as early as July 1944, when it was leaked to the British press, and denounced as a "monstrous offer," or as an unsophisticated Nazi plot to cause a rift between the Western Allies and the

Soviet Union. In the view of some historians, such as Yehuda Bauer, however, the proposal was both serious and ought to have been supported. Even if the specific terms, by which the West was to make available trucks for use only on the eastern front, were unacceptable, Bauer claims that the negotiations should have been prolonged. The refusal to do so, despite pressure from the American War Refugee Board and the representatives of the Jewish Agency, was lamentable.

> The process of negotiation itself, without leading to any concrete result, might have saved lives. . . . The moral imperative, however, of trying to save even one life was ignored by an Allied world that by its lack of action denied the rationale of its war against the absolute evil that was Nazism. The real conclusion is that Brand did not fail. It was the West that failed.[22]

In the view of others, however, such as Braham and Gilbert, these negotiations were never more than a "brilliantly successful deception."[23] The German aim in launching them was to divert attention while the mass of deportations and murders were taking place. Therefore the longer the negotiations, the better for the Germans. To Eichmann, the need to eliminate any possible obstruction of the extermination process, whether from outside or inside Hungary, was paramount. The eventual failure of the "Brand mission," through the Allies' refusal, was predictable. But by that time the majority of Hungarian Jewry would have been, and indeed were, murdered. The lack of response by the Allies did not therefore affect the Germans' plans. And, even if the Allies had been willing to entertain the idea and continued the secret negotiations beyond July 1944, the time involved in these negotiations would have been enough for Eichmann's deception to succeed to an even better degree.

This division of opinion was already apparent between those who urged the necessity of such negotiations and those who rejected them at the time they were taking place. Thirty years of controversy have not yet resolved the issue or produced agreement on what to some was the most spectacular rescue effort on behalf of Europe's Jews, and to others was no more than a discreditable ruse which never deserved to be taken seriously. Both these views were already expressed in 1944 by the officials of the British and American governments, as is made clear in the extensive exchange of memoranda and telegrams, fully described by Wasserstein and Gilbert. On June 3, 1944, the British informed the Americans that

> We realize importance of not opposing a mere negation of any genuine proposals involving rescue of any Jews and other victims which merit serious consideration. . . . We are yet far from indifferent to the sufferings of the Jews, and have not shut the door to any serious suggestions which may be made and which are compatible with the successful prosecution of the war.[24]

On the other hand, the dubious character of this particular offer made by Brand, and the suspicion that it was nothing more than a "sheer case of blackmail or political warfare" reinforced British fears. In earlier accounts, the British refusal to proceed was attributed solely to their opposition to any steps which might lead to a greater influx of refugees into Palestine. But the further evidence shows that equally forceful arguments were made against any form of negotiations with Nazi Germany which might jeopardize the already strained wartime alliance with the Soviet Union. A further important factor was the secrecy surrounding the actual course of events in Hungary. For example, the British only received the news of the decision by Regent Horthy to suspend deportations two weeks after it had been issued. When this news arrived, the plight of the Hungarians Jews was assumed to be less urgent. At the same time, the State Department in Washington disclosed details of the ransom offer, which led the *London Times* to express the official view in no uncertain terms, as "A Monstrous Offer—German Blackmail—Bartering Jews for Munitions."[25] At the time, such skepticism to these devious schemes seemed justified. The plausible objections against any more striking gestures were in fact reinforced by the antagonisms aroused later in 1944, when the British Minister of State in Cairo, Lord Moyne, was assassinated by Jewish terrorists. In such circumstances, any British initiative to extend more generous help to Hungarian Jewry would have created major political problems at home, especially after the adverse publicity given in the press.

By contrast, the reasons for the Allied refusal to bomb Auschwitz have only recently been clarified. This is one of the main themes of Martin

Gilbert's new book, in which he recapitulates the evidence produced by Bernard Wasserstein in discussing the British policy, and by David Wyman in examining the parallel American options.[26] The suggestion of bombing concentration camps, such as Auschwitz and Treblinka, as can now be seen from the recently opened files of the British Foreign Office and Air Ministry, had been considered in 1943. But it was only a year later that the Allied advance in southern Italy made long-distance raids of this kind more feasible. It was just at this point in the war, namely June 1944, when the Allies were fully committed to the invasion in Normandy, that the British authorities received the information that Auschwitz was now the central extermination plant; simultaneously urgent pleas were received to bomb not only the extermination camp in Birkenau (Auschwitz II) where the Jews were being sent, but also the approaching railways. At the very same time they also gained the first-hand detailed accounts of the assembly-line type of technology of mass-murder in Auschwitz, the news of the daily deportation of Hungarian Jews to this extermination center, as well as the "offer" to exchange Jews for trucks. It is noteworthy that the suggestion for bombing the camps was forwarded to London directly by Jewish representatives in Budapest, Jerusalem and Geneva, and was urged on the British government by the leading Jewish authorities in Britain, including Dr. Chaim Weizmann himself.[27] Yet nothing was done.

Wasserstein argues that, after these representations were made, both the Prime Minister and the Foreign Secretary agreed that Auschwitz should be bombed. However, the idea was blocked by the Foreign Office officials in what was "a striking testimony to the ability of the British civil service to overturn ministerial decisions."[28] Gilbert similarly ascribes the lack of action to a few individuals who

> scotched the Prime Minister's directive, because, as one of them expressed it at the time, to send British pilots to carry it out would have then risked 'valuable lives.'[29]

Diligent research by these ctitics did not take long to discover that in fact equally perilous missions, over even greater distances, were being undertaken at the very same time in 1944, particularly to drop supplies to the Polish underground in Warsaw, or to bomb industrial targets in the areas surrounding Auschwitz. Gilbert follows David Wyman in criticizing the American Air Force leaders who refused to make aircraft available for what was considered "a hazardous round trip flight unescorted of approximately 2,000 miles over enemy territory." Both authors prove that in fact the United States Air Force had repeatedly overflown Auschwitz, though the camp itself was only once hit—by accident. These arguments have been recently reinforced by the discovery of aerial reconnaisance photographs taken between April and December 1944, which clearly show the installations of Auschwitz, including the gas chambers and crematoria, and which were taken by American aircraft flying over the camp. At the time this information was ignored. No systematic attempt was ever made to destroy these installations, or the approaching railway lines.

The bureaucratic hypocrisy of both governments, fobbing off pressure with weak general excuses, is here correctly indicted. Both in London and Washington, the leading officials of the air forces refused to consider as realistic proposals made by civilians, or to change their plans accordingly. The choice and location of bombing targets was a sensitive political issue, as the air commanders well knew. The evidence is clear that they neither encouraged nor welcomed what they considered to be the uninformed interference of interested parties at a time when their priorities were directed elsewhere. "To the American military, Europe's Jews represented an extraneous problem and an unwanted burden."[29]

On the other hand, the supposition, which is at least implied in the title of Gilbert's and Wyman's books, is that if the Allied response to the proposal put forward by the Jewish Agency for the bombing of Auschwitz and its ancillary structures had been positive instead of negative, the murder of the Jews would have been significantly decreased or even stopped. The evidence available at the time or since hardly bears out this contention. In fact there were strong technical grounds for doubting the efficacy of this plan. The British Air Ministry had already expressed its opinion that the bombing of the connecting railways was out of the question.

It is only by an enormous concentration of bomber forces that we have been able to interrupt communications in Normandy; the distance of Silesia from our bases entirely rules out our doing anything of the kind.[30]

Even more conclusive was the fact that such destruction as bombing raids might have been able to achieve would only have meant a temporary, at the maximum, a week's interruption of the extermination process in Auschwitz. The Germans had at their disposal an enormous army of tens of thousands of slave laborers (in Auschwitz and in numerous satellite camps within the Auschwitz district) who would at once have been employed to repair the damage. Sufficient labor was available, and as the Commandant of Auschwitz, Rudolf Hoess, observed in his memoirs, "in Auschwitz everything was possible." In addition, the extermination procedures in use for the newly-arrived Hungarian Jews were not dependent on the continuous use of the crematoria, for large numbers of these victims were in fact gassed in makeshift gas chambers or shot and then burnt in huge pits dug in the nearby woods. The possible destruction of the crematoria would not therefore have altered either the scope or the speed of the murders.[31] The Germans realized that for the enormous number of victims brought from Hungary the technology available was insufficient; they therefore reverted to the methods previously practiced in 1942, before the permanent gas chambers and crematoria were erected. The makeshift gas chambers in wooden barracks and the burning pits could be clearly reconstructed within a few days if not hours.

In reality, as the Jewish Agency in London was forced to admit on July 11, 1944, the bombing of the death camps was "hardly likely to achieve the salvation of the victims to any appreciable extent." Instead, it was claimed, the "main purpose should be its many-sided and far-reaching moral effect."[32] But evidently, the likelihood of success of an appeal based on these vague and unverifiable grounds was judged to be slim, for there is no evidence that this note was forwarded to the appropriate British authorities. The conclusion is inescapable that the idea of bombing Auschwitz in order to prevent the murder of any further Hungarian or other victims, was the product of wishful thinking.

In commenting on these events a generation later, none of these writers mentioned above fully examines or evaluates all the negative factors which led to the rejection of both the proposal made by Joel Brand to exchange

trucks for refugees, and the project for the bombing of Auschwitz. Nor
was the illusionary nature of these schemes exposed. Instead, these authors seek to present a picture of realistic plans to save Jewish lives, which
were "sabotaged" by the inertia or deliberate obstruction of Allied officials, whose unfeeling attitude was succinctly expressed in the comment
of the Head of the British Foreign Office's Southern Department in September 1944:

> In my opinion a disproportionate amount of the time of this Office
> is wasted in dealing with these wailing Jews.[33]

But this desire to blame the Allied Powers for their inaction is not match-
ed by any thorough analysis of their actual capacity for determining
events. The gap between polemics and history thus remains unbridged.
In following this line, Gilbert has skilfully interwoven the story of the
reluctance to assist the Hungarian Jewish victims with the simultaneous
refusal of the British authorities to open the doors of Palestine to the few
survivors who managed to make their way out of Hungary. Seeking asylum
on overcrowded ships, they were ruthlessly turned back or incarcerated
elsewhere before they could reach their goal of safety in Palestine. However, insufficient attention is paid to the fact that the number of those
who could leave Hungary in order to seek such asylum was limited to
hundreds, whereas the extermination procedures of Jews in Hungary were
involving many hundreds of thousands.

Gilbert also quotes from the testimony of survivors in Auschwitz whose
sense of being totally abandoned was only heightened when, far overhead,
Allied aircraft passed them by in favor of other targets. In summary, Gilbert claims,

> it was not German policy, but Allied skepticism and disbelief, as well
> as political considerations and even prejudice, that served to inhibit
> action.[34]

These indictments of the Allied authorities are written in a much more
restrained and balanced fashion than was the case in earlier and more sen-
sational accounts of these dramatic events. Nevertheless the authors' con-

tentions have not been unchallenged. One critic suggests that "the model of conspiratorial indifference hardly encompasses the complexity of motives behind the inaction" of the Allied Powers.[35] Another commentator accuses these authors of using "polemical and emotional arguments," and pertinently asks whether the attempt to make Britain, not Germany, the "guilty party" is not playing into the hands of neo-Nazi revionists.[36] Since the historians Laqueur, Gilbert, Wasserstein and Bauer are undoubtedly united in their loathing of Nazi Germany, it may be more relevant to consider other explanations to account for the fate of Hungarian Jewry in 1944. It may be suggested that the concentration of attack on the failures of the Allies may divert attention away from other actors in this tragic history, in particular from the responses and reactions of the Jewish leaders themselves, especially in Budapest, and to a lesser or similar extent elsewhere.

The Conspiracy of Silence

The behavior of the Jewish people in Nazi-occupied Europe has been one of the most sensitive and emotive issues in the whole Holocaust debate. Particularly since the publication of Hannah Arendt's *Eichmann in Jerusalem*,[37] searching questions have been asked about the response of the Jews themselves, particularly of their leaders, faced with the terrible prospects of victimization, deportation and finally murder under Nazi rule. The earlier picture of the Jews being passive and innocent victims of Nazi ruthlessness, herded like sheep to their slaughter, has now been complemented by a number of books, seeking to show the extent, if not the effectiveness of Jewish resistance.[38] If, in the past two decades, the heated quarrels over these issues have lost some of their agonizing and accusatory tones, the historical realities still have to be confronted and accepted. Amongst these is the fact that the vast majority of those murdered in the Nazi extermination camps were wholly unaware of the terrible end that awaited them. The Jewish masses did not go quietly to their deaths in the Polish extermination centers, but rather were tricked into a passive acceptance by Nazi promises that they were going to live and work in "re-

settlement centers." Although millions were murdered, thousands survived, and these survivors, after the war, were unanimous in their view that
they had never been warned of what lay ahead, as they and their families
embarked on these "resettlement" trains. This was as true for Western as
well for Central and Eastern Europe. Despite the publicity given to the
mass murders in the Allied and neutral press, and the consequent reactions
which were current, for example, in France, the facts never reached the
victims. For instance, a prominent French intellectual, George Wellers, was
one of those taken away on the last deportation train to leave Drancy,
near Paris, for Auschwitz, as late as June 30, 1944. He later recalled
categorically: "We had not the slightest suspicion (in June 1944) of the
systematic extermination to which in fact the Jews were destined at the
end of the deportation journey."[39] The secret was well kept.

The fact, however, remains that a significant number of Jewish leaders
in occupied Europe were aware that the deportees were not going to be
resettled but murdered. Indeed, as noted before, the Jewish leaders were
actively passing this information to the West through neutral countries
and continually stressing its accuracy in order to reinforce their arguments
for Allied intervention. Why then were the Jewish masses kept in ignorance of the Nazi atrocities, especially in Hungary in 1944, when everything
was known about the extermination procedures? Why did they never learn
of the eyewitness reports about Auschwitz or the fateful selection for the
gaschambers of almost 90% of the Jews who arrived there daily in the deportation trains from all over Europe?

The explanation for these fateful developments lies, it may be claimed,
not only in the conditions prevailing in Hungary in 1944, but also in the
events which took place two years earlier in the neighboring territory of
Slovakia.[40] In view of the fact that, on both the Nazi and Jewish sides,
the same considerations prevailed, and even several of the same personal
ities were involved, the pattern followed was too similar to be merely
accidental. Indeed the parallels are striking, in the readiness of certain
members of the Jewish Councils of both countries to enter into secret
negotiations with the Germans, their belief in the possibility of rescuing
themselves and a few select members of the Jewish community, or at least
of obtaining a delay in their own favor from the Nazis or the local authorities, in their willingness to suppress their knowledge of the mass murders,

and in the failure to inform the overwhelming majority of the victims
of their probable fate. A brief description of the Slovakian situation
in 1942 is thus called for.

The Geman decision to implement the expulsion and decimation of
Slovakian Jewry had been taken early in 1942. Pressure was successfully
applied both on the Slovakian government and the newly-created Central
Judenrat in Bratislava to begin the deportations at the end of March 1942.
The *Judenrat* was ordered to prepare lists of all the Slovak Jews, on the
basis of which, in the following six months, nearly 60,000 were transported to Poland in 57 trains, 19 of which were sent to Auschwitz, and 38 to
Lublin, from where they were despatched to Treblinka, Belzec, Sobibor,
Chelmno or to the nearby concentration camp of Maidanek.[41] At the same
time, the Slovakian *Judenrat* transmitted German orders that everyone
on these deportation lists should undertake to sign, before boarding the
trains, a declaration handing over to the Central Jewish Committee in
Bratislava irrevocably and for ever their total property wherever situated"[42]—which relinquished property was promptly seized and divided
between the Slovakian authorities and the German government. The deportees were herded into the trains in batches of 40 to 100 per freight car,
with a supply of food supposedly sufficient for 14 days. The secrecy of
their real destiny was complete.

Already in the Summer of 1942, however, only a few months after
the deportation trains left, at least one of these deportees, Dionys Lenard,
succeeded in escaping and returned to Slovakia, bringing alarming news
about the fate of the Jews in Maidanek camp.[43] These revelations placed
the Jewish Council in a highly compromised position. Their collaboration ,
in preparing the lists of deportees, and their acceptance of the role thrust
on them by the Germans, now took on a much more sinister light. It was
clear from Lenard's report that the German promises of "resettlement"
were a total lie. Lenard's testimony stated: 1) the prisoners taken to
Maidanek were permanently separated from their families; 2) they had no
idea of their families' fate, nor any later contact with them; 3) on arrival
at Maidanek, all prisoners were stripped of their belongings and became
convicts with absolutely no human rights. His conclusion was, correctly,
that these deportees who had voluntarily and without resistance joined the
transport in order not to be separated from their families had been grossly

deceived. Far from being "resettled" together in family groups, they were now bestially handled in the dreadful conditions of the concentration camp. What had up to then been only rumors about the fate of the Jews were now confirmed as terrible truths not only by Lenard but also from other sources.

In response certain members of the Jewish Council decided to establish a secretly-operating "working-party" to make use of this information now in their hands in order to oppose the deportations by appeals and bribery. Among the most prominent members were Rabbi Michael Dov Weissmandel and Gizi Fleischmann. On the one hand, appeals were made to leading Slovakians who were believed to be sympathetic. A well-known rabbi, Armin Frieder, for instance, in August 1942 revealed the facts about the concentration camps to the Minister of Education, Sivak, and through him obtained a secret interview with President Tiso in order to describe the appalling situation and fate of the Jews.[44] He received only a non-committal answer. He doubtless, however, left the President to reflect on the likely repercussions on his own reputation and that of his regime if the facts were to be revealed that he had encouraged and condoned the mass slaughter of Slovakians by handing them over to the Germans. On the other hand, other members of the "working-group" believed that such appeals to the humanity or religious feelings of leading Slovakians, or attempts to secure the recognition of legal rights, were of little avail. Money appeared to be a more effective means. It was largely due to their initiative that during the months following the first deportations of March 1942, considerable bribes were paid over to the officials in charge of the deportation process. The commanders of the concentration camps in Slovakia also received bribes and gifts of furniture. By this means, individuals were rescued from the camps in Slovakia, or furnished with letters of protection, exempting them from deportation "to the East." Suitable bribes were also given to non-Jewish couriers to maintain their contacts abroad, and to assist many refugees who had been warned to flee across the border to Hungary, where they came in contact with the Zionist Relief and Rescue Committee. By late summer 1942, the "working-group" resolved to try an even more risky venture, namely to enter into secret negotiations with the Nazis directly, in particular to seek to bribe the co-ordinator of the deportation program, Dieter Wisliceny, who later admitted having received at this time the sum of $20,000.[45]

In order to obtain these resources, pressure was put on the local Slovakian Jewish population, especially the richer members, and appeals were directed to the Jewish agencies abroad for substantial funds. But at the same time, the members of the "working-group" were aware of the risks involved. For their own safety's sake, they dare not reveal the extent of their own complicity in the organization of the deportations, or the extent of their highly devious and secret negotiations with the Nazis. Both considerations propelled them to maintain extreme secrecy about their knowledge of the mass murders lest alarm and resistance should spread throughout the remaining Jewish community. So long as they maintained the hope of some concessions from the SS through bribery, they were prepared to keep to themselves their knowledge of the facts of the atrocities perpetrated in Poland. Whether this was a condition imposed by Wisliceny or self-induced remains a matter of conjecture.

In October 1942, the deportations from Slovakia came to a temporary halt. As we now know, there were several reasons for this, including the reactions of the Slovakian population to the rumors of the deportees' fate, and the protests launched by the Vatican. The members of the "working-group," however, readily believed that the chief cause was the success of their policy of bribes. Because of this, they began to develop even more "grandiose plans." In late 1942, convinced of the "vital" role played by Wisliceny, these men conceived of the idea of a plan to ransom all of Europe's remaining Jews, except those already in Poland. They sought to obtain Wisliceny's approval to suspend the deportations throughout Europe, totally failing to realize that Wisliceny's influence in the SS hierarchy was far too limited to achieve such a goal; in return Wisliceny demanded the sum of $2 million. As it was quite impossible for the small Slovakian Jewish community to raise such an enormous amount themselves, they took steps, which continued throughout 1943, to appeal to the Jewish agencies concerned with relief and rescue work abroad, including the much wealthier Jewish community in Hungary. Although repeatedly disappointed by the response they received, Weissmandel and his associates apparently continued to believe in the possibility of this so-called "Europa Plan." They added to their entreaties detailed information they had received about the mass murders of Jews proceeding in Poland, which was designed to stress the urgency of providing the sums necessary to secure from the Nazis the halting of further deportations. Weissmandel, as Braham has noted,

> wrote heartbreaking letters to the Jewish leaders in Switzerland, practically accusing them of complicity in the mass murders for failure to heed his desperate appeals. He and his colleagues who lived in the midst of the bloodletting failed—with much justifica-tion—to understand the failure of the free world's Jewish leaders to covertly forward large sums of money.[47]

The fact remains that, despite these vigorous efforts to engage support from both inside and outside Slovakia, the "working-group," neither at that time or in the almost two years that followed, revealed the informa-tion brought by Lenard, or by later escapees, to those victims whose names were placed by the Jewish Councils on the deportation lists. This vital information was never shared with the Jewish masses in Slovakia. Vrba, for instance, was deported to Maidanek on June 14, 1942. He re-calls that, in this transport of some 1,000 Jews, including women and children, no one was made aware of their future fate. They were totally ignorant of the fact that, on arrival at Maidanek, the men would be im-mediately separated from their families, or that the mothers and children would be summarily murdered. Five months later, in September and Octo-ber 1942, well after Lenard's information about this camp was in the hands of the Jewish leaders, further transports were sent from Slovakia. When they arrived in Auschwitz, none of the deportees knew what was in store for them, as Vrba, who had been transferred from Maidanek to Auschwitz in the meanwhile, was able to record with horror and dismay.[47a]

The evidence from Slovakia is thus clear that the leading representatives of the "working-group" not only knew the details of the Nazi mass mur-ders from August 1942 onwards, and readily revealed these facts to the highest Slovakian authorities and to their Jewish colleagues abroad, but also restricted the dissemination of this deadly knowledge to a chosen few of their fellow-Jews in their own communities.[47b] This was the tragic pattern to be repeated in Hungary two years later.

The contrast is glaring between the well-prepared Nazi plans for the elimination of Hungary's Jews, which were implemented following the German seizure of power in March 1944, and the lack of foresight which characterized the leading Jewish factions in Hungary itself. Immediately on his arrival in Budapest in March, Eichmann instituted the well-tried procedures which had successfully worked elsewhere, beginning with the selection of a *Judenrat* from amongst the prominent members of the Jewish community, especially from those known to have influence in the various groups, such as the religious Orthodox and non-Orthodox communities, the Zionists and the leading businessmen. The Germans were, however, well aware that in Hungary, because of the acute shortage of Gestapo manpower, two factors were essential: the co-operation of the Hungarian authorities, and the complicity of the Jewish leadership, without which the passivity of the Jewish masses, so startling to later historians, could never have been achieved. To Eichmann's surprise and delight, he found in the responsible Hungarian authorities, particularly in the Ministry of the Interior, officials who gladly put themselves at the Germans' disposal and eagerly collaborated in the ensuing anti-Jewish measures. It was largely due to this fact that the German plans for the round-up and deportation of Hungarian Jewry were carried out more expeditiously and on a larger scale than in any other occupied country. The motives of these Hungarian officials have never been in doubt and the main perpetrators were duly tried and executed shortly after the end of the war.

Far more controversy has continued over the motives and actions of the leading Jews in Hungary. Their readiness to fall in line with Nazi wishes has aroused vehement contention and debate and still leaves many questions unresolved. R. Braham's thorough study of the Hungarian Holocaust comes to the surprisingly mild conclusion that the members of the Jewish Council, although

> shortsighted, too formalistic and legalistic in their attitude, and often mistaken in their judgment, they were nevertheless personally honorable men, who tried, however ineptly, to save what could still be saved given the unpreparedness and atomization of the Jewish community and the overwhelming power of the Nazis and their Hungarian allies.[48]

On the other hand, later in his book, Braham examines the question of how much was known about the realities of the Nazi extermination program by Hungary's Jewish leaders, and concludes that many of them were fully aware of the mechanized extermination well before the German occupation of March 1944. Not only had refugees and escapees from Slovakia, Poland and elsewhere brought a continuous stream of information, but Budapest was the center of the network of contacts with various Jewish organizations, both inside and outside the area of Nazi control. The Zionist Relief and Rescue Committee, one of whose leading members was Dr. Rudolf (Rezső) Kasztner, set up, according to Braham, a special intelligence unit for interrogating escapees, whose accounts of the whole procedure, from ghettoization to extermination, were carefully monitored.[49] These reports were then forwarded to Istanbul, Jerusalem, or Geneva, where they became one of the chief sources of information supplied by the Jewish Agency to the Western Allies and, indeed, to the public in the West. It is unbelievable, but true that no attempt at all was made to supply the same information to those who were most affected, i.e., the majority of the Jewish population in Nazi-occupied territories who really needed it most.

Even if these reports, as we have seen were frequently received with skepticism by the free world, the Hungarian Jewish leaders were in a much better position to obtain verification, and could discriminate with more accuracy on the basis of their knowledge of the sources. For example, close contacts were maintained between the Relief and Rescue Committee in Hungary and its counterpart in Slovakia from early 1943 onwards. The Slovakians as has been shown were particularly active in sending to Budapest the information that in fact "resettlement" meant annihilation, accompanied by repeated pleas for support. Yet despite these warnings, the Hungarian Jewish leaders failed to take any precautionary measures to alert their fellow-countrymen to the mortal danger, or to inform the Regent or other political leaders of what they knew was happening in the Nazi-controlled countries adjacent to Hungary's borders. This failure, even before the Nazi killing machinery engulfed Hungary, remains unexplained, much less justified. In Braham's opinion, it amounted to a "conspiracy of silence."[50]

Some of the Hungarian Jewish leaders continued to indulge in the illusion that, whatever enormities were committed elsewhere, the same thing could not happen in Hungary.[51] Although fully aware of the *Vaada's* activities and their contacts across the Nazi-held borders, which involved large-scale efforts to supply funds for relief and rescue of refugee Jews, the official leaders' trust in the Hungarian state authorities for protection continued, even after the German seizure of power. But when faced with the reality of Nazi occupation and the preliminary demands imposed on the Jewish Council, some at least recognized that reliance on the Hungarian constitution would not be enough.

In this situation, at least three groups of prominent Jews undertook steps to save themselves, which became well-known after the war and caused acrimonious controversy. The owners of the Manfred Weiss Works, one of the Hungary's largest industrial concerns, signed a secret agreement with *SS-Standartenführer* Kurt Becher, Himmler's personal agent, lightly disguised as being in charge of the Commission for the Registration of Remount Horses, Armaments Staff, who had been sent to Hungary to gain control of such enterprises for the SS behind the backs of the Hungarian government. In return, Becher agreed that the SS would arrange the departure to Portugal of 45 members of the Weiss family, where they arrived at the end of June 1944. The successful escape of this group of Jewish millionaires, with German collaboration and mediated by Jewish authorities, at a time when thousands of their co-religionists were being deported to death every day, was then, and still remains, the subject of bitter recrimination.

A second similar attempt was made by Philipp von Freudiger, the President of the Budapest Orthodox Jewish Congregation, and one of the leading members of the Jewish Council established on Eichmann's orders. According to his own testimony,[52] Freudiger had had extensive contacts with his close associate in Bratislava, and a leading representative of the Slovakian illegal "working-group," Rabbi Weissmandel, who passed on the information that certain of the SS leaders, in particular Dieter Wisliceny, who had been in charge of the deportations from Slovakia, "were susceptible to bribes." Wislicency was brought to Budapest by Eichmann in March 1944, and subsequently showed himself no less willing to deal with Freudiger. Indeed, Freudiger recalls that shortly afterwards Wisliceny handed over to him personally a letter written in Hebrew from Rabbi Weissmandel in which he lamented bitterly that it was now apparently the turn of Hungarian Jewry to suffer the same fate as the rest of the Jews in German-dominated Europe. Weissmandel then proceeded to recommend negotiating with Wisliceny for some plan to ransom "worthy elements" in exchange for two million dollars, as Wisliceny was a "trustworthy man." Accordingly, Freudiger paid over a cash bribe as well as jewelry, as a first install-ment. In return, Wisliceny promised to "take care" of Freudiger and his family, and in fact, in early August (after the deportations of Jews from Hungary were stopped by Horthy's government), when Freudiger's useful-ness to Wisliceny was at an end, his departure to Romania was "arranged." Unaware of the background of Freudiger's sudden and secret flight, and in the mistaken belief that it meant the revived threat of imminent deporta-tion for the remaining Jews, who had no such "connections," the unin-formed Jewish masses in the capital fell into a new panic.[53]

These negotiations overlapped with the above-mentioned and later notor-ious "blood for trucks" scheme, arranged between the members of the SS and the *Vaada*. This episode has been extensively studied in all its aspects in subsequent years, and figured largely in a series of legal actions in Israel during the 1950s and again at the Eichmann trial.[54] The emphasis in these accounts was largely to attempt to exonerate the participants, or more lately to criticize the Allied Powers for their lack of response. Never-theless, certain features are still hotly debated and deserve further con-sideration. Particularly controversial are the character, motives and actions of the chief representative of the *Vaada* involved, Dr. Kasztner, whose stormy career was brought to an end when he was assassinated in Tel Aviv in 1957. To some observers, Kasztner was a hero of the Jewish resistance in promoting attempts to rescue Jews from the clutches of the Nazis; to others, such as Hannah Arendt, his actions were morally disastrous in that in his efforts to save "prominent Zionist Jews" from deportation and death, he collaborated with the SS by implicitly accepting the liquidation of a large proportion of the remainder of Hungarian Jewry by his agree-ment to keep the secret of the Auschwitz machinery of destruction from the victims.[55]

Kasztner's own testimony immediately after the war, and in the sub-sequent libel actions in which he was involved in Israel in the mid-1950s, brought to light a great deal of information about the panic-stricken plight of the Jewish community in Hungary following the German seizure of power. It is clear that all the leading figures regarded the situation as catastrophic, and many were paralyzed with fear. The Zionist leaders, on the other hand, were already persuaded that the same initiatives for negotiations with the invading Germans as had operated in Slovakia, should be tried at least as a means for securing their own temporary safety. Accordingly, on April 5, on the same day as all Hungarian Jews were ordered to wear the Yellow Star, Kasztner and Brand were given Immunity Certificates, freeing them from having to wear the Yellow Star.[56] They were also promised that six hundred Jews would be allowed to emigrate to Palestine, to be selected by the Jewish community themselves. A further one hundred could be added if an extra per capita payment of 100,000 *Pengős* was received. The Germans insisted, however, that this offer must be kept entirely secret, a condition which Kasztner would appear to have accepted. In Braham's opinion, the *Vaada* leaders failed to realize that this offer was no more than a trick. By offering minor exemptions in this way, the larger purpose of the liquidation of Hungarian Jewry could be assured and the Jewish masses would be kept unaware of their fate. Other critics claim that the Zionist leaders were perfectly aware of the SS tactics. Rather they willingly enough sacrificed the non-Zionist majority of Hungarian Jewry in order to secure the survival of those "most valuable Zionist elements" who were to become the pioneer founders of the new Israel, and of course their own survival.[57] In later years, Kasztner maintained that since no other avenues of escape remained for all of Hungarian Jewry, the implementation of the Nazi plans could only be mitigated by these negotiations to save a few "prominent Jews." Indeed, he claimed, the speed with which the Germans began the process of ghettoization and round-up of the Jews made such moves even more necessary. He failed to add that this speed was only possible because of his failure to divulge the information in his possession to those Jews earmarked for "resettlement."

In coming to this conclusion, the evidence is clear that Kasztner's tactics were strongly influenced by his intimate knowledge of events in Slovakia, as outlined above. Not only had he been a frequent visitor to Bratislava and in close touch with Weissmandel and Gizi Fleischmann and other prominent Zionists in Bratislava, such as Oscar Neumann and Oscar Krasnansky, but he had been responsible for assisting their contacts with the Jewish Agency offices in Istanbul and Switzerland. There can be little doubt that he sympathized with these proposals for rescue, and was appalled by the disinterest displayed by the more conservative and legalistically-minded Jewish leaders in Budapest. As a result, the news that Wisliceny had been transferred to Budapest at the end of March 1944 led Kasztner and his Zionist colleagues, with Weissmandel's encouragement, to believe that a new and more vigorous effort should be undertaken. The *Vaada* should now take over the opportunity of attempting to achieve the realization of the "Europa Plan," using the same means of bribing the Nazi officials.[58] The connection is made all the more clear by Wisliceny's reiteration at his first meeting with Kasztner on April 5 of his demand for $2 million. Braham is surely correct in stating that the Germans immediately saw the advantages of exploiting the as yet untapped and much larger Hungarian Jewish resources, while purchasing the complicity of these Jewish leaders. The Nazis also believed that the Zionists had greater international contacts and access to foreign currency than the local Jewish Council members.[59] For his part, there can be little doubt that Kasztner was persuaded that the Slovakian example offered a realistic means for saving at least a number of the now seemingly doomed Jews of Hungary. The price, however, was the maintainance of the conspiracy of silence, which was the pivotal point of the German extermination plans, and which was to have such fateful results.

The Secret of Auschwitz Revealed

It was just at this juncture, at the end of April 1944, that two significant developments occurred. To date, their interrelationship has never been clarified. The first was the escape from Auschwitz of the two young Slovakian Jews, Fred Wetzler and Rudolf Vrba, who successfully eluded pursuit and arrived on April 25 in Zilina, Slovakia, where on the same day they met members of the Slovakian Jewish Council hastily summoned from Bratislava, and immediately wrote an extensive report—frequently referred to as the Vrba-Wetzler report.[60]

The purpose of their escape from Auschwitz, and of their Report, was to warn the remaining Jewish population which still survived, particularly in Hungary, of their imminent fate. It was their belief that the widest possible publicity should be given to the Nazi policy of total annihilation so that the proposed victims would be alerted in time, and would then take action to avoid the fate of the rest of European Jewry, in particular by resisting the efforts of the Nazis to segregate and deport them with the help of the collaborating *Judenräte*. At that time, the two escapees still believed that the Jewish authorities were ignorant of the fate of the "re-settled" millions deported to Poland, since none of those deported to Auschwitz between March 1942 and April 1944, from all the countries of occupied Europe, had any foreknowledge of the true nature of "reset-tlement" before they arrived, and none had been warned in advance. It was only later that they realized the fact of the Jewish Council's shocking duplicity.

The Vrba-Wetzler report described with unprecedented exactitude the extermination procedures in Auschwitz, a detailed layout of the camp facilities, and a memorized list of the transports from all over Europe with the numbers (1,760,000) and nationality of Jews killed in Auschwitz between April 1942 and April 1944. In addition the escapees outlined the preparations already underway to murder the Jews of Hungary, whose arrival in Auschwitz was shortly expected. Vrba and Wetzler specifically urged that immediate steps be taken to warn the Hungarian Jews of their imminent fate by the widest possible dissemination of the information in their report. Further, as Vrba recalled, he argued that the Allied Powers should be informed so that they could organize the bombing of the connecting railways between Hungary and Auschwitz.

The report itself was explicitly factual in order to enhance its value as an unparalleled description of the actual situation in Auschwitz. It contained no hypotheses or warnings about the future, lest these detract from its impact. But the implications for both Slovakia and for Hungary were reported verbally and were so understood by the Slovakian Jewish Council. Already on May 22 we find Rabbi Weissmandel writing to Switzerland recapitulating the evidence drawn from the Vrba-Wetzler report, and calling for urgent steps to prevent the mass destruction of the Hungarian Jews.

Gestern hat man mit der Deportation der ungarischen Juden ostlich der Theiss begonnen . . . . Das ist der erste der Deportation aller ungarischen Juden—und diese erste Teil betragt 320,000 Seelen. [Yesterday the deportation of the Hungarian Jews east of the River Tisza began . . . . This is the first of the deportation of all the Hungarian Jews—and this first lot comprises 320,000 souls.]

In paragraph (1) on p. 1 of this same letter Weissmandel drew attention to the special measures taken to build a new ramp at Auschwitz "um die neue Arbeit der Vernichtung der ungarischen Juden vorzubereiten" [in order to prepare for the new task of the destruction of the Hungarian Jews]. Where could he have got this information from? Obviously from Vrba and Wetzler. He could not have derived this information from the two later escapees, Rosin and Mordowicz, who fled from Auschwitz on May 26 and only reached Slovakia on June 6. But they were able to confirm that these murderous developments had in fact taken place, exactly as predicted by Vrba and Wetzler in April. It is clear that the suggestion is untenable that only in later years did Vrba (and/or Wetzler) seek to take the credit for warning of the imminent fate of the Hungarian Jews. They did so at the time.

The interview between the two escapees and the leaders of the Slovakian Jewish Council took place on April 25-26. On the following day, the report was taken to the Council's headquarters in Bratislava, and copies made to be sent to the Jewish Agency in Istanbul, the World Jewish Congress in Geneva, and the Papal Chargé d'Affaires in Bratislava for onward transmission to the Vatican.[61] In addition, as one of the Jewish Council leaders, Krasnansky, stated, he had summoned Kasztner from Budapest and had given him a copy of the report immediately to take back to Hungary.[62] Another member, Neumann, in his memoirs, later recalled that the text was forwarded to Hungary "shortly" afterwards.[63] Yet, despite this new authentic and irrefutable evidence of the imminent disaster facing the Hungarian Jews, the leaders, in accord with Eichmann's intention, kept these revelations entirely secret, and no immediate steps were taken to alert their fellow-Jews. On the contrary, the Central Jewish Council in Budapest and its recognized successor, as of mid-May, the provisional Executive Committee of the Association of the Jews of Hungary, continued to urge calm and discipline upon all Jews, and to advise them to carry out obediently the Council's instructions, such as, for example, the compilation of lists of Jews, which were indispensable for the future deportation plans. As Braham records, despite the warnings against compliance sent by Zionist representatives in Istanbul, the local Jewish communal leaders faithfully obeyed orders to compile these lists.

> In smaller communities, it was usually the secretary or registrar of the congregation that prepared them; in larger ones, they were usually prepared by young men not yet mobilized for service in the military labor service system. They usually acted in pairs, conscientiously canvassing the entire city, eager not to leave out a single street or building. The lists included given names and surnames, mother's name, address, occupation and age.[64]

The second significant development was the decision by Eichmann himself to take over "negotiations" with the Jews in Budapest. He sent for one of the members of the *Vaada*, Joel Brand, and outlined to him his own grandiose scheme for exchanging a million Jews in return for war-essential goods, such as trucks. Eichmann's motives are far from clear. It is conceivable that he was acting on orders from Berlin, where Himmler, allegedly, was convinced of the need for a quick end to the war, and sought to mobilize international Jewish forces in the West for this purpose by offering to liberate a large number of the surviving Jews in Hungary and elsewhere. It is also conceivable but even less likely in view of the measures taken already at Auschwitz, where preparations for the murder of the Hungarian Jews had been made (and were known) as early as January and February 1944, well before the actual invasion of Hungary, that the SS hoped, even if such a plan failed, to establish an alibi by this "humane" gesture. It has, however, also been argued that in the atmosphere of rivalry and corruption prevailing in Budapest, contradictory policies were put into practice and that Eichmann sought to reassert his own control of events, rather than allow them to be conducted by others, such as his SS rivals, Kurt Becher or Otto Clages. Eichmann himself later claimed that he could not recall who originated this idea, but that in any case it received approval from his superiors.[65] More credible, on the other hand, is the view, as suggested above, that Eichmann's offer was never intended to be more than a deliberate deception to lure the Jewish leaders into complicity with the Nazi plans by dangling in front of them a supposedly tempting offer in return for silence on the true destination of the deportees (as revealed meanwhile by Vrba and Wetzler), while in fact the Nazi deportation procedures were being implemented. In view of the lack of German personnel, and the tensions between the Germans and the Hungarians, Eichmann was well aware that he needed maximum collaboration and strict preservation of the secret of the destination of the "resettled" Jewish masses in order to prevent any violence or panic such as led to the costly suppression of the Jewish ghetto in Warsaw a year before.[66] This danger was magnified by the fact, that during the uprising of Jews in the Warsaw ghetto in 1943, only about 50,000 Jews were in the ghetto and the military position of the Germans was relatively more favorable. In Hungary in the spring of 1944 the situation for Eichmann and his collaborators was much more precarious, as the possible active and/or passive resistance of the great mass of Hungarian Jews presented a danger increased by the vicinity of the advancing Russian troops. It is also credible that, by choosing Brand, one of the representatives of the illegal Zionist *Vaada,* with their links to the allegedly powerful Jewish international organizations rather than any of the "establishment" figures in the newly-established Central Jewish Council, whom he treated with contempt, Eichmann hoped to fan the flames of dissention within the ranks of the Jewish representatives.

There is considerable controversy over the date on which this meeting between Eichmann and Brand took place. According to some sources, it was held on April 25, i.e., at the very day that the Auschwitz revelations were being reported to the Jewish Council in Slovakia.[67] Kasztner, however, in his first postwar memoirs, claimed that the meeting was held only on May 8, that is, after the *Vaada* leaders had learned of the advanced preparations in Auschwitz for the annihilation of their fellow Hungarian Jews, i.e., about two weeks after the arrival of Vrba and Wetzler in Slovakia.[68] Some commentators, such as Gilbert, in accepting the earlier date of April 25, argue that the horrendous facts revealed by Vrba and Wetzler arrived too late:

> Kasztner and his colleagues in the Zionist leadership in Hungary were already committed to their negotiations with Eichmann. . . . They therefore gave no publicity whatsoever to the facts about Auschwitz which were now in their possession.[69]

If, on the other hand, Eichmann's proposal was put to the *Vaada* leaders
only after they were fully aware of the Vrba-Wetzler report with its full
and shocking details on the plans for the murder of the Hungarian Jews,
it would appear that the offer of suppression of these facts was a powerful
bargaining counter designed to obtain better terms from Eichmann. It was
not so much a question of a prior commitment, as Gilbert suggests, but
rather a "deal" by which the Jews would be kept in ignorance of their
imminent fate in return for the release of those prominent Zionists in
whom Kasztner was most interested.[70] In fact, Kasztner from the first
expressed his skepticism about the chances of the success of such a grandiose scheme as the saving of a million Jews through Brand's "mission" to
the West. He obviously did not believe that the Allies would agree to
transport a million Jews to any possible haven of rescue at the time when
the invasion in Western Europe was imminent. Moreover, he opposed the
choice of Brand, and suggested others who would "carry more weight
abroad." On the other hand, the terms set by Eichmann should not be
rejected, if there was any hope for saving at least a few while leaving the
others in ignorance of their imminent death. Moreover, such a "mission"
would serve as an excellent alibi for the future. The fact that Eichmann
was prepared to negotiate at all should be exploited. Later in May, Kasztner
was in fact able to obtain Eichmann's agreement to his own plan for the
specific rescue of a prepared list of Jews. As Braham rightly asked: Was
this one of Eichmann's devices to buy off or perhaps compensate Kasztner
for his "services"? Was it his expression of gratitude for the smooth way
he was able to carry out the anti-Jewish drive, avoiding another Warsaw-
type uprising?[71] This move led eventually to the transfer to Switzerland
in August and December of two trainloads of Hungarian Jews, including
Kasztner's own family and friends, amounting to nearly 1,700 persons
in all.

In the absence of conclusive evidence there can be no final proof that
Eichmann's readiness to grant these and other favors to Kasztner, which
included the freedom to travel easily to Germany and Switzerland for the
remainder of the war, was given in order to prevent any Jewish resistance
from this potentially dangerous group while the Nazi annihilation of the
remainder of Hungary's Jews proceeded. Nor can there be any certainty
that the *Vaada* leaders used their willingness to suppress the Vrba-Wetzler

report in order to press for further concessions, including the organization of the "Brand mission" abroad. Yet the fact remains that the Hungarian Jews were not informed, even though Kasztner and others who possessed Certificates of Immunity were able to travel to various parts of the country, where the measures for rounding up the local Jews were already in progress. Nor did Kasztner and his associates avail themselves of a group of young Jews in Budapest who at the risk of their lives were able to travel illegally and disseminate the content of the Vrba-Wetzler report in the provinces outside Budapest. Nor is there any evidence that this information was shared immediately with all the leading members of the Jewish Council. Freudiger, for example, stated that he received the Vrba-Wetzler report only at the beginning of June, and then in a letter directly from Rabbi Weissmandel in Bratislava.[72] Furthermore the evidence is by no means clear that the *Vaada* leaders in Hungary took active steps to bring this information to the attention of the neutral powers and the Allies.[73] The fact remains that the first copy to reach Geneva in late June was supplied, not by the *Vaada* leaders who, as we have seen, had suppressed this information since April 28, but on the personal initiative of the executive secretary of the Palestine Office in Budapest, Miklós (Moshe) Krausz, behind their backs.[74] Krausz, a rival of Kasztner's, claimed later that he had obtained the Vrba-Wetzler report by chance from a Jewish employee of the Turkish Legation in Budapest only one day, June 18, before he forwarded it to the West, using the good will of a Romanian diplomat (Manoliu) who accidentally was passing at that time through Budapest on a trip to Geneva. It is known that his move was prompted by his knowledge that, during the previous four weeks, some 300,000 Jews had already been deported to Auschwitz, and his consequent disbelief in the schemes undertaken by Kasztner and the *Vaada*.[75] The subsequent publicity given by the western press to the Report and its horrendous contents was immediate and striking. But the evidence is clear that the publication was due to the isolated initiative of Krausz and not the result of the activities of the Jewish leaders in either Slovakia or Hungary.

As in the controversy over Allied policy, opinions are still strongly divided over the significance of the Zionist *Vaada* leaders' silence. On the one hand, it is argued that:

To say that Hungarian Jewry had to rely on their leadership for information regarding the 'Final Solution' is to misread the whole historical situation. This mistake has at its roots the confusion between 'information' and 'knowledge.' The information was there all the time, including information regarding the ways in which the Nazis were misleading and fooling their victims. The point is that this information was rejected, people did not want to know, because knowledge would have caused pain and suffering, and there was seemingly no way out . . . . In the light of the general situation, it seems questionable whether the Jewish leadership and the Jewish people were psychologically capable of absorbing as knowledge what they had at their disposal as information: the fact of the Nazi desire to murder them all.[76]

Or, as the Israeli Attorney General, defending Kasztner at his trial, argued:

Kasztner was convinced and believed that since there was no ray of hope for the Jews of Hungary, almost for none of them, and since he, as a result of his personal despair, did not disclose the secret of the extermination in order not to endanger or frustrate the rescue of the few—therefore he acted in good faith and should not be accused of collaborating with the Nazis in expediting the extermination of the Jews, even though, in fact, he brought about its result.[77]

On the other hand, as one Auschwitz survivor later testified:

Had I known what Auschwitz was, no power on earth could have made me get on that train.[78]

By contrast, the few Jews in Hungary who had been informed of the eventual fate of the deportees were well aware of the significance of Auschwitz. Amongst them were the members of the special transport, selected on Kasztner's initiative, which left Budapest on June 30, destined for Switzerland. While still at the Hungarian border, it appeared that the train would be rerouted through the Bohemian junction of Auspitz. Alarm and panic ensued. At least one person escaped to return to Budapest and raise the alert. Similarly, when the train reached Linz, in Austria, and the occupants were ordered to enter bathrooms for disinfection, the same reaction occurred, as these refugees knew that in Auschwitz the gas chambers were camouflaged as bathrooms. In the event, the passengers were reassured, but the incident clearly shows the contrasts in the responses between the few who had been informed about the horrors of Auschwitz and the many who were not.[79] The conclusion is inevitable: there were two "kinds" of Jews in Hungary; those who knew the purpose behind "resettlement" and those who remained in ignorance that "resettlement" was a Nazi euphemism for mass murder.

It can only be a matter of speculation as to how far the Hungarian masses were "informed" but did not "know" the fate in store for them, or alternatively how much active or passive resistance would have been engendered if their leaders had actively disseminated the facts about Auschwitz in their possession, and repudiated the Nazi and Hungarian propaganda that the Jews were merely being moved to resettlement areas to work for the war effort or to be "reeducated" for "productive work." The fact remains that, however extensive or pervasive the disbelief of the common Jews may have been, the majority were not given the chance to judge for themselves. While some of the Zionist and Orthodox leaders took prompt measures to ensure their own survival, the majority of Hungarian Jewry was deluded into a passive acceptance of their fate because the secrecy of the Vrba-Wetzler report was preserved. As Vrba later recalled:

> As an ex-prisoner of Auschwitz-Birkenau, one who was forced to witness from the closest possible quarters the functioning of this annihilation apparatus, I cannot emphasize sufficiently strongly that secrecy was the main key to its successful operation. . . . No doubt before they left Hungary, they [the deportees] were worried about the real nature of their sinister, unknown destination; but there is a critical difference between vague suspicion and exact knowledge. They were people who had spent their lives under civilized influences and thus they were inclined to hope in their darker hours that, by obedience, they might avoid a massacre of their children. The Jewish leaders in Hungary, though knowing the truth, the detailed facts about Auschwitz, did nothing to dispel this unrealistic hope.[80]

No one can now say how many might have escaped the annihilation process if the Jewish leaders had adopted another course, and openly encouraged escape, resistance and disobedience. In the eyes of some, revelation of the true nature of the destination of the transports would have activated the normal biological instincts of self-preservation. At least, it can be claimed, the proportion of casualties could not have been as great as that suffered by those who were deported so unwittingly to their deaths in Auschwitz. As Vrba again commented:

> How many able-bodied men would have remained passive? If one in ten of those 400,000 had thrown a stone, there would have been quite a hail of stones. A massacre might have followed, but at least they would have been hunted like deer, not slaughtered like pigs. Needless to repeat, that to hunt deer is more difficult and time consuming and the final result is less obvious.[81]

An examination of the figures carefully compiled after the war demonstrates conclusively the truth of this contention. According to Braham, the total Jewish population in Hungary on the eve of the German seizure of power, was 762,007. Excluding the 255,500 who were liberated in 1945 or returned from deportation, the net losses during the occupation amounted to 501,507.[82] Of these, however, no fewer than 437,400 were deported to Auschwitz in the short period of less than two months, May 5 to July 9, 1944.[83] To these must be added the figures of the early transports prior to May 5 and the few deportations which took place later despite the Regent's order for their cessation on July 7. It is clear that the total casualties sustained in the remaining months of the war, even under the impetus of the anti-Semitic killings and terror of the Szálasi regime, amounted to a maximum of some 50,000. The conclusion can therefore be drawn that the overwhelming proportion of Jewish losses occurred in the period of successfully organized deportations while the secret of their eventual fate was suppressed. Had the facts about Auschwitz been broadcast as soon as they were reported at the end of April, and had Horthy been subject to the same pressures as happened in July, the majority of Hungarian Jewry, even if subject to the pogroms, thuggery, persecutions and humiliations of the Hungarian Fascists, would never have perished. The search for responsibility for these unprecedented mass murders in May-July 1944 must therefore include those who maintained silence while thousands of their fellow-citizens were daily taken away to be slaughtered.

The publication of portions of the Vrba-Wetzler report in the Swiss press in the last days of June, and by the Western Allies shortly afterwards,[84] produced a spontaneous international denunciation, which led to protests from the Pope, the U.S. Secretary of State, Cordell Hull, the British Foreign Secretary, Anthony Eden, the International Red Cross and the King of Sweden, amounting to a "bombardment of Horthy's conscience."[85] They indubitably influenced the Regent to order the cessation of the deportations from Hungary on July 7. This fact certainly strengthens the arguments of those who have claimed that an earlier dissemination of this report would have been effective. But, by this time, more than half of Hungary's Jews had been deported to their deaths. From the point of view of the *Vaada* leaders, however, these revelations in the world press were to have serious consequences. The breaking of the conspiracy of silence threatened to remove one of the most significant cards in their hands. If Eichmann and his associates were to believe that the *Vaada* leaders had been responsible for this exposure of the Nazi annihilation process, their hopes for the rescue of the group of prominent Hungarian Jews, which had reached a most delicate stage, would have been completely jeopardized, and they themselves would be in great danger of sharing the fate of the other Jews. Indeed Eichmann's anger at this highly unwelcome publicity, even if it was only released in Switzerland rather than in Hungary, was only diverted by the dubious argument that the leak must have come, not from the *Vaada* leaders in Hungary, but from Slovakia, as the Vrba-Wetzler report originated from two Slovak Jews. As a result, Eichmann ordered one of the most prominent Zionist leaders in Slovakia, Gizi Fleischmann, to be arrested, put in chains, and carried off to Auschwitz under special guard.[86] Despite urgent pleas for her release by her friends among the *Vaada* leaders, Eichmann refused to countermand the order for her murder, on the grounds that she was the author and distributor of these calumnious reports against the Third Reich.[87] The fate of Gizi Fleischmann showed clearly enough the limits to which Eichmann's "goodwill" could be exploited any longer, now that the secret was out, even though only abroad. Eichmann demonstrated that he would by no means remain "benevolent,"

if the terrible secret was to be disseminated among the masses of intended
victims.

Horthy's decision of July 7 to order the cessation of deportations also
caused further dissention within the ranks of the Jewish leaders. Some
now argued that their safety lay in the Regent and in the Hungarian
repulse of Nazi orders. Others argued that the Regent was too weak, that
Hungarian anti-Semitism was still rampant, and that the only chance lay
in the maintenance of their secret contacts with the SS behind the Hungarians' backs. Only thus could they bring the "Brand mission" to a successful conclusion, and secure the release of the two special trainloads
of "emigrants" which Eichmann had now transferred to Bergen-Belsen,
although granting them a better treatment than customary in that place.[88]
The Jewish representatives sought to take advantage of the rivalries within
the SS, particularly between Eichmann and Becher, but still maintained
that they were keeping their side of the bargain to keep the secret of the
Nazi plans from the Jewish masses. They relied on the fact that the information about Auschwitz, which was now shocking the free world,
could not reach Hungary. The efficiency of the broadcast messages from
England was hampered by the fact that all Jewish-owned receiving apparatus was long since confiscated and draconian measures were applied
to listeners of foreign broadcasts, Jew or non-Jew alike. The willingness to
suppress the information inside Hungary by mere silence was still a significant bargaining counter.

Later in July, the denunciation by the Western Powers of the "blood
for trucks" proposal demonstrated that even the full possession of information about the Nazi atrocities was not enough to alter the Allied priorities.
It also destroyed the illusionary hope among the Jewish leaders in Hungary
that the "Brand mission" could succeed. The only avenue left was Kasztner's convoluted negotiations with the SS, which now began a new phase
through intermediaries in Switzerland.[89] Throughout, however, Kasztner
and his associates continued to withhold the information about Auschwitz in order to secure the best possible bargain for the handful of Jews,
who did, in the end, reach the safety of Swiss territory in August and
December 1944.

In October, the overthrow of Horthy's regime, and the installation of
Szálasi's Arrow Cross supporters intensified the pogrom-like persecution

of the surviving Jews and removed the final chance for any successful rescue attempts from Hungarian soil. By that time the Germans did not have such organizational and technical means to conduct mass deportations from Hungary, as they had in May-July 1944. Nevertheless, they managed to organize death-marches of Jews toward Austria during which thousands perished. At the end of November a special area of Budapest was established as a Jewish ghetto, which was sealed off on December 10. By the end of January, it contained nearly 70,000 persons. Suffering from starvation and rampant diseases, and subject to constant plundering and violence from Arrow Cross thugs, the surviving Jews of Budapest were finally rescued when Russian troops liberated the city in February 1945.

Conclusion

The staggering losses suffered by Hungarian Jewry in the short months of German occupation have been calculated at over 500,000 persons. They comprise almost one-tenth of the whole tragedy of the Holocaust. Their swift annihilation serves to demonstrate how effectively the machinery of destruction could be deployed in the perpetration of this infamy. As a case study in the politics of genocide, the Final Solution in Hungary was unique not only because of the speed and scale on which it was carried out, but also because of the worldwide attention it so quickly evoked. Already in 1944, the insistent questions were being posed: could more have been done to avert, or at least to mitigate, the tragedy, by the Hungarians, by the churches, by the Allies, by the Jews themselves?

Inevitably, the answers of historians and other writers to these questions have been colored not merely by their analysis of the events, but also by more contemporary concerns. Jewish historians in the State of Israel and elsewhere have sought to portray the Holocaust as the basis of Israel's national identity in order to affirm the need for national survival in a judaeophobic world. Critics of the churches have stressed the bleakly anti-Semitic record of Christian doctrine and practices, lest these again find nourishment in church circles. Critics of the Allied Powers lay emphasis on the failures of British and American policy, for fear that another such "betrayal" might be repeatable. Marxist historians have waged a continuing campaign against the Zionist leaders of the war-time period in order to justify the present wave of anti-Zionist propaganda. Theologians have wrestled with the problem of the irreconcilability of such mass human slaughter with the idea of God's benign providence. Political scientists have been concerned with the implications of the technological and bureaucratic machinery of large-scale annihilation for political purposes.

Jewish writers, in turn, have sought to balance these often theoretical and abstract discussions with a factual emphasis on European Jewry's responses in the daily struggle for survival against overwhelming odds. Over the past two decades, much has been written to show that the earlier picture of the Jews accepting their fate like sheep is no longer tenable. The alleged passivity of the Jewish masses when faced with physical destruction was not caused by their "inferiority" as the Nazis asserted, nor by their "inability to comprehend the truth" as Bauer claimed, nor by their "having lost the will to live" as Bettelheim contended.[90] The facts are less mystical. The strange lack of resistance, so contrary to every biological urge for self-preservation, and so distressing to most later observers, becomes less incomprehensible once it is realized how much the Nazi terror depended for its success on the maintenance of secrecy. Once this was broken, many forms of resistance, both active and passive, both physical and spiritual, were practiced by the intended victims. But the special tragedy of the Hungarian Jews, it may be claimed, was that this conspiracy of silence was maintained for too long, not only by the Nazis' deliberate deception, or by the Allies' skepticism and insensitivity, but also by those of the Jewish leaders who knew only too well the full details of the methodical and ruthless slaughter proceeding in their midst.

Faced with the unprecedented enormity of the Holocaust, we can realize, as Elie Wiesel has said, that "all questions pertaining to Auschwitz lead to anguish." But as the historiography of the Hungarian Jewish Holocaust shows, political interest and emotional resentments still play their part in the continuing debate and controversy which these events have prompted. Yet, as Yehuda Bauer has rightly warned, the result is the danger of mystification and mythification.[91] The pursuit of partial, or politically-motivated explanations diminishes the significance of the Holocaust in its entirety. For, in the years since 1945, the realization has grown that the Holocaust was not just a by-product of a world war, nor just the set purpose of a single German madman, nor just the affair of the Jewish victims, but rather was an indictment of the whole civilized world which failed to prevent the deliberately planned murder of millions of human beings. The desire to pin down the responsibility for all these brutal events by laying the blame on one or another of the participants, or by exculpating others, may stem from the insistent need to find an explanation for such unprecedented horrors, or to respect the political exigencies of today. But, in the long run, such attempts, if they sacrifice objectivity for polemical purpose, do a disservice to the memory of the victims of the Nazi-organized Holocaust and to the total truth about man's inhumanity to man.

The author wishes to express his gratitude to the Social Sciences and Humanities Research Council of Canada for assistance in the preparation of this research.

NOTES

1. Transcript in Franklin D. Roosevelt Library, 'FDR Press Conferences 1933-1945, folios 112-5, quoted in M. Gilbert, *Auschwitz and the Allies.* London: Holt, Rinehart and Winston, 1981, p. 184.

2. Y. Bauer, *Holocaust in Historical Perspective.* Seattle: University of Washington Press, 1978, 181 p.; Y. Bauer, *The Jewish Emergence from Powerlessness.* Toronto: University of Toronto Press, 1979, 89 p.; Helen Fein, *Accounting for Genocide.* New York: Free Press, 1979, 468 p.; Gilbert, op. cit.

3. R. Braham, *The Politics of Genocide: The Holocaust in Hungary.* New York: Columbia University Press, 1981, 2 vols., 1269 p.

4. W. Laqueur, *The Terrible Secret. An Investigation into the Suppression of Information about Hitler's 'Final Solution.'* London: Weidenfeld and Nicolson, 1980, 262 p.

5. M. Broszat, David Irving, Hitler und der 'Befehl' zur Judenvernichtung. *Vierteljahrshefte für Zeitgeschichte,* Munich, vol. 25, no. 4, 1977, pp. 739 ff.; also C. Browning, Eine Antwort auf Martin Broszats Thesen zur Genesis der Endlösung. Ibid., vol. 29, no. 1, 1981, pp. 97 ff.

The Tragedy of Hungarian Jewry

6. See *Daily Telegraph,* London, 25 and 30 June 1942 for the first such reports; also *Palestine Post,* Jerusalem, November and December 1942.

7. *Jewish Frontier,* New York, September 1942.

8. *Jewish Frontier* (Special issue: Jews under the Axis 1939-42.) New York, November 1942.

9. A. Koestler, On Disbelieving Atrocities. *New York Times Magazine,* New York, January 1944.

10. B. Wasserstein, *Britain and the Jews of Europe 1939-1945.* New York: Oxford University Press, 1979, 389 p.

11. Ibid., pp. 132-133.

12. Ibid., p. 80.

13. A. D. Morse, *While Six Million Died. A Chronicle of American Apathy.* New York: Random House, 1968, 420 p.

14. H. L. Feingold, *The Politics of Rescue: The Roosevelt Administration and the Holocaust, 1938-1945.* New Brunswick, N.J.: Rutgers University Press, 1970, 394 p.

15. D. S. Wyman, *Paper Walls: America and the Refugee Crisis 1938-1941.* Amherst, Mass.: University of Massachusetts Press, 1968, 306 p.; *The Abandonment of the Jews: America and the Holocaust, 1941-1945.* New York: Pantheon Books, 1984, 444 p.

16. Public Record Office (P.R.O.), London. Foreign Office 371/42807, Minute by Prime Minister Churchill, 29 June 1944.

17. J. S. Conway, Between Apprehension and Indifference: Allied Attitudes to the Destruction of Hungarian Jewry. *Wiener Library Bulletin,* London, vol. XXVII New Series 30-31, 1973/4, pp. 37-48.

18. Y. Bauer, op. cit., and *American Jewry and the Holocaust. The American Jewish Joint Distribution Committee, 1939-1945.* Detroit: Wayne State University Press, 1981, 522 p.

19. M. Gilbert, op. cit.

20. For example, Z. Steiner in *Financial Times,* August 4, 1979; N. Goldmann interview in *Guardian Weekly,* August 2, 1981.

21. *Sunday Times,* London, 23 August 1981; Gilbert, op. cit., p. 341.

22. Y. Bauer, *The Holocaust in Historical Perspective,* pp. 154-155.

23. M. Gilbert, While the Allies Dithered. *Jewish Chronicle,* London, September 18, 1981, pp. 24-25.

24.   P.R.O.: PREM 4/51/10/1394: Foreign Office to Washington, June 3, 1944.

25.   *The Times,* London, July 20, 1944.

26.   D. S. Wyman, "Why Auschwitz Was Never Bombed" in his *The Abandonment of the Jews,* chap. 15. (First printed in *Commentary,* New York, vol. 65, no. 5, May 1978, pp. 37-46.) The first account in German of these events, written by the radio jounalist Heiner Lichtenstein, *Warum Auschwitz nicht bombardiert wurde* (Cologne: Bund Verlag, 1980, 183 p.) is based almost entirely on the evidence produced by Wasserstein and Wyman. He seeks to lay the principal blame for the failure of the Americans to undertake the bombing of Auschwitz on the then Assistant Secretary in the U.S. War Department, John J. McCloy.

27.   M. Gilbert, op. cit., p. 267. Weizmann's memoris—*Trial and Error,* London and New York: Harper Books, 1949, 493 p.—make no reference at all to this attempt.

28.   B. Wasserstein, op. cit., p. 316.

29.   M. Gilbert, op. cit., p. 341.

29a. D. S. Wyman, *The Abandonment,* p. 307.

30.   P.R.O.: F.O. 371/42809, WR 277, folios 147-148, quoted in M. Gilbert, op. cit., p. 285.

31.   The first crematorium to be built in Auschwitz-Birkenau was erected in February 1943, and the final and fourth was completed at the end of that year. Mass murders of Jews were, however, already begun in April 1942, and the number of those killed did not significantly increase with the new buildings. See also the account by Filip Müller, *Eyewitness Auschwitz: Three Years in the Gas Chambers.* New York: Stein and Day, 1979, 180 p. However, some passages contain inaccuracies, especially about the origins of the Vrba-Wetzler report.

32.   M. Gilbert, op. cit., p. 279.

33.   P.R.O.: F.O. 371/42817.

34.   M. Gilbert, op. cit., p. viii; Wyman's verdict is similar: "Roosevelt's personal feelings about the Holocaust can not be determined. . . . There are indications that he was concerned about Jewish problems. But he gave little attention to them . . . . In the end, the era's most prominent symbol of humanitarianism turned away from one of history's most compelling moral challenges." *The Abandonment,* p. 313.

35.   H. L. Feingold, "The Government Response." In: *The Holocaust: Ideology, Bureaucracy and Genocide.* Edited by H. Friedlander and S. Milton. New York: Kraus International Publications, 1980, p. 245.

36.   See J. P. Fox's review of B. Wasserstein's work in *European Studies Review,* London, vol. 10, no. 1, January 1980, pp. 138-146, and rejoinder in ibid., vol. 10, no. 4, October 1980, pp. 490-492.

37.   H. Arendt, *Eichmann in Jerusalem. A Report on the Banality of Evil.* New York: Viking Press, 1963, 275 p.

38.   See R. Ainzstein, *Jewish Resistance in Nazi-Occupied Europe.* New York: Holocaust Library, 1974, 238 p.; L. S. Dawidowicz, *The War Against the Jews, 1933-1945.* New York: Holt, Rinehart and Winston, 1975, 460 p.; E. Kulka, "Five Escapees from Auschwitz." In: *They Fought Back.* Edited by Y. Suhl. New York: Crown Publishers, 1967, 327 p.; I. Trunk, *Judenrat: The Jewish Councils in Eastern Europe Under Nazi Control.* New York: Macmillan, 1972, 664 p.; Y. Bauer, *The Jewish Emergence from Powerlessness.* Toronto: University of Toronto Press, 1979, 181 p.

39.   G. Wellers, *L'étoile jaune.* Paris: Fayard, 1948, p. 229. Hermann Langbein, *Menschen in Auschwitz.* Vienna: Europa Verlag, 1972, 607 p. Langbein compiled a lengthy list of testimonies to the ignorance of those sent to Auschwitz about their future fates. See especially pp. 84-88, 140-142.

40.   See the account by L. Lipscher, *Die Juden im Slovakischen Staat, 1939-1945.* Munich: Veroffentlichungen des Collegium Carolinum 35, 1980, 210 p. and L. Rothkirchen, *The Destruction of Slovak Jewry. A Documentary History,* Jerusalem: Yad Washem, 1961, 257 p. (Hebrew with English summary.) See also her updated account, The Slovak Enigma: A Reassessment of the Halt to the Deportations. *East Central Europe,* Pittsburgh, vol. 10, parts 1-2, 1983, pp. 3-13.

41.   L. Lipscher, op. cit., p. 121.

42.   Ibid., p. 109.

43.   Ibid., p. 126; Rothkirchen, The Slovak Enigma, pp. 5-6 and fn 12.

44.   Ibid., pp. 132, 189.

45.   Ibid., p. 127.

46.   R. Braham, op. cit., pp. 702-703 and 937-938. See also Rothkirchen, op. cit., pp. 237-242. Those who seek to portray the Slovak Jew-

ish Council's operations more favorably, such as M. N. Penkower (*The Jews Were Expendable. Free World Diplomacy and the Holocaust,* Urbana: University of Illinois Press, 1983, 429 p.) ignore the fact that little was done to warn the victims but rather claim that "The Slovak Jewish underground could do nothing more" (p. 185); see also Y. Bauer, *American Jewry and the Holocaust,* chap. 15.

47. R. Braham, op. cit., p. 938.

47a. Y. Bauer, *American Jewry,* p. 367 states unequivocally that Gizi Fleischmann was aware at the end of August 1942 that deportation was synonymous with death. On August 27 she wrote to her contacts in Switzerland, "The fact that this mass killing continues unabated can drive one to madness. The news received last week from emissaries has no precedent in history." Bauer fails to explain why this information was not transmitted to those deported on these later transports.

47b This silence also extended towards the several thousand Slovakian Jews who had fled to Hungary, where they remained in relative security from 1942 to 1944. But despite the contacts they maintained with the Slovakian Jewish Council, they were never told, nor were they able to inform their Hungarian hosts and relatives, of the policy of total annihilation which might soon, and indeed did, engulf the Hungarian Jews as well. See L. Lipscher, op. cit., and R. Braham, op. cit.

48. R. Braham, op. cit., p. 425.

49. Ibid., p. 700.

50. Ibid., chap. 23.

51. Ibid., p. 92.

52. P. Freudiger, *Five Months,* typed manuscript dated November 1972, p. 6 (Available in R. Braham's possession; for printed version, see pp. 237-287.)

53. R. Braham, op. cit., p. 792.

54. See *Der Kasztner-Bericht über Eichmanns Menschenhandel in Ungarn.* Edited by E. Landau. Munich: Kindler, 1961, 368 p.; A. Biss, *Der Stopp der Endlösung.* Stuttgart: Seewald Verlag, 1966, English translation, *A Million Jews to Save.* London: Hutchinson 1973, 220 p.; W. Laqueur, The Kasztner Case: Aftermath of Catastrophe. *Commentary,* New York, vol. xx, 1955, pp. 500-511; R. Braham, op. cit., pp. 705-724, 932-976; Y. Bauer, *The Holocaust,* chap. 4; and *Jewish Emergence,* chap. 1.

55. H. Arendt, op. cit., revised and enlarged edition 1976, p. 172; H. Fein, op. cit., p. 130.

56.   A. Biss, op. cit., English edition, p. 29; R. Braham, op. cit., pp. 939-940.

57.   This is the tenor of Communist historians and propagandists, especially in the Soviet Union, but also of some non-Zionist Jews. See Reb Moshe Shonfeld, *The Holocaust Victims Accuse,* Brooklyn, N.Y.: Neturei Karta of USA, 1977, 124 p., quoted in R. Braham, op. cit., p. 720. See also R. Vrba and A. Bestic, *I Cannot Forgive.* London: Sidgwick and Jackson, 1963, 278 p. and B. Hecht, *Perfidy.* New York: Julian Messner, 1961, 281 p.

58.   *Der Kasztner Bericht,* p. 72; A. Biss, op. cit., p. 28.

59.   R. Braham, op. cit., p. 938.

60.   This report is frequently described under different names. For example, Braham refers to the Auschwitz Protocols (pp. 708-716); other authors refer to it as the Auschwitz Report. Here it is cited by the names of the two authors. The text was first published in English in November 1944 by the War Refugee Board in Washington, D.C., under the title "German Extermination Camps—Auschwitz and Birkenau." In fact this document includes not only the evidence provided by Vrba and Wetzler, but also a previous report made by an unnamed Polish major which would appear to date from late 1943. Also included was the evidence given by two further escapees, Mordowicz and Rosin, who arrived in Slovakia on June 6, bringing information about the mass murder of the Hungarian Jews, which confirmed that supplied by Vrba and Wetzler. The Vrba-Wetzler Report is discussed fully in J. S. Conway, Fruhe Augenzeugenberichte aus Auschwitz. Glaubwurdigkeit und Wirkungsgeschichte. *Vierteljahrshefte für Zeitgeschichte,* Munich, vol. 27, no. 2, 1979, pp. 260-284. The full text of the Vrba-Wetzler portion of this report is printed in *Zeitgeschichte,* Vienna, vol. 8, no. 11/12, August/September 1981, pp. 413-442. See also R. Vrba and A. Bestic, op. cit., pp. 248 ff.; M. Gilbert, op. cit., pp. 202-225.

61.   This note was forwarded to the Vatican from Bratislava via Switzerland on May 22. See *Actes et Documents du Saint Siege.* Vatican City: Libreria Editrice Vaticana, 1980, vol. 10, no. 204. Unfortunately it would appear that, due to the difficulties in communications, it only arrived at the Vatican in late October.

62.   See R. Braham, op. cit., p. 711; Krasnansky later recalled that "a copy of the report was sent to Dr. Kasztner, to give to the Reich Adminis-

trator Horthy and to Prince Primate Serédi. At the request of Dr. Kasztner, I mayself translated the report into Hungarian." E. Kulka, "Five Escapees from Auschwitz." In: *They Fought Back*. Edited by Y. Suhl. New York: Crown Publishers, 1967, p. 234.

63.   O. Neumann, *Im Schatten des Todes*. Tel Aviv. Olamenu, 1956, pp. 178-182 as quoted in R. Braham, op. cit., p. 711.

64.   R. Braham, op. cit., p. 532.

65.   H. Arendt, op. cit., p. 25.

66.   Eichmann Tells His Own Damning Story. *Life*, New York, vol. 49, no. 23, 5 December 1966, p. 146.

67.   A. Biss, op. cit., p. 39; R. Braham, op. cit., p. 941.

68.   *Der Kasztner-Bericht*, op. cit., pp. 86-89; A. Weissberg, *Advocate for the Dead*. London: A. Deutsch, 1958, pp. 83-89.

69.   M. Gilbert, op. cit., p. 204.

70.   A. Biss, op. cit., p. 43 ff.

71.   R. Braham, op. cit., p. 952.

72.   P. Freudiger, op. cit., p. 19; but Braham questions this statement referring to Freudiger's testimony at the Eichmann trial, when he stated that he had received this letter "a few days before the 15th of May, on the 10th or 11th." R. Braham, op. cit., p. 711.

73.   R. Braham states (p. 979) that Kasztner and the other *Vaada* leaders in both Budapest and Bratislava had sent such reports to the *Hech-alutz*, to AJDC and the World Jewish Congress in Switzerland several months earlier. However, he also asks (p. 715) why the Jewish leaders in Hungary, Switzerland and elsewhere did not publish these reports, nor the Vrba-Wetzler report immediately after they were supposed to have received copies in late April or early May 1944. The lack of reaction in Switzerland until late June suggests that no such report was received there at any earlier date, and indeed may not have been sent at all.

74.   R. Braham, op. cit., p. 712; W. Rings, *Advokaten des Feindes*. Vienna: Econ-Verlag, 1966, pp. 140-148.

75.   R. Braham, op. cit., pp. 712, 741, 978-9. Krausz later appeared as one of the prosecution witnesses against Kasztner in the 1954 libel trial in Jerusalem.

76.   Y. Bauer, *The Holocaust*, pp. 106-107.

77.   As quoted in R. Braham, op. cit., p. 721.

78.   Ibid., p. 973.

79.   A. Biss, op. cit., p. 81, also R. Braham, op. cit., p. 956.

80.   R. Vrba, Footnote to Auschwitz Report. *Jewish Currents,* New York, vol. 20, no. 3, March 1966, p. 23. (The actual figure should be 437,000.)

81.   Ibid., p. 26.

82.   R. Braham, op. cit., p. 1144.

83.   Ibid., p. 607.

84.   See J. S. Conway, "Frühe Augenzeugenberichte aus Auschwitz," op. cit., p. 273 ff. and J. S. Conway, "Between Indifference and Apprehension," op. cit., pp. 41 ff.

85.   G. Reitlinger, *The Final Solution.* London: Vallentine, Mitchell, 1961, p. 432; also R. Braham, op. cit., pp. 1070-71, 1078, 1085, 1110-12.

86.   A. Biss, op. cit., p. 118.

87.   Loc. cit.; see also L. Lipscher, op. cit., p. 180 for a different but not necessarily incompatible version of her fate.

88.   A. Biss, op. cit., p. 81.

89.   Y. Bauer, Onkel Saly—Die Verhandlungen des Saly Mayer zur Rettung der Juden, 1944-5. *Vierteljahrshefte für Zeitgeschichte,* Munich, vol. 25, no. 2, 1977, pp. 188-219.

90.   B. Bettelheim, *The Informed Heart.* London: Thames and Hudson, 1960, 309 p.

91.   Y. Bauer, *The Holocaust,* chap. 2.

ANTI-SEMITIC LEGISLATIONS IN HUNGARY AND THEIR IMPLEMENTATION IN BUDAPEST—AN ECONOMIC ANALYSIS

Yehuda Don

I

In the late 1930s, Hungarian public opinion was obsessed with the Jewish question. In a memorandum to the Regent in January 1939, signed by 11 conservative centrist politicians, among them some very prominent figures,[1] the Jewish question, along with the issue of the agrarian reform, were considered as "the two most fateful questions in Hungary" which were to be treated as "the two undefused timebombs of the Hungarian public life."[2] So, it was only a question of time before anti-Jewish laws were implemented.

The First Anti-Jewish Bill was introduced to the Parliament in April 1938, and was enacted about one month later as Act XV 1938. Its declared objective was to create "more effective safeguards of balance in the economic life" and "conditions to combat unemployment among the intelligentsia."[3] The principal instrument of the law was to be a network of binding chambers in most professions. The very concept of compulsory membership in professional chambers, as explicitly spelled out in paragraph 4 of the law, was designed to restrict the number of Jewish lawyers, physicians, engineers, journalists, and actors. In all these professions the Jews were heavily represented.[4] Therefore, no chambers were founded for high school teachers or for civil servants, among whom very few Jews could be found.

The convergence of the Jewish middle class in the independent professions was not accidental. As of the late nineteenth century "a never explicitly pronounced, yet pragmatically operative, division of labor existed, whereby the jobs in the public sector became the turf of the young 'gentry' class, whereas the so-called independent professions stood open for the children of the Jewish middle class."[5] The difference between these two paths of career was vast. Public-sector jobs provided job security and assured promotion through seniority, while the independent professions were by nature highly competitive.

The First Anti-Jewish Law stipulated that Jews could be admitted to the local chambers, each large locality had its own network of chambers, only when the ratio of Jews in that chamber was below 20 percent. Practioners at the time of the enactment of the law automatically became founding members of their respective chambers, so that the law basically restricted only young Jewish graduates and migrating Jewish practitioners. It was also injurious for the salaried Jewish professionals, who, as stipulated by clause 18 of the implementation regulations, were exposed to a compulsory process of semiannual dismissals. The law allowed for an adjustment period of five years.[6] It adopted basically a religious rather than a racial definition of Jewishness.[7] It represented a brand of "right-wing constitutional" anti-Semitism which was considered a lesser evil even by some Jews,[8] who condoned it as a protective shield against the more radical and violent anti-Semitism.[9]

The official estimate was that the execution of the law would affect 16,000 Jews,[10] while local Jewish sources estimated that the law would disrupt the careers of 15,000 Jewish professionals during the planned five years of implementation period.[11] The law was, however, never implemented.

By the end of 1938 the Second Anti-Jewish Bill was submitted to Parliament. It was designed by the new Prime Minister, Béla Imrédy, the formerly Anglophile financial expert who rapidly drifted to the radical populist right-wing.[12] Imrédy, who was feared and hated by the "constitutional right" for his radical standing on the exceedingly sensitive issue of land reform, was replaced in February 1939.[13] The bill was passed in May 1939 by Imrédy's successor, Count Pál Teleki, himself a long-standing anti-Semite, though of the constitutional rightist school.[14]

The Second Anti-Jewish Act IV of 1939 differed from its predecessor by the fundamental tenet of the notion of "Jew." Jewishness was no longer conceived as a religion. It became, following the German Nazi model, a race:

> A person should be considered a Jew if himself or at least one of his parents or two of his grandparents are members of the Jewish faith, or were members of it, as well as their offspring who were born after the ratification of the Bill, and those children whose Christian parents married after the ratification of the bill.[15]

Logically racial anti-Semitism was quite incompatible with either religious or economic anti-Semitism. The Jews were no longer members of a profane minority religion, or a minority group which unfairly grasped economic positions. Jewishness became an unavoidable destiny irrespective of religious affiliation. Indeed, the Church, which had tolerated without any perceptible misgivings the First Anti-Jewish Law,[16] raised its voice and protested against the "rejudaization" of converted Christians and their offspring.[17]

The principal objective of the bill remained "the restriction of the public and economic functioning of the Jews."[18] However, it went far beyond economic containment, although its most acutely felt constrictions remained economic.

The most immediate constriction was the absolute elimination of Jews from all positions in the public sector, including teaching positions in public schools. All Jewish employees in the public sector had to be dismissed or forced into early retirement (Paragraph 5). Banning Jews from the public sector was more significant as a question of political principle than as a disrupting employment factor, since as indicated,[20] the proportion of Jewish employees in the public sector had been quite unimportant. Absolute banning of Jews made obvious mockery of the argument of "imbalanced occupational structure" and could be logically defended only with the claim that all Jews had been fundamentally disloyal to the Hungarian State. Such an assumption was totally unfounded, since the loyalty of the Jewish leadership and intelligentsia to Hungary was ludicrously persistent even during the critical years of vocal anti-Semitism.[21]

The constrictions on the economic functioning of the Jews in the private and semi-private sectors was, however, of overwhelming importance.

Paragraph 12 of the law stipulated that all licences granted to Jews in the tobacco and liquor trade (State monopolies) had to be revoked in two years. The licenses in other State-controlled commodities were to be withdrawn in five years and in pharmacies in eight years.[22] The share of Jewish firms in the transportation of public sector cargo had to be reduced to five percent of the total public cargo until 1943.[23]

No Jew was granted a licence to open a workshop or a store in any municipality as long as the number of Jewish licensees in that municipality was above six percent of all such licensees. The share of Jewish white collar employees in any single undertaking in the private sector, "such as clerks, sellers, and other professionals," was to be kept down to 12 percent or less.[24] Moreover, to avoid situations in which the "Jewish quota" would be filled by senior, high-salaried employees, the law stipulated that the aggregate wage bill of all Jewish employees in the total wage bill should not surpass their share in the total number of employees.[25] On the other hand, firms with fewer Jewish employees than the stipulated Jewish quota, were not allowed to hire additional Jews and thereby raise the share of their Jewish employees to the permitted level.[26]

As expected, Jews in the independent professions were subjected to the most stringent limitations. Professional chambers of lawyers, physicians, engineers, journalists and actors in each municipality were forbidden to admit any Jewish candidate as long as the share of Jews in that particular chamber was at or above six percent.[27] Jewish artists and journalists were banned from positions of responsibility in the theaters, the motion picture industry, and the press.[28]

Finally, in agriculture, Jews were, in fact, prohibited from holding agricultural property whether as owners or lessees. They were obviously forbidden to acquire such property.[29]

The Second Anti-Jewish Law embraced all walks of Jewish economic existence. It severely limited all sources of livelihood for Jews, with the exception of hired manual labor in agriculture and industry.

II

The empirical examination of the economic aspects of the Second Anti-Jewish Bill on the economic functioning of the Jews was conducted on the census figures of 1935 in Budapest. In that year only the city of Budapest held a census. The date of this census was the closest to the enactment of the anti-Jewish laws. The national census in 1930 was almost a decade before the Laws and did not reflect the employment effects of the great depression, while the national census of 1941 was already influenced by the laws themselves. Therefore we preferred to use the 1935 Budapest census, although it only represented the situation in the capital itself. According to the findings of this census we see that 80 percent of all jobs held by Jews were subject to some sort of limitation as a direct result of the Second Anti-Jewish Law. In fact even this figure is downwardly biased, as it disregards the impact or constrictions upon Jewish undertakings on the employment of Jewish laborers in those undertakings.

What would have been the employment effect of the Second Anti-Jewish Law under the assumption of full implementation? This question, though hypothetical, still has considerable practical as well as theoretical importance. The theoretical importance is the measurement of the depth of economic discrimination through legislation. This same question had a great deal of practical significance at the time of the Bill's enactment. Contemporary sources suggested some rough calculations and used those calculations as a point of reasoning against the law. Two of the leading figures in Hungarian Jewry in 1939, Samu Stern, the President of the Jewish Community of Budapest, the country's largest Neolog congregation, and Dr. Sándor Eppler, the Secretary of that congregation, estimated that the Second Anti-Jewish Law would cause about a quarter of a million Jews to lose their employment.[30]

In this study we attempt to reconstruct the occupational composition of the Jews in Budapest in 1935, and to recapitulate the relative and absolute employment effect of the Second Anti-Jewish Law upon the major occupational sectors. Let us first compare the occupational structure of Jews and Gentiles (Table 1).

The very low ratio of agriculture obviously reflects the fact that the statistics related to the metropolitan area of the city of Budapest.

Table 1 corroborates only partially the conventional wisdom with respect to the unique occupational structure of the Jews.

1. Commerce was, as expected, dominant among Jews, as four out of ten Jewish persons were occupied in commerce. However, the outcry that commerce was in Jewish hands was unfounded. The number of Gentiles in commerce was higher by 10,000 than the number of Jews.

2. The frequent statements that Jews refrained from entering "productive" branches was also unfounded. Well over one-third of all Jewish persons worked in industry. Admittedly, the percentage of the Gentile labor in industry was higher, yet the difference certainly did not support the charge of unproductivity.

3. Jews were heavily represented in the independent liberal professions, journalism, and the arts. However, statistically at least, the situation was a far cry from domination.

4. The figures fully corroborate the accepted view that Jews were kept out of the public sector.

Statistics kept track also of the status of employees at their work. Three categories were distinguished: (1) self-employed, including both owners of large enterprises, independent physicians or lawyers, and tiny shopkeepers, peddlers or artisans; (2) white collar employees, including clerks and salaried professionals as well as salesmen and retail clerks; (3) blue collar employees defined mainly as manual laborers, though including also highly skilled workers and technicians.

The breakdown of the major branches into status at work, by distinguishing between Jews and Gentiles will throw light upon some unique propensities of Jewish employees (Table 2).

Table 2 brings into sharp focus the most outstanding feature of Hungarian Jews with respect to their occupational preference toward entrepreneurship and independence. Jews displayed a strong inclination to self-employment. Whenever possible, they prefered the status of independent operator of an enterprise over that of waged or salaried employee. This tendency is very clearly shown in the high ratio of self-employed Jews in

TABLE 1

Occupational Structure of the Jewish and Gentile Labor Force in Budapest in 1935
(absolute relative figures)

Branch	Jews		Gentiles		Total		Share of Jews
	Numbers I	% II	Numbers III	% IV	Numbers V = I + III	% VI	% VII = I/V
Agriculture	507	0.5	5,537	1.3	6,044	1.1	8.4
Mining and Industry	40,345	35.9	201,703	48.4	242,048	45.7	16.7
Commerce and Trade	45,599	40.9	55,758	13.4	101,357	19.1	45.0
Transportation (Private)	919	0.8	6,456	1.5	7,375	1.4	12.5
Public Sector[a]	2,982	2.6	62,730	15.0	65,712	12.4	4.5
Liberal Professions	9,184	8.2	19,429	4.7	28,613	5.4	32.1
Others[b]	12,995	11.5	65,414	15.7	78,409	14.8	16.6
Total	112,531	100	417,027	100	529,558	100	21.2

a Including Civil Service, Public Transportation, Communication, and Ecclesiastic Services.
b Including four major groups (1) people living from capital (20 percent); (2) Pensioners (42 percent); (3) Unskilled labor (30 percent); (4) Miscellaneous (8 percent). Of the Jews, 52 percent belonged to the first group, 35 percent to the second, 4 percent to the third and 9 percent to the fourth group.

TABLE 2

Status at Work[a] of Jews and Gentiles by Branches (in percent)

Branch	Jews			Gentiles			Jews/Gentiles		
	S I	W II	B III	S IV	W V	B IV	S I/IV	W II/V	B III/VI
Agriculture	66.0	21.9	12.1	34.0	6.7	59.1	1.9	3.3	0.2
Industry and Mining	24.7	24.8	50.4	11.7	6.3	81.9	2.1	3.9	0.6
Commerce	35.7	39.0	25.3	21.5	34.6	43.9	1.7	1.1	0.6
Private Transportation	55.1	15.3	29.6	17.6	5.4	77.0	3.1	2.8	0.4
Civil Service[b]	—	50.5	49.4	—	48.5	51.4	—	1.04	0.96

a S = Self-employed; W = White collar employees; B = Blue collar employees (Manual laborers)

b Including Transportation and Communication, excluding Ecclesiastic Services and the Military.

industry, commerce, and transportation. There were about 10,000 independent Jewish operators in industry. Very few of them were large-scale industrial entrepreneurs. The vast majority ran small workshops in the needle trade, printing, leather, and in a wide array of other industries. Though Jews constituted only one-sixth of the labor force in industry, their share in the industrial self-employed reached close to 30 percent, and the ratio of Jewish to non-Jewish independent operators in industry was 1:9. (See column VII.)

Well over 16,000 Jews entered the category of self-employed in commerce. Again, most of them were small shopkeepers, tradesmen and peddlers. The number of Gentile commercial self-employed reached only 12,000. Thus, although four out of seven persons employed in commerce were Gentiles, when it came to count independent establishments, four out of seven were Jews. In other words, although when taking commerce as a whole one could not speak of Jewish domination,[31] the majority of small retail commercial outlets in Budapest were owned by Jews. This very high visibility created the impression of dominance.

Private transportation and agriculture point to the same preference patterns, though their numerical importance in Budapest was rather limited. As is very clearly demonstrated in Table 2, the ratio of Jews to Gentiles among the self-employed in all branches was larger than one.

The standard explanation for the tendency of Jews to prefer independence and self-employment over the status of employees is that their Jewish status would handicap their advancement if they were employees. Though independent businesses involved much higher risks and greater economic uncertainty, these were, apparently, overshadowed by the disadvantages of being a Jewish employee. The tendency of Jews to prefer self-employment over the status of salaried employees or wage-earners was not unique to Budapest. It was, and apparently it still is, a general phenomenon in the economic behavior of Jews.[32]

Besides self-employment, Jews preferred employment in white collar jobs over blue collar manual labor. The reasons for such preference are quite obvious, as white collar jobs required less physical effort, were conducted in more comfortable conditions and, as a rule, paid more than blue collar jobs. The distribution of Jews and Gentiles between white and blue collar jobs is displayed in Table 3.

TABLE 3

**Jewish and Gentile Employees in White Collar and Blue Collar Jobs
in Industry, Commerce and Private Transportation
(in percent)**

Branch	White Collar			Blue Collar		
	Jews	Gentiles	Total	Jews	Gentiles	Total
Industry	43.9	56.1	100	11.0	89.0	100
Commerce	51.9	48.1	100	35.5	64.5	100
Transportation	28.7	71.3	100	5.2	94.8	100

In fact, about one-third of all Jewish employees in industry were white collar workers, compared to 7.2 percent of all Gentile employees in industry (a ratio of 33.0/7.2 = 4.6). The respective ratio in commerce was 60.6/44 = 1.4.

The greater proportion of Jews to white collar occupations is explained by the educational background of the Jews as compared with that of the Gentiles. Jews were, on the average, better endowed with the qualifications required for white collar occupations in the business sector.[33] This reality was well known to the authorities and to the legislators of the Second Anti-Jewish Law, who imposed the restrictive quotas so that the higher the participation ratio of the Jews had been the lower the permitted quota was set. Thus, the quota for independent businesses, for jounalism, the arts, and the professions was set a six percent. For white collar positions in the business sector it was set at 12 percent, and for blue collar jobs no quota was imposed by the law.

III

The conclusion of this paper is that the Second Anti-Jewish Law was not, in fact, implemented in a systematic fashion. Nevertheless, hypothetical questions about the accumulated direct effect of the full implementation of the law upon the employment structure of the Jewish community remains of great interest. We have attempted to calculate the total

number of Jews subject to elimination from their professions or dismissal
from their positions assuming full implementation. Unfortunately, we can
only estimate the direct and immediate effects of such loss of employment,
and cannot go into speculations, either as to the alternative employment
opportunities of those who were to lose their jobs, or with regard to the
multiplier effects of such massive transformations in the employment
structure of one one-fifth of the total labor force in Budapest. Table
4 summarizes the estimated job losses under the assumption that the
Second Anti-Jewish Law was consistently implemented.

According to Table 4, of the close to 100,000 economically active Jews
in Budapest the law would have deprived over 61,000 of their positions.

Assume that the law were indeed fully implemented. How would it re-
shape the economic structure of the Jewish population in Budapest? Table
5 attempts to suggest some approximations.

Although plans were drawn up about the "productivization" of the
Jews, i.e., forcing them to enter into manual workers' occupations, as
one of the main objectives of the anti-Jewish legislation, such programs
were never even begun to be implemented. The reasons were obvious. The
skills of those who would have lost their jobs were either highly specialized
(professionals and white collar) or they had no specific skills at all (commerce). The only feasible employment options for these persons—without
lengthy retraining programs—would have been unskilled manual labor to
which most of the unemployed were physically as well as mentally unfit.
Besides, the supply of unskilled manual labor of Gentile workers was
plentiful and the entrance of Jews into this market would have pushed
others out of it into unemployment.

The introduction of forced labor service for Jewish males in 1939 removed tens of thousands of men of the economically active age groups
from the labor market and alleviated any potential pressure of unemployment created by discrimination and anti-Jewish legislation.[34]

The actual impact of the law obviously depended upon the rigor of
its implementation, which was not consistent, at least not until the German occupation in March 1944. Two subperiods are distinguishable from
the enactment of the law in May 1939 to March 1944. The first lasted
until the appointment of Miklós Kállay as Prime Minister in March 1942,
and the second, the Kállay era, ended with the formal occupation of
Hungary by the Germans on March 19, 1944.

TABLE 4

Estimated Job Losses Following Implementation of Act IV 1939 in Budapest, by Branches

Branch and Status at Work	Before Implementation Jews Employed	After Full Implementation Jews Employed		Employment Loss
		N	%	
Agriculture				
S (self-employed)	335	0	0	335
W (white collar)	111	58	12.0	53
B (blue collar)	61	61	Free	0
Mining and Industry				
S	9,984	2,020	6.0	7,964
W	10,024	2,737	12.0	7,287
B	20,337	20,337	Free	0
Commerce				
S	16,289	1,610	6.0	14,679
W	17,765	4,444	12.0	13,312
B	11,545	5,071	14.1[a]	6,474
Private Transportation				
S	506	99	6.0	407
W	141	59	12.0	82
B	272	272	Free	0
Liberal Professions	9,184	1,717	6.0	7,467
Public Sector	2,980	0	0	2,980
Ecclesiastic Service	101	101	6.0	0
Total	99,653	38,586		61,049

a Of the Jewish blue collar employees in commerce 2,736 were registered as workers (No limitation of percentage). The rest, 8,809 employees, were registered as retail personnel whose percentage had to be reduced to 12 percent.

TABLE 5

Jewish Employment Structure of the Economically Active Labor
Force in 1935 and After the Implementation of the Second
Anti-Jewish Law by Economic Branch (in percent)

Economic Branch	in 1935	After Implementation
Agriculture	0.5	0.1
Industry	40.5	25.2
Commerce	45.8	11.2
Private Transportation	0.9	0.4
Liberal Professions	9.2	1.7
Public Sector	3.0	0.0
Ecclesiastic Service	0.1	0.1
Unemployed[a]	unknown	61.3
Total	100.0	100.0

a   The statistics do not distinguish between Jewish and non-Jewish unemployed
    workers in 1935.

During the first subperiod, under the premiership of Teleki, and as of
April 1941 that of László Bárdossy the law was enforced rather in a haphazard fashion. Alongside with accidental and intentional slackness in
certain sectors, we observe some major transgressions, often not stipulated
by the law. In the public sector the implementation was swift and thorough.
The civil service, the legal system, the public transportation network, the
post office and the telecommunication offices all got rid of their Jewish
officials and workers in one year or less.[35] The military establishment, a
traditional haven of virulent anti-Semitism, was the first to throw out the
few Jews they employed. Even the licences of the Jewish cab drivers were
revoked under the pretext they were civil servants.[36]

In the private sector, implementation was more accidental and sloppy.
President S. Stern complained in August 1941 of massive revocations of
practicing licenses of Jewish artisans and merchants.[37] In numerous villages and townships Jewish shopkeepers were forced to display signboards
indicating that theirs was a "Jewish store." Commodities in shortage, such
as kerosene, hides, soap, and textiles, were distributed among retailers "in
consideration of Act IV 1939."[38] The Jewish newspaper sellers lost their

licences, together with some 15,000 peddlers as did most retail grain merchants and merchants of heating material.[39]

Notwithstanding, and despite the frequent very cruel overkills, the role of the Jews in the Hungarian economy did not go through radical changes until March 1944. There were two main reasons for this:

1. Full implementation of the law would have been in sharp conflict with the economic interests of the country, and would have been possible only at prohibitively high costs, at least for the foreseeable future.
2. During the second subperiod, from mid-1942 to March 1944, the thorough execution of all regulations of the law were, apparently, no longer among the major policy goals of the Hungarian government.

When the time for the full implementation of the anti-Jewish discriminative economic steps arrived, there was no more economic need for "the restriction of the . . .economic functioning of the Jews."[40] Much of the pressure to contain the Jews in their economic activities was created by the employment effects of the great depression. The depressed agricultural production, sharp declines in the output among the metal, engineering, construction, and lumber industries,[41] and above all the heavy underemployment in the rural sector[42] and the high rate of unemployment in the urban sectors[43] intensified the sense of actue economic rivalry of the Jews, and enhanced anti-Semitism. However, more than a year before the ratification of thc Sccond Anti-Jewish Law, the Hungarian government approved a five-year development plan involving one billion *Pengő* (about $175 million) of public expenditure, two-thirds of which was earmarked for rearmament. Increased public expenditure revived economic activity and bolstered growth.[44] The phenomenon of unemployment vanished in 1939. So did the difficulties of overproduction and insufficient purchasing power. They were replaced by problems of labor shortage, insufficient productive capacity, and inflation.[45]

Utilization of excess capacity enabled rapid industrial growth in the first two to three wartime years at stable prices. As of 1941 output growth was in fact halved and inflation gradually accelerated. The figures in Table 6 demonstrate the course of development.

TABLE 6

Industrial Price Index and Real Industrial Growth Index in Hungary During 1938-1943 (1938 = 100)

Year	Industrial Price Index	Industrial Real Product Index
1938	100.0	100.0
1939	98.6	120.7
1940	106.8	132.8
1941	126.1	128.1
1942	146.3	135.2
1943	206.4	137.5

Source: Berend and Ránki, n. 41, p. 216.

Under such circumstances the productive capacity of the Jewish enterprises became a vital asset to the national economy and the rearmament efforts. Furthermore, in terms of economic pragmatism the Second Anti-Jewish Law proved to be quite unimplementable in the short run, unless the politicians were willing to pay a very high price in terms of economic stability and growth. Regent Horthy in his well-known letter to Prime Minister Teleki, in October 1940, admitted that "it is impossible to discard the Jews . . . in one or two years and to replace them by incompetent, vulgar and boorish elements, because we could flounder. Such a project requires at least one full generation."[46]

Consequently, changing economic conditions, together with the realistic approach of the Regent led to a discriminatively selective policy in the implementation of the anti-Jewish economic restrictions.

After the appointment of Kállay as the Hungarian Prime Minister in March 1942, the foreign policy of the country gradually shifted from the explicit dogmatic pro-Gemanism of Bárdossy to a more pragmatic, opportunistic course known as the "seesaw policy."[47] Prime Minister Kállay, following the German defeat at Stalingrad and El Alamein in early 1943, initiated some cautious moves to open new avenues for Hungary to the Western Allies. Kállay's Jewish policy was, apparently, instrumental to his foreign policy. His oratory in public was as anti-Semitic as that of his predecessors, yet in practice he refrained from putting into effect those anti-Jewish restrictions which could jeopardize strong economic interests

of the country. As of 1943 the tenor of the government's Jewish policy
was that of apology. The ideological validity of racial anti-Semitism was
wholeheartedly approved and praised. On the other hand they refrained
from removing those Jews from their positions who were considered to be
essential to the economic welfare of the country. The authorities felt an
urge to apologize to the Germans for leaving indispensable Jews in their
positions in the economy, and reasoned that radical implementation of the
anti-Jewish laws would have upset the normal functioning of the country.
A typical example of this apologetic tone of the leadership is the following
memorandum, which was, apparently, written by the Hungarian Minister
of the Interior, Ferenc Keresztes-Fischer in 1943.

> The Jewish question is one of the most difficult problems in Hun-
> gary. Nowhere in Europe could be found such high proportion of
> Jews as in our country, where they constitute at least 10 percent
> [sic] of our genuine Hungarian population, and where they have
> penetrated thoroughly into all walks of our life. Thus, it has been
> an exceedingly complex operation to completely uproot them from
> the intellectual, literary and cultural life (the press, the theaters,
> the motion pictures, etc.), and to reduce them in the industry and
> the economy to their legal proportion which is now considerably
> lower than their numerical proportion. Racially they were separated
> by racial legislation. Instead of military service, they serve in special
> labor service companies, their landed property was 100 percent con-
> fiscated. In other words they were harshly pushed back in all walks
> of life. Exactly because of their multitude, and the high level of their
> integration into all strata of our life, if we do not want to upset the
> functioning, the working capacity and the law and order of this na-
> tion, it is impossible to effectuate against them such restrictions that
> are in force in other countries and first of all in Germany where their
> relative weight is less than ten percent of that in our country. The
> introduction of yellow armbands, of concentration camps, or any-
> thing alike are technically unimplementable and they would lead to
> the total collapse of law and order in Hungary.[48]

The same type of language of apology was used by the Regent in his reply to Hitler's complaint about the untolerably lenient treatment of the Jews in Hungary.[49]

Thus, the Jewish Law was not systematically implemented until March 1944. As late as in 1941 over 91 percent of all operating Jewish industrialists of 1939 were still in control of their enterprises.[50] The authorities turned a blind eye to the widespread practice of using Gentile persons as straw men—as fictitious heads of Jewish firms.

The instruction to gradually reduce State orders from Jewish firms proved to be impractical with the sharp upswing of the Hungarian economy and the exceptionally rapid growth of public expenditure for rearmament. As shown in Table 7, public sector could not afford to chose among potential suppliers, and it purchased merchandise from any firm which was capable of producing it. Even the explicit injuctions to expropriate all Jewish

TABLE 7

The Share of the Public Sector Expenditure in the National Income

Year	Budget Expenditures in Fixed Prices, Index	National Income in Fixed Prices, Index	Percentage of Budget in National Income
1938-39	100	100	33.1
1939-40	146	112	43.3
1941	175	115	50.5
1942	228	123	61.5
1943	244	120	67.4

Source: Berend and Ranki, n. 41, p. 211.

landowners or *rentiers* was apparently not carried out. Contemporary sources indicated that in 1942 the landed property under Jewish control was well over one million acres.[51]

IV

The Second Anti-Jewish Law was not fully implemented because its implementation would have conflicted with the economic reality, because the Regent, and later also the government, were disinclined to pay the economic price of implementation, and also because—as late as 1943— implementation was intentionally sloppy, in order to show the Western Allies that Hungary was not a German puppet. None of these reasons included any element of remorse or admission of moral misconduct in the very act of racially discriminative legislation. Ideologically Act IV 1939 remained impeccable. Practically, it was unimplementable. However, partial implementation had its effects upon the economic structure of the Jewish community, as it was by no means random or haphazard. Lack of execution had its very clear-cut tendencies.[52]

The general characteristic of the implemented measures of the Second Anti-Jewish Law was regressive. It apparently widened the economic differences within the Jewish community and increased inequality both in income and wealth. Substantially unharmed were the Jewish industrial magnates, large commercial establishments, and apparently the self-employed, well-established members of the professions. They remained members of their respective professional chambers, and continued to practice without very major disturbances. Until 1944 the big Jewish firms countervailed attempts to oust their original directors and key workers, by bringing in fictitious or genuine—though usually redundant—directors with clear Christian pasts, preferably with an aristocratic pedigree.[53] The "straw man" system was also intensively utilized by the well-to-do business firms. These groups were also exempted from the economic afflictions of the anti-Jewish law because they were irreplaceable if chaos and economic collapse were to be avodied.[54] Even the institutions of the Jewish community, dominated by the Jewish plutocracy, remained in good financial shape.[55]

The other group relatively unaffected by the anti-Jewish law was the manual-worker class. The law itself regarded the shift of Jews from self-employment and white collar work to manual labor as one of its goals. However, the numerical weight of the blue collar Jewish workers, particularly in industry, was not great.[56]

The brunt of the anti-Jewish laws was felt by the middle and lower middle classes. They made a decent, though modest, living as tradesmen, journeymen and clerks, and were the elements most likely to be deprived of their livelihood. They could seldom afford to hire a straw man and were not regarded as essential to the national economy. Journalists and actors were also systematically removed from their posts. However, quantitatively they were quite insignificant.

One more factor is worth mentioning in this respect. Until May 1944 the anti-Jewish laws affected only employment and income, and not wealth. Since income from property was not jeopardized, the regressive tendencies of the implementation were thus intensified.

It seems that the regressive impact of the anti-Jewish laws upon income distribution within the Jewish community, were probably not conceived intentionally. Yet, they were certainly condoned, even probably approved, by the legislators. It was the "constitutional right" who initiated the economic dimensions of anti-Jewish legislation, and they could apparently not forget their own terms of reference with respect to the distribution of income.

NOTES

1. The Memorandum written as a critical denunciation of the political measures of the Imrédy Cabinet, was submitted to the Regent on January 14, 1939. Among its signatories was Count István Bethlen, the most powerful politician of the interwar years, and Zoltán Tildy, later the President of the post-World War II Republic of Hungary. The Memorandum was published in M. Szinai and L. Szűcs, eds., *Horthy Miklós titkos irati* (The Confidential Papers of Miklós Horthy), Budapest: Kossuth, 1963, pp. 205-211.

2. Ibid., pp. 206-207.

3. A short overview of the First Anti-Jewish Law is in *Fegyvertelenül álltak az aknamezőkön* (Armless They Stood in the Minefields). Elek Karsal, ed., Budapest, 1961, p. 753.

4. In a national survey of professionals, conducted in 1928, 49.3 percent of all lawyers and 38.1 percent of all physicians were Jewish. See O. Szabolcs, *Köztisztviselők az ellenforradalmi rendszer társadalmi bázisában, 1920-1926* (The Civil Servants in the Social Basis of the Counterrevolutionary Regime, 1920-1926). Budapest, 1965, p. 124. In Budapest

itself, according to the city census of 1935, 51 percent of all lawyers and 38 percent of all physicians were Jewish. The proportions for other independent professions were: pharmacists, 27 percent; engineers, 33 percent; journalists, 35 percent; artists, 24 percent; writers, 28 percent.

5. Szabolcs, ibid., pp. 123-124. The share of Jews in public sector jobs was insignificant. According to the 1928 survey, only 1.9 percent of all civil servants were Jewish. Ibid., p. 124.

6. See Regulation 4350/1938.

7. See R. L. Braham, *The Politics of Genocide–The Holocaust in Hungary.* (New York: Columbia University Press, 1981), 2 vols., p. 125.

8. Katzburg quotes some clear-cut evidence to the effect that "Hungarian Jewish leaders. . .in view of the political circumstances. . .were prepared to accept a tolerable level of anti-Jewish measures. See Nathaniel Katzburg, *Hungary and the Jews* (Ramat Gan: Bar-Ilan University Press, 1981), p. 98.

9. The Hungarian Minister to Washington promulgated this view to the U.S. Assistant Secretary of State claiming that "it was for the Government to undertake measures of this character." Ibid., p. 110.

10. *American Jewish Yearbook 1939,* p. 278.

11. The estimation appeared in the *Egyenlőség* (Equality) on April 14, 1938 and in the *Zsidó Szemle* (Jewish Review), no. 21, 1938.

12. On the unique course of the political career of Imrédy, see P. Sipos, *Imrédy Béla és a Magyar Megujulás Pártja* (Béla Imrédy and the Hungarian Rejuvenation Party) (Budapest, 1970), esp. p. 98.

13. Imrédy:s radical views on the land distribution issue were first given publicity in his famous Kaposvár speech on September 5, 1938. In January 1939 he submitted a relatively moderate plan for land reform. The real reason for Imrédy's dismissal was his Land Reform Bill and not his Jewish ancestors. See Szinai and Szücs, op.cit., p. 215.

14. Teleki was the sponsor of the forerunner of the anti-Jewish laws, the notorious Law XXV 1920, better known as the Numerus Clausus Act.

15. This is the first sentence of a special book devoted solely to the text of the Bill, its related regulations and supplemented by a brief comment. See S. I. Székely, ed. *A II-zsidótörvény és a végrehajtási utasitás* (The Second Anti-Jewish Law and its Implementation Ordinances), Budapest, 1939, p. 5. The most perverse aspect of this book is that fact that E. Bródy, a Jewish member of the Hungarian Parliament wrote its preface.

16. See Braham, pp. 123-125.

17. Ibid., pp. 152-154. During the incubation period of the Bill, in January 1939, the Hungarian Synod of Bishops discussed the Bill and approved it with some reservations. The Catholic Primate, Jusztinián Cardinal Serédi, drew the attention to the fact that if the Bill "intended to hamper Jewish immigration and end the social and economic preponderance of the Jews in general 'it' ought to have been based on other principles." The Bishop of Csanád protested openly against what he called "the rejudaization of Christians." See *The American Jewish Yearbook,* 1939, p. 281.

18. This was the official name of the Bill and its introductory sentence. See Karsai, op. cit., vol. II, p. 755.

19. No Jew could acquire any more Hungarian citizenship; no Jew was eligible to be elected to the Upper House of the Parliament (except the official representative of the religion who sat there *ex officio;* no Jew could exercise his voting right unless he proved that his family had been residing continuously in Hungary from 1867 onwards; no Jew could become a candidate for any municipal elected or appointed post, not even the members of the group of "virilists" (citizens who carried the main financial burder of the municipal budget).

20. See note 5 above.

21. For a detailed description of the super-loyalty syndrome of the Hungarian Jewish leadership, see Braham, pp. 90-103.

22. Székely, op. cit., p. 43.

23. Ibid., pp. 46-47.

24. Ibid., p. 51 (paragraph 17, passage 1).

25. Ibid., (passage 2).

26. Ibid., (passage 6).

27. Ibid., pp. 37-38, (paragraph 9, passage 1).

28. Ibid., pp. 40-42, (paragraphs 10, 11).

29. Ibid., pp. 48-50 (paragraphs 15-16).

30. The figures were quoted in a letter sent by N. Lasky, the President of the Board of Deputies, to the Marquis of Reading, the Chairman of the Council for the German Jewry. The letter is cited in Katzburg, op. cit., p. 279.

31. A detailed statistical study on the "Role of Jewish Capital and Entrepreneurship in the Hungarian Economy," in preparation by this au-

thor, corroborates the statement that there was no Jewish domination in the wholesale trade and the large commercial undertakings.

32. The preference of independent status at work is being emphasized by Professor S. Kuznetz in his pathbreaking paper on Jewish economics. See S. Kuznetz, "Economic Structure and Life of the Jews," *The Jews— Their History, Culture and Religion,* L. Finkelstein, ed. New York, 1960, vol. 2, pp. 1067, 1069. The same results were shown by E. Bennathan, *Die demographische und wirtschaftliche Stellung der Juden in Entscheidungs- jahr 1932.* Tubingen, 1966, p. 123, whereby in 1933 the percentage of self-employed among the German population was 16.4 percent, while among the Jews it was 46 percent.

33. For a brief statistical account of the Jewish educational structure in Budapest in the thirties, see V. Karady, "Jewish Enrollment Patterns in Classical Secondary Education in Old Regime and Interwar Hungary. Some Long Term Trends," *Studies in Contemporary Jewry,* 1984, pp. 363-367. Bennathan, op. cit., came to similar conclusions with respect to the prefer- ence of Jewish employees for white collar jobs. Defining white collar workers as "clerks" and blue collar workers as "workers," the figures for Germany in 1933 were the following (percent of total participants in the labor force).

	German Population	Jews
Clerks	12.5	33.5
Workers	46.3	8.7

34. For a very detailed documentary account of the forced labor ser- vice system, see E. Karsai, op. cit. See particularly the Introduction in Vol. I, pp. vii-cxxvii. R.L. Braham devotes a long and very informative chapter to the forced labor service system. See pp. 285-361.

35. *American Jewish Yearbook,* Vol., 1940-41, p. 361 and Vol. 1942- 43, p. 260. See also F. Grünwald, *Az elmult év története* (The History of the Year That Passed), Vol. 1940, p. 297.

36. *American Jewish Yearbook,* Vol. 1942-43, p. 260.

37. *Védelmünkben* (In Our Defense). J. Lévai, ed., Budapest, 1942, p. 16.

38. *American Jewish Yearbook,* Vol. 1942-43, p. 260.

39. Ibid.

40. From the preamble of Act IV 1939.

41. For a brief summary of the output, productivity, and terms of trade of Hungary during the years of the Great Depression, see I. Berend and G. Ránki, *A magyar gazdaság száz éve* (The Hungarian Economy 100 Years). Budapest, 1972, pp. 129-144.

42. According to contemporary sources, the Hungarian agricultural workers had, on the average, 150-180 days of work per year. See ibid., p. 189.

43. The number of unemployed in the first half of the 1930s was estimated above the 200,000 figure, about one third of the Hungarian industrial labor force. During the second half of the 1930s unemployment figurges were somewhat lower, but still close to 100,000. See ibid., p. 191.

44. The following figures reflect the impact of increased public expenditure on economic growth.

Real Changes in Budget Expenditures and Economic Growth in Hungary
1938-39 to 1942 (Index, 1938-9 = 100)

	Budget Expenditure	National Income
1938-39	100	100
1939-40	146	112
1941	175	115
1942	228	123

Source: Berend and Ránki, op.cit., p. 211. For price index of manufactured goods, see ibid., p. 216.

45. The principal sector of growth was obviously the heavy industry, particularly steel, iron, engineering, and coal mining. The output of some of these industries doubled in a few years, the light industry, including food, contracted because it lacked sufficient inputs.

46. Szinai and Szucs, op. cit., pp. 261-262.

47. See R. Braham, pp. 222-223.

48. See Szinai and Szucs, op. cit., pp. 363-364.

49. Ibid., p. 392.

50. The data relate to the 1939 boundaries and were collected from different volumes of the Hungarian Statistical Yearbook.

51. The total surface of large Jewish estates (90 acres or more) was estimated in the forties at about 1.2 million acres by Jewish sources (Grünwald, op. cit., p. 341). They were estimated by anti-Semitic sources at about 1.5 million acres. (M. Matolcsy, *A zsidóság házvagyona* (The Real Estate Capital of the Jews). Budapest, 1942, p. 8.

52.   The following analysis contains a rather strong element of speculation. Further field research on the level of individual firms seems essential
to corroborate or reject our conclusions. E. Karsai, in his conversation
with the author, suggested the same idea.

53.   The largest and most important engineering firm in Hungary, the
Weiss-Manfréd Works, the prototype of Jewish industrial initiative, was
technically, a Christian establishment, because "the majority of the Weiss-
Manfréd capital is at present in the ownership of family members who are,
according to the existing regulations, Christians." So wrote F. Chorin, the
head of the Weiss-Manfréd Works and the former President of GyOSz (National Alliance of Industrialists) to the Regent in a letter, dated May 17,
1944. See Szinai and Szücs, op. cit., document no 83, p. 441. In fact, even
members of the Horthy family accepted remunerative directorships in
large Jewish industrial and banking firms. See ibid., fn, 1, p. 399.

54.   The argument of irreplaceability is mentioned in several documents. It it even repeated in Chorin's letter to the Regent in May 1944.
See Note 53 above.

55.   See the report of S. Stern, the President of the Neolog Congregation of Budapest in August 1941. Quoted in *Védelmünkben,* op. cit., p. 16.

56.   The total number of Jewish blue collar workers in Budapest, in
agriculture, mines, industry and private transportation was in 1935 20.670,
a mere 18.6 percent of the economically active Jews, and only 10.6 percent of all blue collar workers in the same industries. See Table 4 above.

Some Social Aspects of
Jewish Assimilation in Socialist Hungary,
1945-1956

Victor Karady

This study focuses on the conditions of Jewish assimilation under Communist rule in Hungary.[1] It deals with three interconnected though rather specific problems pertaining to the process of Jewish assimilation under the new regime. The first part of this essay contains a sociological inquiry into the socioeconomic frustrations certain sections of Hungarian Jewry suffered under the pre-Holocaust regimes and which prepared many of the survivors to seek career compensations within the emerging Communist power structure. The second section focuses on the situations of conflict produced by the integration of Jewish groups which were historically deprived of any tradition of legitimate violence into a regime exerting State terror. The third section attempts an analysis of the political economy of Jewish commitment (and the forms of disengagement from it) as they were experienced both before and after the 1956 October Revolution.

I

Class-Related and Occupational Conditions of
Jewish Integration in the New Regime

A number of stereotyped ideas concerning Jewish-Gentile relations survive in present-day Hungary. They are often closely determined—one could
even say "over-determined"—by actual group interests. These include the
idea that Hungarian Jewish survivors of the Holocaust sought and found
positive integration within the Communist establishment. In contrast one
should clearly note that such integration into the new system has *not* encompassed the whole of the Jewish population—or probably even a majority of it. Even before 1950 there was a considerable Jewish emigration,
which increased after 1956. At least a quarter of Jewry was thus out of
the running, as far as "positive integration" was concerned. If one adds to
this the numbers of surviving Jewish capitalists, professionals, and self-
employed, as well as the independent lower middle class, the number of
would-be "integrationists" was reduced even further. These were some of
the groups economically expropriated and suppressed by the new regime;
thereby they became socially depressed.[2] Many of them sank to the level
of the proletariat or had to adopt different forms of "enforced mobility."
Some of them were actually persecuted as "class aliens" or "cosmopolitan
agents." It is well known that the Jewish middle class in Budapest was a
particular victim of the 1950-1951 forced "relocations": these survivors
had been largely concentrated in the capital; many families had been
decimated; many elderly persons lived alone; and they mostly occupied
fairly large central city apartments. Thus, they became an easy prey for
the new wave of persecution directed against the former "bourgeoisie"
during the first years of the Hungarian Stalinist regime.

We may therefore deduce that the part of Jewry willing to adopt integration was comparatively small—certainly smaller than is commonly assumed. Furthermore, the tendency of *dissimilation*—fueled mostly by religious feelings or the desire to maintain the identity of the traditional
community—never ceased. This tendency was mostly prevalent in the older
generation whose demographic importance suddenly increased because of
the Holocaust.

Positive integration thus encompassed the numerically small youngest generation that passed through the process of "socialist transformation" and a section of the intermediate age groups of the active population. In terms of social class categories, the remnants of employees and workers were touched by this process to a larger extent (their proportion within Jewry had probably increased, owing to selective emigration) than were the economic, technical and artistic intelligentsia, many of whom had been earlier in indepedent occupations.

In order to establish the correct sociological perspective, our analysis must also deal with the vital connections trying this positive integration to the process of radical social restratification of society ensuing after 1945 and accelerating after 1949. There is, perhaps, one overwhelming reason why positive integration became common with a segment of Hungarian Jewry. The process directly benefited their collective interests. Their primary sympathy toward the new regime (a reflection of their alienation from the old one) served as a ticket into the dazzling world of opportunities created by the violent sociopolitical upheaval and the ensuring burst of social and economic mobility. Furthermore, Jews were particularly favored in the new socialist market of careers, owing to their group-specific social stratification.

If there had been a simple changeover in the seats of power following 1945 (as had happened in the 1918 and 1919 revolutions), probably only the narrow, politically active, oppositionist elements of Jewry would have shared in the fruits of power. The competitive social situation of the rest of Jewry would also have improved somewhat, owing simply to the disappearance of negative discrimination. In this radically new situation, however, all those Jews who became attracted to a new-style assimilation found that that they could identify their group-specific interests with those ascribed to the global scoiety or to the nation as a whole.

There may have been traces of a "secular Messianism" in this, but in practical terms their own social advancement and integration was part and parcel of a process that affected the position and condition of all layers of society. Although this process was enforced by an external power through despotic measures, it did mean a genuine and thoroughgoing opening up of the channels of social mobility. In the old dispensation, whole social groups had either been fully excluded or severely restricted in social advancement, even within their own class, let alone beyond it. The poor peasantry, unskilled laborers, women and national minorities found the doors were now thrown open to them.

The extension and democratization of the educational system (which also involved a kind of intellectual downgrading) was one very effective scheme for change; but so was extensive industrialization, land reform, and later the collectivization of agriculture, State control and development of welfare, communications and the media, as well as the reshaping of the administrative structure. Within the latter, an unprecedented inflation took place in the personnel of the so-called forces of law and order, of trade union establishments and of the propaganda apparatus—as in all other agencies of centralized power.

Old barriers were lifted by these changes for other, non-Jewish disadvantaged groups too: for Gypsies, women, children of the "lower orders," or members of "unrecognized" religous groups. All in all, this artificially induced but nevertheless revolutionary transformation radically reshaped the whole edifice of society, creating new relationships, power-linkages and opportunities. And, *within* these changes, it granted a special premium to assimilant Jewry by virtue of their being the collective possessors of a kind of "social capital," the use of which had been limited in the old order but particularly favored in the new one.

An attempt will now be made to interpret the positive ideological and political integration of some sections of Jewry in the light of chances for mobility tied to particular interests and expediencies.

The general conditions for social advancement in the new regime were in many ways similar to those prevailing in the last period of the prewar system. They were based on quite comparable principles. Admittedly, during the Horthy regime, the part played by inherited social "investments" was still quite strong, next to individually attainable "social capital," including educational achievements and professional skills. Noble ancestry, family patrimony, the "old boy" network, non-Jewish origins, a genuinely Magyar (and not Magyarized) surname were all assets helping the advancement both within the ruling elite and within the middle classes in general. However, according to recent studies, in the last phase of the old order, the importance of "inherited social capital" was of diminishing significance, even in leading posts of officialdom.[3]

The ideology of the new system after 1945, concerning the allocation of leading positions—and generally speaking concerning the whole question of mobility—was *formally* meritocratic. Social capital not acquired by individual effort was to be disregarded. This ideology—like all principles of revolutionary social selection—was aiming at the radical devaluation of all class and status privileges: the ruling forms of social capital in the collapsed old regime. This goal was only partially achieved by the abolition of the most archaic forms of discrimination prevalent in the old, nonmeritocratic, selective processes. Among these, one can count the abolition of all anti-Jewish restrictions. During the Second World War, a very large number of positions in industry, trade, finance, and the indepedent professions had been passed into "Aryan" hands, with complete disregard for competence. A similar drive fueled the nationalization of all elements of production. While this move did not do away with large numbers of managers with real competence, it also cut the ground from under the feet of *rentiers,* financiers, and capitalists who had been the beneficiaries of inherited wealth. The abolition of titles and legal privileges, the equality of women before the law, the denial of social influence to Church hierarchies, the introduction of universal suffrage (and its symbolic, formal maintenance even after the elimination of free elections) were all carried out under the aegis of the same meritocratic ideology. Some of the its effects have remained permanent.

It was less simple to apply the same rules to those processes of social selection that had always been based on education, culture, professional competence, or entrepreneurship—that is, on "individual" merit—but that in essence had belonged to the collective social capital of the privileged groups in the old society. One cannot organize an industrial revolution and a new state administration without professional competence. Therefore, the new system partly devalued and partly revalued the functions of professional competence. By its extensive—and selective—educational policies it also attempted an accelerated "output" of revalued forms of competence. In the old regime, legal education and competence had been paramount; now these had lost their primacy and the emphasis was put on technical and scientific training, on applied skills and knowledge. The new regime, so to speak, modernized and reinforced the selective principle of "competence." This, of course, contributed to its self-image: the legitimation of a "revolution of equality."

It had been clear, however—even before the change in power—that it is not possible to recruit a dominant new elite purely by meritocratic methods. The new regime, supported by the bayonets of a foreign occupier, possessed a monopoly of power but lacked legitimacy. Only its technical personnel (or part of it) could be selected according to the traditional rules of certification of competence. The forcible industrialization of the 1950s, the collectivization of agriculture, the obligatory mass mobilization for purposes of economics and politics alike, could be pursued only by the use of police terror and the total control of all social life. These odious tasks could be carried out only by a new political elite. The collective future of the apparatus of power depended on the success of these new policies; the reward for individuals within the system was the optimization —if not the maximization—of their chances for advancement in the abject situation of a country groaning under Soviet occupation. Obviously, the old ruling elite, recruited according to the traditional rules of selection, could not be relied on to carry out the new policies. The system could not rely on a purely technocratic elite either, this having been selected on the basis of competence alone. The regime did not pursue the policy of a rational reallocation of the national product (or that of a rational reinvestment of unconsumed surplus value) which, according to leading theoreticians, would have conformed to the class ideology of a modern professional-technocratic elite.[4]

Its policies fluctuated all the time, often completely ignoring proper economic criteria. On occasion they were voluntarist, but the purposes of voluntarism were subjected to the whims of Soviet demands and instructions. Policymaking was wholly arbitrary, without coherence, and without the inner logic and rationality of "technostructural" systems. Therefore, in the first period of the new regime, competence as a selective criterion was of secondary importance in building up the new power elite. The criterion of competence played some part only in areas far from the decisionmaking centers, where no political power was exercised. The first principle of selection was that of "political reliability." This did not exclude professional competence, but severely limited its application. One may say that "political reliability" functionally replaced most forms of the —largely inherited—"social capital" that had been important in the old system. On the other hand, the functions of professional competence were partly restricted, partly extended in the new order.[5]

"Political reliability" itself, according to the official ideology, could be partially acquired, and partially represented by inherited social capital. It could be acquired by membership in the Party, by activism in the mass movements, "voluntary" social work on behalf of the Communist movement; it could also be attributed to past participation in the movement—especially in the 1919 Commune—or in the Communist emigration. But in order to be recognized as "politically reliable," one had to show one or more of the acquired criteria too. This proved to be essential in applying the strategies of social advancement, as far as the individual was concerned. Besides this, however, the value of the "acquired capital" could be increased by "inherited" criteria, which were, so to speak, the collective property of a family, a social class, or of a community.

Those criteria associated with "working class" or "poor peasant" origin included past political activity of one's forebearers or relatives, and/or having been personally persecuted during the old regime: the new-style "inherited" social capital functioned in much the same manner as letters patent of nobility before the onset of capitalism. It served to demonstrate the unity, the historically predestined oneness of the new ruling elite. In the past, being a nobleman had meant the birthright to a place—and to mobility—within the ruling elite. Similarly, this new kind of inherited social capital served as an entry card to the ranks of the new elite.

Of course, there was no obligation to use it, nor was its use automatic. This new fangled social capital in a way demonstrated one's rejection of the old order. Furthermore, it played an important part in the legitimation of the new power-elite. The unpopular forced accumulation of productive capital was carried out by the "best representatives of the people"; enforced collectivization by peasant chairmen of the so-called "cooperatives" (in reality, collective farms); the liquidation of independent trade unions by worker managers; and the political control of the churchs by "peace priests." Similarly, the fight against Zionism was led by Jewish apparatchiks.

To come back to our original subject: by virtue of their past harassments and—thus, indirectly—of their origins, surviving Jews became the possessors of this new kind of inherited social capital. And this meant that they became a *natural* reservoir of selection for the new ruling group.

This, of course, did not mean an exclusive privilege for Jews willing to accept positive integration. Nor did it ensure a place within the bastions of power for all Jews. It meant simply that being of Jewish origin had lost its negative connotation, while Gentile middle-class elements (the potential competition for Jewry), especially those who had been active in the old regime, acquired that negative connotation. Jewry thus did not automatically gain power, but only a better position from which to start. The positive integration that could result was not achieved in the wholesale manner that has been suggested by a certain social stereotype current in Hungary (no doubt of anti-Semitic inspiration). Jewish origins were but one element in the process. In borderline cases, in which there was competition among equally strong candidates, being Jewish may have done the trick, but it was far from being a necessary condition for success.

The moral judgment inherent in the prejudiced stereotype mentioned above is untenable. In light of recent historical research, the facts point to the other way. Jews simply made good use of the social opportunities available to them as a group. The temporary advantages gained by the survivors, owing to the change in power, did not lead to naked opportunism or a wild drive to grab what they could. In glaring contrast, broad masses of the Gentile middle classes, the so-called "petty Nazis," the bustling radical wings of bourgeois parties, did their level best to compensate for their servility toward the old regime by a barefaced reversal of their position.

A 1949 survey on people in public service showed that the proportion of those who did not belong to a political party—42.5 percent—was the lowest among those who had worked in public offices before 1945; while the proportion of public servants of the same category was the highest among the members of the united Socialist-Communist party: 46.5 percent.[6] These people *had* to be middle class Gentiles. As the author of the survey states: "taking absolute numbers, by 1949, among all those public servants who belonged to the Communist Party, 67 percent had been in public service before 1945." It is something of an understatement when the author comments: "Readiness to adaptation is nothing strange for public servants."[7]

The recruitment policies of the coalition parties between 1945 and 1948 offered many an example for the *volte-face* performed by middle class people attempting to save—or trying to further—their careers. It is true that the division of the spoils of power among the parties of the coalition did work on the basis of *Cuius regio, eius religio,* and this naturally influenced the political orientation of the middle classes. Belonging to no party carried the brand of being "politically suspect" with it.[8] Therefore, public servants rushed to join the party which commanded the ministry or institutions in which they worked. Often this took the form of enforced recruitment. For instance, the number and proportion of Communist Party members was very high among physicians, mine manages, and policemen, as the relevant government departments they were working for happened to be under Communist control.[9]

In the months of gradual Communist takeover of power—in the wake of the 1947 elections—practically the whole Gentile middle class stampeded into the Communist Party, its "future steward." Otherwise usually apolitical officials, like notaries or teachers (among whom there were hardly any Jews) scrambled to join the Party.[10] It is superfluous to point out that the middle class "reacted very sensitively to the changes in power" and "joined the strongest battalions."[11]

In this rush for Party membership, the "political capital" of assimilated Jewry was a great help toward far-reaching opportunities for mobility. This was, of course, due not only to their advantageous situation as a consequence of the persecutions, but also to quite a few other objective factors connected with other social assets of post-1945 Jewry and with the special circumstances of the thoroughgoing social reorganization.

We have discussed elsewhere the sizable specific potential for mobility as an asset of the Jewish survivors. The upward shift in class status after 1945, their high levels of education, their political motivation, are just as good indicators as the high proportion of "reproductive social investment" per head among Jewish youth. Owing to these factors, Jews as a group (having already been in a high state of mobility that had been arbitrarily throttled down) could offer many more suitable candidates for responsible positions in the new system than any other politically fit social group. Professional competence, political knowhow, organizational talent, qualities of leadership, verbal skills—these, and other, endowments of a metropolitan middle class culture and social practice—gained additional importance with the newly introduced forms of mass mobilization and political manipulation. New Jewish functionaries of middle-class origin almost always outshone the new "working-class cadres" that were just graduating from crash courses. In fact, many of the latter were also Jews, thanks to the fact that the proportion of working-class Jews as a percentage of the total Jewish population—about 31 percent[13]—was very much the same as that in the total population.

Naturally, they were better fitted for responsible jobs. Although in 1945 only about a third of the Jews of Budapest were working class, as we have seen, the relative position of Jews in the whole working class was much better. Therefore, their potential for mobility was also that much greater. Significantly, the proportion of Jews among the least skilled elements of the working class had been and still was strikingly low.[14]

These differences between categories of workers—always advantageous for their Jewish members—no doubt had a beneficial effect on the chances of the Jewish working class in the transformations of 1945 and 1949. The new regime elevated the criterion of "working-class or peasant origin" to a predominant principle of selection, particularly in contrast to the "class alien" tag. But this principle could easily be the subject of manipulation,[15] particularly in borderline cases, like those of independent artisans and so on; and, again, Jews were strongly represented among these.

An additional advantage for Jewry was the concentration of survivors in Budapest. The consolidation of one-party rule meant the sudden growth and overweening authority of the centralized governing bodies—all, of course, located in the capital.

It would be worth further study to consider the cultural pattern of lower-class and lower-middle-class Jewry, in the light of the demands set before them by the new social situation. These groups—like small traders, commercial employees—possessed certain specific skills: business sense, readiness to haggle, a nose for the market. They also practiced ascetism in consumption, abstention from drinking, a good knowledge of the ground, a sober assessment of the given social situation, quick learning, and a talent for adjustment—all of these qualities are typical of oppressed minorities worldwide. Their scholastic successes also demonstrate these qualities.[16]

The question is, in what way was this bundle of collective assets a match for the demands set before the new cadres of a radically reshaped bureaucracy. It goes without saying that, in terms of career prospects, some of these qualities represented manifestly strong advantages over non-Jewish new cadres in many areas. In the network of commerce, in industrial reorganization, in communications (journalism, publishing, printing) Jews had always had strong traditions, thanks to their class structure.

Soon enough, a kind of "dual cadre" system emerged: the "working-class cadre" performed the duties of representation and promotion, and maybe some tasks of administration, while the Jewish professionals managed the business. This was not very different from the boards of banks and large concerns in the old regime, with their aristocratic "dummies" whose only task had been to draw their stipends. Now, the "dual cadre" system was a direct result of the crying need for new cadres. In the course of a few years not only was there a changeover of the power elite taking place, but also a large-scale increase in bureaucratic personnel as well. The network of control radiating from the center in the years of forced industrialization and planning required an untold number of intermediate cadres for its operation. The growth in State bureaucracy from the beginning of the coalition period in 1945 up to 1947 was quite spectacular.[17] Only a small part of the new upper and middle level positions could be filled by "worker-peasant" cadres. According to an accurate and detailed survey, "in 1949, 7.3 percent of the new administration was working-class by previous occupation;" even in leading positions (heads of departments or higher) only 21.5 percent came from the working-class. According to the author, "in the course of two years, 1947 to 1948, 72,500 new administrative positions were created; about half of these were filled from the ranks of originally independent or self-employed people who had to become State employees. The rest were recruited for *entirely new* administrative jobs."[18]

Without relevant data it is not possible to demonstrate the measure and extent of the attractions of these opportunities specifically for the lower and middle class groups of Jewry. Over and above the political and social "capital" of Jewry mentioned before, the factors of its group culture and of its historical-social experiences must have played an appreciable part in their attitudes toward the demands of new cadres. Even since the end of the last century, an intellectual, or at least semi-intellectual, reserve army had developed from the ranks of lower- and middle-class Jews, owing to their propensity to a measure of "over-schooling." The ruling official (or latent) anti-Semitism denied then the "pensionable" jobs; the private sector could employ only some of them. Language teachers, private tutors, newspaper stringers, music instructors, and occasional publishers had been typical instances of this function-less "marginal," semi-profes-sional intelligentsia.[19]

Between the wars many university and high school graduates swelled the ranks of the unemployed intellectuals. The proportion of Jews among them was much higher than that of Gentiles, according to 1928 figures. Moreover, the 1920 *Numerus Clausus* Law forced a good number of potential Jewish intellectuals to choose the route of emigration or to take menial jobs. (See Table 1.)

TABLE 1

Unemployed Israelite White Collar Workers, Professionals and Others in Intellectual Occupations, 1928
(in percent)

	Counties	Towns	Budapest	All of Hungary
Unemployed Jews	15.7	36.0	38.1	29.9
All Jews	9.8	25.2	28.7	18.2

Source: My own calculations based on *Magyar Statisztikai Közlemények* (Hungarian Statistical Reports), Budapest, no. 79, 1930, pp. 43,57.

Between 1928 and 1945, this critical state of affairs could only have worsened, partly for well-known reasons, partly as a result of the kind of "social investment" practiced by Jewish middle class families. The main external reason, of course, was the onslaught of institutionalized anti-Semitism which eventually led to the anti-Jewish laws. These laws—from 1938 onwards—drastically restricted the employment of Jews in intel-lectual, or any other white collar, jobs and shut the doors of universities before most of them. However, the secondary schools remained largely open to them, at least up to the time of the German occupation on March 19, 1944. The available indicators testify to the increase in the number of Jewish children (let alone the baptized ones) in secondary school, in all age and sex categories. Indeed, between the two world wars, Jewish girls caught up with Jewish boys at university entrance level. Ever since the 1880s Jewish boys had always been more heavily represented at this stage than the Gentiles, thanks to the class structure of Jewry and its much greater "social investment" in schooling.

For example, in 1943 there were 3,585 Jewish secondary school students in Budapest; a good proportion, 41.3 percent were girls. In the corresponding Gentile group the percentage was only 37.[20] In 1942, according to figures for the then enlarged Hungary, 28.2 percent of Jewish students reaching university entrance level were girls; among Gentiles, this proportion was only 11.1 percent.[21] In the smaller Hungary of 1938, the same proportion had been 38.3 percent among Jewish girls and 23 percent among Gentiles.[22]

In consequence, the proportion of Jewish males and females suitable for posts among the higher and middle cadres was much higher than that of the total population. In fact, in the 1940s this proportin reached its historical maximum. This coincided with the expulsion of the Jews—both Israelites and baptised—from most white collar jobs. Their jobs were taken over by Gentiles; thereby the sizable unemployment among non-Jewish white-collar workers was as good as liquidated during the war years.[23] Of course the boom created by preparations for war and an increase in civil service personnel also contributed to this.

According to our figures, in 1930, nearly one-third of Jewish male students had acquired a university entrance certificate, and half of them were at school at least to the age of 14. We can assume that, by the war years, Jewish female students also reached similar levels. Taking into account the selective nature of the bloodletting, it is pretty clear that an *absolute* majority of Jewish survivors, thanks to their level of education, were capable of immediately taking over middle level management positions.

Following 1945, their chances actually improved in this respect, for two main reasons. On the one hand, there was a natural drive to catch up in education and to compensate for earlier disadvantages. Long before 1937, they had already been excluded from the army academy and from select colleges.[24] From 1939 to 1945, they had been barred from the universities.[25] The younger ones could not complete their secondary education, as they were herded into forced labor service companies. Many of them had to leave school owing to the unemployment of their parents or the disappearance of the breadwinner while serving in the labor service companies. Others again were turned away from the *gymnasia* (high schools)—especially from Catholic institutions (which had started discrimination against non-Catholics early in the century)—and to content themselves with enrollment in the inferior "civil schools."[26] Now they all wanted to rectify these enforced omissions.

This rush into schooling was to some extent influenced by the fact that white collar unemployment did not immediately cease after the Second World War.[27] The reduction of the territory of Hungary meant redundancy for many officials. Later on, a steady stream of those who had escaped to the West returned home again. Large numbers were dismissed for their "Nazi past" or for their "unreliability."

On the other hand, the formal criteria for white collar jobs were swept away following the changeover of power—at least for positions in the power structure.[28] Brand new institutions, including Party schools and the so-called Red Academy were established—institutions which inculcated no administrative skills proper, but endowed their students with a measure of the then much more valuable "political competence." The fresh social capital of Jewry, however tragically acquired, offered a strong initial advantage for entry to these institutions. Those Jewish youngsters who had had to miss part of their schooling but were highly motivated politically, found their "compensatory" education in these outfits. This kind of schooling lifted many of them almost immediately into the ranks of the power elite.

By 1947-48 the shortage of cadres became well-nigh critical. The sheer disposability of Jewish survivors after 1945 made them natural candidates. All those who, during the persecution, had been brutally kicked out of their jobs and had to scrape out a living on the margin, now found it easy to "switch jobs," maybe aided by some political crash course, and thus satisfy the need for personnel trained in the new spirit. It is also understandable that those who returned from the shadow of death in the extermination camps or in the labor service companies gravitated toward the safety offered by the power structure, even if they were not fueled by a wish for vengeance.[29] The multitude of widowed women among Jewish survivors, having no breadwinner, were also forced to look for jobs. Their education and culture—or simply their urban background—that made it easy for them to adapt to new jobs or tasks, gave them a good start in bureaucratic jobs requiring no great competence. The large and increasing numbers of female Communist Party functionaries in the 1950s had quite enough to "compensate" for—also in the Freudian meaning of the term.

In summary, the mass entry of "overeducated" middle class Jews into the power apparatus was strongly correlated to the social and professional frustrations caused by institutionalized anti-Semitism. The so-called "Jewish rule"[30] whispered about in the 1950s had, in fact, been prepared by the historic ruling classes of old Hungary.

Group-Psychological Aspects of Jewish Integration into the New System

This study has so far only attempted to indicate the outlines of an important question, without trying to fully explain it: under what conditions did Jewish survivors carry through their integration into the power structure of the new system; more precisely, what group-specific inhibitions had to be overcome by them and what moral conflicts may have arisen on the way? Their rejection of all the works of the old system that had been based on force and duress is easy to understand in the light of the persecutions they suffered. It is less easy to explain their unconditional acceptance of the new system—also based on a somewhat similar kind of force and duress. Their participation in the apparatus of oppression was active—indeed voluntary. Even consideration of the social and professional gratifications described above, arising from the great change, will not explain fully the behavior of this group of Jewry.

In the recent past, communist ideology had been alien to most of them; particularly its aspects of Stalinist terror. The lack of any traditions of naked individual and collective violence had in fact been a dominant characteristic of their subculture. One can argue that the largely Jewish leadership of the 1919 Commune had laid the groundwork for a sectarian-communist tradition of political violence; that may have induced many Jews, having lived through the collapse of the old order, to adopt this stance after 1948. Their reasons may have been a demand for compensation and wish for a defense mechanism against the possible rebirth of anti-Semitism.

This kind of reasoning, although attractive, is far from satisfactory. Historically speaking, it is a deficient explanation: it does not tell us how and why the cult of violence had arisen among the Jewish leaders of the Commune, in view of their overwhelming bourgeois origin. This was almost the first instance in Hungarian history when force could be used against members of the opposition—indeed, all those who had held different views. On the other hand, this kind of reasoning implies that the victims of revolutionary violence were exclusively Gentiles, an impression anti-Semitic propaganda did its best to convey. "Revolutionary violence" from 1949 onwards—just like its predecessor in 1919—was directed in equal measure against the Jewish bourgeoisie or Jewish "deviants" and all the other "deviants" among the Hungarian people. Indeed, this violence was directed, in a very sophisticated manner, against all those who were arbitrarily branded "deviants" by the communist leadership, for their own ulterior purposes.

The theory of "violence in reverse," has had some vogue. It contends that Jewish secret policemen were the people best suited for carrying out actions of terror, as they had suffered the murderous brutality of guards and officers of the wartime forced labor service companies. Thus the "revolutionary violence" practiced by the Jewish henchmen of the regime was nothing but legitimate "counter-violence." This fantasy illustrates only too well the attempts at self-justification carried out by the new rule of oppression. As is well known, high-ranking Jewish secret policemen did not hesitate to make use of "repentant" petty Nazis or Horthyist "hanging judges." The need for cadres was probably greater in this field than elsewhere. The "old" cadres thus embraced could be expected to be superefficient; they had plenty to "compensate" for. One cannot look for the attractions of this oppressive system, which affected so strongly certain elements of Jewry who desired positive integration, purely in terms of the ideology of revenge: one has to look for a group-psychological variable affecting the changing collective *attitude to violence.* In the circumstances of a rather new form of assimilation, this attitude suffered a reversal, of both in its appearance and in its order of values. In my view, it is indispensable to treat this shift as an important intermediary variable.

The attitude to violence, defined by accepted or preferred forms of violence in a particular social group, must be interpreted in the same sociohistorical context as, for instance, religious practice or family structure. Having no room for a detailed historical study, I indicate only the outline of a working hypothesis, showing the *weakness* of the tradition of violence among Jews in Hungary.

The question is, how far does a hypothesis of this sort cast light on the group-specific political behavior of Jewry in our age? Without going into historical detail, it can be stated that the weakness of the tradition of violence is not a "racial" characteristic and has nothing to do with Jews. Functionally speaking, it seems that originally this may have been the self-defense mechanism of a barely tolerated, oppressed status group, eventually admitted to the margins of society. Willy-nilly, this attitude assumed the form of an ideal, a canon of group morality. This age-old tradition had been reinforced, or rather, reshaped, by the moral canons of an emerging middle class of traders and artisans, as well as professionals, in our times. The ethos (and the practice) of these groups consisted in neutralizing conflicts arising in the course of exchanges, by the use of the contract or the law; of expressing violence verbally or in writing, anyway in a *symbolic* form; of attempting to blunt arbitrary power by their fight for equality before the law.

These features of a "bourgeois" moral culture were, of course, not absent in the other social groups either, but probably they were strongest among Jews—not only because this ethos did not run contrary to their traditions but also because Jewry had been the strongest motive force of "embourgeoisement" in Hungary, even since the Age of Reform in the 1830s. Between the two world wars, bourgeois elements made up the greater proportion of Jews, while among Gentiles the parallel group (including those of German origin, who had had the longest and strongest civic traditions) represented only the narrow tip of a broadly based social pyramid.

Following these historically well attested generalizations, we can attempt to elucidate the characteristic weakness of the Hungarian Jewish tradition of violence. Indicators taken from different areas of social behavior can illustrate this more closely: for instance, the direction of social mobility, the nature of the historical-military tradition, the collective definition of manliness as it affected the individual and the rate and nature of criminality.

To begin with: the social mobility of Hungarian Jewry was never directed toward the armed forces or police while these occupations offered important avenues of social advancement to the offspring of the gentry and civil servants. This was due partly to anti-Semitic discrimination, always extant in these occupations, and partly to the specific patterns of social mobility among Jews, mentioned above. These facts are well enough known not to demand detailed treatment. Maybe a few key data are worth mentioning: for example, toward the end of the liberal period in 1900, only 4.5 percent of civil servants were Jews[31] and in 1910 5.4 percent.[32] In the armed forces, however, the proportion of Jews showed a declining tendency, from 4.2 percent in 1900, to 3 percent in 1910.[33] Between the two world wars, the ranks of the senior police and of the officer class were exclusively Gentile—as was the civil service in general.

In the modern forms of the Jewish religious subculture there was no place for the "martial virtues" or "soldierly spirit." These had been natural features of the ideology of the traditional nobility, and were adopted later on by the rising Gentile middle class. This martial spirit played a strong rule in the socialization of Gentile boys; family attitudes, the school system, and the Boy Scout movement deflected this toward an irredentist political ethos; thus the ideology acquired official status. In the teaching of national history, and in the historical consciousness of the Gentile middle class, the glorification of aggressive manliness played a very strong part, mostly by belittling other ethnic groups. Legendary heroes of Hungarian history are paradigms of a national cult of violence and a xenophobia (directed mostly at neighboring peoples). Not even the ethos of the great colonial powers can match this cult. In Hungarian historical tradition, the ideal of collective violence as an expression of virility was self-centered. The ideals of conquest, of a nation ruling other nations, only served the political ideology of dominance. It proclaimed the historical privileges due to a "martial folk," embodied in the legal continuity of a "thousand years right to rule" (and right to oppress other nations), accorded to the Magyar nobility. It contained nothing of the ideology of "spreading civilization among the benighted," which is characteristic of the colonial spirit of the West.

The slogan of "cultural superiority" surfaced only towards the end of the last century, when the hegemony of the Magyar ruling elite became threatened and, with the dissolution of the Habsburg Empire, eventually vanished.

It was Vilmos Vázsonyi, the respected Jewish liberal politician, who dared to denounce publicly, for the first time, these excesses of the national ethos and the accompanying militaristic customs of feudal origin such as the cult of formal duelling.[34] This was another proof of the fact that the recognition of the right to individual violence was just as much absent from the traditions of Hungarian Jewry as that of group violence. Traditional Jewish morality rejected—or, at least, severely controlled—the formal opportunities for aggression (or for a ritualized release of inhibitions) prevalent in Gentile society: pub-crawling, riotous parties, alcoholism in general. These were the features not only of peasant or working-class life; they were practiced equally by the middle classes (except perhaps by those of German origin). Knife-fights, brawling, rowdiness (more or less accepted outlets for aggressive impulses in other social groups) were as good as forbidden by the moral rules of every Jewish social stratum.

Moral control of sexual behavior was probably also much stronger among Jews than among Gentiles; and sexuality may serve everywhere as a main source for socially approved individual violence. Indirect proof for the latter may be found in the fact that the number of illegitimate births was the lowest among Jews. Comparable data for 1925, for example, show the proportion of illegitimate births among Jews was 3 percent of the total; in 1938, only 2.6 percent. This compares with 9.2 percent and 9.3 percent respectively in the Gentile population in the same years.[35] Other indicators of the social control of sexuality reinforce this assumption.[36] An even stronger proof is contained in the figures on criminal (collective or individual) deviancy. It is well known that tendencies toward criminality are different among middle class people, and their incidence is generally much lower than that of other social classes. Indicators of criminality among Jews were always the lowest of all religious groups (next to the smaller Protestant denominations like the Lutherans, the Unitarians, and Baptists). Analyzing the composition of criminal acts, we find that "acts of violence committed against the person or against the public" are almost completely lacking among Jews. Proof of this is Table 2, summarizing final sentencing in two periods of institutionalized anti-Semitism.

This picture explains, perhaps to some extent, why "Jewish aggressiveness" was such a feature of the fantasy world of anti-Semitism. The ac-

TABLE 2

Types of crime committed	1930				1942			
	Catholic	Calvinist	Lutheran	Israelite	Catholic	Calvinist	Lutheran	Israelite
Rape	261	83	16	9	155	51	12	1
Murder, manslaughter	190	41	26	–	164	46	12	1
Infanticide, abortion, exposure of infants	271	89	24	3	392	122	37	5
Grievous bodily harm	3,481	823	224	34	2,489	755	161	38
Assault on persons	58	7	6	–	70	29	–	–
A. Total of convicted of all crimes	30,300	8,525	2,060	1,859	59,895	18,428	4,333	3,728
B. Total of convicted for crimes of violence	4,261	1,043	296	47	3,270	1,003	222	45
Percentage of B as compared with A	14.1	12.2	14.4	2.5	5.4	5.4	5.1	1.2
C. No of convicted over 15 yrs. of age per 100,000 heads of population	106	79	74	13	–	–	–	–

Source: *Magyar Statisztikai Évkönyv* (Hungarian Statistical Yearbook), 1930, p. 48, and 1942, p. 299.

cusation of "ritual murder" in particular: the notorious scandal of Tiszae-szlár in the last century (1882-1883) was a case in point. A cultural tradition built on the cult of violence could interpret another tradition that rejects open violence in only one way: by projecting into it the idea of an even greater violence shrouded in religious mysticism, as if it were a command of that religion. By the same token, the stereotypes of the "aggressive Jew" took on the character of "symbolic aggression." Irony, business sense, sharp dealing (as contrasted to open, physical violence) had, in fact, been characteristics of Hungarian Jewry, developed through its history and kept alive throughout the process of assimilation.

It is not our task to analyze in detail these features of symbolic violence. No doubt they were defense mechanisms of a strongly mobile group that had been partly kept in a state of pariahdom, while it had also functioned as a dominant motiving force of the economy. This state of affairs would probably account for the collective suppression—or control—of open aggressiveness too. Both the lack of objective, external possibilities and the subjective, culturally determined, sanctions concerning violence resulted in a symbolic compensation. The projective mechanism of anti-Semitism found this duality handy. On the one hand, it supported the idea of the "cowardly Jews" (who does not hit you back); on the other, it reinforced the stereotype of the "aggressive, cunning" Jew (who cheats or pulls a fast one on Gentiles).

Of course, the practice of symbolic aggression was not alien to Gentiles either. This carried the stamp of the ruling groups and of the power relationships which existed. In the villages, the Jewish grocer or innkeeper did have some economic power over the poor peasantry. Indeed—on occasion —he could exploit his customers (mostly by credit at steep interest rates) since he often benefited from the local monopoly of commerce that the Magyar "gentlemen," who considered trade degrading, declined to perform. At the same time, the peasants could despise and look down on the Jews; on occasion—at the time of anti-Semitic hate-campaigns—he may have had the chance to loot the Jewish shops (as sometimes happened in the months following the Tiszaeszlár incident).

The system of symbolic aggression as practiced by the ruling classes had, as its main features, "keeping at a distance from the proletarian;" condescending behavior toward the "common folk"; discrimination against Jews; and—last but not least—the use of arbitrary power. It cannot be said, therefore, that only the Jews applied the techniques of symbolic aggression, while all strata of Gentile society were practitioners of physical violence only. The cult of symbolic violence was just as strong among non-Jews; only its nature differed from that of the Jews. Gentile symbolism was based on the institutionalized, collective superiority of the majority—first of all on that of the ruling groups. The symbolic violence of Jews had been determined by the objective factors of their subjection and defenselessness. Therefore the forms of symbolic violence among Gentiles could be more straightforward, more open. The Jews could never be secure in their application of symbolic violence. They could never rely on the accumulated social authority and power of the historical ruling classes.

The best example of the Jewish attitude was their reaction to anti-Semitism. They hardly ever stood up and attempted to fight it openly, with whatever weapons may have come to hand (even if only verbal ones), although they had every reason to do this. They restricted themselves to passive resistance, to an appeal to—often inadequate—legal remedies or to a kind of verbal vengeance (suited to their subculture), expressed in jokes or in religious quietism. If we look at the figures on emigration, these will show that not even the forms of resistance or withdrawal embodied in Zionism did appear in Hungary to the extent as elsewhere in Central Europe. Shorn of all collective power and authority, their relations with Gentiles were largely restricted to contractual, businesslike contacts. The manifestations of symbolic violence among Jews were mostly expressed in individual adroitness, enterprising spirit and in the use—or abuse—of individually acquired or inherited material capital.

This contention is aptly mirrored in the statistics on criminality. Of course, the incidence of economic crimes is rather high, as is to be expected in a community the majority of which was made up of economically independent, self-employed people. Table 3 clearly shows this.

We have no room for a detailed analysis of these figures. Still, in order to exclude any shadow of misunderstanding, we must point out that—while Table 3 illustrates well the specific character of Jewish criminality—it is far from offering any proof for supporting the anti-Semitic stereotype of the "deceitful Jew." The opportunity for committing crimes of "symbolic" violence is a function of one's class position. For instance, peasants and workers may hardly have the opportunity for committing embezzlement or fraud. Looking at the social distribution of opportunities for such

TABLE 3

Types of crime committed (economic or symbolic)	1930				1942			
	Catholic	Calvinist	Lutheran	Israelite	Catholic	Calvinist	Lutheran	Israelite
Libel and Slander	2,647	1,073	179	195	2,044	627	156	86
False accusation, Perjury, False Testimony under Oath	67	22	3	8	89	41	5	11
Forgery of Handwriting	430	130	34	60	572	206	36	84
Blackmail	395	96	23	79	458	197	26	48
Embezzlement, Misappropriation	2,848	828	207	531	2,496	782	157	229
Larceny	1,014	288	54	16	1,129	399	98	49
Fraud	1,703	435	122	270	2,074	619	126	315
Extortion	11	7	–	7	8	7	2	6
Extortionate Pricing	6	2	1	9	14,763	5,291	1,337	1,091
Total	7,188	2,889	626	1,256	23,633	8,169	1,943	1,919
Percentage of convicted for crimes of "symbolic" violence compared with total of all convictions	23.7	33.8	30.3	67.2	39.5	44.3	44.8	51.5
Proportion of convicted over 15 yrs. of age per 100,000	178	219	158	342	–	–	–	–

Source: See Table 2.

crimes, we may conclude that—according to our data on "symbolic" violence—even the *propensity* to commit crimes was lower among Jews than among the rest. No one could accuse the Hungarian courts of bias in favor of Jews in this period, and a much greater proportion of Jews was engaged in those areas of the economy where opportunities arose for malfeasance —where relationships were based on trust or contract. The statistics on criminality do not properly show this fact. We know that in 1930, 11 percent of self-employed in industry, 33 percent of office staff in industry, 46 percent of self-employed in trade, 47 percent of employed in trade and commerce and 49 percent of lawyers were Jewish.[37] Compared to this, the percentages of Jews among those convicted for crimes of symbolic violence were extremely low: 12 percent of embezzlers, 9.2 percent of forgers of handwriting, 13 percent of blackmailers, 10.7 percent of frauds and only 1.2 percent of misappropriators were Jews. It was probably a consequence of the economic squeeze following the anti-Jewish laws that, by 1942, even this scale of propensity decreased. If we leave out "extortionate pricing"—by then the most widespread offense—the number of symbolic crimes committed by Jews fell from the 1930 figure of 1247 to 828 in spite of a large increase in population. It is quite striking that, by 1942, the share of Jews among the profiteers was an insignificant 4.9 percent. It is difficult to explain this, even if we consider the increasing severity of policing and the ensuing Jewish self-control. After all, the network of retail distribution was still largely in their hands. It is, of course, understandable that the war boom led to an increase of economic and symbolic criminality among Gentiles too.

Summing up our arguments drawn from social history, we may say that institutionalized anti-Semitism gradually stripped the Jews of every chance to indulge in a symbolic gratification of their aggressive drives. This, of course, is a characteristic feature of every oppressive system. The exclusive rights to personal, official, or symbolic violence were reserved for those in power; they applied it, first and foremost, against the Jews—especially during the Nazi terror after October 1944.

At this point, our train of thought meets that of István Bibó, the greatest Hungarian sociological thinker of our time, who has analyzed the process of social selection applied to fascists which brought to the fore a special type of man of fascist drives and of fascist morality.[38] Being by nature violently anti-Semitic, this counter-selection only applied to non-Jews.

Bibó draws two interlinked conclusions from this phenomenon: first, in view of the shortage of good democrats and Jewish immunity to fascist contagion, Jews found themselves in a favorable situation when it came to the selection of personnel for the new, democratic political system; second, it allowed "people of a fascist bent to act in the name of democracy."[39] We can accept both statements and underline their importance. However, Bibó's premise that among the victims of the anti-Jewish laws there were "plenty of them of a fascistic *Gestalt*" cannot be accepted without strong qualifications.[40]

What is objectionable is that Bibó implicitly attributes a psychological character to people "of a fascistic *Gestalt*," and thereby—so to speak—"naturalizes" this phenomenon in the social spectrum. "Fascistic *Gestalt*" is not something "innate": it is a product of social history. Its appearance and spread is tied to certain modern societies in a state of crisis, where violence and counterviolence becomes a legitimized outlet for aggression. Of course, this need not mean that—*potentially*—the "fascistic *Gestalt*" would be less frequent among Jews. It only obliges us to clarify the actual social conditions that give rise to the practice of violence. We must analyze (over and above the immediate interests of the participants) the totality of social practices which apply to the perpetrators of violence: their culture, customs, moral tenets, etc.—in short, their historically developed attitudes to violence. Otherwise one cannot properly understand the origins and evolution of *any* fascist political system—old or new.

If we apply this viewpoint to Jewry between the wars, in an intuitive manner, it seems obvious that individuals of a "fascistic *Gestalt*" among them was not less frequent only because true fascists were also anti-Semites; more importantly, there was simply no room for "fascistic" behavior in the social makeup of traditional—or assimilated and urbanized—Jewish communities. Thus the mass entry of Jews into a different system of institutionalized violence—as it happened in the Communist regime—must be based on a drive for an "anti-bourgeois" type of assimilation and all those concerned had to pay the price of a radical break with the previous social behavior of that group. The ideology justifying this break had then to be a universalist "state religion": the Bolshevik variant of Marxism, with its legitimized practice of terror. This had already been foreshadowed by the Commune of 1919, which set up the model of political action for its commissars.

In 1919, however, only a tiny handful of Jews attached themselves to Bolshevism. After 1945, large sections of the traditional upper and lower Jewish middle class chose the path of positive integration rather than that of remaining outside the system, or that of dissimilation: Zionism. In order to understand why broad masses of Jewry accepted the legitimacy of the new system and undertook the task of supplying its cadres, we have to take into account another, entirely new, intermediary, historical variable: Auschwitz.

The period after the Second World War became a historic turning point for surviving Jewry in every area, including opportunities for the release of their aggressions and their general attitude toward violence. This change can be assessed in the terms of three concepts mentioned above: in the transformation of the moral sanctions of their sub-culture; in the falling away of the opportunities for the release of their aggressions in an economic, i.e., symbolic manner; and their new relationship with the officially approved violence.

It is self-evident that the moral controls asserted by the Hungarian-Jewish subculture, the caution-counseling moderation, the rejection of wild excesses of the "Goyim," (which, incidentally, contributed to positive Jewish self-image) lost their force for those who had staggered back from the death camps or from the horrors of the forced labor service companies. Destroyed was the traditional balance of Jewish-Gentile relationships, which in any case, had been built on a very unequal "social contract." It, nevertheless, represented an uneasy equilibrium between the different forms of aggression/abreaction. In the aftermath of Auschwitz, the old-fashioned use of symbolic aggression must have looked completely absurd and grotesque. The taboo on open aggression could not be upheld any longer. No doubt this transformation was determined by the specific factors of age group and social group, in the nature of common experiences affecting a social unit, stratified along the lines indicated above.

For the elderly, and for those who stuck to their traditions, the moral commands and reflexes of their subculture remained more-or-less in force

—surviving, as it were, their objective obsolescence. For assimilated Jews, particularly for the younger generation, these commands largely lost their relevance. The latter group had undergone its process of moral socialization in the worst period of institutionalized anti-Semitism. For the young, this about-face could lead toward collective dissimilation, channelized by Zionism of an often quite aggressive mentality. One of the main arguments of the Zionists was a rejection of Jewish passivity, of a "stance of martyrdom." It could also lead them toward positive integration, as advocated by the new regime.

It could be an interesting avenue to investigate—from an ethnographic viewpoint—the changes in lifestyle and in value systems shown by Jews in the process of this integration. But even without such a special study, we can easily interpret the cult of collective (and officially sanctioned) violence, or rather that of counter-violence. This was a new script offered by the new system. This new kind of integration was militant—indeed, militaristic—both in spirit and in practice. The main tenets of its ideology were such Marxist dialectics as the class struggle and the dictatorship of the proletariat. Besides these, the symbolic mass activities of the new system celebrated combativeness and "battlereadiness": the mass rallies and demonstrations, the organized handclapping, the rituals of "unmasking and destroying our enemies," the tribunals in schools and factories, the witch hunts and show trials, the breast-beating self-criticism. Of course, in borderline cases, we may even note a mimetic role change adopted by the newly recruited members in the forces of suppression. This behavioral model may easily have been supplied by Nazi camp guards or officers of forced labor companies.

The group-psychological aspects of militant behavior were probably twofold: once more, in the course of their history (as in the 1848-49 War of Independence or in the 1918-1919 revolutions) Jews willing to integrate could rally to a "great cause," could join a fighting comradeship, could rise above petty self-interest. Companionship in such a fighting force is always one of the most effective routes to maximum integration. At the same time, mobilization for a great cause always demands maximum emotional identification and investment. On occasion, an actual overinvestment in certain social roles may also occur.

The gradual weakening of chances for economic success after 1945, followed by their complete disappearance with the wholesale collectivization of the economy, also helped to destroy traditional forms of symbolic counter-aggression that may have allowed a collective group defense of some effectiveness. The official ideology of the Leftist parties, expressed in an anti-capitalist demagogy, allied with the anti-urban demagogy of the former populist movements, reviled and devalued private enterprise, risk-taking, individual investment in work and skills; in many ways, they followed in the footsteps of the anti-urban, anti-Semitic hate campaigns instigated by the erstwhile Gentile ruling elite. The small—or large—Jewish entrepreneur had been hounded on account of his origins in the recent past; now he was being houded as a "class alien." The economic manifestations of symbolic violence, based on individual accumulation of capital, had to disappear completely for a while so that even their memory was branded with ignominy.

Against these minuses, the great plus beckoning to Jews (the first time in the history of Hungary) was the opportunity to live out their aggressions in the name of the State, in an official or a police capacity. Indeed, young Jews as a group—being a small cohort of "natural anti-fascists"—were summoned to occupy the leading positions in the newly formed bodies of "law and order." I mean this summons literally: for instance, a Jewish entrant into an elite college could become a senior police officer, without any preparation or training. How could a sociologist interpret the role change and about-face in moral attitude that fashioned a member of the new secret police's terror squad from a promising art student?

In the first place, loyal service to the new system demanded an identification with the aims and methods of the ruling power. Being a policeman or an official obviously demanded this kind of loyalty. But a similar loyalty was demanded from Party secretaries, block wardens, and Pioneer leaders too. The behavior of these people in the days of Stalinism proved no less brutal—though mostly "symbolic" in its nature—than police violence.

It may have been comparatively easy to identify with the aims—the distant dreams of a perfect society—in spite of possibly disturbing circumstances. Maybe other members of one's family were branded "class aliens;" one had to hush up the existence of relatives living in the West;

one had to brush aside the strong traditions of group solidarity; on occasion one was even forced to dishonor the memory of the martyrs: "Why did they not resist?" Identification with the methods was more difficult. In the light of our previous findings it is clear that open and often physical violence had been alien to the collective social heritage. In any case, an inevitable break had to be made with everything Jewry represented in Hungarian life—culturally, spiritually, and socially. Indeed, in that old ethos, open violence had beeen always considered to be wrong and impermissible.

There were two avenues toward this decisive break with traditional attidues. They were not inherently contradictory: indeed, sometimes they ran parallel to one another. Ideologically assessed, one form was "maximized assimilation;" the other, "maximized dissimilation"—even if this latter differed radically from any known form of Jewish dissimilation (opting out, seclusion), in so far as it also required a particular form of *assimilation,* that is, the acceptance of a non-Jewish value system. Both ideological "solutions" were based on a theoretical fiction justifying "counter-violence" and legitimizing the practice of violent behavior. Without this fiction, the lifting of inhibitions created by the cultural heritage would have been impossible.

The "maximized assimilant" attitude justified the forcible application of power by claiming that this was done "in the name of the Hungarian people" and "its vanguard"; ultimate legitimation was ensured by the guidance of the "best pupil" (Hungarian Party leader Mátyás Rákosi) of the "wise leader" (Stalin). In this context, Jewry as a referent group of social action ceased to exist. It was replaced by a somewhat mythical abstract idea of "the community": "the masses," "the Party," "the international working class" or just "the working people." "Counter-violence" became the rightful tool of a similarly mythical "dictatorship of the proletariat." Violence had to serve the aims of this entity, whose interests (in an even more mythical fashion) coincided with the Marxist dialectic.

It is evident that all these aspects of the theory of "counter-violence" had to exclude every trace of identification with Jewry as such. (It had to exclude every other kind of identification with folk or nation too.) These were replaced by a strongly "sublimated," essentially universalistic identification of interests. The scope of actually—and personally—experienced

sublimation varied, of course. Probably it happened to the greatest extent
among the intelligentsia, particularly the young among them; those members of this group who had undergone a somewhat abstract kind of education—in the arts or in the law—had anyway a much more scanty experience
of social realities. They were habituated to build these up from their own
biased imagination, from reading nothing but the newspapers, or from
fleeting visits to "model villages" set up—*à la* Potemkin—by the Party.
The process of sublimation was probably much weaker among those Jewish cadres who had a direct role to play in industrial production or, who
were active in the forces of "law and order," or in the central agencies of
power. In their case, the other approach to the ideological fiction of
"counter-violence" played its due role.

This approach was a peculiar variant of the ideology of "revenge."
Strictly for internal use, its slogan was: "We are the masters now." It can
be called "maximized dissimilation," because its point of reference was
exclusively Jewishness. Political violence gained its full justification (i.e.,
the offspring of the urban elite could turn into a secret policeman) from
the battlecry: "We beat them instead of their beating us!" The peculiarity
of this concept—its exclusive Jew-centeredness—lies in the identification of
the "We" with the mythical community: a kind of abstract idea of Jewry
that had never existed in reality. This "We" excludes, for instance, traditional and religious Jewry, those who refuse to engage in counter-violence
("the cowards"); it also excludes the Zionists, especially those who emigrated to Israel (comments on them are unprintable); also the "reactionary-
bourgeois" Jews. In this value-system the true representatives of this "We"
is the secret policeman or the Party secretary. Everyone who dares to oppose these authentic representatives of the mythical confraternity must be
excluded from the community and, on occasion, can be safely persecuted.
Jewish party functionaries hardly ever used categories derived from religion—not even among themselves. Nevertheless, in this instance we cannot
but recognize a borderline case of the concept of the "good Jews" in contrast to the "bad Jew."

A correct definition of authentic identity is always a very important
factor in the internal tensions of a threatened social group. Within a majority, or within a ruling elite, this problem hardly arises. Within the minority
in question, the problem disguises a conflict of strategies, essential for the

sake of the survival of the community as such (that is, not that of its individual members, but that of the integrity of a whole community). Without any hair-splitting, one can conclude that the category of the "good
Jew" means, in this instance, a Jew who actively supports—or actually
participates in—the regime. This is why this kind of dissimilant behavior
is "maximally assimilant." According to this interpretation, the "We"
consists of those whom the regime accepts as "progressive-minded people."
The definition of the "good Jew" is very much the same as that of the
"decent Goy." Everything specifically Jewish has been drained from this
concept, whether religious, cultural or moral. Indeed, even the semblance
of such specifically Jewish traits must be carefully censored. (For example,
the children must remain ignorant of their Jewish origin; if they happen
to know it, officially they are "atheists.") Jewishness in this case is only a
contingent factor: the once persecuted person now takes his revenge.

Even this residual trace of Jewishness can be dissolved by assuming the
role of a representative of the "oppressed working masses who have now
become masters of their own fate." What we find here is a confluence or
overlap in the assimilant and the dissimilant interpretation of the fictional
"counterviolence." Analytically speaking, we may discover the difference
in the rate of sublimation. The assimilant behavior continued to be exclusively oriented toward the defense of universal interests; the attitude of
the dissimilants supported an artificially created particularism. The overlap
found its expression in the identical stand of both groups: they distanced
themselves from Jewry as such, on occasion even approved of the persecution of its own members according to Marxist doctrine.

These strands of positive integration led to a twofold consequence of
a sociopsychological nature. The newly recruited party cadres of Jewish
origin (that is, those who had no prior involvement in the Social Democratic or illegal Communist movements) were induced to make an "over-
investment" in their new role, maybe to compensate for the loss of their
cultural heritage. On occasion, these new cadres showed the over-enthu-
siasm of neophytes. Another manifestation of this over-investment may
have been an almost pathological public play-acting. There was many an
instance of conflict between their private *persona* and their official behavior, with troublesome cross-currents afflicting the individual. Their
voluntarist positive integration swept them up as individuals only, while

their families, friends, and their broader cultural affiliations remained untouched by it. This poorly disguised confusion and perplexity of the new cadres came to the fore in a striking manner at the time of the "thaw" following the new government program proclaimed by Prime Minister Imre Nagy in 1953. Among other things, this program involved a thorough-going reassessment of the previously sanctioned very vague rules governing the proper behavior for party cadres.

This basic uncertainty may have been one source of the many arbitrary acts perpetrated by the new cadres (often without the approval of their superiors). The probably deliberately vague definition of their role may also have contributed to this uncertainty, amid almost revolutionary changes affecting them. The "party line," the working principles, directives, and oppressive practices of the highly centralized despotic regime had been arbitrarily changing all the time. These twists and turns made it virtually impossible to lay down clear rules for the exercise of power. To cap all this, the concept of the "cadre," as the executor of an uncommonly broad application of power, had been earlier quite unknown in Hungary. The new despotic system was Manichean in nature, not pluralist. It was characterized by the slogan of the Rákosi-Stalinist period: "He who is not with us is against us." It was not unusual that the local party secretary in a factory became at one and the same time a manager in back-seat control of production, an investigating magistrate, a detective, a factory owner, a representative of the workers, a government commissar, a local councilor—all rolled into one, all difficult to reconcile. The difficulties of playing the role of a cadre were thus structurally determined.

Furthermore, it was not only the concept of the "cadre" and the new manner of exercising power that was alien to the historical traditions of Hungary: power was now exercised by new men as well. In the eyes of the Gentile middle class, shorn of *its* power, these were "proletarians and Jews." We should leave aside the question, how far this was really true, considering the entirety of the new cadres. It is enough to say that for the cadres of Jewish origin this role was radically new and—in social terms—unauthentic. It could rely neither on a historically acquired status of Jewry, nor on specifically Jewish norms of behavior, nor on the collective value system of Jewry. The members of the erstwhile ruling classes found it easy to slip into the seats of power; they as good as inherited them. Their family background, their environment, their education, their value-system, their tastes and habits were in accordance with the exercise. And it was not only this subjective feeling of unauthenticity (a further source of their uncertainties) that confronted the new Jewish cadres. The majority of Hungarian society living outside the magic circle of power—and not only the members of the discredited old ruling class—considered their role to be preposterous and somehow "not right." István Bibó grasped this view best, when he wrote: "Probably the old rule applies here, according to which individuals, grown up in a feudalistic atmosphere, find it easier to accept leadership, superiority, even high-handedness, from others having an authority sanctified by history. They resent the same coming from someone of their own kind, especially if they have well-established characteristics, making them somewhat different."[41]

This unauthenticity of the new power elite was also aggravated by its demographic constitution. There were far too many young people and women among them—both groups carrying a negative sign in the canons of social authority. In addition, formal scholarly achievements as a basis for selection had been done away with. The crying need for cadres, created by the takeover of power, offered the chance for some quite spectacular careers; and these ran in complete disregard of all the hallowed definitions of competence for power positions.

On top of all this, the legitimacy of the new elite remained doubtful for quite a long while. They claimed a kind of "revolutionary legitimacy" —but no revolution from below had actually taken place in the country, only a takeover of power supported by an alien occupier. No revolution was ever sanctioned by the popular will expressed in free elections—as required by the democratic system installed in 1945. The question of doubtful legitimacy is important only in this context, because—the new elite possessing no traditional authority—a bureaucratic exercise of power had to be clothed in a "quasi-charismatic" garb. Power as such came to be tied not to a person or to persons but to an exalted institution. This system, slavishly copied from the Soviet model, was installed in Hungary by people amost exclusively Jewish in origin. It therefore became easy to draw a sign of equality between "communists" and "Jews."

It is therefore no wonder that a conviction took root among Jews and Gentiles alike that the new regime and the new elite represented something alien and transient in the history of the nation.

The Profit-and-Loss Account of Commitment:
The Crises of Being a Cadre: Jewish "Solidarity"

In order to understand the working principles of this new kind of as-similation—implying a severe alienation from Jewish moral and cultural traditions—we have to analyze a number of factors in more detail. First of all, the function of a quasi-charismatic leading personality (or person-alities) of Jewish origin for the legitimation of the power structure; the way in which the "folkloristic" ideology, tied to the "cult of personality" fitted into the social awareness of Jewish survivors; the self-induced and self-sustaining personal profit-and-loss accounts—and personal crises—generated by identification with the despotic regime. I intend to pursue these largely hypothetical concepts from the point of view of those Jews only who were active participants in positive integration (disregarding other historical developments in the country as a whole).

To begin with, we may state the fact that commitment to totalitarian-ism must be complete, that is, unconditional. Totalitarian systems do not allow conditional identification (except for those, whose existing social capital—authority or artistic or political prestige—makes them useful adjuncts to the regime, so that their partial support can be tolerated).[42] These anti-liberal, non-permissive, non-eclectic ideologies are exclusive: they deny legitimacy to any other system. Identification with a system of this kind means complete commitment, if only because this adherence utterly compromises the individual in the eyes of all those who do not share this loyalty.

To make things more difficult, the regime itself was being subjected to constant change. The political system called "people's democracy" under-went many twists and turns between 1947 and 1956. These were due not only to shifts in local power relations, but also to the worldwide strategy (and ideological mirages) of the occupying Soviet power. These bore no relation whatsoever to the situation in Hungary. In consequence, the "Party line" was wavering all the time, without visible rhyme or reason; but the utter devotion to this "Party line" itself was never allowed to waver. The opposite of devotion is disillusionment; just as the opposite of economic or emotional investment is breaking away, that is, disin-vestment.

I mention this, because the logic of identification with a totalitarian regime that is chopping and changing all the time, can be best approached via the logic of economic investment. The greater the investment, the more difficult it is to cut one's losses, although there is no profit in the enterprise. The investor is "running after his money" and is willing to invest even more, in the hope that in the end he can amortize his capital.

Identification with the totalitarian system can be considered a form of social investment. The measure of the value of an investment is, of course, its *price* (in our case, this can be "objectified"). The measure of political commitment is the value of what the "investor" has given in exchange, i.e., what price he had to pay: the rejection of group loyalties, a change in self-identity, the denial of certain values, or a change in lifestyles. Furthermore, *in what manner* has he been obliged to express his loyalty—and what was the price of *this*? The profitability of such an investment will be expressed in the relation of price with social gain.

Even if we rely on intuition only, it seems clear that the price paid by the Jewish party cadres, who had gone along the route of positive integration all the way, up to the specific assimilation mentioned above, was at least as high as the one paid by new cadres of "worker-peasant" origin, or the one exacted from the civil servants of the old regime who had undergone their political conversion. But the social gain they could expect was equally high, considering the "added value" of their moral-psychological sublimation or the "profit" of physical and social safety accorded to erstwhile pariahs who now became "shareholders" of total power.

Let us examine a few examples to illustrate our thesis.

The price of a similar "investment" for an erstwhile Nazi stormtrooper was negligible. All he did was to change uniforms. His tasks were very much the same. His peasant or servant origins made him well fitted to carry out commands without demur. Physical force and violence (passive or active) were part and parcel of his social experiences. He had hardly any other job prospects except the one of carrying arms. Probably his family background—that of servility—had been shaped by his (positive or negative) dependence on the powers-that-be. His traditions dictated that he should always keep on the right side of the "masters"—so a change of uniform was no skin off his nose.

The elevation of someone of "worker-peasant" origin into the job of factory manager or something similar meant a huge social gain and very little personal investment. Therefore, the marginal losses suffered through his break with his class—cultural shock, social isolation—seemed at first of little consequence. Of course we know that in real life this has not worked out so smoothly. The genuine "worker-peasant" cadres (not the "pseudo-" ones who had acquired the social capital of being a "son of the people" through some clever cosmetic manipulation of their class origin) had to carry the burden of their sudden jump up the ladder throughout their whole life, in being social outcasts, in role-insecurity, in nervous breakdowns.

The "old" public servant or professional who accepted the role of the "progressive intellectual" usually did not gain much, but did not lose either: he avoided loss of class status. Being a political turncoat, however, may still have carried a fairly high moral price. (It should be pointed out that all the parties in the coalition government, not only the Communists, had been busy in persuading the "old" civil service to change sides.) It may have meant estrangement from one's family, often a complete break with one's nearest and dearest. Of course, the members of the Gentile middle class were hardly ever put into positions of real power or trust, unless—and this was very rare—they could call on the "acquired" capital of participation in the illegal Communist movement. Mostly they played the part of technical or administrative experts, at some distance from central power; so their role was less "degrading" and did not require the same wholesale political commitment. Those who may have joined the Communist Party in the Coalition period (before 1948) and had done work in "political" jobs were usually shifted to nonpolitical positions after the Communist takeover. The group-psychological conflicts of positive integration therefore cannot be said to have affected the Gentile middle class in a comparable manner.

Unconditional solidarity with the new regime took a very different form in the moral and social "household economy" of the surviving Jews. We must, however, make a distinction between those Jews who had already been politicized and thus, in a manner, prepared for social and political tasks on the one hand, and the more traditional, culturally more conscious Jews who had, earlier, followed the route of "bourgeois assimilation" on the other.

An empirical analysis would find many representatives of the technical or legal intelligentsia (and their scions and relatives) in the first group. In the second group, those of the commercial and industrial middle classes, middle managers, and other office workers and their relations probably were more numerous. This difference is, in a way, a reflection of political engagement by Jews between the wars.

The members of the first group had already belonged to the leftist opposition, whether immersed in political action or just emotionally engaged. They hailed, therefore, the change in power as a self-fulfilling prophecy. They had already left behind them several landmarks on the political road toward integration, well before the shift in power. The abandonment of Jewish religious and moral traditions, as a price paid for their assimilation, had been an essential element in their social environment. For those who had not participated in the working-class movements, this usually meant a cosmopolitan culture, the artistic or literary *avant-garde,* not the catechism of dialectic materialism. Some members of this group may have fallen by the wayside. They abandoned positive integration, disgusted and revolted by the depredations of the Russian soldiery and the "salami tactics" of the Communists. The majority, however, was swept along by the utopian radicalism of the "new dawn."

It should be stressed that, after October 1944, the Communist Party was the only one whose ideology and social program promised a *total* break with the practices of the old regime. The three other constituent parties of the Coalition had legally existed and operated in the Horthy period. Therefore the Communist Party seemed the ideal rallying point for all those who had become completely alienated from the old system: all those who had suffered under it from anti-Semitism, who had belonged to the left, who had been the victims of racial and political persecution. They could easily accept the tenets and the practices of "revolutionary violence" in the spirit of "counter-violence"; especially those who had already been prepared for this in some measure by their political awareness or their illegal past.

The price of becoming a cadre was, therefore, comparatively low from the point of view of group psychology—the more so because for many of them this was a collective act, involving families, friends, and peers. They could also salvage something of their moral principles (with the help of a good dose of "false consciousness"). The new role could satisfy not only their—broadly or narrowly conceived—group interests, but could serve distant and desirable goals too, with vistas of moral and political sublimation.

This group, however, made up only a minority of all those Jews who set out on the road toward positive integration[43] —but they had the best chance of swift career advancement. Over and obove their "primary social capital" (i.e., their Jewishness) they also possessed an appreciable political capital. It may be said of this group that, among the new cadres, their earlier, so to speak "anticipated," political investment was the greatest— and so were their expectations of success.

When we come to consider the other Jewish group, ready and willing to embark on positive integration, we find that the symbolic costs of a changed identity and of a break with moral and cultural traditions were much higher. For them, the price of new loyalties involving a different kind of assimilation was rather steep. No doubt this did cause many a conflict within families and among friends. Group solidarity had been one of the fundamental values of their traditional subculture. Feelings for this had been much strengthened by common suffering during the physical and moral persecution. Family traditions, including continued adherence to religion, had been the mainstay of an ideology whose central tenet had been the maintenance of spiritual continuity with one's forebearers. On the other hand, the destruction of extended families must have led to a loosening of the ties of kindred. This may have lessened the pain of dissension with those who wholeheartedly joined the Party. (It would be of interest to explore how many of the new cadres had no relatives left. Altogether, an analysis of the linkage between demographic factors and political mobility would be a worthwhile subject for inquiry.)

At the same time, certain features of the social stratification, of pre-vious experencies in migration and mobility affecting the survivors, may have exacerbated dissensions with the "renegades." As we have seen, practically the whole of Jewry had been in a state of mobility—geogra-phically as well as socially. Even the poorest, proletarian, elements of Jewry had some kinship with "bourgeois" Jews. Most families had rela-tives abroad, including some (the Lord forbid) in Israel. The "bourgeois" came to be condemned to serious loss of class status. The emigrants— especially those to Israel—became "enemies" or "traitors" after 1949.

A good cadre was obliged to break all links with such elements. Sometimes they even had to deny the martyrs in their own families, as these could hardly be said to have represented Communist ideals.

This attitude, allied to a positive evaluation of their break with the past and present, explains why the loyalty of Jewish cadres toward the new regime was that much stronger than that of Gentiles. "Never again another Auschwitz," or "We shall never submit the way they did"—if slogans like these were signs of distancing themselves from the martyrs, rather than just expressions of defiance, they also carried a powerful commitment.

People of this kind had to leave behind their identities, their moral traditions, just as they were bereft of any other kind of emotional investment. Let us not forget the disintegrated families, the numbers of widows, 7000 orphans in the capital alone—they had no other choice than to identify fully with the new regime, hoping for some sort of emotional compensation for their grievous losses.

In their new role, the price of loyalty, as well as the reward that could be expected, was largely symbolic. Without a previously acquired political capital, their career prospects in the political field proved to be limited. On the other hand, however, the reward (and the price) may have looked emotionally greater, in so far as they could be linked to the *messianistic* elements of their traditional subculture (factually, or as a means of sublimation). In this context, those economic and professional frustrations that may have found their release after 1945 can be said to have played a negligible part in the price/reward equation. This majority group of Jews, ready for positive integration, would have become the stalwarts of the new regime even if their chances of mobility had not improved considerably. In fact, in many cases this did not even happen. The widow of a shopkeeper, now in a low-grade clerical job, may have been a "sentimental Communist," may have mourned Stalin, may have been proud of his Pioneer son, without her attitude having any bearing on her "objective interests."

If we accept the conclusions of our analysis, it will become self-evident why *some* of the Jewish cadres can be found among the most extreme supporters of Rákosi's rule of terror and why they often remained his faithful acolytes to the bitter end. Total commitment was a "social

contract" heavily paid for; it could not be canceled at the first disappointment. Moreover, the greater the number of moral compromises, the
greater the social ostracism for their slavish execution of hateful policies
(i.e., the "price" paid for their commitment up to a critical threshold).
It became important to justify the profitability of the investment—at least
subjectively. This justification then demanded further and bigger compromises, thereby adding to the "investment." In the meantime, the
chances of reward gradually shifted toward an indefinite future—especially
those of the nonmaterial kind; and these were the important ones (because they were best suited for sublimation). Material rewards, the fruits
of participation in power, could be taken for granted. This, however, was
not cause enough for self-justification. So the fervent belief in the "new
dawn" grew ever stronger—the obverse of their blindness toward the misdeeds of Stalinism. With the self-destructive degradation of the regime,
this fervent belief, as the only remaining support for their loyalty, took
on the character of an *independent sociological variable.*

The show-trial of József Cardinal Mindszenty, the general "struggle
against clerical reaction," the forcible relocation" of "class enemies," the
hate campaign against Tito, the expropriation and pauperization of the
peasantry could all be carried out in the name of the "international class
struggle." Less so the execution of László Rajk and his comrades. Least
of all the preparations for a show trial of Jewish physicians—"the criminals
in white coats"—especially when one could easily become a candidate
for liquidation oneself, as one of the "medical gangsters."

As is well known, many of the new cadres had this experience. The
victims of the so-called "conceptual trials," who uttered the wildest self-
accusations incriminating themselves, were tragic—and paradigmatic—examples of those beyond-the-borderline cases when the ideology fueling
public behavior becomes completely divorced from reality. Even plain
human self-interest—indeed, the instinct for self-preservation—will be suppressed, for the sake of a mythical identification with a fictitious social
entity that claims to transcend the interests of real people. The unconditional belief in "true socialism" thus turned into our independent sociological variable, *in spite* of the day-to-day experience of social reality.

Our cautious working hypothesis can be stated therefore as follows:
new cadres of Jewish origin, by virtue of their great social investment in

political commitment, and in their expectation of a strongly sublimated set of rewards, were bound to occupy such an extreme stance—much more than anybody else.

If all this is true, we can guess that their disillusionment with the regime must have been an even more searing experience than that of the others. After awhile, the accumulation of unfulfilled hopes reached the critical threshold—any further "investments" would only have meant emptying the beaker of shame to its last bitter dregs (*toute honte bue,* in the words of François Villon). Their attitude, having lost all its sense and reason, had to change. Commitment and loyalty, in particular their emotionally over-invested—and socially degrading—forms, had to give way to something different. One can distinguish four variations of new attitudes.

The first variant did not directly involve any kind of spectacular public switch of behavior. It simply meant that from the role of a party-centered *apparatchik* (while retaining official power positions) they transmuted themselves into job-centered professionals. Party trusties in enterprises and institutions, who had been feared and hated in the early 1950s, turned themselves, in the next decade, into popular researchers or engineers—often without leaving the Party while regaining the trust and esteem of their peers. Emotional engagement diminished or vanished completely. Its place was taken by the prospect of a professional or scientific career. This came about much more easily for Jewish cadres than for the other, "worker-peasant" cadres, as the majority of the former did not have proper qualifications—and competence—for doing their job in a satisfactory manner.

The second avenue of "disinvestment" did not require any visible about-face in attitude or behavior. The role played by the cadres did not change, only the spirit driving it. In other words, the enthusiastic, eager, faithful cadre became the cynical agent of power. He kept up appearances not for the sake of "Socialism" but for the sake of his own selfish interests. By the 1960s, the members of this second group made widespread use of the dichotomy between "internal" and "external" morality (*Binnenmoral* and *Aussenmoral*). This was, of course, nothing new. Even since the 1950s, practically the whole community applied this social technique. The Jewish cadres in question behaved quite differently in their private lives from their public *persona*—sometimes one was in sharp contradiction to the other. However, nothing could replace the emotional engagement for these people; the collapse of "investment" in the movement led to a total moral vacuum. This type represented a special aspect of positive integration: one with either very high or with very low mobility. Age also came into it. So we could find this type both among elderly professionals and among young unskilled workers who had become cadres.

The third group forced to "disinvest" displayed a much more dramatic shift in behavior and attitudes. Former loyalty and commitment turned into moral indignation. With them, the greater the rate of original investment and its more zealous exercise, the stronger became the feeling of loss, of having been deceived, of moral crisis. There were two ways of resolving this crisis. One was to leave the Party, to become apolitical; the other, to return to the original community. A very sizable part of the mass emigration in 1956 and after was made up of disillusioned Jewish ex-cadres, in particular of those of the younger generation. The parents—owing to their advanced professional careers and the stability of their social investments— were reluctant to leave the country. They adopted one of the new attitudes described above—or the one described below—and stayed at home.

The shock of the 1956 revolution also meant a parting of the ways for the whole Hungarian Jewish community, including the new cadres. They had to choose between reintegration or separation. This situation became even more critical for the whole of Jewry (including those who did not take part in positive integration), as the ghost of a new wave of anti-Semitism arose from the shadows. We know now that this fear was quite groundless, but its effect was real. We should not forget that 1956 was only half a generation away from 1944. The impact of 1956 brought to the fore, in a dramatic manner, the demand to break away from the Party, as well as from the whole past. This impact was much greater among the handful of surviving Jews—first and foremost among the new cadres—than among Gentiles.

All this leads us to the fourth form of disengagement. A good part of the Jewish cadres, now bitterly disillusioned with the despotic rule of Rákosi (among them the militant Communist leader of youth movements) turned their moral indignation into political action. Precisely on account of their previous commitment, they became the most radical, effective, and bravest critics of Stalinist political practices—*in the name of true Socialist ideals.* It is very likely that a scrutiny of the list of victims executed or imprisoned in the course of the Soviet-inspired savage repression in the wake of 1956 would show a sizable overrepresentation of young Jew-ish cadres.[44] Many of them had indeed been among the moving forces in the preparation and effectuation of the revolution.

It is not too difficult to interpret this phenomenon in the light of our sociological disquisitions on the social circumstances of positive integra-tion. In the motivation of this fourth group, political awareness had *pre-ceded* adherence to the new rule. They had already distanced themselves from traditional Jewry; they had as good as given up their Jewish identity. All this made it impossible for them to choose any of the available routes: disengagement, emigration, an apolitical stance, or cynical resignation. In the new social environment after 1945, their cultural and historical identi-fication with the country became complete. This closed the route of Jew-ish dissimilation—there was no doubt about their identity with the nation.

On the other hand, their parallel identification with the ruling system was of a more sublimated nature. It was quite blinkered, considering that for them their "belief"—the purely political interest—had played a much stronger part than natural and "healthy" self-interest in terms of a socially acceptable career. Their violent reaction against discredited despotism could only find resolution in an equally intensive counteraction, carried out by political means. De-Stalinization from 1953 onward created the possibility for such political activity. The strength of this reappraised sub-limation was demonstrated when—following the defeat of the revolution in which many of them had played a leading part—very few of them left the country. They tried to carry on the fight for a "Socialism with a human face," under constant threat to their mere existence, often suf-fering heavy prison sentences, loss of jobs, continuous censorship, early retirement and so on. Certainly, they had had the requisite assets for their enterprise: their previously strong links with the Communist movement helped them to convey their political demands upwards; their Jewish origins and their social capital acquired through participation in the move-ment meant that they could not be accused of wishing "to bring back the old order." In addition, they had an intimate knowledge of the situa-tion, including the workings of the Stalinist political mechanism (in their criticism, they knew how to act "according to the inner rules of the Party"), and they succeeded in hanging on to such powerful positions as their leadership of highly esteemed institutions (the press, the writers' guild) which proved to be the best instruments in shaping opinions in *Party* ranks.

In contrast to appearances and to general public belief (not only of anti-Semitic inspiration), the Jewish majority of the Communist leadership—in the first phase of the new dispensation—had an ambiguous effect on the motives and the success of positive integration. It is true that both among the returning emigrants and among the leaders of the legal and illegal movements, Jews were in the majority. This leading group had no need for positive integration. They had prepared themselves for their role for several decades. From the point of view of a successful positive integration opening up before the Jewish survivors, the presence of the "Muscovites" represented thus an independent, external variable.

Viewing the matter historically, it is fairly well documented that progressive movements in Hungary had been intertwined with certain elements of emancipated and assimilated urban Jewry (*not* with the whole spectrum) even since the end of the last century. Most of the leaders of the 1919 Commune came from the ranks of Jewry. Between the wars, the part played by Jews in both the legal and illegal leftist organizations was quite considerable. It falls outside my subject to attempt a closer scrutiny of this comparatively small group, who, after 1945, became the main protagonists of the Communist course. Nor do I wish to attempt a scrutiny of their impact on the evolution of the despotic regime between 1949 and 1956. The only problem raised here is related to their links with Jewry—as far as these existed—and to the objective role they played in furthering or obstructing the course of positive integration.

It may be said that the rigid, sectarian, bureaucratic, and inhuman nature of their rule of terror was the joint outcome of their social uprootedness and the brutal historical process of selection they had undergone before acceding to power. Their rule proved to be utterly alien to the historical traditions of the country, even in its rituals and forms of appearance. Their economic policies followed alien models and interests. So did their insistence on needlessly harsh repression. Policies of this nature could be executed only by a leadership that had been completely divorced from the Hungarian comity—*alienated* in the strict sense of the word, and so much so that no proper analogies can be found in the course of Hungarian history. In the alienation of these people the influence of a universal ideology of the State (Lenin's internationalism) was quite conspicuous. This theory denies the interests of all local or national entities which are to be subordinated to "historical progress," represented by the day-to-day politics of the Soviet Union. The members of the emigrant group had spent a large part of their lives away from their homeland, in the shadow of the Kremlin. Those of the "internal" illegal movement had also usually adhered to the cult of the "great Socialist fatherland"—many of them for a quarter century.

Their stance was, of course, also shaped by the Soviet-type "selection" process. The nonconformists among them (or simply those who—with or without reason—could be denounced as nonconformists) were liquidated. Those who succeeded in staying alive were so intimidated that their attachment to the "Party line" became second nature for them—built into their inner nervous system, so to speak. From the ranks of the illegal movement in Hungary, only those who themselves had developed similar reflexes were allowed into the closed circle of power.

Many of these highly doctrinaire Party leaders were mostly the scions of strongly assimilated Jewish families. Their estrangement from Jewry, however, was largely due to their devotion to the "movement." This became a lifelong identification for them, encompassing their emotional, intellectual, and social beings. Indeed, it would be wrong to describe their attitude to Jewry as one kind of "assimilation." They were completely indifferent to all manifestations of Jewish identity or Jewish particularism. This indifference was quite genuine on their part, although it could also be labeled as a kind of political color blindness. They felt no qualms about occupying all the seats of power in the newly created Hungarian state, without the slightest regard to the historical symbolism—and to the great sensitivity—of these key positions. They behaved as if they did not have to give a thought to their Jewish origins.

Beria called Mátyás Rákosi in 1953 "the first Jewish king of Hungary"— his overlordship signified not just the "Jewish rule" (a slogan busily spread by the anti-Semites): it also signified, for the nation as a whole— even for Gentiles who were far from being anti-Semitic—that the continuity of the nation was thereby broken; the country had become subject to an alien rule. "The commands of the occupying power are carried out by their Jewish proconsuls."

It should be stressed that this image of the "Rákosi system" prevalent throughout the country supplied not only additional weapons to latent anti-Semitism: it also led to a revulsion, and a retreat—amounting to a kind of dissimilation—from the ruling system by the majority of the Jews. The strongly traditional, religious, elements of Jewry—as well as the best educated, most assimilated middle-class Jews—came to distance themselves equally from the power structure. The traditional groups simply considered the doctrinaire party leaders as "Godless renegades." The groups which had no identity of interest with the rulers, and which refused to compensate this lack of interest with positive integration, withdrew their passive support from them. This applied mostly to that elderly or middle-aged generation which—in spite of the persecutions—retained the ideals of liberal radicalism and the accompanying desire for an independent national life. These were the people who continued to value their cultural heritage. Not for nothing had they been the pioneers of the Hungarian artistic *avant garde* or of the Hungarian school of psychoanalysis.

Rákosi and his gang were completely lacking in the peculiarly Jewish habits of mind: the self-mocking humor, the cultural tastes, the critical appraisal of their own social role, the ambivalence of values. On the contary: perhaps to prove their rootlessness "upward" and "downward" in equal measure, they directed the fight against every single manifestation of modern Jewish identity with the greatest diligence. They called their targets "imperialist Zionism," "robber capitalism," "cosmopolitanism," "decadent art"—all dangerous masks for the bogey, "Reaction." They decreed an almost complete taboo on the great tragedy of Jewry. School textbooks were allowed to mention only the "victims of Fascism." This as much as drew a sign of equality between hundreds of thousands of murdered Jews and the few dozen martyrs of an embryonic anti-German resistance.

It would be an entirely false conclusion thus to borrow the bogey of "Jewish solidarity" from the storehouse of anti-Semitic slogans. The positive integration of assimilate Jewry was very far from having been due to its complicity with the Muscovite leadership. Indeed, the leadership was as much a straw man as a desirable model for many of them. Many of the Jewish emigrants after 1956 were motivated in their escape by a fear of this new-fangled official "Communist anti-Semitism," or by a refusal to be

branded an accomplice of the "Jewish rule." There were indeed signs that
—as a reaction to Rákosi's despotism—a new kind of spontaneous anti-
Semitism began to raise its head among professional people and the peasantry, even among those who had not been anti-Semitic at all.

In spite of all this, one cannot deny that this alienated leading group of
Jewish origin did have some attraction for certain Jews desiring positive
integration. *Ex hypothesi,* we may identify three aspects of this phenomenon.

The Jewish party bosses represented one borderline case of assimilation;
in the given historical situation, having become the possessors of unlimited
power, they offered the *most successful* example of this trend. Any form
of social success may offer an attractive model for an upwardly mobile
group, particularly when this group had, earlier, been physically threatened. Taking part in power meant collective security for them. I have to
admit, though, that this somewhat trivial comment may not fully explain
the attraction of this new model for assimilation.

The pseudo-charismatic power, called the "cult of personality," must
have played a part over and above this. Many Jews who, not very long ago,
had trembled in the ghetto, or suffered in the unspeakable labor service
companies and the death camps, could now feel (rightly or wrongly) that
they had something in common with the figure of the Great Leader cut-
ting capers on the pedestal of public rituals—or with his lieutenants whose
names were quoted with reverence in all textbooks, putting into shadow
the names of hallowed sovereigns resting in the national Pantheon. For
certain elements of Jewry (probably the political innocents) who had been
symbolically and physically cast out from the body of the historical
nation, the figures of these "Jewish heroes" may have appeared as a confluence of their traditional Messianism and of their thirst for freedom
from fear (possessed by all pariahs of history). The cult of the "wise
leader" and of his underlings, obligatory for Jews and Gentiles alike, may
also have created the illusion of a renewed integration, now carried through
according to "our" interests, on "our" conditions. A whole status group
may have felt the drift of its own collective mobility which, in a dream-
like fashion, carried them all now into the groves of sanctified power.

Probably this was the point—the forced adulation of the Party leaders—
where Jewish and Gentile political sensitivity parted company. The "cult

of personality" demanded the adoration of people who had really been just "imported aliens." They were supported by the bayonets of an alien power; often they had alien nationality; they followed alien policies and obviously served alien interests. Regardless of the anti-Semitic jibe that they were also "racially alien," their conceits could evoke only revulsion in the non-Jewish masses. No fully legitimate ruling body had ever been surrounded by this kind of adulation in the history of the country. On the contrary, for many Jews, including those who did not favor the system, the enthronement of this Jewish leadership may have *objectified* in some manner the fact of liberation—no matter that this "liberation" had its drawbacks (expressed in many jokes of bitter irony). To all intents and purposes, what looked like provocation or historical sacrilege to many Gentiles may have seemed a positive achievement in the eyes of many Jews. One must not forget that they owed their survival to these "aliens"; anyway, they were not that much "alien" by virtue of their origin. This may have supplied an additional motive to the desire for identification.

Last but not least, we should consider the problem of "Jewish solidarity." According to this idea, the Jewish leadership followed the principle of "racial solidarity" in selecting Party cadres. The sociologist cannot call this factor into doubt (every group "hangs together": that is the essence of being a group). I call this issue a "problem" because it is very difficult to say anything worthwhile about it. On the one hand, the whole idea is shot through with anti-Semitic fantasies so much so that it appears, at first sight, as a biased projection of the experience of totalitarian rule. It is easy to attribute the baffling despotism to an already well-established scapegoat: the Jews. On the other hand, the rulers constantly manipulated their own Jewish character; sometimes they emphasized it, at other times they minimized it. For instance, on the few occasions of anti-Jewish pogroms occurring in 1946, the Party rushed to the defense of those Communists—often ex-Nazis—who had perpetrated the outrages. And this happened when the police, and the other organs of the law who handled the matter, had an overrepresentation of Jews in their ranks. (In the whole new system of tribunals, &c. charged with dealing with war criminals, Jews played a disproportionate role.)[45] After 1949, an entirely new course was initiated and many cadres of Jewish origin were replaced by those of "worker-peasant" origin. According to one witness, after 1949 a *numerus nullus* was introduced at the Party High School (the chief training ground for new leading cadres), that is, candidates with a "bourgeois" background (meaning Jews) were refused entry.[46]

Without sufficiently detailed and precise historical evidence, it is difficult to interpret this confusing picture. All one can do is to try and identify the revelant facts of social reality, peeling off the accretions of popular legend. Four main factors can be isolated, if we attempt to separate ideology from reality.

The first of these is the "social capital" mentioned before. Jewry came into possession of this in the new system, owing to the persecution (whether they liked its possession or not). In the initial selection of cadres, especially at the lower levels, this factor no doubt turned the scale in favor of those Jews who had been ready to embrace positive integration.

The second factor is perhaps nearest to the imaginings of "Jewish solidarity." This was not the case of a "Jewish conspiracy" against "Christians"—a favorite accusation of anti-Semites—but simply the natural social reaction: "Who trusts whom?" and "Who sympathizes with whom?." This is a universal feature of group dynamics. In our case, it came about as a consequence of Jewish historical experiences. The only peculiarity of the case is that, while it goes unnoticed in any other group, it will be picked out as significant in the instance of Jews. What may seem normal among Gentiles will become a monstrosity if practiced by Jews. Of course it is true that, while in other groups this can be considered normal behavior, it will have an added content when it comes to Jews. For them, it is an indispensable, almost obligatory reaction, part of the defense mechanism of a constantly threatened group. Especially when members of this group had not only been threatened but actually *subjected* to mass murder, from which only one-third of them escaped—and just barely.

A Jewish party official or business manager could obviously put greater trust (and, objectively, he was right in this) in a candidate or colleague of Jewish extraction. Common suffering, common culture, perhaps common past or family links, bound them indissolubly together. All these contributed to a kind of social sensitivity—the understandable gut feeling that *they* could not be suspected of anti-Semitism. Whatever measure of solidarity may have actually existed, past and present anti-Semitism was really responsible for it.

This, of course, did not exclude the possibility of an almost natural human failing. Once "Jewishness' came to represent a kind of social capital—according to the criteria of "trustworthiness" set out by the new regime—quite a few Jewish functionaries utilized this capital for excluding Gentile rivals from career-competition (sometimes going to the extent of smearing them, in some cases with fatal consequences). For some Jewish functionaries, this was nothing but a deliberate application of a "group-specific" strategy for their own advancement. A good example of this was the regular smear campaign directed at the political and intellectual leadership of the Populist movement, harping on the family background or past associations of Gentile colleagues at the workplace, and so on. It was of course easier to pick out compromising tidbits about Gentiles—after all, *they* had not been persecuted *as such* in the bad old days.[47]

These manifestations of "Jewish solidarity" thus fueled the vicious circle of "reaction" and "counter-reaction." Not only the wheels of traditional anti-Semitism were oiled by this antagonistic practice. Very often it created indignation—indeed, a new kind of alienation—from Jews among the new, democratic intelligentsia and among political cadres themselves. Almost a new form of anti-Semitism could be witnessed, relying now on fresh arguments.

This phenomenon may offer further proof of the inevitability of a kind of social "logic" appearing in a development of this nature. Social capital (especially if it is group-specific, like "Jewishness" in 1945) is there to be used or, on occasion, to be misused. In the atmosphere of Stalinist despotism, it was fatally easy to misuse arbitrary power. This led to a large-scale corruption of certain Jewish cadres. They abused their advantages to the detriment of their rivals, for the acquisition of ill-gotten gains, flaunting the unassailable and often cynically applied argument of having been a "persecutee." In other words, they behaved in exactly the same manner —now that the circumstances favored them—as countless members of the Gentile middle classes had behaved at the time of the anti-Jewish laws. In that past period, being an "Aryan" had suddenly acquired an increased social value. This led to denunciation of Jews and to their exclusion from professional and business competition—the fruits of which had been eagerly gathered up by a good part of the Gentile middle classes.

In addition, we should appraise—as the third factor—the manner in which the Party hierarchy manipulated this "solidarity." At the very top,

"Jewishness" did not represent any kind of advantage or social capital. Quite a few of the victims of the show trial of László Rajk and his comrades were of Jewish origin—and so were the local authors of the plot against the "conspirators."[48] It is possible that family links and long acquaintance may have played some part in the cohesion of this caucus. It was, however, of greater importance for the Party leadership that they were offered the chance of playing off one clique against another. Taking part in one of the "Jewish coteries" may now have been an advantage, now a drawback. Jewish origins may have opened some doors to careers or, conversely, may have closed them. We have already mentioned the figurehead role thrust upon some "worker-peasant" cadres. But there were also figureheads of Jewish origin. They were deliberately put into positions outstripping their competence, in order to do away with the appearance of non-Jewish professional, local, or institutional lobbies.

Finally, we should never forget that in "Judeo-Bolshevism" (a favorite expression in the dictionary of anti-Semitism) the force of solidarity was always much stronger in the second half of the term: Bolshevism (not, of course, in the anti-Semitic interpretation). If we consider the life histories and careers of Rákosi and his band, it seems clear that their rootlessness and social alienation led willy-nilly to a loss of their "Jewish-awareness." It was their militant ideological solidarity that motivated them, overcoming all their inner conflicts. The determinant effect of social origins cannot be very strong in the case of a group that had been subjected to the kind of severe and brutal process of "selection"—quite indepedently from their Jewish origins—such as most Communist leaders underwent in their period of emigration. Those of them who succeeded in surviving the show trials of the 1930s and did not disappear through the trapdoor, as well as those of them who remained afloat in the murky waters of a sectarian Party, understandably followed the logic of their own best political interests in selecting their advisers, confidants, and successors, or in creating alliances among themselves. Obviously, they did not take the slightest notice of the question of whose grandparents had gone to pray in which church or synagogue."

We may say that the appearance of "Jewish solidarity" here had simply been a cover for "political solidarity," quite independently of the presence or absence of Jewishness. This solidarity linked together certain people who had developed common interests in their past political life and just *happened* to be often of Jewish origin. (Although this may not have been purely an accident, considering their social background; but for our purposes this remains a contingent factor.)

In the course of the Rajk trial, the conflict of interest between two groups came rudely to the fore. There were Jews in both groups, but the root of the conflict had been most probably the tension between "home-grown" and "Muscovite" Communists. Jewish origins, or the proportion of Jews in either group had nothing to do with the clash. As is well known, a very similar situation developed in Czechoslovakia, in the trial of Slan-sky. Indeed, the whole tenor of the accusations had a strongly anti-Semitic undertone there, although many Jewish functionaries ranged themselves on both sides of the struggle within the Czechoslovak party.[49]

NOTES

1.   This study is based on three chapters originally published in 1984. See my "Szociológiai kisérlet a magyar zsidóság 1945 és 1956 közötti helyzetének elemzésére" (A Sociological Attempt at Studying the Situation of Hungarian Jewry Between 1945 and 1956) in *Zsidóság az 1945 utáni Magyarországon* (Jewry in Post-1945 Hungary). Introduction by Peter Kende. Paris: Magyar Füzetek, 1984, pp. 36-180.

2.   It should be noted that small capitalists and self-employed independent professionals were almost fully expropriated in 1948-1949. During the same period, independent Jewish communal life was also liquidated. In March 1949, the Zionist movement was suppressed; in February 1950, the three historic religious groups (Orthodox, Liberal or Neolog, and the *status quo ante,* in existence ever since the Jewish Congress of 1867) were forcibly united and the new religious body subordinated to State control. Jewish institutions—schools and hospitals, first and foremost the renowned Jewish Hospital, rebuilt by the Joint (The American Joint Distribution Committee)—were taken into State ownership. The collectivization of the private sector was as good as completed by the end of 1949. All businesses employing more than 10 people were expropriated. For further details, see J. Fisher, "Hungary," in *European Jewry Ten Years After the War.*

New York: Institute of Jewish Affairs, 1956, pp. 71-72; and E. Duschinsky, "Hungary," in *The Jews in the Soviet Satellites*. Syracuse: Syracuse University Press, 1953, p. 466.

3. For data on the social position of the political elite between the wars, see A. C. Janos, *The Politics of Backwardness in Hungary, 1825-1945*. Princeton: Princeton University Press, 1982. See also, S. Szakály, "A második világháborús magyar katonai felső vezetés összetétele" (The Social Composition of the Hungarian Army Leadership in the Second World War), *Valóság* (Reality), Budapest, 1983, pp. 78-91.

4. G. Konrád and I. Szelényi, *Az értelmiség útja az osztályhatalomhoz* (The Road of the Intelligentsia Toward Class Rule), Bern: European Protestant Magyar Free University, 1978.

5. The treatment of professional competence and of the part played by the various "inherited" or acquired forms of social capital in the new regime can only be somewhat superficial in relation to my main subject. A detailed and thoroughgoing study of this problem has not yet been done. The whole picture is complicated by the fact that the policies affecting the new cadres very often served the purposes of legitimation only, in order to camouflage the essentially illegitimate nature of the regime.

6. M. Kovács, "Közalkalmazottak 1938-49." (Public Servants, 1938-49). *Valóság*, no. 9, 1982, pp. 41-53.

7. Ibid.

8. M. Jakab, *Társadalmi változás és magyar értelmiség, 1944-1948* (Social Change and the Hungarian Intelligentsia, 1944-1948). Budapest: Kossuth, 1979, p. 226.

9. Ibid., p. 216. On forcible recruitment, see ibid., pp. 54, 216, 276, and note 48.

10. The timing of the mass entry into the Communist Party by the middle class and the intelligentsia can be fairly accurately pinpointed. For details see M. Jakab, op. cit., p. 196.

11. Ibid., pp. 219-221.

12. Cf. Victor Karady, Class Structure, Restratification and Potential for Social Mobility in Post-Holocaust Hungarian Jewry (1945-1948). *Studies in Contemporary Jewry*, Bloomington, Ind., no. 3, (forthcoming).

13. See the tables. According to a Hungarian scholar, a large part of the favored "worker-peasant" personnel was of Jewish origin in the Stalin-

ist period. This is supported by our findings: the Jewish working class had been more active in political movements, and its education and culture had been of a higher standard. It is interesting to note that in 1948, more than half of industrial managers of "working-class origin" (53 percent) possessed a university entrance certificate and only a fraction of them (8 percent) had no secondary education. M. Jakab, op. cit., p. 234, and note 129.

14.   *Budapest Székesfőváros Statisztikai Évkönyve* (Statistical Year-book of Budapest), Budapest, 1941, p. 52.

15.   First of all in the cities, where bureaucratic scrutiny of social origins was not supported by public knowledge of a certain family's status, as usually was the case in the provinces. The destruction of Jewish families, the uprooting of many survivors (most of them were flocking to the capital), made manipulation of "social origins" that much easier.

16.   The statistics covering the 1900-1938 period, for example, show with some regularity that Jewish and Lutheran (and, where data are reliable, the few Unitarian) pupils achieved the highest grades; Catholic and Calvinist pupils were much less successful; Greek Orthodox students the least. See also scholastic successes in my study "Jewish Enrollment Patterns in Classical Secondary Education in Old Regime and Inter-War Hungary." *Studies in Contemporary Jewry*, Bloomington, Ind., no. 1, 1984, pp. 225-252.

17.   Once the wave of political dismissals was over, public service jobs increased rapidly. In 1947—in the course of one year—the number of State employees increased by 55,000, of which 15,000 were brand-new jobs. M. Kovács, op. cit., p. 50.

18.   Ibid., p. 51.

19.   For data substantiating these ascertions, see *Magyar Statisztikai Közlemények* (Hungarian Statistical Reports), Budapest, no. 64, p. 205, and no. 114, pp. 194-195. See also my study cited in footnote 1.

20.   *Budapest Székesfőváros Statisztikai Évkönyve* (Statistical Year-book of the Municipality of Budapest), Budapest, 1944, p. 236.

21.   Ibid., p. 224.

22.   Ibid., 1938, p. 294.

23.   T. Hajdu, "Az értelmiség számszerű gyarapodásának következményei a második világháború előtt és után" (Consequences of the In-

crease in the Numbers of the Intelligentsia before and after the Second World War), *Valóság* (Reality), Budapest, no. 7, 1981, pp. 1-22, and M. Kovács, op. cit., pp. 43-46.

24. Before the First World War, very few Jews were admitted (and very few applied) to the Military Academy. However, in 1903-1905, we find 12 Jews among 300 cadets. To graduate into the officer class inevitably meant conversion. After 1919, no Jewish officer cadet was to be found —probably not even among converted Jews. For further details, see my study under footnote 1.

25. Up to the period of the anti-Jewish laws, the proportion of Jewish university students was near 10 percent of the total. For example, in 1935—excluding theology and the vocational high schools—9.2 percent of all students were Israelites. By 1941-1942, this figure had sunk to 2.9 percent. In practice, this meant that those who had enrolled in universities could still complete their studies (the "continuity of rights" was still in force). Students branded as Jewish by the laws (of whatever religion) were rejected, perhaps with a very few exceptions. For statistical data, see *Magyar Statisztikai Évkönyv* (Hungarian Statistical Yearbook), Budapest, 1936, p. 330, and 1942, p. 230.

26. Education statistics clearly prove the flocking of Jewish pupils into the so-called "civic" (*polgári*) schools (a peculiarly Central European institution for 10-14-year-old pupils who could not gain entry—or could not afford—secondary education at high schools called *gymnasia*. The civic schools granted a simple certificate: it entitled school leavers to enter only commercial colleges. Only about half of high schools were State-supported; the others were denominational. Owing to this fact and to their smaller number (260 in all in 1942), the high schools were much more discriminatory, as far as the Jews were concerned. The civic schools were practically all local-authority-supported; they numbered 564. In spite of the increase in territory of the country (1938-41), the number of Jewish pupils in high schools decreased from 11,525 to 9,616 between 1940 and 1943. In the civic schools, however, their numbers increased from 9,133 to 10,436 in the same period.

27. We can accept the statement by T. Hajdu that ". . . intellectual unemployment was moderate and transitory" in the years following 1945, see his study, op. cit., p. 16.

28. "In the 1950s, official jobs, especially in leading positions, were not strictly dependent on qualifications. Many people qualified in crash courses, often lasting only a few weeks." T. Hajdu, op. cit., p. 17.

29. As T. Hajdu states: "the majority of survivors among the Jewish intelligentsia looked for jobs in the civil service; indeed, many of those who had lost their jobs in economic fields after 1938, preferred this to restarting their old activities." See p. 15 of his study cited above.

30. This theme is explored in depth by István Bibó. See his Zsidókérdés Magyarországon 1944 után (Jewish Question in Hungary After 1944). *Válasz* (Response), Budapest, vol. 8, Oct.-Nov. 1948, pp. 778-877. This essay is reproduced in: *A harmadik út* (The Third Road), edited by Zoltán Szabó (London: Könyves Céh, 1960), pp. 227-354, and in *Bibó István összegyüjtött munkái* (The Collected Works of István Bibó), edited by István Kemény and Mátyás Sárközi (Bern: Az Európai Protestáns Magyar Szabadegyetem Kiadása, 1982), pp. 389-504. See also the following two essays by András Kovács, "La question juive dans la Hongrie contemporaine." *Actes de la Recherche en Sciences Sociales,* Paris, no. 56, March 1985, pp. 45-57, and "The Jewish Question in Contemporary Hungary." *Telos,* St. Louis, no. 58, Winter 1983-84, pp. 55-74.

31. *Magyar Statisztikai Közlemények,* no. 56, pp. 712-781, passim.

32. Ibid., no. 16, pp. 135-263, passim.

33. *Publications statistiques hongroises,* Budapest, no. 64, p. 276.

34. Vilmos Vázsony (1868-1926), Member of Parliament for a Budapest district from 1901 to his death. In 1917 he was Minister for Electoral Law, in 1918 Minister of Justice. He was the only member of a Government in the old regime who was a profession Jew. See *Vázsonyi Vilmos beszédei és irásai* (Speeches and Writings of Vilmos Vázsonyi), Budapest, 1927, passim, esp. p. 110.

35. Based on *Magyar Statisztikai Közlemények,* no. 74, p. 62, and *Magyar Statisztikai Évkönyv,* 1940, p. 28. For further details, see my study cited in footnote 1.

36. For instance, among the officially registered prostitutes in Budapest between 1930 and 1942, only 5.1 percent were Jewish, while the proportion of Jewish women between the ages 15 and 50 was three times as high in the whole female population of the city (1930: 17.8 percent, 1941: 15.6 percent). Source: *Budapest Székesfőváros Statisztikai Évkönyvei* (Statistical Yearbooks of Budapest).

37.   A. Kovács, op. cit., pp. 64-66.

38.   I. Bibó, op. cit., p. 494.

39.   Ibid., p. 495.

40.   Ibid., p. 494.

41.   Ibid., p. 491.

42.   There is plenty of evidence for this. The Communist party methodically courted the leading lights of the intellectual community, either to recruit them as party members or to attract them as fellow travelers. For this purpose, the Party leaders were willing to shut their eyes to the political past of the candidates. The best known example was that of Professor Gyula Szekfű, the conservative historian. He was "turned around" and praised as one of the "honest converts." So much so that he accepted the appointment of Ambassador to Moscow—a largely symbolic office. See M. Jakab, op. cit., pp. 56-58. Similar efforts were exerted to win over university professors. Ibid., p. 215.

43.   The question is: can we accept the estimate that, in May 1945, the Communist Party had altogether 12,000 members who had some part in the movement? (See M. Jakab, op. cit., p. 369, note 75.) Furthermore, can we-at least hypothetically—apply our measure of one-third to this group (according to data presented in Gy. Borsányi, "Ezernyolcszáz kartoték a budapesti baloldalról" (One Thousand Eight Hundred Police Files on the Left Wing in Budapest). *Valóság,* no. 89, 1983, pp. 19-31, in order to estimate Jewish participation in the Communist movement? If so, we may deduce that, from 1945 onwards, about 4000 Jewish "cadre-candidates" were active in the Party, who did have some political experience. We should also take note of the active membership of the Social Democratic party and of hundreds of emigrants coming home (mostly from the Soviet Union). In addition, there was a sizable number of "sympathizers" who also had some political awareness, although at that stage could not be listed as full "converts." Perhaps we are not far out in our guess that about 10,000 Jews belonged to this cohort. This is not a negligible number: about one-seventh of adult Jews at that time. Nevertheless, this constituted a minority within Jewry—even among Jews ready for positive integration.

44.   F. Fejtő, *Les Juifs et l'antisémitisme dans les pays communistes,* Paris: Plon, 1960, p. 95.

45. Jewish participation in the forces of the new law and order was indeed conspicuous for contemporaries. Even István Bibó thought that the very large number of Jews taking part in the legal structure, charged with dealing with the punishment of war crimes, was somewhat preposterous. I. Bibó, op. cit., p. 487.

46. It is worth quoting in full one part of F. Fejtő's report on the years following 1951: "About 30 percent of the 'relocated' were Jews. . . . When, at the beginning of 1952, anti-Semitism started to gain ground in Russia, Rákosi decided that he himself would carry out the 'liquidation' of Jews in Hungary. In preparation for this dirty work, he caused his own life history to be rewritten. He now claimed that his parents had not been petty Jewish traders but had belonged to the lesser nobility. He sent to prison the (Jewish) head of the secret police; his own brother-in-law; Dr. István Benedek, the chief of the Jewish Hospital in Budapest, the president of the Jewish Community; Lajos Stöckler (who has utterly compromised himself by his servility to the Communists), and many others." Fejtő, op. cit., p. 94.

47. The competition between Jewish and Gentile middle-class political converts proved that the social capital of Jews was more effective in the Stalinist period. Many Gentiles had had family links and associations with the heavily compromised old civil service, the petty nobility, or the expropriated landed gentry. Many of those who had a more modest, petty bourgeois background or, indeed, were of "worker-peasant" origin —especially the Catholics among them, who had owed their social advancement to religious high schools—could easily be branded with being "servants of the clerical reaction." Many Gentiles—whether they liked it or not—served in the army on the Russian front. Others—more willing—were guilty of misdeeds, if not worse, committed during the Nazi terror. Jewish cadres lacked these stigmata. Their family background was more likely to have been "progressive" (doctors, engineers, etc.). Those whose parents were entrepreneurs or employees could sometimes transmute their origins into the category of "exploited masses."

48. The chief defendants in the Rajk trial, apart from László Rajk himself, many were of Jewish origin, e.g., Tibor Szönyi, Pál Justus, András Szalai. In spite of this, the trial was looked upon by many people as the victory of the "Jewish faction" in the Party elite over the "non-

Jewish faction." László Rajk had, in fact, been rumored to be anti-Semitic —most likely, without reason. One of his brothers, however, had been an active Nazi. While he was in charge of the Ministry of the Interior, Rajk directed the campaign against the Zionists. He also protected the culprits of the 1946 anti-Jewish pogroms from prosecution. E. Duschinsky, op. cit., pp. 421, 457, 425, 435, 443.

49.   For details on the Slansky trial, see *Encyclopaedia Judaica,* vol. 5, p. 1202. See also my essay cited in footnote 1.

THE UNFINISHED PAST—JEWISH REALITIES IN POSTWAR HUNGARY

Péter Várdy

My subject[1] is the significance of self-censorship, and the forms of its manifestation, as it affects Hungarian Jewry. Following a short outline of the scene, I shall attempt to sketch a map of Jewish realities in Hungary, then investigate the blank spaces on this map. The pattern of these blank spaces may then cast light on the linkages of self-censorship: the heritage —and now the guardian—of a deep social division of long standing. We may also ask: in whose interests is it worth maintaining public dissension? And finally: what are the chances of a clarification and of a healthy social consensus?

The complicated geography of Jewish realities, with their peaks, troughs, and fissures, would require an investigation involving an institutional approach. In the present essay all I can attempt is an outline. In my own case, a distance of 25 years makes the task that much more difficult.

Anyway, the methodological problem of the right approach involves in this case the whole question. Those who carry memories of the early forties are at least not neutral observers. Quite the contrary: they will actually play one or another role. I, for example, am of christianized Jewish origin.

The Remnants of Hungarian Jewry

The Hungarian Jews of today are the fourth—perhaps to be the last—generation whose forebears migrated to the country largely in the eighteenth and nineteenth centuries. Hardly any Jews survived the preceding Turkish wars. The number of immigrants—from Moravia, Austria, and especially Poland, and of their offspring—was about 900,000 by the beginning of the twentieth century, roughly five percent of the total population, In the Hungarian Reform period of the middle nineteenth century and afterward, in the prevailing spirit of liberal nationalism, these immigrants were received with open arms. The social establishment of Jewry concluded a tacit treaty with the ruling liberal-nationalist nobility on the rather temporary footing of mutual interests. On this basis Jewry played a dominant part in the industrialization of the country, making good use of its competence in this field. It enthusiastically supported the ruling nationalistic culture.

In consequence, the bulk of Jewry adopted the Magyar language and considered itself to be a constituent part of the Hungarian nation, Jewish only in its religion. In recognition of this, the ruling classes ensured the Jews equality before the law. The first generation of Jewish immigrants thus became a party to a "social concordat," ensuring its own progress. The second generation wholeheartedly supported the Hungarian reform movement according to the spirit of Jewish enlightenment[2] and became assimilated to Magyar society.

The bankruptcy of the liberal nationalism in 1918 also meant the collapse of the drive from complete assimilation—a reversal of fortunes for the third generation. The heyday of bourgeois radicalism gave way to the tribulations of World War I, the 1918 revolution, the 1919 Commune. Then followed the cataclysm of the counterrevolution of Miklós Horthy and the inexorable descent of the often murderous persecution at the end of World War I. Finally, came the fatal developments during World War II.

About 60 percent of the Jews within the area of present-day Hungary perished—nearly 300,000 souls; if the territories temporarily attached to Hungary during the war—parts of Slovakia, Transylvania, and the whole of Carpatho-Ruthenia—are added in, then the corresponding number who perished in the persecutions is 560,000, or 67 percent of Jewry living on these territories in 1941.[3]

Almost 80 percent of provincial Jewry was exterminated, and more than 100,000 from Budapest (where, however, nearly 60 percent survived the Nazi terror). In 1946, less than 200,000 Jews were living in Hungary, including about 50,000 converted Jews. There have been no separate census figures since 1949 indicating religion or racial origin. Therefore, we can make only educated guesses about their numbers today. There are perhaps 100,000 Jews in Hungary, according to strict religious demonination—maybe half of them observant of their religious laws.

The social position of Jews in the Hungary of today is determined by four factors. First, a split in identity (the age-old concomitant of assimilation). Second, the tragedy of 1944 and the diffuse notion of a hostile social surrounding. Third, the modernization of the actual Hungarian society. Fourth, government policies, which hold the fate of religious Jewry in a state of dependency on changing national and great-power interests.

In view of all this, we must ask: how does the disrupted past, troubled present, and problematic future of Hungarian Jewry manifest itself in the consciousness of Hungarian society?

Jewish-Magyar Realities and the Blank Spaces on the Map

I shall attempt to draw a sketch of this "map of realities" and indicate the blank spaces. My first concern is the relationship between society as a whole and the Jews, and how this relationship manifests itself in public opinion. For this purpose I shall review the scientific and political literature of the post-1956 era. Of course, publications before 1956 must also be taken into account. My purpose is not to write the history of the Jewish question, nor to analyze its historical roots or to give it a solution, only to try to elucidate how it appears today in the mirror of social consciousness. Therefore I have, with certain exceptions, excluded literature dating from before 1945. There is also a very respectable volume of work pursued abroad, of high scientific value. Many of these works will also serve as pointers to the shortcomings of developments in Hungary itself. I regret that the scope of this treatise allows me only a somewhat summary survey.

A comprehensive, up-to-date scientific history of Hungarian Jewry has still to be written.[4] There is, however, a wealth of source publications, data banks, partial approaches and works on certain matters of detail.[5] A good part of these have appeared abroad. Some of these partial attempts to assess the social history of Hungarian Jewry deal with particular problems, like the demography of Jews,[6] or Jewish education between 1848 and 1948 (the latter analyzed in a monograph published in the United States).[7]

The great bulk of all works dealing with the social history of Jewry—treating the period from the 1830s to the 1920s—may be summarized under the heading "assimilation or the genesis of the middle class." This question dominates the approach both within and outside Hungary.[8] Most researchers agree that, given the contradictions of an unevenly developing feudal order, Jewry was the standardbearer of modernization, but also the butt of tensions created by this drive. M. Horváth and G. Bárány concur that it was not so much the uneven progress of assimilation but its very success that created social tensions. Some of the works deal very thoroughly with the structural indicators which prove a rapidly growing degree of assimilation: the rate of urbanization of Jewry, its levels of schooling, its language divisions, its participation in trades and professions. The part played by Jews in industry, trade, and finance—even in landed property —was very significant. The ratio of Jews on the increasingly overcrowded market of the learned professions far surpassed their percentage in the population.[9]

The role of Jews in the economic history of Hungary is nowadays largely being dealt with outside the country. General economic reviews written in Hungary also offer a rich source material.[10] Jewish participation in the modernization of Hungarian economic life has always been a sore point, not only for the conservative establishment, but to a lesser extent this was still the case in the eyes of the orthodox Marxists. Today, this attitude has become largely irrelevant, seeing that the modernization of the country has reached a more-or-less satisfactory level.

Very little has been written on the mainsprings and patterns of assimilation. Bibó's treatise does mention conversion as an escape from traditionalism; the prevalence of free-thinking; intellectual community; mixed marriages; common schooling; the effects of the workplace and the working-class movements.[11] McCagg significantly deduces the activism of many socialist Jews from the failures of assimilation by their fathers' genera-

tion.[12] A critical point occasionally touched upon by the scientific literature: what was the essential *purpose* of assimilation? In the spirit of Hungarian liberalism, fully adopted by assimilating Jews, this purpose was
complete absorption. This is the judgment of Marxist social studies too.[13]
Curiously enough, dogmatic Marxism on this point rather continues the
nationalism of the nineteenth century, more than true dialectical traditions.

The "social contract" between the liberal ruling class and assimilating
Jewry declared the Jews to be Magyars in *nationality* and Israelites in *denomination*. This gave rise to the challenge about "dual loyalty," raised
again and again by—among others—the Populist movement in the thirties.[13a]

Today, Jewry again officially denotes a denomination and, as such,
operates under the suspicious supervision of the State, jealous about every
aspect of its sovereignty. This attitude, and the 150-year process of assimilation broken only in the fateful years between 1920 and 1945 has in
truth very little to do with "dialectics."

Another view considers that the ultimate purpose of social harmony
relies on a social model wherein each community safeguards its own
identity and respects that of the other.[14] In reality, the process of assimilation in Hungary resulted—in the words of Bibó—in a "continuous state
of ambiguity" that, confronted with the false alternative of "either Jew
or Magyar," struggled under the burden of a chronically false social consciousness.[15] The distortions of assimilation gave rise to examples of
grossly overdoing "Magyarism," to abject conformity or a feeling of hopeless outsiderhood. The gentrified Jew, the Jewish contractor raised to the
peerage, the rancorous internationalist, the bourgeois closet-Bolshevik,
the international celebrity writing in several languages at once, the Habsburg partisan, irredentist, Stalinist, and anti-Zionist Jew—not to speak of
the secretly observing high Party functionary—have all been conspicuous
examples of a crisis of identity of the whole Hungarian society which has
especially been dogging assimilating Jews for more than a century.

One should also consider more thoroughly the group of "renegade"
Jews. Rejection of religion has been up to the present day one of the main
avenues to assimilation. Before 1945, this had meant conversion to Christianity; today, adoption of Marxist materialism. "Conversion," however,
means rather a way out than a way in. As Bárány points out: "More re-

search would be needed to analyze the social consequences of rejection of religion and/or conversion, both from the point of view of the Jews and from that of non-Jews."[16] To our knowledge there has not been any recent study of this aspect in Hungary.[17]

According to W. Rabi, it is an omission on the part of Jewish historians to have disregarded the problems of seceding Jewry by concentrating on those of the remnants of the faithful.[18] The Magyarization of surnames has been completely discredited as a possible subject of investigation by the Hungarian Nazis—which is a pity, because a study of this aspect would probably cast interesting light not only on Jewish assimilation, but on assimilation in general.

The assimilation and *embourgeoisement* of Jews in Hungary took place within the frame of a developing Hungarian society toward a modern industrial capitalism and constituted one of its conspicuous factors. The two interwoven processes naturally created their own tensions. We can date the rise of *political* anti-Semitism to this period. Here lies the other chief area of interest for studies in this subject in present-day Hungary.

By about 1880, "modern" anti-Semitism started to emerge in the country. Based on the idea of "race," soon enough it became the central force for certain political parties. This new—and international—wave had a short run in Hungarian parliamentary life, with little practical success; but from then on, a vociferous anti-Semitism became a permanent feature of Hungarian public affairs. The end-of-century liberalism was strong enough to resist this, but its collapse at the end of World War I nullified the resistance. From the early 1920s, political anti-Semitism became the guiding tenet of the so-called "Christian course." Its proclaimed character was conservative, Christian, anti-capitalist and anti-modernist, drawing on deep social rancor. The counterrevolutionary regime of 1919 adopted this anti-Semitism based on the racial theory corresponding at this point to the right wing of the many-colored political Right, until it debouched into the infamy of the Arrow Cross terror late in 1944.

Various historians have recently dealt with many aspects of this process.[19] The emergent anti-Semitism, which eventually degenerated into mass murder, was a symptom of the arrested development of Hungarian society. Its causes should have been explained by the theory of anti-Semitism. Within the theoretical endeavors we can distinguish several strands.

Today it is the Marxist analysis which, with all its merits and wants, still dominates the Hungarian scientific publicity.[20] There are two main themes in it. The first one is of a socio-economic nature emphasizing the unevenness of development toward a "bourgeois" society. According to this view, the laws of movement within feudal society lead to an inevitable clash with the emergent forces of capitalism. Stubborn defense of the caste system prevents the rise of the masses but allows the infiltration of "foreigners" as new allies. The Jews, being the standardbearers of capitalist development, emerge at the very areas of major social frictions and struggles.

The other theme relies somewhat more on social psychology. According to this, whenever a crisis hits the traditional class system, the ruling class artificially fuels anti-Semitism, in order to divert popular passions—originating in oppression and exploitation—toward the Jews. The weakness of this theory is its methodology, whereby it tries to deduce the "false consciousness" from purely economic sources. Furthermore, it is in immanent conflict with the officially approved doctrine, which alleges that fascist ideology infected only a small, *lumpenproletariat* element in society. If this were so, anti-Semitism could not be termed a major factor of the psychology of the masses; if, on the contrary, it can be, there had to be some sort of a mass basis for anti-Semitism.

It is very interesting that M. Horváth in his essay accepts the latter point, at least for the first year following the liberation. He attributes mass starvation and misery to the reemergence of the market economy in 1945, i.e., to the phenomena linked to the market economy, including free enterprise, capital, free trade and commerce on the other hand to Jewry. His conclusion: once the capitalist economy is abolished misery will cease to exist and so will anti-Semitism. We know the consequences of this view. Here again, there surfaces the not unknown undercurrent in socialist thought, linking capitalism with Jewry. The origins of this veiled anti-Semitism go back to Marx himself.[21]

The "unevenness" motive appears in the works of Bibó and Száraz too. Uneven development east of the Rhine resulted, in the case of Hungary, in a weird mixture of traditionalist and capitalist strands: "Capitalist exploitation of social relationships within a feudal system" (Bibó). The unsolved problems and permanent crisis of society found their false answer in anti-Semitism. Next to the predominance of Jews in Hungarian capitalism, Száraz emphasizes the role played by the *fin de siècle* mass immigration of Jews from Southern Poland as an additional factor in emergent anti-Semitism.[22] He adds the notion that the ruling "historic" class perceived a danger both from aggressive capitalism and from radical social criticism. And Jews were prominent in both.[23] McCagg deals with this problem in a different manner.[24] According to both Hungarian and foreign research, anti-Semitism is a symptom of the anomalous development not only of the Jews but of the whole society.[25] The Jews shared the uncertain development of the middle classes;[26] besides, they represented a new form of the old feudal exploitation to the peasantry;[27] capitalism, going from strength to strength, endangered the livelihood of the artisan class; medium-sized landowners fell more and more deeply in debt to the Jews. Anti-Semitism on the part of the gentry is the consequence of this.[28] On all sides, Jewry was up against the mainstays of the traditional order. Its radical spirit, the harbinger of modernity, only aggravated social resentment.

The essay of M. Szabó is an important contribution to the theory of anti-Semitism, as it appeared in Hungary. In addition to the passions of the class conflict, he emphasizes the social psychology of these resentments. While he writes about "bourgeois society" in the past, his description of the various mechanisms at work may just as well be applied to the present. He analyzes, with special skill, the ossified and bureaucratic groups in society. Common-interest groups and lobbies do require a rival "Jewish lobby" in their infighting for advantages. In rigid societies, the anti-Semitism of bureaucrats and officeholders is reinforced by arrested development: "mobility *between* the classes is the primary problem; mobility *within* the classes only secondary. But wherever the social order, the nature of the ruling system and the institutional set-up is inviolable, open or disguised conflicts can only arise in the context of the secondary field of mobility. These conflicts of interest easily crystallize on an ethnocentric pattern. Resentment about the lack of mobility may find their excuse and self-justification in the suspected intrigues of rival lobbies based on ethnic groupings. In these circumstances, anti-Semitism not only survives but it is being re-created over and over again" (p. 362). The fairly virulent anti-Semitism manifesting itself in Hungarian intellectual life is proof of the truth of his statement.

The weak point in the argument of dogmatic Marxists is its one-sided economic motivation,[29] which ignores social psychology. The criticism of

Poliakov is quite justified: Marxist theory disregards the "elementary passions of a tribal nature."[30] Bibó and Száraz also mention—alongside psychological or religious motives—this instinct for "rejecting the foreigner."[31] This is the main weakness of all the theories: they fail to pull the multiplicity of motives together.

In practice, one result of this theoretical shakiness is the curious fact that official Marxist ideology in Hungary agrees with the past liberal-nationalism and with the Zionism which forced the Jews to choose between the false alternative of migration to Israel or joining the Magyar community, in which latter instance, it should give up its group identity.

A few more unresolved problems: Can we equate the official, "conservative" anti-Semitism forming part of government policies after World War I, and the horrific excesses of anti-Semitism between 1941-1944? How far can we draw a sign of equality between the anti-Semitism of the past and its fresh manifestations after 1945? On which specific conditions does the diversion of social resentment really work? What factors make up present-day anti-Semitism? What might be the conditions for its disappearance? Before we attempt to deal with questions of the present, however, we must deal with the confused heritage of the years of persecution.

During World War II, an alleged 825,000 people living under Hungarian administration were stripped of their civil rights and their livelihood, and finally cast into the jaws of death. Before the liberation and, as far as Jewry was concerned, it was exactly that liberation, more than half a million Jews perished. This was nothing less than a national catastrophe. In spite of this, no single work of scientific import has up to now appeared in Hungary on the subject of the persecutions.[32] This is a glaring omission if, for instance, we compare it with the treatment accorded to the persecution of Jews in the Netherlands.[33]

The state of bibliographies,[34] scientific editions of documents,[35] memoirs, and similar source material[36] extant in Hungary is somewhat more reassuring. Fiction and fact (mostly remembrances) dealing with the persecution and the Holocaust is quite copious in Hungary, so far without detailed assessment.[37] The flow of this literature ebbed only during the reign of Rákosi (1949-1954) when the Jewish question was definitely "not on the agenda." Those years of oppression had a harmful effect on the scientific study of primary sources for quite a long period. Even today, scientific life in Hungary has not completely recovered from the after effects of

Stalinism. This, of course, may have other, perhaps deeper, reasons too (see below).

Public life has been unable to face the traumatic subject of the persecutions squarely. The treatment of the source material mentioned above has definitely been patchy. For instance, Geyer's bibliography was put into the shredder immediately on publication, because of a sensitive article quoted by him: a diatribe published in *Szabad Nép* (Free People, the official Communist daily) on March 25, 1945, attributing to the returning Jews the behavior of concentration camp guards. It was written by one of the leaders of the populist Peasant Party (closely allied to the Communists), J. Darvas.

Another bibliography, compiled by Gy. Landeszman, remains in manuscript. A collection of documentary data by Benoschofsky and Karsai has been awaiting publication since 1967. Besides, it is significant that *all* source material that has been published in the last 25 years dealing with the persecution has been financed by Jewish foundations abroad, and has appeared as a publication of the Jewish religious community.[38] In consequence, these works were usually not distributed through the usual channels, the bookshops. While this does not diminish their value, it is a clear indication of the marginal importance that used to be attributed to the problem by the official publicity.

There is hardly any organized research on the subject in Hungary, while in New York, Boston, Haifa, Tel Aviv, and Jerusalem, universities are engaged in a serious and continuing study of Jewish history in Hungary. To all evidence the catastrophe of Hungarian Jewry is not acknowledged by the whole of Hungarian public opinion as being essentially a Hungarian problem. That is why the bulk of research on the problem is pursued in the USA and in Israel.[39] The comprehensive history of the persecution of Jews in Hungary, the work of Braham (1981), was published in the United States, not in Hungary. The estimates about the human losses date back to 1947;[40] its revision is long overdue.[41]

In the last 25 years, only certain aspects of the whole question have been dealt with, in a piecemeal fashion, in Hungary itself. There are memoirs, essays, or treatises on the first deportations in 1941;[42] on the antecedents and the history of the Hungarian labor service[43] system; on the part played by successive governments during the war;[44] on the period of German occupation, March-December 1944;[45] on the Arrow Cross era during the Szálasi government.[46] Many more publications have appeared abroad on similar subjects.[47]

The first, and so far the only, attempt at a summary made in Hungary was the work of J. Lévai, *Zsidósors Magyarországon* (Jewish Fate in Hungary, 1948), a very well balanced work of a high standard. He treats the questions of guilt and merit in an objective fashion; he touches on sensitive aspects of the tragedy which later were given a wide berth by official historians. With its wealth of data and documentation, this was up to Braham (1981), the most comprehensive survey of the facts. It is, however, a 40-year-old work; besides as recently as the early seventies, it was kept sequestered in the "closed" collection of the antiquarians.

Later works, instead of correcting or adding to it, usually fell far below the standards of Lévai. The schematic Marxist treatment imposed from the Rákosi regime[48] onward put a serious brake on scientific life anyway. A praiseworthy exception is the work of Ránki who treats the history of the half-year following the German occupation in 1944 in a serious and well-balanced manner.[49] Ránki, to the best of my knowledge, is the first—in his second edition—for more than 30 years to give chapter and verse for the Zionist attempts at saving Hungarian Jewry. He is also free of that kind of bias which, in a schematic manner, summarily condemns the whole Horthy regime, puts the onus for the Jewish tragedy on the Germans alone,[50] tries to reduce the merits of many courageous Church people,[51] and does its best to blow up, out of all proportion, armed resistance by the organized working class or else the role played by armed Jewish freedom fighters.[52] These ideological distortions are characteristic of most scientific works too, not only of apologetic broadsheets aimed at influencing the Paris Peace Conference; the official Jewish position especially was not exempt from this bias.[53] Ránki is thus a refreshing exception—something that cannot be said about the official *History of Hungary* (Volume 8), which shows a sad decline in standards.

The whole question of the resistance is a sore point for public opinion, largely for two reasons. In the first place, resistance was pitifully weak, both by the organized working class and by Jews in general. Secondly, the only courageous, though sporadic, resistance was shown by the Churches and the Zionists. Their role, however, had to be played down.

Accustomed to summary and simple answers, public opinion—including the scientific community—shied away from the detailed analysis of complex facts and multiple factors; for instance, the moderately anti-Semitic Churches, which had originally condoned the "Jewish laws," turned out to be comparatively the most active in saving Jewish lives. Even the mere existence of the Zionists, who had practically formed the only one Jewish organization capable of some effective resistance, was hushed up. Had their efforts been made public, it might have put on the agenda, the unresolved (and wrongly put) question as to where the Jews belong. The true history of the resistance is far from adequately established. There are a few contributions concerning the role played by certain Jewish social organizations, the Jewish Councils, or the resistance shown by the Zionists—or again the role of R. Kasztner.[54]

The history of protective measures taken by the Churches is somewhat better known—mostly written in self-defense—but no serious review has been published on this subject.[55] Recent publications in the scientific or popular fields sometimes devote a cursory sentence to this aspect, as well as to occasional attempts to save lives made by individuals or the public in general.[56]

All this is a serious debt yet to be discharged by the Hungarian scientific community.[57] For example, there is no recent work assessing the interventions of the Red Cross and the embassies of the neutrals in 1944.[58]

The fundamental reason for this deliberate neglect of the history of persecutions is, of course, the unresolved question: how far was Hungarian society as a whole responsible for them? Speaking of this responsibility, I must also include that of Jewry too. It has been well-nigh impossible to account for the responsibility because, with a few exceptions, almost everybody carried part of the guilt for the persecution: the victims for lack of self-defense,[59] the surrounding society for its indifference or hostility; the state administration and the civil service for being deliberate accomplices in mass murder;[60] the Allied Powers for their cynical inaction;[61] Jewish bodies in Palestine for dangerous amateurism;[62] working-class organizations for their lying low; the Churches for their political and spiritual support of earlier anti-Semitic government policies, including the first two anti-Jewish laws; even the Zionists for being unprepared. Cultural leaders and intellectuals, writers in particular, cannot escape their guilt, first for indulging in the "populist-urbanist" dispute tinged with anti-Semitism, and then for their failure to stand up and be counted.[63]

The burning question of social responsibility not only created a chasm between persecutor and victim; it also charges the Hungarian society with self-reproach for sheeplike submission, lack of courage, of lukewarm attempts at resistance to evil. Designated war criminals did not carry the guilt alone: it belongs to society as a whole.

The treatise of Bibó in 1948, and the essay of Száraz in 1975-76 were courageous acts in a moral sense, because in spite of all the obstacles, they put forward, fairly and squarely, the question of guilt burdening Hungarian society in its behavior toward the Jews. Their effect was definitely beneficial.

L. Márton took up the thread of Bibó's arguments in the early sixties and, being a Jew, pointed out the shortcomings of the Jews themselves during the persecution. Unfortunately, his essay remains unknown in Hungary.[64] More than ten years have gone since Száraz wrote his articles and the question of responsibility has remained untackled in the meantime. It would certainly clear the air if this dialogue, proceeding by fits and starts, resurfacing every ten years or so, were to be supported by sober, objective, straightforward scientific research. I am convinced that clarification of this vexing question is a social task of prime importance: it should be the basis for a genuine reconciliation within and between society and Jewry. Without this, the question of responsibility will remain a running sore for contemporary Hungarian society.[65]

There is an unbroken line leading from the persecutions of the cardinal year 1944 to the present Jewish reality. The attitude of all Jews living in Hungary today is still fully determined by the experiences of those years in which two-thirds of Jews under Hungarian administration had perished. The burden of Jews consists in finding a way through a past marked by gas chambers and mass graves. To raise the "Jewish question" once again is a near impossibility for those who have seen one "solution": Auschwitz and the other extermination camps. This fact must be squarely faced before we try to assess the heritage of a sore past including new problems raised by a multiform present-day censorship.

The main problems of Hungarian Jewry—much simplified—may be viewed as two interlocking elements. One of these is the self-awareness of Jewry: how does it perceive its own identity? The other one is its relationship to Hungarian society as a whole.

Clarification of the first problem area, that of self-awareness, may require transcending a bankrupted assimilation, as well as of a not generally valid Zionist model, that is, transcending of a nationalist concept of nation. Whoever attempts to ask the relevant questions about self-identity must relate it to the concepts of ethnicity, social and religious adherence, and the historical roles and functions of groups.

The other problem area—Jewry's position in society today—must also play a part in the clarification of Jewish identity. This complex question is also dominated by the shadow of 1944. There will be no solution to the Jewish question until a clarification of social responsibility for the mass murders has taken place. This means that historians must deal, without fear or favor, with the details of the persecution, and thereby force society to face up to some searing questions: "Why did we allow—and often help along—the deportation of the Jews?" "Why did we not protest and resist?" "Why did we allow ourselves to be driven to the slaughterhouse like sheep?" In other words, what is required will be a further rising standard of social responsibility with a simultaneous abandonment of comfortable self-censorship.

In the present-day area of Hungary, about 119,000 Jewish civilians and about 11,000 members of forced labor service companies were liberated. Another 65,000 deportees also stumbled home. Therefore, at the end of 1945, nearly 200,000 Jews were present in the country; 114,000 of them were religious Jews.[66] The distribution of this group, by age, sex, and location, was very uneven. Among those who perished, children and males were predominant.[67] About 42 percent of Jews in the capital and 79 percent of Jews in the provinces never came home.

This sad remnant was ravaged by war, German and Russian occupation, bombing, pillage, and then the greatest runaway inflation in history. Although in all this they shared the fate of the majority, they had also, from 1938, been traumatized by the "Jewish laws," discrimination, loss of jobs, then of property, finally of family members.

We have no solid data on the subsequent history of Jewry in Hungary. We can only make guesses as to how many of the survivors did not return; how many have emigrated;[68] how many left the religious community. The last census, in 1949, gave the number of Jews as 134,000,[69] strictly on denominational grounds. There were 30 percent more women than men. These data were kept strictly confidential for a long while. From the next census onward, religion has no longer figured in census data, so we are limited to guesswork. Officially, they set the number of Jews in Hungary at 100,000, of whom 80 percent live in the capital.[70] Unofficially, not more than 30,000 are thought to belong to the religious communities; less than half of this number figures on parochial rolls.[71] The state of Orthodox communities and of provincial groups is particularly grave.[72] On the whole, however, the situation of Jewry in Hungary—from the institutional point of view as well as in respect of equality before the law and lack of discrimination—can be said to be better than in many other countries of East Central Europe. Indeed, it might be said to be slightly improving.[73]

The miserable remnants of Jewry in 1945 shared very much the same problem.[74] There were various attempts, though, at solving them. Many of the Jews emigrated; others tried to build a new life, remarried, then either joined the civil service or entered trade and commerce; most tried to get some compensation for their sufferings; some sought restitution of their expropriated properties. Those who were unable to start anew sunk in hopeless despair, and just waited for the end—in perpetual mourning, disabled, or mad.

Only a minority were willing to face up to the problems of persecution; the majority escaped into furious activities, trying to adjourn the confrontation. Many of them—understandably—thought to find a safeguard against anti-Semitism in Soviet armed power and Communist social systems: they joined the Party, especially the Party-dominated police force.

However, the unsettled psychological problems confronting both Hungarian Jewry and Hungarian society soon enough took revenge, in the form of new distortions. These manifested themselves partly in a new-born anti-Semitism, partly in all Jewish problems becoming taboo. An old division of social consciousness was cemented anew, which meant that there was no unified public opinion, only several particular group attitudes. In consequence, past, present and future were looked at through very different colored spectacles. And this is still valid today. Perhaps the 1954-56 period was an exception—but already, in an evaluation of the events of 1956, this ambiguity has reappeared.

Official Jewish leadership offered the sad spectacle of a divided, quarreling, frightened minority after the liberation. This minority allowed itself to become a ward of the State, both materially and spiritually. State power, according to its whim, supported, tolerated, intimidated, and protected it against the possibility that anti-Semitism would rear its ugly head again. Jewish religious life, and its international links, became subject to the day-to-day changes in State policy, regardless of the proper interests of Jewry itself. The official stand of Jewish authorities—in respect of Zionism, international Jewish bodies, or of West German compensation—coincided only accidentally with the true interests of Jewry.

The military valor of Israel shown in the Arab wars of 1967 and 1973 gave a strong boost to the self-confidence of Hungarian Jews. This, however, was not enough to settle, once and for all, the problem of identity for them. It is not a question of the slogans but of the unspoken problems. Freedom of public opinion in Hungary has been showing an improvement since 1964, albeit with its ups and downs. Today, a stage has been reached where almost everything could be openly said about the Jewish question. That this is still not happening is, in my opinion, to some extent, due to the inner blockages and interdictions of intimidated Jewry.

These anxieties and inhibitions go back, in equal measure, to internal and external causes. The relationship of Jewry and Hungarian society is still burdened by many unsettled questions—first and foremost, that of the responsibility for the persecution and the inner crises of Jewish self-awareness. Since 1945, not a few additional aggravating factors have arisen.[75]

There are many people who blame Jewry on account of the numerous judicial and penal retaliatory measures taken after the liberation for the past persecutions, its eager participation in the political police, in civil administration, and political power. Up to the end of the Rákosi regime, Jews were rather prominent in high-ranking positions of public life; all this used to be called "the vengeance of the Jews."

The Jews too have had many grievances. Governments after the war offered no compensation to the survivors;[76] in 1946, the new wave of anti-Semitism flared up into anti-Jewish pogroms at several places in the

provinces;[77] various discriminatory measures were taken during the
Rákosi era (such as the severe limitations of the Jewish religious organization, an embargo on international links, anti-Zionist trials, sequestra-
tion of communal properties, the evictions in 1951-52,[78] and so on).
Unfortunately isolated anti-Semitic excesses did take place during the
1956 revolution[79] as well. Anti-Semitism is still endemic in several social
strata, and last but not least there certainly has been a tendency not to
face the question of social responsibility for the persecutions: an attitude
of "let bygones be bygones." From time to time an official taboo has
been put on Jewish problems.

By consequence of a divided public opinion none of these grievances
are shared by the various groups who harbor them. Rather, they are
unconscious even of the existence of such reciprocal grievances. There
is a sore need for a thorough investigation to uncover this hidden fer-
ment.

I suggest that the articulation of the "Jewish question" today involves
the relatively favorable social situation of Jews, especially in the professions.
In other words, the findings of Karády and Kemény concerning the twen-
ties are still valid: anti-Semitism today still has largely a middle-class bias.
In today's bureaucratized society, the struggle for jobs in the fairly satu-
rated professional market is still a main source of anti-Semitism.[79a]

Since 1949 (as census data have omitted questions on religious adherence), we have no hard facts about the social position of the Jews, in
terms of their educational attainments, income structure, job distribution, social mobility, and so on. One cannot find out what are the true
numbers behind the informal social bookkeeping with regard to the
presence of Jews under the university professors, theater directors, export
representatives, or publishers. Nor is there a possibility of measuring the
extent to which the Jewish anguishes, the inner crises of identity, the carefully concealed traumas of past persecution and present insult afflict
society.

I must emphasize that, in my eyes, the lack of statistics on Jewish occupational distribution is quite justified. Although one reason for this is
the probable official view of "let bygones be bygones," another—and a
better one—is the treatment of such data for the evaluation of social
mobility, for the purposes of rational organization on the basis of personal
merit and not racial or religious origins. The problems of national minorities

in Hungary before 1919 were similarly not caused by the "predominance" of itinerant Slovak repairmen, German artisans, or Gypsy musicians within an educational branch.

On the other hand, it cannot be denied that the status of professional and intellectual elites is a key question for all developed societies; therefore it is not quite irrational that public opinion is keeping a tab on the ratio of Jews in various occupations, especially the professions. In the political field, the Communist Party pursues a deliberate pragmatic policy of being very careful about official appointments of Jews in posts of high visibility.

Of course, it would be desirable to know what exactly these ratios are, and how society at large keeps account of Jews in jobs. Keeping these things under wraps, pursuing undisclosed policies, "keeping social peace and quiet"—does this not mean that the wounds are still festering under the skin?

Another gaping blank in Jewish reality is the complete lack of Jewish sociography.[80] There is not much to be found either in documentaries, written or filmed, or in reportages on aspects of the past: Jewish life in the provinces, the cultural aspects of Jewry, Jewish family life, the characteristic Jewish quarters of the capital, their traditional occupations—all these are conspicuous by their absence. This is all the more remarkable as the Hungarian school of sociography had a strong tradition and high standards. It is difficult to say whose fault this hiatus may be; in any case, history is that much the poorer.

A similarly deplorable failure is an almost complete absence of any sociographical or sociopolitical analysis of the question: "What does it mean to be a Jew?" (exceptions are two books written abroad). This is one of the most sensitive questions. On the one it touches the Jewish identity crisis, which has been chronic for more than a hundred years. On the other hand, it would cast light upon the structure of the still virulent anti-Semitism of today. How does the "Jewish question" manifest itself at the place of work, on the football field, on the buses, at house parties?

This question isn't given enough attention within the field of scientific investigation in Hungary. Surely, the suppression of the problem can never achieve a solution for the "false consciousness"; it can only convey permanence to a divided social awareness. Under these circumstances

Száraz deserves special credit for sketching out the typology of social awareness in respect of the "Jewish question."[81]

In the last 25 years, there have been only two works which cast some light on the extent of anti-Semitism. One of these tried to assess prejudices among the Catholic farming population; the other did the same among city youth. The results show that anti-Semitism stands somewhere halfway between the slight prejudices against Protestants and other nationalities and the great hostility to Gypsies.[82]

The scarcity of numerical and qualitative data is a symptom of something of a continuing crisis affecting both Jewry and society at large. The "Keep Out" signs marking the boundaries of permissible serious assessment can, of course, maintain only a semblance of social peace. Only a self-confident social awareness can break them down: a mature public opinion would be needed to disperse these veiled prejudices.

In trying to sum up the charting of Jewish realities in Hungary, with all its blanks, one must find, regrettably, a negative balance as far as studies in Hungary itself are concerned. Failures and omissions are preponderant over positive achievements. A comparison with foreign results does not seem to be favorable either. There is no institutional approach or organization in Hungary—again in sad constrast to what is going on abroad. The omissions seem to be most significant in the fields of the theory of anti-Semitism; the history of the persecutions; the question of social guilt and responsibility; the sociography of Jewry; Jewish self-awareness and the facts connected with the social reality of Jewry. Cautious repression, circumlocution, imposed silence signify the false consciousness that has been the order of the day for far too long.

The undoubtedly significant work, mostly preliminary though, that has been done in the field of source-gathering, has usually been financed from abroad. The distribution of such material falls outside the range of the normal book trade. Even earlier works have disappeared from the market: for instance, Bibó's treatise (1948) was before 1984 available only in exile publications. It is just as difficult to measure the effect of the available literature on its readership.

The passage of time may relieve the cramps and disperse the phantoms from the soul of society—and this may make it possible to repair the omissions. In any case, the problems of Jews in Hungary will not be solved by science and publicity alone.

Self-Censorship and the Jewish Question

There are many blank spaces on the map of Jewish realities. This is no accident. There is an assumed identity of interests between the whole of Hungarian society and the Jewish part of it: They both mistakenly think that it is better to sweep certain questions under the carpet. I shall analyze these components of this web of deceit, reticence, or inhibition. As indicated before, there are two interwoven subjects of a traumatic nature: one is the problem of identity for the Jews, the other the question of responsibility for society as a whole. Friction still exists between Jews and their environment. However, as an outspoken discussion of this matter would immediately cast these traumatic problems to the surface, there is a conspiracy of silence that works to the supposed "mutual interest" of both parties. Where both of them evade the questions, there can be no communication—not even within themselves.

Let us try to disentangle this wicked web, first of all the two "core" questions. The crisis of Jewish identity has its origins in the development of the medieval concept of *natio*. The era of liberal nationalism turned this into an all-encompassing idea,[83] allocating only a religious identity to Jews. The route to assimilation became thereby narrower and finally proved to be a dead end. Loyalty to the Magyar nation was, eventually, rejected by society: the Jews were excluded from the body politic, their rights were curtailed, then abolished, finally they were physically destroyed. The Jewish consciousness, reduced to a membership in the religious community, proved to be incapable of defense during the persecution. Rejection and defenselessness—they define the crisis of identity for Jews following 1944. The inner crisis of identity coupled with anti-Semitism from outside add up to the two sides of something of a "Jewish question."

Trying to analyze the essence of the "Jewish question," which is much like wandering into a bottomless pit, frightens even the bravest. Every detailed explanation immediately finds a telling counter-argument. Bruno Bauer, broaching the Jewish question in 1843, suggested, as its main cause, the stubborn adherence of Jews to their ethnicity and religious exclusiveness. He could not know that before long it would be the runaway success of assimilation that would stoke the fires of anti-Semitism. Marx, in 1844, pointed at the "capitalistic nature" of Jews as the root of the problem. This is the officially adopted theory nowadays in Hungary. If, however, this were true, why is it that the main attacks of anti-Semitism were directed at the millions of wretchedly poor Jews in the ghettos of Eastern Europe, and—later in Hungary—against the professionals and the intelligentsia of Jewish origin? In this swamp of base passions, every single argument, and every counter-argument, is a good enough stick to beat the Jews with.

In a fanciful way it may seem that whatever the Jew does, it is his ill fate to incite anti-Semitism. Whether he is humble or arrogant, proud of his Jewishness or denying it, assimilating or Zionist, pious rabbi or imperial baron, capitalist or Communist, he can never be right. Sartre called this *culpabilité juive:* the real original sin of Jewry that cannot be washed away and certainly not by baptism.

This cruel mixture of ideas may be true or not, but the Jews were trapped in its physical consequences. In the view of the anti-Semite Jewry equals evil. This *a priori* statement in effect creates an image of the Jew constructed from the vile instincts of the anti-Semite himself. This sinister caricature of the Jew represents all aspects of evil: he is accused of spreading pestilence, of deicide, blood libel, and usury; later on, during the irresistible burst of industrial development, of *parvenu* arrogance, capitalist exploitation, Judeobolshevism, a worldwide conspiracy, and sexual perversion. Now, having deserved sevenfold death unto the fourth generation there is this handful of impertinent and loudmouthed survivors who have the gall to demand the restitution of stolen property, who speculate on the black market, and enrich themselves once more. Full of revenge, Jewry is the prime mover at the Peoples' Tribunals, at the secret police; at the same time Jews are the lackeys of imperialist powers, Zionist agents one and all—in short, they are the embodiment of aggressiveness, of time-serving spinelessness, of cowardly cringing, of all indecenies. All the nightmares of a bad social conscience are transformed to the Jew. This is the trap from which the wretched Jews cannot escape and, in the end, may make even them believe this demonology.

This wicked caricature, appearing in the crooked mirror of the social

environment, is both effect and cause of the Jewish crisis of identity. By
the end of the nineteenth century, the Jewish religious communities were
shaken by the successive shocks of Jewish migration, Jewish enlightenment, Zionism, and a corresponding anti-Semitism.[84] Jewry could not
find its own self in the way that other peoples did: they had no country
of their own, and their spiritual folk culture, deeply rooted in the religious
mode, was thoroughly disoriented by the effects of enlightenment. This is
why McCagg calls the overweening liberal spirit emerging within Jewry an
inverse or rejectionist nationalism. This Jewish enlightenment denies a
separate nationhood to Jews—in the spirit of the age, it urges adherence
to the surrounding national communities, demands modernization of religious rites and of the Jewish way of life. In the course of this development, "the Jewish identity, in 1800 one of the most distinct in Greater
Hungary, was reduced by successive generations of reformers to one of
the least definable."

The second generation of Jews limited its Jewishness to its religion.
Otherwise it wanted to identify itself with the Magyar nation. Religious
Jewishness combined with secular Magyar nationalism: this was one aspect
of the "inverse nationalism" professed by enlightened Jews. The third
generation turned this on its head; they were free-thinkers and interna-
tionalists. By that time, the Jewish crisis of identity had acquired a chronic
permanence.[85] McCagg points out that the anti-capitalist stance of radical
Jews was the reverse of the slogan "Jews equal Capital"—another aspect of
this "inverse nationalism." All this was a symptom of uncertainty and disequilibrium. The pure idea of the Nation allows no room for Jewry; but
there is a profusion of other options, like the ones listed by Karády and
Kemény in 1978. According to them, the defining traits of Jewish identity
—religion, ethnic traditions, anthropological characteristics, legal position—
are all shifting attributes, subject to the self-awareness defined by events
and class relationships.

W. Rabi analyzed the question of Jewish identity based on empirical
investigations; he assessed the concept of "Jewry" on the basis of religion,
communal behavior, language, common history, folk affinity, and psychological self-awareness. Sometimes it is related to bloodline (child of a
Jewish mother), at other times it means belonging to a national minority
(Poland, Soviet Union), often Messianic, or simply defined by a feeling

of persecution. Its social functioning is also manifold. In Israel, it is the basis of citizenship; in the United States, a mode of social integration. Its character is changing too: in the U.S. and in Britain, its social function grows in comparison with its religious importance. The many-colored linkages give added weight to the factor of self-awareness. Karády and Kemény come to the same conclusion as Sartre: "You are a Jew if you consider yourself to be one, or if the others take you for one." This self-consciousness is linked to objective factors, but there is also an element of arbitrariness.

In the conditions prevailing in Hungary, this "mental construct" has developed within a medium, the Hungarian society, which itself was experiencing a chronic crisis. Unfortunately, there have been hardly any sociographical investigations, nor are there other firm data for assessing the true meaning of Jewishness to Hungarian Jews.[86] Evidence from fictional writings and occasional essays only demonstrate a deep bewilderment[87] —far from a new phenomenon. The internally supporting ties of Jewry had already started to loosen in the first generation of immigrants, once other factors of a secure existence came to hand.[88] It is a characteristic of development in Hungary (and in other countries too) that social ascent and the rate of assimilation proceeded in equal measure. However, in Hungary, a not at all self-evident fact soon appeared: one of the basic conditions of assimilation demanded the abandonment of Jewishness. This is corroborated by the contrary demand of Zionism: dissimilation as a necessary condition of self-preservation.

It may be that assimilationist Jewry honestly tried to safeguard its Jewishness while identifying itself with the Magyar nation. It was Magyar society that rejected this identification, perhaps because it had lost its own way itself in the successive waves of language renewal (a conscious national drive early in the nineteenth century), in the growth of cities, in industrialization. It then transferred its own waywardness to the "landless" Jews. This dissociation from Jewry became the official policy of the ruling governments from 1920 on. First in 1920, then from 1938, subsequent laws were designed to diminish and eliminate the equality of rights.

By the time of World War II, dissimilation had become all too real. The remnants of Hungarian Jewry could not face this even after 1945—the trap of "Where do I belong" had snapped shut.[89] Those who accepted that the "host nation" had cast them out, had to accept the logic of Zionism too (like the otherwise clear-thinking and honest authors, I. Kulcsár and B. Dénes; their works offer the best situation report of Hungarian Jewry immediately after 1945, next to Bibó's treatise).

During the Rákosi regime, Zionism became a crime by 1946, the Communist Party had already adopted the model of absorption as a solution to the Jewish question. Zionist trials took place, in the wake of the trial and execution of László Rajk. The reports of such party hacks as E. Balogh and G. Makai equated Zionism with American imperialism and racism. Since 1948, no publication favoring Zionism has been permitted. Israel remains the only conceptual alternative to complete absorption. This in turn means that Jewish identity in this sense has become a plaything of geopolitics. Jewish official bodies carefully give a very wide berth to Zionism; this is one of their most vulnerable points.

Jewry in Hungary today is definitely just a religious community.[90] Officially, we are back to the conceptual level where we started a hundred years ago.

This confusion and the continuing crisis of Jewish self-awareness is a sign of fractured relationships with the society, just as political anti-Semitism was something of a symptom of inner crises and uncertainties within the surrounding Magyar society. The identity of self can be defined only in relation to others. Jewry has gone through a process of assimilation, for more than 150 years now, within a partly hostile and discriminatory ambience. The humiliating experiences of prejudice constantly surrounding one scar one's consciousness from early childhood.

The distorting effects of discrimination have largely been explored by psychological investigations in other countries.[91] Among their more serious symptoms one can find quite a range of neurotic disturbances, depressive syndromes, and character changes.[92] A more widely observed effect is the loss of self-confidence,[93] a low threshold of frustration, behavior shifting from abasement to aggression, dissimulation,[94] and self-hatred—this last a subconscious acceptance of the hostility of the environment.[95]

Anti-Semitism can even affect the individual's views of his own body: certain physical characteristics are capable of triggering hostile discrimination. In the period of persecutions, such bodily features were quite often decisive for life or death. The mere acceptance of a "moderate," everyday discrimination carried with it the seeds of self-hatred. This psychological distortion, leading to a virtual surrender of self, is a multiform phenomenon. It might manifest itself in various symptoms, like the tinting of one's hair, surgical straightening of one's nose, or just the change of one's name;[96] one could also find Jews mouthing anti-Semitic slogans.[97] A contributing factor may have been the internal division of emergent Jewry in the last century when assimilated Jews would disparage "those Polish finks."[98]

A permanently discriminatory social environment will cause fairly general psychological and communal traumas, even in its passive state. When it turns to active persecution, the effects are much more serious. There is much literature on this subject abroad, but in Hungary nothing has been published on the psychology of the persecuted. The only exception is the work of I. Kulcsár (1946), which sums up, in four short pages, the aftereffects troubling the survivors.[99] First he mentions the spiritual regression of those who succeeded in returning from the extermination camps: primitive instincts and primary needs are dominant; people are emotionally frozen, incapable of mourning, their senses are deadened, they live only for the present. Certain secondary mental disturbances appeared early on, like the so-called "KZ syndrome," aggressive outbursts, impotence, and often suicide.

According to Kulcsár, the majoirty of the survivors suffered from a pointless, impotent, generalized resentment. Their erstwhile crisis of self-confidence deepened further, since they were still at loggerheads with the "host" society. Those who came back from the anteroom of Death for the most part tried, with desperate mental effort, to disguise their outcaste status. There was a pathetic attempt at a rushed assimilation. These serious conflicts led quite often to squalid internal quarrels among Jews. In Kulcsár's words: "Deeply etched memories, un-realized losses, sterile resentment, dole (or relief) neurosis, false illusions, inner civil war—these are the features of a cross section of returned Jews, in the autumn of 1946."[100]

These few pages are the entire contribution to the problem by Hungarian experts, while psychiatry in other countries has accumulated a whole library on it. We should mention the important findings of Bettelheim about social and psychological effects, based on those who had returned from Buchenwald. Like Kulcsár, he points out their regressive infantilism,[101] their crushed personalities, the suppression of compassion,[102] the predominance of primary needs,[103] the uncontrolled aggression,[104] the soul-destroying effects of fear.[105] He also points out that the victim will often identify himself with the executioner,[106] and that mostly the price of survival was compromise.[107] These are important elements for the understanding the spiritual burdens carried by surviving Jews.[108]

Dutch studies on orphans who survived in hiding have established a range of mental disturbances, depending on the age of the children during concealment: traumatization, dysfunctions in character development, depression and anxiety syndromes, arrested psychic and social development, confused affectiveness, disturbed social behavior problems of identity, and so on.[109] Another study in 1960, investigating 50 deportees who were 5-to-25 years old at the time of the persecutions found the following mental disorders:[110]

Symptoms	Percent
High irritability, oversensitiveness, quick to take offense, bouts of aggression, depressions, withdrawal	100
Headaches	98
Apathy; dizziness	92
Memory confusion, insufficient concentration	88
Insomnia	84
Nightmares	82
Disorders of other-relatedness	66
Easily tired	64

Unfortunately, it is not only the children of that time who show the after-effects of their sufferings.[111] Many of these traits can be found in *their* children too.[112]

Every paper emphasizes the heightened disorientation of the persecuted in their social relationships and behavior.[113] They become liable to drop out and become isolated. This, in turn, leads to chronically broken relationships with others, further feeding their mental disturbances.

Psychiatric investigations into the pathogenic effects of persecution only demonstrate in a heightened form, the general spiritual burden, the inner conflicts, and mental distortions that had always been the psychological luggage of a minority discriminated against, albeit in a milder way, by "everyday" anti-Semitism. It is worth mentioning that discrimination and pesecution have had an increased impact on the unprepared assimilating Jews. They have been doubly vulnerable.[114] Jews in Hungary had been the epitome of successful assimilation.

We can only understand properly the inhibitions,[115] the forgetting,[116] the evasion—in short, the self-censorship of Hungarian Jewry—if we take into account this deep spiritual conflict, reinforced by the persecution,[117] wounded even in its religious perceptions.[118] By the turn of the century the mere word "Jew" had pejorative echoes. The "Jewish question" was already on the agenda.[119] Since the end of World War II, there has been a delicate avoidance of the word. Artificial circumlocutions are being used instead: "Israelite, Talmudist, Hebrew, martyr, deportee, racially persecuted," and so on. This ungainly distortion of straight talk is not limited to Jewry only: the whole of Magyar society uses these weasel words, in the same manner.[120]

It is not only the Jewish commonality that is laboring under the inhibitions of self-censorship—which is rather characteristic of public life in Hungary. Only the deeper lines of cause-and-effect are different. In my view, Jewry is shackled by its problems of identity (including the unsettled question of "Us" and "Them"), while Hungarian public life is embarrassed by the still unanswered question of responsibility.

The first chapter of Bibó's treatise clearly established the moral bankruptcy of the whole Magyar society in respect of the persecutions, and its inability to face the questions of guilt and responsibility. The essay by Száraz brought up this unsettled sociopolitical question with great moral force, demanding a solution. Very few people have dared to challenge public opinion in such a creditable manner. Let us hope that these rare utterances have contributed to something of a thaw.

It may be a step forward if hidden self-accusations were spelled out. After all, apart from the self-reproaches of Jewry, Hungarian society itself had even weightier reasons for self-accusation. The Nazi terror, the cowardly fear, corrupted even those who may have been full of compassion—or just remained neutral—among the population.[121] Száraz sets this out in uncompromising terms: decent people were also tainted by the abject behavior of the Christian middle classes: their impassivity toward the robbery of Jewish property, their participation even in the looting of Jewish flats, houses, and so on.

In 1959, even in 1966, the tendency toward forgetfulness, toward disguise, was still too strong.[122] Perhaps it would be correct to say that since then the self-reproach of Magyar society has here and there become more obvious.[123] The passage of time makes it easier to recollect certain things.

The "Jewish question," as it manifested itself over the last 100 years, was essentially the repugnance of feudal society to the easy mobility, the free-thinking, the industriousness, of the process of *embourgeoisement*. This painful transition was then accentuated by a lost war in 1918, two revolutions, and the great economic crisis of the thirties. A maladjusted society reached the limits of self-mutilation, in its vain attempts to cast out the falsely perceived "evil"—and in the process these attempts themselves became the essence of evil.

In this way the inner crisis of the nation paralleled that of Jewry. Magyar self-delusions, sterile nationalism, the empty superiority of a "county" or gentry way of life, a fist-shaking self-pity—all ran aground on the sandbanks of reality. When these collective hallucinations were over and the accounts were drawn up, it turned out that half a million Hungarian Jews were on the debit side. And they were discounted into death by this same society. How to face this examination report? This question has been adjourned *sine die*.

The questions of Jewish identity, of Jewry's relations to society on one side, or the responsibilities of this society for the persecutions on the other, are still open ones, putting constraints on public opinion, whenever the existential problems of Jewry come to the fore. There is a parallel false consciousness, equally burdening the nation and its Jewish component. Neither of them is ready to shoulder the task of disentangling the situation that is tying them into knots. Is it not better to close one's eyes, rather than thresh about impotently?

An old sore spot has become encysted in this way, covered by the hard membrane of self-censorship. That is why these problems still cannot be opened up and dealt with. In vain are the frequent calls for straight talk, for public honesty, for clearing up the moral mess—their hammer blows have not been enough to break the carapace of self-censorship that is re-inforced by other public interests.

The Jewish Question Today

What about the Jewish question today? Even if the utterly cynical aphorism "1944 solved the Jewish question in Hungary" were true, the very fact of this "solution" would put it on the permanent agenda. As it is, we have a double view of history, a double public opinion, a double self-awareness in the country. Neither society as a whole, nor Jewry as such, has clarified the relationships within and between themselves.

There are many signs of this dual consciousness. Take for instance the question of responsibility. According to *A,* Hungarian society has never accepted the responsibility for the persecutions. According to *B,* dwelling on the question of responsibility is constantly humiliating people, by brandishing the stick of "collective guilt" in order to break its national self-esteem. One is fed up with something the other urgently wants to tackle. Another consequence of this unresolved past (and a further sign of a divided consciousness) is the dual evaluation of the Rákosi years, According to *B,* that reign of terror was the vengeance which the Jews wrought on the Magyar people, carried out by the "Jewish" political police. *A* asserts that, on the contrary, Rákosi's rule was anti-Jewish: look at the Zionist trials, the large number of Jews who were deported, the suppression of Jewish religious life.

Another aspect of this dual vision concerns jobs and positions. Natur-ally, there exist the usual networks of mutual interest, often involving discrimination. The role of nepotism, quid pro quo, and the old boy net-work has always been traditional in Hungary. There are many repugnant but spellbinding stories going the rounds, whispering how *X* got his ap-pointment, or why *Y* did not get it. Such stories are rather usual in Hun-gary but they are not mutually shared by the two coexisting networks. Each camp is unaware that discrimination operates against the other one too.

There exists no real *public* opinion in Hungary, only this dual percep-tion—like the two intercommunicating vessels that nevertheless do not intercommunicate.

The mere fact of this division may prove to be a more serious problem for society than the content of the problem dividing it. The unresolved Jewish question and the fractured nature of Magyar society mutually reinforce one another. The lack of a unified public opinion may be the more acute problem today, but the continuing suppression of the Jewish question in itself is nothing less than a latent catastrophe. It would be in the real interests of all concerned, to open up and deal with this state of affairs. Why cannot this be done?

Self-Censorship and Dual Consciousness—Their Social Impact Today

Who is profiting from this divided consciousness? In whose interest is its continuance? What are its consequences? What actually does the "Jewish question" *mean* today?

The Jewish question played an important part in the development of goverment in Hungary following the war.[124] It was one of the consequences of the persecutions that the Soviet Union and its local power source, the Communist Party, were regarded by Hungarian Jewry as the best safeguards for its liberation. This is the very reason why the new regime could draw on Jewry (among others) for competent collaborators in the speedy rebuilding of a new civil administration. The armed police forces too recruited large numbers of enthusiastic and loyal Jews into their ranks.

The Jewish question persisted in not fading away, however, and the divisions of public opinion greatly helped the Communist policy of "divide and rule." The revolution of 1956 was made possible, among other things, by the thaw in these conflicting opinions.

Anti-Semitism had thus become important in the establishment of the "People's Democracy." Its regeneration was guaranteed by the entry of many Jews into positions of authority and into the ranks of the political police. All this generated a new wave of anti-Semitism among the people. Jewry had a vested interest in the new regime, which formed something of a safeguard against open anti-Semitism. Lest they forget this, the state-controlled media reminded them from time to time. *Szabad Nép* (Free People), the official daily of the Communist Party, prominently reported the news of the 1946 provincial pogroms. Official literature stressed isolated anti-Semitic manifestations during the 1956 revolution. The smouldering anti-Semitism in society, with its occasional flareups, was very handy to the regime on three occasions: during the reconstruction, at the time of the Communist takeover of power, and during the restoration of Communist rule after 1956. In other words, anti-Semitism in Hungary has given stability to the regime.

News about manifestations of "popular" anti-Semitism today is exceedingly rare. It would be a sociopolitical task of the first order to investigate those manifestations to determine how anti-Semitism reveals itself in social, political, and economic life, and how it relates to class composition. In the absence of such data, I shall relate two anecdotes in hopes of characterizing the state of affairs:

Imre Berger is the director of publicity for the trade union of workers in biscuit manufacturing. One day he organized a roundtable conference with various factory managers. During the meeting, the shortcomings of production and distribution were discussed with unusual frankness. The trade union paper—with the aim of encouraging improved performance—reported the proceedings in full; whereupon Berger was dismissed.

The participants strongly disapprove of this, saying that if they had said something unacceptable, they should be taken to task, not the editor who only reported what was said. They sent a delegation to the Buscuit Division of the Ministry of Food, led by J. Talpas, the managing director of the Honey-Cake Factory. When they set forth their grievances, the divisional head, D. Léc, a veteran of the working class movement, turns on the spokesman, saying "What the hell bugs you, comrade? What's this Berger to you? You were born in the provinces, not in the ghetto!"

The other story occurred in another industry, the Trust for Carriage Drivers. István Szabó, the very competent, well-liked director of the Trust, was suddenly dismissed in favor of László Rónai. The latter was an ignoramus, inexperienced, and incompetent. There was, of course, no previous scrutiny in the trade and no public discussion about the change. The general secretary of the Carriers' Trade Union then suggested that the appropriate authorities should give their reasons for the appointment. Whereupon he was discreetly warned to desist: any open discussions of the matter would be branded as anti-Semitism.

The first story illustrates the operation of *post facto* censorship. Personal freedom of opinion (increasingly tolerated in recent years) is one thing; but the editor of a semi-official publication must not be allowed to

transgress the invisible boundaries of press freedom. And it also touches
upon another transgression: the equally invisible boundary dividing the
provinces from the "ghetto," dividing Jews from Gentiles, became for a
moment visible. The solidarity shown by the biscuit-makers overstepped
this limit. Unless we attribute the irritation of Comrade Léc to a personal
whim, we can see here the workings of a hidden policy, uneasy about a
loosening of social divisions.[125]

Similar sinister mechanisms may be discovered at work in the second
example. One is the cynical use of anti-Semitism in aid of the reinforce-
ment of social divisions. The bogey charge of anti-Semitism is not an
argument which would be effective in intimidating everybody alike; the
charge is obviously aimed at non-Jews only. That means, some authorities
subtly take account of who is and who is not a Jew, and of who can and
who cannot be intimidated by the charge of anti-Semitism. Such manipulation not only reckons with an effective social division between Jews and
non-Jews but induces and perpetuates it at once. Our story shows, by the
way, that the authorities presumed that the knowledge Rónai was a Jew was
widespread. But the really interesting aspect of our story appears as soon as
we realize that Szabó is also a Jew. Thus, the threat of anti-Semitism to the
trade union secretary lay not in its logical validity, which is nought, but in
something different: in the additional presumption that people take account of the origin only of Jews who undeservedly hold high positions.

The rhetorical threat of branding someone as anti-Semitic lies here in
the fact that a person's Jewishness is taken into account only if he is incompetent. Many people earnestly declare that they are not anti-Semitic:
they have many friends, honest fellows all, who may be Jews, but they
could not care less. The decent, the deserving, the Olympic champions,
the Nobel prizewinners—they all are undiscriminately Magyar even in the
eyes of anti-Semites. Our stories are proof of the survival, indeed the
induction, of the false consciousness. One may not have thought of it,
but is now strongly reminded—with a severe warning not to mention it
openly—that the "unworthy" are Jewish.

A further aspect of this web of contradictions casts light on the question: *cui prodest*? Anti-Semitism is a rhetorical trick, liable to shift the
dispute on to the false grounds of *ad hominem* arguments. The question is
not, any longer, whether X or Y are worthy, competent, expert people,

fit for the appointment: all attention will be concentrated on an irrelevant factor.

Anti-Semitism—in the guise of philo-Semitism in one case—is a mechanism for diverting attention from the essentials. Its main use consists of switching to the sidings the often discussed principle of "selection of the unfittest." The more unworthy you are, the easier to get into a leading position, because it ensures your subservience to the powers-that-be.

Within the ranks of the civil administration, a system of neofeudal vassalage has been developing, in bureaucratic form. At the top of the heap sits the feudal lord, in full possession of privileges: unconditional decision-making, levying of tithes, judgment over life and death, a court with favorites. In charge of various social sectors there are his vassals, enfeoffed in offices, factories, institutions; they owe unconditional obedience to their liege lord for their benefices. The pledge of their faithfulness is their unworthiness. Once the telephone rings, they have to jump up and do what they are told. If one loses the august favor, one automatically loses one's job too—after all, one has no personal merit for holding onto it. It goes without saying that this bureaucratic feudalism is the strongest brake on every effort toward healthy development.

The principle of "selection of the unfittest" has become a cardinal factor in public life. Fighting against it is still well-nigh hopeless. This social disease affects scientific and cultural life, the civil service, factory management, religious institutions, the health services—you name it, they practice it.

Following the Communist takeover of power, it became a deliberate policy to appoint incompetent, morally tainted persons to leading institutional or managerial positions: suspended lawyers, embezzlers, police narks, and suchlike became top dogs.

The revolutionary workers' councils of 1956, as well as the most recent Polish attempts, wanted to cure this social disease and put competent, honest people into leading jobs.

I have come to the conclusion that the political leadership in Hungary would like to undo this system but does not know how to go about it. And, in our case, anti-Semitism plays much the same part as the "selection of the unfittest." The warning sign of "anti-Semitism" freezes the question of competence. The unworthy person in a cushy job is—if he is a Jew—at the mercy of his superiors twice over: he has no leg to stand on, in terms of expertise or personal worth, therefore only the grace and favor of his bosses can protect him from the anti-Semitism of his environment. This new anti-Semitism is a kind of Sword of Damocles, a pledge for unconditional subservience, constantly reinforcing the dependence of the subject. Thus anti-Semitism has become today one of the mainsprings of social manipulation.

If it is true that some of the essential conditions of further advance of the Hungarian society today are "selection of the unfittest" on the one hand, and an undivided social consciousness on the other, it is important to assess the chances of healing the social disease called the "Jewish question," and of doing away with the accompanying cancer of self-censorship.

The Prospects

Lost wars and failed revolutions have brought little balm to Jewry in this century. For the sake of a healing process, let us hope that Hungary will live in internal and external peace in the near future. Let us put our trust in the curative properties of inner consolidation and slow material improvement. Although not without interruptions, this has been an undoubted achievement of the last 15 years. Since the middle sixties, social reorganization has made great strides in Hungary. The problems of the landless peasantry have been largely solved. The modernization of society, in spite of what we said before, is developing apace; the social consciousness is capable of reflecting its own reality. Industrialization has ceased to be a subject of unease and hostility. These favorable items may also help in loosening the social cramp of the "Jewish question."

One of the points made by the various theories of anti-Semitism was the middleman role Jews played between landowners and poor peasants. For this reason, it had looked for a long time as if the emancipation of the Jews and the rise of the peasantry were conflicting ideals.[126] This conflict is bound to disappear, following the rational reorganization of production and ownership of the land, leading to a decrease in numbers of the peasantry, to the modest but increasing affluence of the remainder, to the falling off of the shackles of rural traditions at the impact of greater social mobility. The distance between city and country has been diminishing most of the time. The sons of peasant fathers are becoming industrial workers or office hands; the fathers themselves have been getting used to machinery and communications technology. Conservative cultural criticism—which previously feared for the "poor-but-honest" simple sons of the village, lest they be corrupted by the wicked city and soulless industry—has become irrelevant. This particular battle has been won: Hungary today is a country of industry, of the cities, of mass education—no one in his right mind can say that all this is nothing but the poisoning of the wells by wicked foreigners.

I suspect that these developments may have a thawing effect on the latent anti-Semitism within the dominant official ideology. Here I shall dwell briefly on an inner conflict within State ideology itself: between Marxist theory and actual developments. According to dogma, in the immutable historical process the task of the unfolding bourgeoisie within feudal society is to effect the original accumulation of capital, then—with the help of the working masses—to overthrow the feudal system and establish the rule of bourgeois society. Within a capitalist system, capital accumulation proceeds by leaps and bounds, thereby creating an overweening centralized power; however, mass social production and private expropriation of surplus value will lead to an ever-increasing contradiction. The historical role of the proletariat, gathering strength in the bosom of bourgeois society, is to "expropraite the expropriators"—to restore societal product to society proper and thereby to abolish the capitalist system of production.

In Hungary the "year of decision" (1948-49) occurred *in lieu* of a proletarian revolution. The means of production were expropriated—taken over by the State, not the working class. And the unspoken slogan "Capitalist equals Jew" worked, in the course of the fight against private property, in the direction of raising anti-Jewish sentiments.

History, however, may have given a twist to the cunning prescription of Marx and his followers. What if, in "objective" terms, the role of the proletarian revolutions consisted not in gathering up the harvest sown by the capitalists, but in carrying through the original accumulation of capital? The centralized social state tackles this task wherever the bourgeoisie has failed to perform its historic duty or, simply, failed to come into existence at all. In a country like Hungary, the even more urgent tasks of socialism were the solution of the agrarian problem and the introduction of a rational economic spirit. The essence of this spirit lies in cost-benefit analysis. As it happens, this is the guiding principle of capitalism too. Besides, no social system can be satisified with discharging the purely quantitative, material task: it must also tackle the hard task of satisfying social and personal needs beyond daily bread.

In this sense, the key question for both social systems is the utilization, in a socially acceptable way, of surplus value in the public interest. The solution to this problem is far from being warranted by nationalization— there are many socially acceptable outcomes in the world of free enterprise too.

The task of political leadership in Hungary today is to improve the organization of production and distribution and thereby ensure a socially acceptable satisfaction of all major needs, spiritual as well as material. Unfortunately the effectiveness of productive investment is in contradiction to the wholesale nationalization of productive factors, to bureaucratic direction, and to centralized planning. Nowadays these ideological contradictions are palliated by an apology for limited free enterprise. Further nationalization of production has fallen into abeyance. This does not mean an abdication from the ultimate goals of social policies, simply the abandonment of their dogmatic treatment. This process in turn may blunt the edge of the anti-Jewish element in State ideology, as the "Capitalist equals Jew" association loses its force.

On account of its relatively well developed industrial structure and the balance of its requirements, Hungary maintains a fairly lively economic exchange with the Western world. A component of commercial goodwill toward Hungary is its record of relative respect for human rights. Although the relationship between the State and its Jewish subjects is regulated by the interests of the State, the current external links of the country act at present in a favorable manner in respect to certain freedoms enjoyed by Jews. International links with world Jewry have been permitted again. The main synagogue in Budapest is usually crowded at the Jewish New Year. Hungary can boast of the only rabbinical seminary in East Central Europe. All these form the visiting card of the "liberalism" of the regime in support of the State's interests in the West.

These developments have certainly restored to some extent the bruised consciousness of Jews. As we have seen, their self-doubts contributed to a renewal of anti-Semitism and social division. Jewish consciousness was further strengthened by the existence and military valor of Israel and ample Jewish literature abroad. Further, the broken, discouraged, and mistreated older generation of Jews has been fading, and the new generation has grown up in a somewhat different social atmosphere. There is no denying that these young Jews have also inherited the bitter experience of exclusion, but they had not experienced the shattering of the illusion of social acceptance during the persecutions nor were they burdened by the feeling of having been willing victims. The new generation finds it easier to face up to facts. In the reshaped society, the social and psychological pressures on Jews have been lessening, both in objective terms and in personal perceptions.

The common fight against the abuses of the Rákosi regime, carried on jointly by Jews and Gentiles, also contributed to the thaw. So did the 1956 revolution and its bloody repression. This revolution was a kind of purifying storm with regard to the social relationship of Hungarian Jewry. Perhaps the cautiously increasing Jewish self-confidence may be a token of the slowly disappearing secular identity crisis.

All this may offer a more fruitful seedbed for the growth of healthier social relations than previous alternatives like a vulnerable assimilation, empty apologetics ("Whatever one might say, we are good Hungarians—look at our sacrifices at the altar of the fatherland—look at our achievements for the sake of the nation"), spasmodic self-denial, excessive touchiness, or Zionism which simply denies the possibility of such a relationship.

At the same time another generation has grown up on the Gentile side of society too, freed from the burden of guilt. These young people may be faced with stiff competition from their Jewish peers in the professional and intellectual job market—but the area of that market is wider. They need not bear a grudge against the Jewish tenant who buys up the bankrupt gentleman's property; against the Jewish shopkeeper who is their creditor; against the bloodsucking Jewish employer. Most of this anti-Semitic rhetoric is something of the past for them. They have had no personal part in the persecution of Jews, nor have they been indifferent onlookers of their misery. They can even afford to say: "Yes, in this country many people were Fascists." For both young generations, the cardinal task is to admit and accept the past—in the hope that the grip of the past will fall away.

Of course it would be self-delusion to assume that these young people are all free from inhibitions, prejudices, and memories. They are not quite ready yet to tackle fearlessly all the troubled problems of the community. Old wounds and failures come to the inherited, making a fresh start far from easy. Usually it is the task of a courageous and confident minority to initiate clarification of age-old questions of historical self-awareness. They also need favorable circumstances. We have seen that the words of Bibó and Száraz were greeted by silence: neither in 1948, nor in 1975-76 were conditions ripe for a reckoning of this nature.

False social consciousness is still prevalent. But ironically, even on the right wing there are signs of a change in opinion toward the Jews (an ambiguous change fed by resentment though): many of those in opposition to the regime have evolved a sympathetic stance toward Israel, in opposition to official anti-Zionism. As the Soviet Union has been siding with the Arabs, they are siding with Israel; and there are groups among these who were traditionally a strong source of anti-Semitism. They associate Israel with the Jews, in a favorable sense; likewise, of course, Israel is a source of pride for Jewry.

The voice of the people often bursts forth in curious ways: following another Jewish victory, one could hear the comment in the pubs: "The rag-and-bone men beat the bloody Arabs hollow."

We may say, therefore, that historical, social, political, and psychological factors are, by and large, favorable to the resolution of old problems. And, in spite of all that has happened, there is a residue of public moral capital that has found its voice, demanding honesty and frankness in public life.[127]

No amount of such positive events can solve the "Jewish question" in Hungary with one stroke; the burden of the past is still too heavy. But they may help toward a change in public consciousness. Then, eventually, the fundamental questions can be asked: that of social responsibility, social relations, and self-awareness of Jewry. Let us hope that we shall see acts of real public courage. Otherwise, I fear, the "Jewish question" might outlive the last Jew in Hungary.

NOTES

1.   This essay consists in part of a lecture given to the Kelemen Mikes Circle in The Netherlands, on December 7, 1980. It attempts to provide more of the details of scientific investigations about Hungarian Jewry than was possible in the lecture, although it is far from complete in that sense. Discussion about the part played by radio and television as well as Hungarian films is, regrettably, omitted. Personal communications and the observations of others, on the other hand, are relied upon to a large extent.

2.   "Reform Jewry" was a parallel of the liberal reform movement active in the last century. It fought for the modernization of traditional Jewish schooling, urged the use of the Magyar language, and supported social progress. See Lipót Löw, *Der jüdische Kongress in Ungarn, historisch beleuchtet*. Pest, 1871.

3.   The data are partly obsolete and would require a more detailed scrutiny. See notes 40 and 41.

4.   Earlier works on the subject include: Sámuel Kohn, *A zsidók története Magyarországon* (The History of the Jews in Hungary). Budapest, 1884; Sándor Büchler, *A zsidók története Budapesten* (The History of Jews in Budapest). Budapest, 1901; Lajos Venetianer, *A Magyar zsidóság története a honfoglalástól a világháború kitöréséig* (The History of Hungarian Jewry From the Time of the Creation of a Magyar State to the First World War). Budapest, 1922. These works collectively deal with the history of Hungarian Jewry from 1526 to the end of the last century. A volume, edited by Sándor Scheiber, concerning the subject up to 1945, remains unpublished to this day. See his "A magyar zsidóság történetének kutatása" (Researching the History of Hungarian Jewry). In: *Évkönyv 1971/72* (Yearbook, 1971-72). Budapest: Magyar Izraeliták Országos Képviselete, 1972, p. 257.

5.   Among the most valuable sources are the series *A magyarországi zsidó hitközségek monográfiai* (Monographs on the Jewish Communities of Hungary) and the *Évkönyv* (Yearbook) published by the Magyar Izraeliták Országos Képviselete—MIOK. The following references are especially pertinent to the study of this subject matter: A. Scheiber, "Juden und Christen in Ungarn bis 1526." In: *Kirche und Synagoge. Handbuch zur*

Geschichte von Christen und Juden. Darstellung mit Quellen. Edited by K. H. Rengstorf and S. v. Kortzfleisch. Stuttgart, 1970, vol. II, pp. 559-568; György Száraz, *Egy előitélet nyomában* (In the Footsteps of a Prejudice). Budapest: Magvető, 1976, 287 p.; *Pinkas ha-kehillot Hungaria* (Encyclopedia of the Jewish Communities in Hungary). Edited by Theodor Lavi *et al.* Jerusalem: Yad Vashem, 1976, 557 p.; *Yehudei Hungaria: mechkarim histori'im* (The Jews in Hungary: Historical Studies). Edited by M. E. Gonda *et al.* Tel Aviv: Lahav Press, 1980, 312 p.; and *Encyclopaedia Judaica.* Jerusalem: Keter Publishing, 1972, vol. 8, pp. 1088-1110.

6. Ernő László, "Hungarian Jewry: Settlement and Demography, 1735-38 to 1910." In: *Hungarian-Jewish Studies,* Vol. I. Edited by Randolph L. Braham. New York: World Federation of Hungarian Jews, 1966, pp. 61-136; "Hungarian Jewry: A Demographic Overview, 1918-1945." Ibid., Vol. II, 1969, pp. 137-182. See also Ernő Marton, "The Family Tree of Hungarian Jewry." Ibid., Vol. I, pp. 1-59. These authors' treatment of the demographic data is influenced by particular interests. Assimilating "official" Jewish opinion stressed a thousand-year-long continuity of cohabitation with Magyars; the Zionists emphasized the racial and national identity of Hungarian Jewry.

7. Aron Moskovits, *Jewish Education in Hungary, 1848-1948.* New York: Bloch, 1964, 357 p.

8. Cf. Márton Horváth, Zsidóság és asszimiláció (Jewry and Assimilation). *Társadalmi Szemle* (Social Review), Budapest, no. 7, July 1946: 495-501; István Bibó, Zsidókérdés Magyarországon 1944 után (Jewish Question in Hungary After 1944.) *Válasz* (Response), Budapest, vol. 8, Oct.-Nov. 1948: 778-877. This seminal essay was reprinted in *A harmadik út* (The Third Road). Edited by Zoltán Szabó. London: Könyves Céh, 1960, pp. 227-354. All references in this essay are to this latter source. Péter Hanák, Vázlatok a századelő magyar társadalmáról (Sketches on Hungarian Society at the Beginning of This Century). *Történelmi Szemle* (Historical Review), Budapest, vol. 5, no. 2, 1962:210-245 (see especially, pp.224-226); G. Szabad, *Forradalom és kiegyezés válaszútján, 1860-61* (At the Crossroads Budapest, vol. 5, no. 2, 1962: 210-245 (see especially, pp. 224-226); G. Szabad, *Forradalom és kiegyezés válaszútján, 1860-61* (At the Crossroads of Revolution and Compromise, 1860-61). Budapest, 1967, pp. 359-368; Iván T. Berend and György Ránki. A magyar társadalom a két világháború

között (Hungarian Society Between the Two World Wars). *Új Irás* (New Writing), Budapest, vol. 13, no. 10, 1973: 92ff., no. 11, 1973: 107ff.; G. Szalai, A hazai zsidóság magyarosodása 1849-ig (The Magyarization of Domestic Jewry up to 1849). *Világosság* (Light), Budapest, no. 4, Apr. 15, 1974: 216-233. Of the works written outside of Hungary consult the following: Robert A. Kann, Hungarian Jewry During Austria-Hungary's Constitutional Period (1867-1918). *Jewish Social Studies,* New York, vol. 7, no. 4, Oct. 1945: 357-386; William O. McCagg, *Jewish Nobles and Geniuses in Modern Hungary,* New York: Columbia University Press, 1972, 254 p.; ——, Jews in Revolutions: The Hungarian Experience. *Journal of Social History,* New Brunswick, N. J., vol. 6, no. 1, Fall 1972: 78-105; George Barany, Magyar Jew or Jewish Magyar? To the Question of Jewish Assimilation in Hungary. *Canadian-American Slavic Studies,* Toronto, vol. 8, no. 1, Spring 1974: 1-44; Victor Karády and István Kemény, Les juifs dans la structure des classes en Hongrie: Essai sur les antécédents historiques de crises d'antisémitisme du XXe siècle. *Actes de la Recherche en Sciences Sociales,* Paris, no. 22, June 1978: 25-59; ——, Antisémitisme universitaire et concurrence de classe. La loi du numerus clausus en Hongrie entre les deux guerres. Ibid., no. 34, Sept. 1980: 67-96. The last three references are especially valuable. See also "Studien zum ungarischen Judentum." In: *Studia Judaica Austriaca,* Vol. 3. Eisenstadt, 1976.

9. Cf. Karády and Kemény, op. cit., 1978, pp. 52-59; and 1968, passim; Barany, op. cit., pp. 36ff.; László, op. cit., 1969, p. 155. See also M. Szabó, Az 1901-es egyetemi "Kereszt Mozgalom," Adalék a magyarországi szélsőjobboldal előtörténetéhez (The "Cross-Movement" at the Universities in 1901. A Contribution to the Early History of the Ultra-Right Movement in Hungary). *Történelmi Szemle,* no. 4, 1970: 483-516; T. Hajdú, Az értelmiség számszerű gyarapodásának következményei az első világháború előtt és után (Consequences of the Increase in the Number of Professionals Before and After the First World War). *Valóság* (Reality), Budapest, vol. 23, no. 7, 1980: 21-34; and Andor Ladányi, *Az egyetemi ifjúság az ellenforradalom első éveiben, 1919-1921* (University Youth During the First Years of the Counterrevolution, 1919-1921). Budapest: Akadémiai Kiadó, 1979, 234 p.

10. István Végházi, "The Role of Jewry in the Economic Life of Hungary." In: *Hungarian-Jewish Studies,* op. cit., Vol. II, pp. 35-84; McCagg,

Jewish Nobles and Geniuses in Modern Hungary, op. cit.; G. Kiss, *A buda-pesti várospolitika, 1873-1944* (The City Politics of Budapest, 1873-1944). Budapest, 1958; and K. Vörös, *Budapest legnagyobb adófizetői, 1873-1917* (Budapest's Largest Taxpayers, 1873-1917). Budapest, 1979. See also the works of G. Mérei, I. T. Berend, Gy. Ránki, and M. Szuhay on the economic history of Hungary during the nineteenth and twentieth centuries.

11.   Bibó, Zsidókérdés Magyarországon 1944 után, op. cit., pp. 305ff.

12.   McCagg, Jews in Revolutions, op. cit., pp. 94ff.

13.   E. Molnár, Zsidókérdés Magyarországon (Jewish Question in Hungary). *Társadalmi Szemle* (Social Review), Budapest, no. 5, 1946: 326-334, and M. Horváth, Zsidóság és asszimiláció (Jewry and Assimilation), ibid., no. 7, 1946: 495-501.

13a.   I. Vas, Mért vijjog a saskeselyű? (Why Does the Vulture Screech?). *Kortárs* (Contemporary), Budapest, no. 4, 1974: 520ff. These very remarkable reminiscences by Vas—a major Hungarian poet—are an important contribution to the history of attitudes among Jewry in the thirties—first and foremost that of a dual loyalty. Vas saw himself confronted with the choice according to the principle: "No one can belong to two communities, least of all to two nations" as stated by another great poet, Gyula Illyés. Illyés apparently still holds on to this view. See his play "Sorsválasztók" (Choosers of Fate). *Kortárs,* Aug. 1981: 1171ff. In Illyés's view, the crisis of consciousness affecting the Jews culminates in the dilemma of having to choose between the Magyar nation and the Israeli nation. This false dilemma is his starting point in using the Jewish question for a paradigm of the Hungarian minorities oppressed in the Successor States.

14.   G. Barany, Magyar Jew or Jewish Magyar? To the Question of Jewish Assimilation in Hungary, op. cit., p. 44.

15.   McCagg, Jews in Revolutions, p. 92.

16.   Barany, op. cit., p. 33.

17.   For an interesting treatise containing important empirical data relating to the proportion of religious weddings, mixed marriages, conversions, and general vital statistics, see J. Katona, *Zsidó megújhodásért. A Fővárosi zsidóság lelki képe* (For a Jewish Revival. A Spiritual Portrait of Jewry in the Capital). Budapest, 1947; *Zsidó Világkongresszus (Magyarországi Képviselete) Statisztikai Osztályának közleményei* (Reports

of the Statistical Department of the Hungarian Section of the World Jewish Congress), Budapest, no. 12, Mar. 1949; László, op. cit; Kárady and Kemény, op. cit.; and I. Vas, op. cit. For a thorough assessment of the statistical data of Hungarian Jewry after 1945, see V. Karády, "Szociologiai kisérlet a magyar zsidóság 1945 és 1956 közötti helyzetének elemzésére" (A Sociological Endeavor to Analyze the Situation of Hungarian Jewry Between 1945 and 1956). In: *Zsidóság az 1945 utáni Magyarországon* (Jewry in the Post-1945 Hungary). Paris: Magyar Füzetek, 1984, pp. 37-180.

18.   W. Rabi, Modes et indices d'identification juive. *Social Compass,* vol. 18, no. 3, 1971: 337-356.

19.   On the Jewish question and the rise of anti-Semitism following the Compromise of 1867, see J. Kubinszky, *Politikai antiszemitizmus Magyarországon, 1875-1890* (Political Anti-Semitism in Hungary, 1875-1890). Budapest, 1976; M. Szabó, Az 1901-es egyetemi kereszt-mozgalom, op. cit.; Barany, op. cit.; P. Hanák, Vázlatok a századelő magyar társadalomról, op. ct., and N. Katzburg, *Hungary and the Jews, 1920-1943.* Ramat Gan, Israel, 1981.

20.   E. Molnár, op. cit.; M. Horváth, op. cit.; E. Andics, *Nemzetiségi kérdés, nemzetiségi politika* (Problems and Policies of National Minorities). Budapest, 1946; G. Mérei, Szekfű Gyula történetszemléletének birálatához (On the Critique of Gyula Szekfű's Historical Approach). *Századok* (Centuries), Budapest, vol. 94, nos. 1-3, 1960: 180ff.; P. Hanák, op. cit.; and I. T. Berend and Gy. Ránki, A magyar társadalom a két világháború között, op. cit.

21.   In his "Zur Judenfrage," Karl Marx indicated (in the second part of his comments sent to Bruno Bauer) that "dirty commerce" was the essence of "real particularity" (as generalized by the French Revolution) and associated this with Jewry. E. Molnár vulgarizes this dubious theory to such an extent that he deduces the origins of the Jewish religion from the commercial practice of traders. Over and above the known anti-Semitism of Marx, this has Aristotelian undertones. Marx is influenced here—obviously via Adam Smith—by the theory of naturalistic productivity of Aristotle.

22.   Bibó, op. cit., pp. 292-294. Száraz wrote about the monopolistic position the Jews occupied in the world of capital. See his essay—*Egy*

előitélet nyomában (In the Footsteps of Prejudice)–in *Valóság* (Reality), Budapest, no. 8, 1975: 70. He repeats the same mistake in his book cited above (p. 184). This erroneous–though fairly universal–belief mistakes the appearance for the reality; the actual proportions tell another story. Jews did play a predominant part in the capital formation inside the Habsburg Monarchy, although not in Bohemia.

23.   Gy. Száraz, *Egy előitélet nyomában* (In the Footsteps of Prejudice). Budapest: Magvető, 1976, p. 207.

24.   McCagg, Jews in Revolutions, pp. 93ff. The inverted nationalism of the second generation finds its counterpart in the internationalism and irreligious free-thinking of the third generation.

25.   E. Gyertyán, *Szemüveg a porban* (Eyeglasses in the Dust). Budapest, 1975, p. 374. "It is not a Jewish question–it is an anti-Semite question. Hungarian anti-Semitism is, first and foremost, a problem for Hungarians." Cf. J. P. Sartre, *Reflexions sur la question Juive.* Paris, 1946, p. 197: "Anti-Semitism is not the Jews' problem. It is *our* problem." Sartre refers here to the American black writer Richard Wright. See also the motto of Mária Ember's *Hajtűkanyar* (Hairpin Bend). Budapest, 1974.

26.   Hanák, op. cit., pp. 224-226. See also footnote 9.

27.   Barany, op. cit., pp. 13, 35.

28.   Ibid., p. 35ff. See also Karády and Kemény. Les Juifs dans la structure des classes en Hongrie, p. 49.

29.   M. Horkheimer and T. W. Adorno, *Dialektik der Aufklärung Philosophische Fragmente.* Frankfurt am Main, 1944, p. 177ff.; *Elemente des Antisemitismus. Grenzen der Aufklärung,* 1969, pp. 177ff. The authors derive popular anti-Semitism from the sharpening class conflict and oppression of the masses in late capitalism.

30.   "Des elementaires passions paratribales." See L. Poliakov, "J'ai vecu cette histoire en temoin avant de la relater en historien." Entretien avec Lucette Finas. *La Quinzaine Littéraire,* Paris, Nov. 16-30, 1977: 21ff.

31.   Bibó, op. cit., pp. 259-263 and Száraz, op. cit., pp. 192-200.

32.   See *Magyarország története,* op. cit., p. 1347. This grave omission of Hungarian historiography was rectified by a political scientist living in the United States. See R. L. Braham, *The Politics of Genocide. The Holocaust in Hungary.* New York: Columbia University Press, 1981, 2 vols. (1369 p.)

33. In his ten-volume work on the history of The Netherlands during the Second World War, Professor L. de Jong devotes close to 1500 pages (Volumes 4-8, 1972-1978) to the persecution of the Dutch Jews. In contrast, *Magyarország története* cited above, devotes only five pages to the extermination of Hungarian Jewry—although five or six times as many Jews perished in Hungary as in The Netherlands.

34. A. Geyer, *A magyarországi fasizmus zsidóüldözésének bibliográfiája, 1945-1958* (Bibliography of the Persecution of Jews by the Fascists in Hungary, 1945-1958). Budapest: Magyar Izraeliták Országos Képviselete, 1958, 167 p. See also R. L. Braham, *The Hungarian Jewish Catastrophe. A Selected and Annotated Bibliography*. New York: Institute for Holocaust Studies on The City University of New York, 1984, 521 p. (Distributed by Columbia University Press.) Cited hereafter as *RLB-Bibliography*. For other related bibliographies, see Refs. no. 15-22 in *RLB-Bibliography*.

35. For the most important documentary collections, see Refs. no. 504-515 in *RLB-Bibliography*.

36. See Refs. no. 996-1097 in *RLB-Bibliography*.

37. This author is acquainted only with two relevant articles: O. Zsadányi, "A magyar zsidóság tragédiájának visszhangja a magyar irodalomban" (The Reflection of the Tragedy of Hungarian Jewry in Hungarian Literature). In: *Évkönyv 1975-76* (Yearbook 1975-76). Budapest: Magyar Izraeliták Országos Képviselete, 1976, pp. 411-421, and P. Várnai, A zsidóüldözés évei a mai magyar irodalomban (The Years of Jewish Persecution in Contemporary Hungarian Literature). *Menora,* Toronto, Nov. 18, 1978: 7.

38. This applies not only to the *Magyar Zsidó Oklevéltár* (Hungarian Jewish Archives) series, but also the monographs and yearbooks. All these are published under the auspices of the *Magyar Izraeliták Országos Képviselete.*

39. For the relevant materials published in the United States and Israel consult *RLB-Bibliography*.

40. See *Zsidó Világkongresszus* cited above, no. I, 1947. Its data, which are to some extent obsolete, are reproduced in many works, including Braham's *The Politics of Genocide* cited above.

41. It is regrettable that Braham's comprehensive work relies on the outdated 1947 figures.

42. A. Geyer, "Az első magyarországi deportálás" (The First Deportation From Hungary). In: *Új Élet naptár, 1960-61* (New Life Calendar, 1960-61). Budapest: Magyar Izraeliták Országos Képviselete, 1960, pp. 75-82.

43. E. Karsai, *Fegyvertelen álltak az aknamezőkön...* (They Stood Unarmed in the Minefields...). Budapest: Magyar Izraeliták Országos Képviselete, 1962, 2 vols. See especially introduction.

44. Gy. Ránki, *Emlékiratok és valóság. Magyarország második világháborús szerepéről* (Memoirs and Reality. The Role of Hungary During World War II). Budapest, 1964.

45. Gy. Ránki, *1944. március 19* (March 19, 1944). Budapest: Kossuth, 1978, pp. 238-275. See also the introductory essay in *Vádirat a nácizmus ellen* (Indictment of Nazism). Vols. I-II. Edited by I. Benoschofsky and E. Karsai. Budapest: Magyar Izraeliták Országos Képviselete, 1960, 1967.

46. É. Teleki, *Nyilas uralom Magyarországon* (Arrow Cross Rule in Hungary). Budapest, 1974. See especially chapter 7.

47. Consult *RLB-Bibliography*.

48. See, for example, conceptualizations like "the first fascist regime," "the last accomplice of Hitler," "the attempts at guilt-transference," "the responsibility of the Germans," "Horthy-fascism," etc.

49. Ránki, *1944. március 19,* op. cit., pp. 238-275, a chapter titled *Szeretettől áthatott fajvédelem* (Love-Imbuded Defense of Race).

50. Putting the blame on the Germans was fairly widespread. See, for example, Law No. XXV of 1946 as reproduced in J. Lévai, *Zsidósors Magyarországon* (Jewish Fate in Hungary). Budapest: Magyar Téka, 1948, pp. 471-473; *Vádirat a nácizmus ellen,* vol. 2, p. 25 (the groundless statement by Karsai that the forced labor system was introduced on the German model); and the official Jewish position represented by G. Seifert, "A magyar zsidóság harminc éve" (Thirty Years of Hungarian Jewry). In: *Évkönyv 1975-76* (Yearbook 1975-76). Budapest: Magyar Izraeliták Országos Képviselete, 1976, pp. 318-353. See also *Memorandum of the Hungarian Government Concerning the Jewish Question in Hungary.* N.d., p. 2.

51. *Vádirat a nácizmus ellen,* vol. 2, omits completely, or quotes incompletely, various documents, including the circular of the Prince Primate to the bishops, May 17, 1944; the Prince Primate's memorandum to the Prime Minister, April 23, 1944; and the protest of the Calvinist bishops, May 17, 1944. The omissions highlight those aspects of Church interventions that may appear contrary to the views of the editors. On the Prince Primate's interventions, see also T. L. László, *Szellemi honvédelem. Katolikus demokrata mozgalmak és az egyházak ellenállása a második világháború idején Magyarországon* (Spiritual Defense of the Fatherland. Democratic Catholic Movements and the Resistance of the Churches During the Second World War in Hungary). Rome, 1980, p. 82 and note 57. The essays were first published in the 1978-79 volumes of *Katolikus Szemle* (Catholic Review). See Refs. no. 1556-1557 in *RLB-Bibliography.*

52. G. Makai, *Fajelmélet-fajüldözés* (Race Theory—Racial Persecution). Budapest, 1977, p. 266. Makai writes: "Tens of thousands of Jews participated in resistance movements." As a consequence, he also exaggerates the Warsaw Ghetto Uprising.

53. A typical example is G. Seifert's "A magyar zsidóság náci-üldözésének 25. évfordulójára" (On the 25th Anniversary of the Nazi Persecution of the Hungarian Jews). In: *Évkönyv 1970* (Yearbook 1970). Budapest: Magyar Izraeliták Országos Képviselete, 1970, pp. 3ff.

54. Cf. Benoschofsky's introduction to vol. 2 of *Vádirat a nácizmus ellen* and Geyer's "Az első magyarországi deportálás," p. 81. From earlier years see *A Hásomér Hácáir a zsidó ellenállási mozgalomban, 1942-1944* (The *Hashomer Hatsair* in the Jewish Resistance Movement, 1942-1944). Budapest, 1946.

55. The rather biased exception is I. Kádár. See his *Egyház az idők viharaiban. A magyarországi református egyház a két világháború, a forradalmak és ellenforradalmak idején* (Church in the Storm of History. The Hungarian Reformed Church During Two World Wars, Revolutions and Counterrevolutions). Budapest, 1957. On the attitudes of the Christian churches in Hungary see Refs. no. 1551-1632 in *RLB-Bibliography.*

56. *Mementó. Magyarország 1944* (Remember. Hungary 1944), edited by Ödön Gáti, *et al.* Budapest: Kossuth, 1975, pp. 120ff. See also Telcki, op. cit., pp. 342ff., and *Magyarország története,* op. cit., p. 1195.

57. Yet there is a growing number of publications about opposition forces in other fields. See, for example, Gy. Kádár, *A Ludovikától Sopron-*

kőhidáig (From the Ludovika [Military Academy] to Sopronkőhida). Budapest, 1978, and *Ego sum gallicus captivus.* Budapest, 1980, dealing with French refugees in Hungary. However, neither the rescue activities of Jewish organizations nor those of Christian institutions (e.g., the Holy Cross Association an the Good Shepherd Society) have yet properly been investigated. I am grateful to I. Szépfalusi of Vienna who drew my attention to an evaluation of the Good Shepherd Society by G. Sztehló, one of its leading figures. Parts of this personal overview are quoted by E. Bozóky in *Diakonia,* nos. 1-2, 1981.

58.   One of the first books dealing with the subject was J. Lévai's *Fehér könyv* (White Book). Budapest: Officina, 1946, 175 p.

59.   See L. Márton, "Zsidó sors, zsidó kérdés a háború utáni Magyarországon" (Jewish Fate and Jewish Question in Postwar Hungary). In: *Eszmék nyomában.* (In the Wake of Ideas). Edited by S. Németh. The Netherlands: Hollandiai Mikes Kelemen Kör, 1965, p. 121. See also H. Feingold, "The Roosevelt Administration and the Effort to Save the Jews of Hungary." In: *Hungarian-Jewish Studies.* Vol. II. Edited by R. L. Braham. New York: World Federation of Hungarian Jews, 1969, p. 211ff., and B. Bettelheim, *The Informed Heart. Autonomy in a Mass Age.* New York: Avon Books, 1960, 304 p.

60.   Cf. Bibó, op. cit.; Száraz, op. cit.; Karády and Kemény, Anti-semitisme universitaire, pp. 81ff.; Gy. Moldova, *A Szent Imre induló* (The Saint Emerich March). Budapest: Magvető, 1975, 215 p.; Y. Z. Moor, The Catholic Church and the Extermination of the Jews in Hungary. *Quadrant,* Sydney, May-June 1966: 67-73; and B. Zsolt, *Kilenc koffer* (Nine Suitcases). Budapest, 1980.

61.   Feingold, op. cit.

62.   R. Vago, "The Destruction of Hungarian Jewry as Reflected in the Palestine Press." In: *Hungarian-Jewish Studies.* Vol. III. Edited by R. L. Braham. New York: World Federation of Hungarian Jews, 1973, pp. 291ff.

63.   It is interesting that the dispute between the populist and urbanist writers during the 1930s has not been properly researched so far. See the debate between V. Juhász and I. Kovács in the *Új Látóhatár* (New Horizon), Munich, 1965: 164-175 and 357-362. See also M. Lackó, Az Új Szellemi Front történetéhez (Contributions to the History of the New

Intellectual Front). *Századok* (Centuries), Budapest, vol. 6, no. 4-5, 1972: 919ff.; and I. Vas, op. cit., p. 507. A major contribution to the question of the inadequate response of the populist writers to the persecution of the Jews has recently been made by Gyula Juhász. See his *Uralkodó eszmék Magyarországon, 1939-1944* (Dominant Ideas in Hungary, 1939-1944). Budapest: Kossuth, 1983, 343 p., and A barbár korhullám (The Barbarian Epochal Wave). *Új Irás,* vol. 24, July 7, 1984, pp. 68-92.

    64.   See Márton's article cited above.

    65.   B. Horgas, A film és közönsége (Films and Their Public). *Valóság* (Reality), Budapest, no. 12, 1966: 81-90. Horgas reviews public reactions to A. Kovács's film *Hideg napok* (Cold Days), dramatizing the Újvidék (Novi Sad) massacres of January-February 1942. In spite of his faulty methodology, one thing is clear: the question of responsibility for this outrage has not been tackled at all and the public rejects even a whiff of guilt. For a more favorable evaluation of public attitudes, see P. Köteles, *Forditott optika* (Reverse Optics). *Mozgó Világ* (World in Motion), Budapest, vol. 7, no. 2, 1981: 62-65. Köteles emphasizes the negativistic national awareness of Hungarian school children in contrast to their French counterparts.

    66.   See footnote 40. See also *Memorandum,* op. cit., p. 4.

    67.   I. Benoschofsky, "The Position of Hungarian Jewry After the Liberation." In: *Hungarian-Jewish Studies.* Vol. I. Edited by R. L. Braham. New York: World Federation of Hungarian Jews, 1966, pp. 237ff. See also Zs. P. Pach, "A magyarországi zsidóság mai statisztikájának szembetünő jelenségei" (Some Conspicuous Aspects of the Statistics on Hungary's Jewry Today). In: *Maradék Zsidóság* (Remnant Jewry). Edited by Imre Benoschofsky. Budapest, 1946, p. 22; and N. Robinson, *The Jews of Hungary. Survey of Their History and Postwar Situation.* New York: Institute of Jewish Affairs of the World Jewish Congress, 1952, p. 9. In 1945, half of those below the age of 18 were orphans.

    68.   See Robinson, op. cit., pp. 18ff. Chief Rabbi L. Salgó reckoned that 15,000 Jews emigrated from Budapest alone. In 1956, about 20,000 of them left the country. L. Salgó, "A fővárosi zsidóság vallási élete" (The Religious Life of Budapest's Jewry). In: *Új Élet naptár, 1959* (New Life Almanac for 1959). Budapest: Magyar Izraeliták Országos Képviselete, 1959, pp. 140ff. Salgó's figures coincide with those in *Encyclopedia Judaica,* op. cit., p. 1107.

69.   Statistical data on the Jews are provided by L. Thirring in his "Magyarország népessége 1869-1949 között" (Hungary's Population Between 1969 and 1949). In: *Magyarország történeti demográfiája. Magyarország népessége a honfoglalástól 1949-ig* (Historical Demography of Hungary. The Population of Hungary from the Time of the Magyar Settlement to 1949). Edited by J. Kovacsics. Budapest, 1963, p. 306.

70.   See G. Seifert, op. cit., p. 329. *Encyclopaedia Judaica,* p. 1107, gives the number of Jews in Hungary in 1967 as 80,000-90,000, including about 10,000 nonpracticing Jews.

71.   Salgó, op. cit., p. 144.

72.   J. Schindler, "A vidéki zsidóság" (Provincial Jewry). In: *Új Élet naptár 1959,* op. cit., pp. 147ff., and J. Schück, "Az ortodoxia a felszabadulás után" (The Orthodox Community After the Liberation). Ibid., pp. 156ff.

73.   I. Héber, "A magyar zsidóság élete" (The Life of Hungarian Jewry). In: *Évkönyv 1979-80,* op. cit., pp. 167ff. See also I. Benoschofsky, op. cit. The official Hungarian picture is completed by works published abroad. See, for example, S. Szamet, *Ezt láttam Magyarországon 1955 januárjában* (This Is What I Saw in Hungary in January 1955). Tel Aviv: The Author, 1955, and P. Lendvai, *Anti-Semitism Without Jews.* Garden City, NY: Doubleday, 1971, pp. 301-325.

74.   I. Kulcsár, "A maradék zsidóság lelki keresztmetszete 1946-ban" (A Psychological Cross-Section of the Remnants of Jewry in 1946). In: *Maradék zsidóság,* op. cit., B. Dénes, "Politikai helyzetkép" (The Political Situation). Ibid. See also N. Robinson, op. cit., and I. Benoschofsky, op. cit.

75.   Bibó, however gently, does go into the question of mutual grievances. The same subject is tackled by B. Dénes, op. cit. See also F. Fehér's "István Bibó and the Jewish Question in Hungary." *New German Critique,* Milwaukee, Wis., no. 21, Fall 1980: 3-46, and P. Bárdos, *A második évtized* (The Second Decade). Budapest, 1981, pp. 23-33.

76.   Act XXV of 1946 assigns unclaimed Jewish legacies to a fund for compensation, which, in fact, was never implemented. See Braham, *Politics of Genocide,* pp. 1154 and 1178. However, by this act the Hungarian state did not accept in principle the duties of legal continuity; it only resigned the benefits of mass murder. American Jewry on the other hand

contributed $52 million to the rehabilitation of Hungarian Jews. A part of these American contributions became state property. This was, for example, the case with the newly equipped Jewish hospital which was nationalized.

77.   Cf. the interesting analysis of M. Horváth, op. cit., pointing at a new, populist, anti-Semitism, assigning this to the miseries of the aftermath of the war. For him this is a good reason for liquidating the market economy. Bibó goes into some details abut this "new" anti-Semitism that culminated in local pogroms (see pp. 337ff. of his essay). Robinson (p. 12) says that the origins of this populist fury include a residue of Nazi propaganda, the demands for restitution by the survivors, the dominance of Jewish members among the Communist Party leaders, and the presence of Jews in the political police. Bárdos' memoirs cited above are very enlightening on this point. In his view, both the self-accusations and the anti-Semitism were the effects of the moral trap the Hungarian population was caught in. On the one hand it deplored the deportations, on the other, it was a beneficiary of confiscated Jewish property.

78.   Robinson (pp. 19-21) deals in great detail with the policy of "relocation." He claims that between May and July 1951, 40,000 to 65,000 people were forcibly relocated, and that of these, 3,000 were Jews. Including the ones deported in 1952, *Encyclopaedia Judaica* claims that the total number of Jews relocated was 20,000.

79.   The anti-Semitic manifestations during the 1956 revolution have not yet been sufficiently investigated. During the years of reprisals following the revolution, the government strongly emphasized them. See *Ellenforradalmi erők a magyar októberi eseményekben* (Forces of Counterrevolution During the October Events). Budapest: Office of Information of the Ministerial Cabinet of the Hungarian People's Republic), n.d., vol. 4, pp. 70-78. The source of this material was a memorandum prepared by the *Magyar Izraeliták Országos Irodája* (The Central Office of Hungarian Jewry), the official Jewish representative body. Besides the one murder of a Jewish salesman in Miskolc, which is well documented, Jewish official representatives had some apologetic interest in exaggerating anti-Semitic manifestations in order to explain the flight of 20,000 Jews following the Soviet attack on November 4, 1956. See L. Harsányi, "Adalékok a hajduvárosok zsidóságának történetéhez" (Contributions to the History of Jews in the

Hajdu Towns). In: *Évkönyv 1970*, op. cit., pp. 116, 127, 136, 161. See also his "A nyíregyházi zsidók történetéhez" (Data on the History of Jews in Nyíregyháza). In: *Évkönyv 1973/74*, op. cit., p. 87, and Imre Benoschofsky, "Beszéd a szegedi Öregtemplomban tartott nagygyülésen" (Address to the Mass Meeting Held at the Old Temple of Szeged). In: *Új Élet naptár, 1959*, op. cit., p. 157. A typical prejudiced source is J. Weidlein, *Der Aufstand in Ungarn und das ungarländische Judentum Wiederaufflammen des madjarischen Rassennationalismus.* Schorndorf, 1957. There is no doubt that the 1956 revolution was on the whole free of anti-Semitism. Cf. F. Fejtő, *Les Juifs et l'antisemitisme dans les pays communistes.* Paris, 1960.

79a. For an overview of the Jewish question in postwar Hungary, see A. Kovács essay in *The Holocaust in Hungary. Forty Years After.* Edited by R. L. Braham. New York: Institute for Holocaust Studies of The City University of New York, 1985, pp. 205-232.

80. The lack of sociographic studies relating to Jewry was pointed out by G. Borbándi, Mit fedeznek fel Magyarország felfedezői? (What Are the Discoverers of Hungary Discovering?) *Új Látóhatár*, no. 3-4, 1977: 331. Taking into account the exceptionally rich sociographic tradition of Hungary, it appears that self-censorship is a decisive factor for these lacunae. There is a striking contrast, for example, between the lack of Jewish sociography and the frequency of documentary studies, written or filmed, treating the problems of the Hungarian Gypsies. The latter is an institutionally approved subject. See *A cigányság társadalmi helyzete. Tematikus szociológiai bibliográfiák* (The Social Position of Gypsies. Thematic Sociological Bibliographies). Vol. 4. Budapest: Fővárosi Szabó Ervin Könyvtár, 1975.

81. Száraz, *Egy előítélet nyomában*, pp. 249-284.

82. M. Márkus, Büszkeség és előítélet (Pride and Prejudice). *Valóság*, no. 4, 1967: 63-65; P. Józsa, Ideológiai áramlatok városi ifjúságunkban) (Ideological Trends in Our City Youth). *Világosság* (Light), Budapest, Mar. 1979: 175ff.; Á. Havas, Nacionalista hatások gyermekeinkre (Nationalist Influences on Our Children). *Társadalmi Szemle*, vol. 22, no. 3, 1967: 97-111.

83. L. Péter, "A magyar nacionalizmus" (Hungarian Nationalism). In: *Eszmék nyomában*, op. cit., pp. 191-193.

84.   Rabi, op. cit.

85.   McCagg, Jews in Revolutions, pp. 91-94.

86.   Two recent studies are exceptions. See A. Kovács, op. cit., and J. Simon's *Zsidókőzérzet 1981* (Jewish Self-Awareness 1981). The latter, a manuscipt in possession of this author, is based on a survey of 50 professionals. Simon's survey revealed that these professional Jews tended to distance themselves from Israel and showed a complete lack of knowledge about the past history and traditions of Jewry.

87.   I. Sanders analyzes A. Gergely's *A tolmács* (The Interpreter) in this manner. See his Tétova vonzalmak. Zsidó témák a kortársi magyar irodalomban (Vague Affinities. Jewish Themes in Contemporary Hungarian Literature). *Új Látóhatár*, no. 5, 1975: 430ff. In his *Egy előitélet nyomában* (pp. 284ff.) Száraz quotes a letter from one of his Jewish correspondents in desparate state about his own identity. The hero of Gy. Moldova's novel—Elhúzódó szűzesség (Protracted Virginity). *Kortárs*, vol. 24, no. 11, 1980; vol. 25, no. 1-2, 1981—shows clear signs of uncertainty about his own Jewishness.

88.   Karády and Kemény, Les Juifs dans la structure des classes in Hongrie, p. 39.

89.   Kulcsár, op. cit., p. 37.

90.   Imre Benoschofsky, op. cit., p. 106. See also the interview with Rabbi L. Salgó in *NRC-Hadelsblad*, Rotterdam, Oct. 20, 1979: "We have chosen. We are Hungarians of the Jewish faith, not Jews of Hungarian nationality." Further: "There are no Zionists among us."

91.   Bibó emphasizes this effect. See pp. 268 and 282ff. of his essay. Zwi Rudy points to the lack of any social study investigating the distorted attitudes and social relations of Jewry living in the Diaspora. See his Bemerkungen zu einer Soziologie des jüdischen Volkes. *Kölner Zeitschrift für Soziologie und Sozialpsychologie*, Cologne, no. 21, 1969: 1-15.

92.   W. v. Baeyer, H. Häfner, and K. P. Kisker, *Psychiatrie der Verfolgten. Psychopathologische und gutachtliche Erfahrungen an Opfern der nazionalsozialistischen Verfolgung und vergleichbarer Extrembelastung.* Berlin-Göttingen-Heidelberg, 1964, pp. 370ff.

93.   F. Kafka, "Briefe an Milena." *Gesammelte Werke.* Edited by W. Haas. 1952, vol. 1, p. 45. See also the novels by Ember and Moldova and the essay by Száraz cited above.

94. C. Bondy, "Versagungstoleranz und Versagungssituation." In: *Psychische Spätschäden nach politischer Verfolgung* by H. Paul and H. J. Herberg. Basel-New York, 1967, p. 2. See also Száraz, op. cit., p. 222.

95. Cf. Th. Lessing, *Der jüdische Selbsthass.* Berlin, 1930. About persecuted Jewish orphans see H. Keilson, *Sequentielle Traumatisierung bei Kindern.* Stuttgart, 1978, pp. 66ff. On the psychoanalysis of anti-Semitism in Jews, see B. Székely, *Az antiszemitizmus pszichoanalizise* (The Psychoanalysis of Anti-Semitism). Budapest, 1936.

96. Sanders, op. cit., p. 430, quoting from Gergely's *A tolmács.*

97. Ibid., p. 435, quoting M. Ember.

98. See, for example, I. Goldziher, *Tagebuch.* Edited by S. Scheiber. Leiden, 1978. In this early diary, this slur is often repeated. See also L. Nagy, *Az antiszemitizmus négyszemközt* (Anti-Semitism Between You and Me). Budapest, 1920, p. 7; Száraz, op. cit., pp. 200ff.; Barany, op. cit., p. 20; and Karády and Kemény, Les Juifs dans la structure des classes en Hongrie, p. 38.

99. *Maradék zsidóság,* pp. 34-38.

100. Ibid., p. 37.

101. Bruno Bettelheim, *The Informed Heart. Anatomy of a Mass Age.* New York: Avon Books, 1971, pp. 131 ff., 168 ff.

102. Ibid., pp. 159ff., 184ff.

103. Ibid., pp. 180, 233 (note).

104. Ibid., p. 212.

105. Ibid., pp. 281, 284ff.

106. Ibid., pp. 169ff., 217ff., and 230ff. See also W. v Baeyer, et al., op. cit., p. 17.

107. Inmates are supplying the camp with goods; the price for advancement in the prisoner hierarchy is factional fighting and treason. See Bettelheim, op. cit., pp. 178ff., 183, and 187. There were also instances of mutual assistance in higher circles by sacrificing others. Ibid., p. 235. There were humane SS guards, but they were in a tiny minority; but so were the decent ones among the prisoners (ibid., pp. 241ff.) Bettelheim agrees with Kogon (p. 186) that "in the camps one prisoner was the fiercest enemy of another prisoner, not the SS."

108. On the self-accusations of persecuted Jews, see M. Avi-Shaul, *Aranytó. Válogatott irások* (The Golden Pond. Selected Writings). Trans-

lated from the Hebrew by L. Jólesz and A. Mezei. Budapest, 1975, pp. 108, 121ff., 197. See also E. Kolozsvári-Grandpierre, "A Duna-parton" (On the Banks of the Danube). In: *Évkönyv, 1979/80,* op. cit., pp. 230ff. It is not a necessary condition of self-accusation that the survivor escaped through the sacrifice of others. The internalization of rejection is sufficient in the case of any person discriminated against, or that of a stepchild. It is well known in psychiatry that survivors may not be able to live down the death of others (the "survivor syndrome"). S. Csoóri noted the same phenomenon among Hungarian soldiers who survived the ordeal along the Don in 1942. See his A magyar apokalipszis (The Hungarian Apocalypse) *Látóhatár,* Nov. 1980: 128.

109. Keilson, op. cit., pp. 424ff., and W. v Baeyer, et al., op. cit., pp. 370ff.

110. H. Paul, "Psychologische Untersuchungsergebnisse 15 Jahre nach der Verfolgung." In: *Psychische Spätschäden nach politischer Verfolgung,* op. cit., pp. 218ff.

111. *Der Spiegel,* no. 12, 1979, 98ff.

112. J. van Tijn, De tweede generatie (The Second Generation). *Vrij Nederland* (Free Netherlands), Nov. 25, 1978.

113. Paul, op. cit., note 110; v. Baeyer, pp. 50ff., and Keilson, pp. 424ff.

114. Bondy, p. 20; Keilson, pp. 36ff.

115. The following quote from the confessions of a noted writer of great integrity illustrates the point. In his A pálya végén (At the End of the Field), published in *Új Irás,* no. 10, 1973: 112, A. Komlós writes: "Being Jewish has been a barrier too. It meant that my origins were marginal to Magyar society. I was unable to tell all I had become aware of about the Jewish question, in part because of external censorship, but in part also because of my own self-censorship. This arose because I could never be sure whether my prejudices as a Jew would not distort my critique of society."

116. Avi-Shaul, op. cit., pp. 106, 108.

117. Keilson, pp. 2, 424ff.; Kulcsár, pp. 36ff.; Bibó, p. 324.

118. "They have chosen Jesus, instead of Jehovah, who had turned his eyes away from his chosen people." Sanders, p. 430, quoting Gergely's A *tolmács.* Further: "The camp killed my faith. In 1945, I still went to the

synagogue, but I ceased to believe in God. My God had died when I was forced into the ghetto. I cannot carry on with religion" (Bárdos, p. 38). This writer suspects that Hungarian theology has carefully avoided the problems of "belief after Auschwitz." By the same token, psychiatry has failed to adequately deal with the problems of persecution. With respect to the former point, see J. Schweitzer, Istenhit Auschwitz után (Belief in God After Auschwitz). *Theologia* (Theology), Budapest, no. 4, 1974: 207-211, which is an apologetic work. For a more informative source see *Auschwitz als Herausforderung für Juden und Christen.* Heidelberg: G. B. Ginzel, 1980.

119.   F. Brámer, "Zsidó élet Pesten a század elején" (Jewish Life in Pest at the Beginning of the Century). In: *Évkönyv 1977/78,* op. cit., p. 94, and F. Katona, op. cit., pp. 218ff.

120.   Bibó (p. 324) indicates that this was then a well-established taboo. We could adduce countless examples of it today. J. Simon, cited above, demonstrates that self-censorship reaches down to the most intimate family relationships.

121.   Avi-Shaul, p. 204.

122.   Imre Benoschofsky, p. 105. See also Horgas's survey cited above about public attitudes relating to the film *Hideg napok.*

123.   Avi-Shaul, p. 220. In his autobiographical work *Sirjaim* (My Graves), a peasant says: "What is the difference between my killing others as a soldier in the Ukraine, and killing or pillaging Jews in the next village? . . . The whole country ought to be cleaned, scrubbed, scoured." The testimony of the Israeli writer, who was born in the provinces in Hungary, sounds convincing. See also Bárdos, op. cit., pp. 30ff. Besides Száraz's essay a more recent survey among elementary school children corroborates my thesis of the presence of strong latent self-reproaches within Hungarian society. I find, however, displeasing the manner in which the Hungarian press commented upon the social response to the film *Holocaust* in West-Germany. See *Élet és Irodalom* (Life and Literature), Budapest, Feb. 17, 1979; *Nők Lapja* (Women's Journal), Budapest, no. 8, 1979. These articles failed to note that in the course of the past 35 years there had been hardly any real *social* echo of the persecutions in Hungary; neither did they comment on the desirability of a similar scrutiny of the Hungarian Holocaust. This shows that it is perhaps still too early to speak about a definite breakthrough on this point.

124.   On this subject I rely on information supplied by L. Péter (London), indicating the important part played by the Jewish question in the new social structure evolving in the year 1945-49.

125.   Our assumption is supported by the report of the Scientific, Cultural, and Educational Department of the Central Committee (1981) on a memorial volume on Bibó. This report is concerned about the wideranging cooperation of opposition groups and recommends—by grading the contributions—certain sanctions aiming at dividing this "coalition of opponents" (Cf. *Irodalmi Ujság* (Literary Journal). Paris, July-Oct. 1981:24).

A very interesting comment can be found in P. Ignotus's essay (Népiség; Populism. *Új Látóhatár*, no. 1-2, 1959: 132), discussing the conflict between the populists and urbanists during the 1930s and 1940s. The Chief of Police Hetényi—in charge of political matters—prohibited during the war a public opposition meeting scheduled to feature Ignotus, the urbanist, and Péter Veres, the populist, as the main speakers. Ignotus wrote: "It was in the interest of certain people to add fuel to the fire of this antagonism. Clearly, this was the interest of the ruling circles . . . . Obviously we shouldn't have done the favor for Hetényi in remaining in our opposing corners."

126.   See footnote 27.

127.   I. Csurka, *Házmestersirató* (Dirge for a Building Superintendant). Budapest, 1980, vol. 2, p. 480. "Who will draft the real questions, the relevant questions?" I could also list Konrád, Szelényi, Haraszti, Száraz, Kenedi, Réz, Kósa, and many others of the intellectual opposition; honesty in public life is one of their chief concerns. The poet S. Csoóri sums up their common efforts best when he writes: "We must do away with the gap between Truth revealed and Truth uttered . . . . Let us grasp these half sentences—what do they disguise?" The meaning of this is amply elaborated in his valuable essays. See his Egy félfordulat hátrafelé (A Half Turn Backwards). *Látóhatár*, Nov. 1978; A panaszos hangról (About the Complaining Voice). *Élet és Irodalom*, Aug. 1980; A magyar apokalipszis, op. cit., pp. 120ff.

DOCUMENTS

A FOILED JEWISH POLITICAL VENTURE IN HUNGARY, 1939-1942

Denis Silagi*

Introduction

In August 1939, two books were published in Budapest in the "Jewish Nation Publications" (*Zsidó Nemzet-kiadás*) series. During 1940, five more books appeared in the pocket-size "Spinoza Booklets" (*Spinoza-Füzetek*) series. In January 1941, a team named "Jewish Work Collective" (*Zsidó Munkaközösség*—cited hereafter as JWC), put into action by the promoters of the publishing venture, made its appearance in the Hungarian capital. During 1941, one last "Spinoza-Booklet" and two impressively made-up "Jewish Yellow Papers" (*Zsidó Sárgakönyv/Második Zsidó Sárgakönyv*) were published by the team. Some members covertly ran a "Jewish Public Opinion Research Station" (*Zsidó Közvéleménykutató-Állomás*) that began to function toward the end of 1941.

---

* The author's last name appears as "Szilágyi" on publications prior to 1944. Only in 1945 did he succeed in having the internationalized spelling legalized and officialized.

For the first time since 1919, outspoken and uncompromising Jewish nationalism had made its voice heard in Hungary. This attracted considerable attention, was discussed in Jewish quarters and in the Jewish press, and was also dealt with in gentile newspapers of conservative and right-wing leaning. The activities of the JWC (and also of the Jewish Public Opinion Research Station) ended abruptly in June 1942. It was, so to speak, a posthumous stirring when a book titled "The Personality of the Jewish People" (*A zsidó népegyéniség*) was produced on behalf of the team in the fall of the year (with—as was customary—a 1943 publication date). Eventually, the horrors of 1944 suppressed the memory of the short-lived and frustrated political experiment.

A few years ago, however, scholarly interest in this vigorous, though abortive, venture in nationalist Judaism in Hungary began to emerge. Inquiries have been reaching me as a surviving protagonist, and a few publications have dealt with the subject, such as a contribution by Gershon Weiler of Tel Aviv University in *D'var ha-Shavua*[1] and an essay by Nathaniel Katzburg of Bar-Ilan University in *Yad Vashem Studies*.[2] In gauging the difference between the policies of the Budapest arm of the World Zionist Organization and the approach of the JWC, Professor Katzburg comes to a conclusion that, in my opinion, is an apt evaluation of the matter. In his words, there was something "unique in the ideological platform" expounded in the Jewish Yellow Papers, namely "its perception of the need to dissolve the Magyar-Jewish partnership, to recognize the Jewish collectivity as a national minority, and to engage in preparations for an organized exodus of Hungarian Jews after the war. Those ideas were forcefully stated in the [Yellow Papers,] which provided a sober analysis of the reality of the Jewish conditions in light of the positions held by non-Jewish society. These ideas injected new elements into the Jewish-Hungarian debate . . ."[3]

In view of the attention recently given to the JWC and its activities, and in view of misunderstandings arising for lack of adequate source material, Professor Randolph L. Braham suggested that I present my pertinent recollections and a digest of the sources still extant. Without his prompting, this memoir would probably never have been written. For its contents and for the value-judgements, of course, I alone am responsible.

It is a pleasure to acknowledge the aid and the encouragement I have received from many people (a few contemporaries whom I could contact and numerous younger friends and colleagues) who showed stimulating interest in the completion of my memoir. Some of them assisted me with small bits of information, which proved to be "missing links" and bridged gaps of memory; some helped by letting me use their treasured personal papers; some traced for me hidden documents and forgotten publications in archives and libraries in Jerusalem, Tel Aviv, Frankfurt, and Budapest. For offering support or answering inquiries I would like to thank Dr. Elizabeth E. Eppler, Yitzhak Guttman, Ferenc Katona, Professor Nathaniel Katzburg, Dr. Martha Kreilisheim, John D. Makkay (János Makkai), Dr. Francis Ofner, Miryam Schütz-Weinberg, Dr. Rafael Vago, and Professor Gershon Weiler.

Denis Silagi
Munich, May 1986

A Jewish Tour D'Horizon in Hungary in 1937

The officially recognized leaders of the Jews in Hungary stubbornly stuck to what may be called the fallacy of the Napoleonic Sanhedrin of 1807: the thesis that Judaism was a religious persuasion like Christianity or Islam and that its ethnic dimensions had been accidental and could now be ignored. The Budapest Jewish leaders took themselves for Hungarians, they revelled in Magyar patriotism, and even preferred to be called "Israelite'. rather than Jewish. They branded as an enemy of the Jews anyone who would even consider the possibility that such a thing as a Jewish people existed, and they abused and persecuted even moderate and timid Zionists within the congregations, in which the Jews in Hungary—about 445,000— were organized. The vast majority of the members of the congregations, knowing no better, accepted this. The official Israelite leadership's approach to Nazi anti-Jewish measures was to issue condemnations not out of Jewish solidarity, but on general humanitarian grounds.

The Hungarian authorities not only approved of, but actually insisted upon, the tabooing of Jewish ethnicity by the Israelite assimilationists. Since 1919, one outstanding feature of the politics of Horthyite Hungary was irredentism. And since the inherently anti-Semitic Budapest regime was eager to statistically buttress its claim to the provinces lost in 1920 to Czechoslovakia, Romania, and Yugoslavia, it labeled as rascals and traitors those Jews in the formerly Hungarian territories who professed to belong to the Jewish rather than to the Magyar national minority.

The Horthyite establishment was double-tongued. Although it demanded the upholding of the fallacy of 1807 by the assimilationist leadership, it fostered anti-Semitism in the country. But benevolent, non-anti Semitic Magyars also shared the theory that there was a Jewish religion, but no Jewish people—at least not anymore. They fell for the rhetoric of the assimilationists, who equated the recognition of the existence of the Jewish nation with Jew-baiting, as if equal rights for non-Magyar citizens of Hungary could have by any reason been made dependent on their disavowing their nationality.

The Communist Party was banned in Horthyite Hungary, active communism was a criminal offense, and under such circumstances one can assess the weight of the accusation by a leading member of the Israelite establishment and deputy of a small Hungarian liberal party, Béla Fábián, who publicly declared that "every Zionist is a communist." It is true that Fábián was called to order by decent assimilationists, but his mean and stupid denunciation was characteristic of the political climate in which the small group of Zionists had to work in Hungary. In view of the two-pronged pressure coming from the Jewish assimilationists on the one side and from the irredentism-obsessed gentile regime on the other, the Zionists were compelled to camouflage their belief in the existence and the values of Jewish nationhood. Consequently, in the eyes of both the gentile and the Jewish public, Zionism's image degenerated into one of Palestine-loving sentimentality and non-political philanthropy. The Budapest branch of the World Zionist Organization, the "Magyar [sic] Zionist Association" (Magyar Cionista Szövetség), an umbrella for the Zionist parties, was void of prestige and influence; from among the 445,000 registered Jews in the country, about one thousand had joined it. Even so, the assimilationists and especially the leadership of the largest congregation—that of Pest, the Eastern half of the capital—headed, since 1929, by the business magnate Samu Stern (1874-1948), held Zionism to be a menace for their position and ostracized its followers. (In 1932, Stern seized the chair of the central bureau of all Neolog congregations, the Országos Iroda, too.)

The pretense of mere religion was doubly false in the case of the Pest Neologs. Not only did their leaders make a mockery out of Judaism by denying its ethnic essence, but the majority of the members were near-nonbelievers, ignorant of the religious traditions as well. An incident that threw a light on this occurred during the congregation's general assembly on January 15, 1938. This is what I reported on it to the Berlin revisionist weekly *Das Jüdische Volk:* [4]

> Almost every member of the presidium piled quotation upon quotation in his speech, more or less humdrum sayings by Magyar poets and statesmen, also words from King Stephen [a Saint of the Catholic Church]. The one speaker on the presidential platform who cited Jewish prayers, the bible, and, pointedly, the *Kohelet* was the congregation's secretary general and, according to widespread belief, its very master, [Sándor] Eppler. Upon catching the word "Kohelet," the weaver-baron [Leó] Buday-Goldberger bent toward his neighbor, the member of parliament [Béla] Fábián: 'What's this?' Fábián, well-known to Zionists and a rather displeasing figure, offered an answer. I could not catch what he said but I would make a bet that it was false. A couple of days later, I had a visit with one of the top brass of the congregation, a very clever and learned gentleman, a brilliant writer whose broad erudition was widely admired, yet without the faintest idea of Jewish essentials. I mentioned the shameful little occurrence in connection with the word "Kohelet." He stared at me with a somewhat embarrassed expression and at last brought himself to say: 'Well—what does it mean? I don't know either.' [5]

At the time the report was prepared for *Das Jüdische Volk,* we did not know that Eppler's display of familiarity with the Scriptures was an, albeit subdued, protest against the absence of Jewish spirit at the head of the congregation, and not until four years later did we realize that Eppler was not the manipulator of both the affairs and actions of a dummy president, but that Samu Stern was indeed the boss, a despot as intractably self-willed as he was conceited, and thirsty for power, too. He treated Eppler as a subordinate who had to obey. Not until four years later did we learn how the secretary-general would try, more often than not in vain, to restrain the autocrat whenever Stern's behavior would have fitted Haman rather than Mordecai.

This parallel may sound uncharitable; it is not. Of course Stern was no Haman; he is said to have had merits in the fields of charity, and he certainly did not have evil intentions. He undoubtedly had the firm belief he was serving the public well. But he fanatically wished to be first and foremost a Magyar patriot, and to dictatorially pursue policies aimed at holding back the Jews in the country and at thwarting attempts at Jewish emigration. In his obsession, he did act Haman-like. Let me quote here, breaking for once the chronology, a particularly stunning instance of Samu Stern's Hamanish demeanor from Aron Grünhut's memoir.[6]

Grünhut was no Zionist. He was a leader of the orthodox congregation in Bratislava (Pozsony; Pressburg), then capital of the Nazi protectorate of Slovakia. After receiving confidential information on the imminent deportation of Slovakia's entire Jewish population to German-occupied Polish territories, a rescue operation was conceived. Preparatory negotiations had to be started from Budapest. Slovak Jews were barred from traveling; Grünhut, who was entrusted by the Bratislava Jewish leadership with going to the Hungarian capital, took the risky mission upon himself and reached Budapest, after illegally crossing the border, early in February 1942. His Orthodox friends arranged for him a meeting with the leaders of all Hungarian Jewish groups in Samu Stern's office. He reported on the Slovak situation, outlined the rescue project, and asked for help of the Budapest Israelite leadership, adding that participation in the project could prove beneficial also to the Hungarian Jews in the future. Stern objected strongly to such an allusion since in a state with a thousand-year-old constitution and men like Horthy at her head, events like those in Slovakia could never occur; besides, so he said, the Slovakian Jews had hastened to join the Czechs after their territory was separated from Hungary in 1920, instead of siding with the Magyars.

Eventually, Stern emphasized he would not grant Grünhut and his friends any aid whatsoever, because he was not prepared to get involved in illegal doings. Grünhut hereafter raised the question what assistance could be expected from Stern should the Slovakian Jews be forced to flee illegally to Hungary. Stern retorted: "We shall see to it that they be caught and sent back right after crossing the border."

Then Stern wanted to know how Grünhut had come to Budapest because, to his knowledge, Slovak Jews were not permitted to travel. When Grünhut admitted his illegal entry, Stern ordered him to get out. It was Eppler who tried to bring Stern to reason by telling him that Grünhut, whom he knew personally, had, in former days, rendered great services to the Pest congregation. Stern calmed down and Grünhut was allowed to address the gathering again. But when he repeated his warning that one day the Hungarian Jews themselves might be in need of help, Stern flew into a rage and Grünhut had to leave for good.

Eppler and other participants asked him to wait in the lobby while they tried to convince Stern to change his attitude—to no avail. Stern insisted that it was not for him to grant aid to Slovakian Jews and that he would not allow anybody to intimidate him.

The episode, described in Aron Grünhut's memoirs, was hardly unusual. In fact, it was all too typical of Samu Stern. When my friends and myself learned of it, we were neither surprised nor shocked; Stern's unconditional refusal of solidarity with Jews beyond Hungary's borders was a rather unusual phenomenon even among the other Israelite Magyar patriots, but he worked his will, if not upon the entire Neolog community, then certainly upon the all-important Pest congregation.

Under such circumstances, I decided to temporarily withdraw from active participation in the Zionist movement in 1937. I had been a member of the Hungarian branch of Vladimir Jabotinsky's youth organization *B'rit Trumpeldor (Betar)*, but after five years of *Betari* service I came to the conclusion that for the time being it was hopeless to strive for creating a Zionist mass movement in Hungary. While I continued to contribute to the Jabotinskyan (Zionist-Revisionist, after 1935, "New Zionist") press and kept in touch with leading Revisionists such as Dr. Joseph B. Schechtman, Jabotinsky's right-hand man, I drafted plans for an educational campaign adapted to the level of consciousness of the Jews of Hungary.

Everything that could be said about, and against, the self-humiliation of assimilationists—in our own case that of the Israelite establishment vis-a-vis the Hungarians—had been superbly put in writing by Theodor Herzl and Max Nordau. Their spirit was to be revived, according to the requirements of the 1930s and of the peculiarities of the Hungarian situation. My friends and I were motivated not just by a feeling of honor and pride incompatible with assimilationism, but also by the feeling of an increasingly hostile attitude of the surrounding populace. One of the factors that stimulated us was disgust of the Israelite behavior, lacking in dignity, sincerity, and determination to defend ourselves—to hit back and if necessary to hit first.

After Hitler's ascent to power, an expulsion of Jews from their countries of birth was no longer inconceivable. One Jewish-Hungarian politician, Pál Sándor, a man not without merits, cried out: "Even in the deportation freight-car, I shall sing the Hungarian national anthem!" We found such an attitude nauseating.

So did a few other Jews, too. Our assessment of the situation was, up to a point, shared by some other co-nationals who otherwise were far from our *Weltanschauung*. In the year of the Nuremberg Laws, 1935, one noted Jewish author, Aladár Komlós (1892-1980), went so far as to write in a book-review in the then most prestigious Budapest literary journal: "This is not the proper occasion to ponder why not even impending deadly peril can awaken the Hungarian Jews to consciousness. Their press is not capable of anything but of celebrating the Great Men of the congregations or fruitlessly whimper on account of anti-Semitism when Jews are called Jews."[7] But Komlós and the others who might have sympathized with his views had little in common with what I could call, in retrospect, our activism and militancy. However, when Komlós spoke of "deadly peril" in 1935, it was only rhetoric. After 1937, the peril became real.

The Gathering Storm

Until the Nazi occupation of Austria, official Budapest seemingly adhered to the theory that between Jews and gentiles in Hungary there was no other difference than their denomination: legally they were equal. Actually, however, Nazi racialism had begun to influence the Budapest authorities much earlier. The first symptom was an editorial in the German-language daily paper of the government, *Pester Lloyd*, at Easter 1937. Its author, a parliamentarian of the ruling party, Imre Németh, explained that Hungarian society suffered from a "lack of equilibrium" caused by the disproportionately high proportion of Jews in the professions and white-collar jobs. On April 18, Prime Minister Kálmán Darányi himself delivered a speech in the same vein; he put on record that a Jewish problem did exist in the country but its solution must be

achieved "constitutionally." In the summer of the same year, the government arranged for a statistical survey to determine the exact number of
Jewish employees in commercial, industrial, and banking enterprises.
And in December, several hundred Budapest Jews were expelled to Poland
for not being in a position to prove their Hungarian citizenship.

Still, at the same time the Hungarian envoy to Great Britian solemnly
asserted to the London press that the expulsions had nothing to do with
the victims' being Jewish; the measure concerned aliens, illegal residents,
and there was no discrimination whatsoever against indigenous Hungarian
Jews.

That kind of official eyewash and make-believe was dropped overnight
after Hitler's occupation of Austria. Almost immediately, preparations
for drafting an anti-Jewish law got underway in Budapest. The bill was
presented to the House of Representatives on April 8, 1938, and was enacted into law on May 29. The new law did not offer a clear definition of
what Jews were—a religious community? a race? a nation?—but established
criteria as to who was "to be regarded as a Jew" (some converts to
Christian churches were, others were not) and introduced a *numerus
clausus* of 20 percent in the economic field. In government quarters,
they swore by all gods that this was the ultimate concession to placating
the Nazi-type radical rightists: the Israelite establishment swallowed this
and continued to profess their Magyar patriotism and their faith in "Hungarian chivalry."

My reports from Hungary published by the Berlin weekly *Das Jüdische
Volk* from December 1937 through April 1938 closely followed the
events preceding the promulgation of the First Anti-Jewish Law. I warned
that the law would never take the wind out of the sails of the Hungarian
Jew-baiters, who would refuse to acquiesce in the 20 percent limit. I also
stated that the law would not awaken the bewildered Jewish masses, because it did not unequivocally contradict the Israelite delusion. (My diag-
nosis proved tragically correct. In less than a year, the law—ostensibly
aimed at correcting a mere "social disequilibrium"—was abrogated, and
on May 4, 1939 the Second Anti-Jewish Law, bluntly racialist and bluntly
aimed at curbing Jewish role and influence, was enacted).

It was not until the end of 1938 that the project of the educational
campaign I had thought of took shape. The final plan materialized in the

course of an intensive exchange of ideas between the lawyer and Revisionist ("New Zionist") leader, Dr. Imre Kálmán (1894-1956), the physician,
Dr. Imre Varga de Tamási (1897-1944), my wife, and myself. We conceived a kind of ideological shock-therapy to awaken the dormant Jewish
masses lulled to passivity and an illusion of safety by the assimilationist
establishment. A publishing venture was to become the starting point. We
wanted to hammer in the truism that honesty was the first precondition
of constructive Jewish politics, and that the basic truth of our existence
was that we were Jews, not Magyars; to pretend that it was otherwise was
to lie. We wanted to stress that the Jews of Hungary were loyal Hungarian
citizens who differed from other national minorities insofar that most of
them were Magyar-speaking but differed essentially from the Magyars,
too. They were a national minority *sui generis,* but still a national minority—a group sharing a common ancestry and a common destiny. By loudly
proclaiming this, we were determined to break the grand taboo equally
sacred to the powerful and wealthy Jewish leaders and the irredentism-obsessed gentile regime.

The coming of the new Jewish state in Palestine was to be presented as
a matter of course, though we would avoid the term "Zionism," so sadly
compromised in Hungary. Our slogans were to be "Jewish nationalism"
and "Jewish *realpolitik.*"

Dr. Varga had never been a Zionist; he was raised a Magyar—and a few
years earlier, he would have deemed it inconceivable that an anti-Jewish
bill could have been debated, let alone passed, in the Budapest parliament.
That this did happen—and that a wave of violent anti-Semitism swamped
Hungary, carrying away not just the mob but the body politic as well—
made him search for, and find, his Jewish identity.

But Dr. Kálmán was the leading authority of "New Zionism" in Budapest, mentor of the *Betar* organization in Hungary, and prime promoter
of *Aliya Bet* in the country. (For the British, and for the World Zionist
Organization, *Aliya Bet* meant "illegal immigration to Palestine." We
combatted this. After all, it was the British policy of preventing Jews from
freely entering Palestine that was illegal as contrary to the explicit provisions of the Mandate of the League of Nations and therefore to be con-
travened by every means.) And I was a *Betari* "in reserve." Both of us
wanted to consult the New Zionist leadership before embarking on the
campaign.

Dr. Schechtman visited us in March 1939. He came to discuss *Aliya Bet* problems with Dr. Kálmán but I was able to brief him on the matter of the "autonomous" publishing project. Dr. Schechtman was in agreement with my evaluation of the Hungarian Jewish situation and thought it reasonable to try to turn the Jews into Jews before attempting to win them over to Zionism. He volunteered to inform Vladimir Jabotinsky and to ask him to write a foreword to a collection of my essays as a mark of assent. In a few weeks' time, the typescript of the foreword (in German) arrived from Jabotinsky's London headquarters. We had no more reservations, and in August 1939, "Jewish Nation Publishers" (*Zsidó Nemzet-kiadás*) made its début.

It issued two books: "The Unique Way / The Book of Jewish Nationalism" (*Egy az út / A zsidó nacionalizmus könyve*) by "D. Sabbatai," the pen-name I would frequently use in the course of the following campaign; and "Education for a National Revolution" (*Nevelés nemzeti forradalomra*), the collection prefaced by Jabotinsky. (When the Press Section of the postwar Budapest Prime Ministry issued a series entitled *Register of Fascist, Anti-Soviet, Anti-Democratic Publications* in 1945, my "Education for a National Revolution" was singled out for distinction, being listed on page 19 of the second issue.)

"The Book of Jewish Nationalism" was drawn up as a *vade-mecum* for the absolutely uninitiated—as were the vast majority of the Hungarian Jews. A "National Catechism" familiarized the reader with the fundamentals of Pinsker's, Herzl's, and Jabotinsky's thinking. A chapter on "The Country of the Jews" offered a nutshell-geography of Palestine. A history of the Jewish nation, also told in a nutshell, followed, with the firm promise of the coming of the new Jewish State as its message. Then "The Basic Documents of Building Palestine After the World War" (the Balfour Letter and the League of Nations' Mandate for Palestine, suitably commented upon) were presented. A chapter entitled "The Hebrew Language" was meant to dispel the widely held opinion that learning Hebrew was beyond an average person's reach. The concluding "Remedy for the Ghetto Spirit" brought 24 snappy aphorisms on "Self-esteem," "Self-Reliance," "Truthfulness," "Jewish Unity," "People and Religion," "We and the Magyars," "We and the anti-Semites," "We and the Racial Argument," and "We and the Apostates." It was a dramatic end, supplemented

EGY AZ ÚT

ארץ־ישראל

A ZSIDÓ NACIONALIZMUS KÖNYVE

Facs. 1. Title page of *The Unique Way. The Book of Jewish Nationalism* by D. Sabbatai, Dr. Silagi's pen-name.

S Z I L Á G Y I

NEVELÉS
NEMZETI
FORRADALOMRA

VÁLOGATOTT CIKKEK ÉS BESZÉDEK

JABOTINSKY ELŐSZAVÁVAL

BUDAPEST, 1939

A ZSIDÓ NEMZET KIADÁSA

Facs. 2. Title page of Dr. Silagi's *Education for a National Revolution* with a preface by Vladimir Jabotinsky.

ZSIDÓ MUNKAKÖZÖSSÉG

ZSIDÓ SÁRGAKÖNYV

1941 JÚLIUS

Facs. 3. Title page of the *Jewish Yellow Book* published under the auspices of the Jewish Work Collective.

A
ZSIDÓ NEMZET
TÖRTÉNETE

SPINOZA-FÜZETEK

Facs. 4. Title page of the *History of the Jewish Nation*,
one of the "Spinoza Booklets."

by illustrations of the Jewish national emblems, and also the score and text of "Ha-Tikwa."

A selection from "Remedy for the Ghetto Spirit" may give a taste of the publication:

We and the Magyars

If you love, and your love is not reciprocated, then—if you are of sound mind and a person of integrity—you will keep your love to yourself. Perhaps this will kill you, but you won't run after a carriage from which you have been chucked out amid abuse.

Do you really believe that 'here you must live and die' [words of a poem by M. Vörösmarty, Hungary's 'second' national anthem]? Then grind your teeth, but do not humiliate yourself, for no patriotism can demand that the patriot be spineless. Live then, while they let you, then die here, but shut up.

Refrain from criticizing matters relating to the internal politics of Hungary. Do not mingle in Hungarian cultural affairs. Do not attempt to build Hungary's national economy in place of the Hungarians. It is not your duty as a loyal citizen to work for the Magyars against the will of the Magyars. They know better than you do what they need. Do not foist your work upon them, no matter how beneficial you think it is.

We and the Racial Argument

For goodness' sake, do not argue when they say that the Jews are a race and did not assimilate. For one thing, what they say is true and you yourself know this and you would not lie—or would you? Secondly, it is no more serious a charge to say that we are a race than to say that we are six feet tall, or that we have two eyes. For none of these circumstances can constitute, on the basis of law, humanity, or logic, a justification for depriving anyone of his rights. And if, in addition to that, the conclusions of the anti-Semites are not even really based upon this presupposition, why, then, bother yourself to refute that presupposition?

We and the Apostates

Jews' baptism is to be regretted for one reason only: the apostate no longer pays any dues to the synagogue. Otherwise, Jewry never loses anything by getting rid of those who get themselves baptized. Without them, we are stronger. For it is always the weak who fall away, those who prove, by the very fact of their apostasy, that they are unfit to be Jews. And the departure of the unfit need never be regretted.

"The Unique Way" sold well by September 1939, but the promising initial response was cut short by the outbreak of World War II. Still, the effect of "the book of Jewish nationalism" lingered on. Telephone inquiries reached Dr. Kálmán's office, letters arrived at the printer's, and the volume of correspondence handled by my wife was growing.

For a while, that was all. The message was being spread mostly by word of mouth. Already during the preparation of the first publications a few active supporters had been recruited among friends and acquaintances— all of them, with the exception of one former *Betari*, hitherto "unawakened" Jews with no links to Zionism. More turned up from among the readers of "The Unique Way." And whenever a member of our team went to a shop, a bank, a repair service, it naturally came to a conversation with a Jewish shop assistant, bank clerk, or apprentice. "What will happen to us?" was the standard question, and it was a matter of course that one recommended "the book of Jewish nationalism" to the perplexed and got their addresses for our mailing list.

Early in 1940, Jewish Nation Publishers resumed its activities. We started the series Spinoza Booklets, the first two being expanded reprints of the initial chapters of "The Unique Way" that by now was out of print. Five such pocket-size pamphlets were issued during the first half of the year, namely:

"A History of the Jewish Nation in a Nutshell" (*A zsidó nemzet története dióhéjban*), by D. Sabbatai; "Jewish National Catechism"

(*Zsidó nemzeti káté*), by D. Sabbatai; "Auto-Emancipation!" (*Auto-emancipációt!*), by L. Pinsker (translated by Silagi); "The Jews' Country: Palestine" (*A zsidók országa: Palesztina*), by Silagi; and "Jewry and Socialism" (*Zsidóság és szocializmus*), by V. Jabotinsky (translated by Silagi).

In 1941, one last Spinoza Booklet came out: "The Jewish State" (*A zsidó állam*), by Th. Herzl (a condensed edition, translated and annotated by Silagi). Pinsker's and Herzl's masterly works had been published in Hungarian earlier, but those translations were inadequate, and we considered it of great importance to make these classics available in faultless and readable Hungarian.

The booklets carried a post-office box number as a correspondence address as well as the address of Budapest's one Zionist bookshop, whose owner, Sándor Gondos, did not share our "radicalism" but loyally supported the venture. He promoted our publications, and forwarded letters, messages, and inquiries.

The cover of every booklet advertised the following concise declaration of intent:

THE JEWISH NATION'S PUBLICATIONS

serve Jewish *realpolitik*. The basic tenet of Jewish *realpolitik* is this:

JEWRY IS A NATION.

The principal task of Jewish *realpolitik* is to organize the migration of the young Jews of Hungary to their homeland, Palestine, and to safeguard fair living conditions for the older Jews remaining here.

In the summer of 1940, ominous developments halted our activities. Jewish men of military age were drafted into an army-controlled "labor service." This name sounded innocent; in fact it stood for forced labor. Treatment was harsh, though almost humane in comparison with what was to come two years later. It aimed at humiliation, not yet murder. Still it was another step in the process of disillusionment for many young Jews. They suddenly realized the emptiness of the phrasemongering of the assimilationist leadership, whose spokesmen incessantly preached that "it can't happen here" and that the generous and noble Magyar race would never tolerate outrages of the Nazi brand. Although by the end of December 1940 virtually all forced laborers had been demobilized, the sobering shock could not be undone anymore. Some of these men, and their wives, became responsive to Jewish *realpolitik*.

A "Qualitative Leap"

When Dr. Schechtman visited us in March 1939, he warned us that should a war unleashed by Hitler break out, the Nazis would try to carry out an all-European pogrom of unprecedented dimension. (After the war I asked him whether he could recall the source of this information, and he told me that he probably had it from friends in the Polish intelligence community.) We were not really alarmed and concentrated upon preparing our educational project. In the meantime, Dr. Kálmán worked on securing ways for *Aliya Bet*, in cooperation with the *Betar* organization. He was a highly decorated infantry captain of the First World War, and some of his former comrades who now occupied important positions in the army and the government were his devoted friends. Thanks to them he was able to pave the way for *Aliya Bet* by having travel documents for stateless persons issued to the Jews who had fled to Hungary from Nazi-dominated territories and naturally did not have national passports, and by obtaining a green light for the technically illegal transports.

A first such transport of about 750 Hungarian *Betar* members and sympathizers got to Palestine via Austria in the summer of 1937, and a second made it via Yugoslavia a year later. About 150 *olim* (immigrants) could take ship for the first time in Budapest in December 1938; they sailed on the Danube as far as Sulina, where they changed boats and boarded a seagoing vessel. That was to become the routine up to the Nazi invasion of Hungary in March 1944. Until then, only about 4500 Hungarian *olim* had been able to go that way, on account of the resistance of the Jewish establishment, while from among the "foreign" Jews who had escaped to and then hid in Hungary, about 35,000 could join *Aliya Bet* transports through the good offices of Dr. Kálmán, since the departure of the aliens was not obstructed by the Israelite leadership.

Before December 1938, Dr. Kálmán had to pull many strings until the proper authority, the Ministry of the Interior, resolved to patronize the affair by removing bureaucratic hurdles and passing over transgressions incidental to such an undertaking. Samu Stern's emissaries made great efforts to bring about a ban. They warned the Ministry against all kinds of risks, from official British protests to the death of all passengers. But Dr. Kálmán's authority and the Magyar willingness to painlessly get rid of Jews prevailed. The *olim* put to sea and on January 5, 1939, a cable from Tel Aviv confirmed the arrival of the group. It had disembarked near Natanya and was received and brought to a safe place by men of the *Irgun Ts'vai Leumi* (the Revisionists' National Military Organization). Dr. Kálmán presented the cable to the Ministry and, in the hope of making him see reason, to Samu Stern. In the Ministry, Dr. Kálmán was assured that from now on he could rely on further official toleration; at the same time Samu Stern vowed to do everything in his power to block Jewish emigration from Hungary.

For the early participants, *Aliya* was the fulfillment of the Zionist dream; for some of them it also was a way out of an economically hopeless personal situation. It was not yet a matter of life and death.

However, toward the end of 1940 ill-boding news signaled what might be called in quasi-Hegelian terms a qualitative leap in Nazi *judenpolitik,* a mutation in policies that affected Hungary, too. Up till then, it could be taken for granted that the wildest Nazi activists were not demanding more than the departure or, at worst, the expulsion of the Jews. Now, almost overnight, physical extermination appeared to become a thinkable alternative to expulsion. Historians of the Third Reich reached the consensus that the Hitlerite regime dropped the emigration plans and switched to a mass-murder project some time in 1941; but the winds must have changed well before then. Dr. Kálmán received confidential information about secret meetings of the supreme command of the Hungarian army, who discussed military aspects of a forthcoming Third Anti-Jewish Law, this time to be faithfully patterned after the German model. Certain generals, along with their Chief of Staff, Henrik Werth, envisaged the possibility of ridding the army of Jews by putting them, one way or another, to death. (Werth's successor, Ferenc Szombathelyi, was tarred with the same brush.) Although no final decisions were taken, many officers present were scandalized but kept silent. Dr. Kálmán's former comrades passed word to him on these confidential utterances. We took them seriously.

Now we could no longer content ourselves with a long-range-project aimed at the ideological enlightenment of the Hungarian Jews. We had to high-pressure *Aliya Bet.* And we had to win more gentile allies. If the Jews of Hungary were to survive the war influential Magyars had to be persuaded that they must, in their own patriotic interest, listen to us.

It was a matter of course that handpicked Magyar anti-Semites were to be included in our target group. We wanted to reach people in key positions, in the press, in parliament, in the administration; few of them liked the Jews. After all, anti-Semitism had existed in Hungary well before 1918; after World War I, it became virulent, although lately some contemporaries have tended to deny this. After the Holocaust, Miklós Kállay (1887-1967), Prime Minister from 1942 to 1944, produced an affidavit to the effect that anti-Semitism was a German import, unknown in Hungary before Hitler's advent; Kállay did this in support of former Hungarian Jews' claims to damages against Germany, and he seemed to really believe such nonsense. But I also came across Jews who saw their Magyar years prior to 1938 through rose colored glasses, and emphatically denied to have sensed dislike or discrimination in those days—a strange case of self-deception.

A famous quip, usually attributed to the great novelist Kálmán Mikszáth (1849-1910), comes much nearer to the facts. It says that an anti-Semite is a person who hates the Jews more than it is appropriate. While this sarcasm came from a gentile source, after 1919 an analogous household word, of Jewish origin, cropped up in Hungary: the Jews themselves wanted to differentiate between the murderous Jew-baiting of the White Terror and the former manifestations of antipathy that could be easily endured, and they coined the term "peacetime anti-Semite."

"Peace-time," *békebeli,* was an epithet widely used in Hungary after 1918 and did not refer to historical chronology but denoted "good quality." In other contexts, it designated "excellent prewar standard" of goods, living conditions, manners. The phrase "peacetime anti-Semitism" implied the ironic admission that some snubbing and discrimination was tolerable (*vide* Mikszáth's quip) in contrast to the violent anti-Judaism of the early years of Horthy's regime.

A mark of the truly moderate *békebeli* was to open conversation on the subject with "I am no anti-Semite, but. . . ." The less moderate peace-timers admitted that they had reservations concerning Jewry in general and especially its influence upon Magyar affairs, but they often had Jewish friends whom they genuinely liked or respected and would not like to see emigrate. One could rate Gyula Illyés (1902-1983), an outstanding literary representative of young Hungary between the wars and the grand old man of Magyar literature after the crushed anti-Soviet upheaval of 1956, a model *békebeli*. During the disastrous 'forties he aided and patronized Jewish friends and colleagues and did not flinch from rabid and menacing attacks of the pro-Nazi press, although in 1935, he had said in a book re-view: "For lack of evidence, I do not believe in the intellectual superiority of Jewry. Money-making is no proof of such an attribute but of some-thing entirely different. I do not think that the leading role of Jewry in Hungary's economic life or in the management of modern Hungarian cul-ture reflect Magyar incompetence. I do not think that in the absence of Jewry, no Hungarian industry, journalism, or revolution would have come into being. It is quite possible that everything would even have become far superior, although possibly a little later."[8] No matter how question-able the logic of that argument was, Illyés' anger was revealing and his sincerity commendable.

Such were the views of a leftist-populist author; one could not expect fonder feelings when turning to conservative Magyar politicians—parti-cularly not after 1938, when their irredentism had made them dependent on Hitler's favor. Not only could we not help dealing with anti-Semites, we could not even stick to contacting *békebeli* only.

Still we drew a sharp dividing line between those anti-Semites with whom we were ready to try a dialogue and those to whom we did not even deign to speak. We refused to have anything to do with Hungarians whose will to bring about the Magyar-Jewish divorce was imbued with hatred and ill-will toward the Jewish individual and with theories of Jewish racial inferiority and noxiousness.

Those whom we wanted to approach had, then, to meet two criteria: they had to share our absolute confidence in Hitler's eventual defeat; and they had to rule out cruelty in the process of the divorce. Such Magyars were numerous. Even Count Pál Teleki (1879-1941), a more than moderately anti-Semitic politician who was Prime Minister when the Second Anti-Jewish Law was passed, stressed after its promulgation that it would be fully implemented, but without cruelty, because cruelty was alien to the Magyar (this being a broad anti-German innuendo). We wanted to take Teleki and his like at their word.

The Jewish Work Collective

At this point it became clear that our project had outgrown the framework of a diminutive publishing enterprise. By now our team consisted of a sizable group of active supporters and we had a mailing list of over 200 sympathizers who were eager to receive further information (and, so we hoped, might be mobilized at a later stage), and we needed a respectable "visiting card" for our next moves.

Getting established was a delicate problem. Freedom of assembly and association had not existed in Hungary since 1919. A society or club was to be licensed by the Ministry of the Interior. Applications for a Jewish association were, invariably, submitted to the Israelite central bureau for a report; and the reaction of the bureau to every nonassimilationist application was, invariably, anathema. That's why we started our activities in the summer of 1939 in the guise of a publishing house. Now we were on the search for a formula that would meet our public relations requirements yet be a legal nonentity so that it would not require a government-issued licence and could not be objected to by the authorities either. We decided that we would assume the name of JWC, something evasive that could not be prohibited or disbanded—as long as the authorities could discover no conspiracy behind it.

As a precautionary measure, we arranged for a call to the head of the political police, Dr. József Sombor-Schweinitzer, an exceptionally intelligent officer and an anti-Nazi. Dr. Kálmán, Dr. Varga, and myself briefed him about our intentions and thus warded off a possible police action should the assimilationists inform against the Jewish nationalist campaign (something they later tried).

Although Sombor-Schweinitzer assured us of his understanding, we had to shun the risk of being reprimanded for holding illegal gatherings. Therefore we usually met with our friends in minute groups in our offices or private homes.

The JWC had no constitution or formal hierarchy, but it did have an organically grown structure. The prime impulses always emanated from the nucleus of four that had begun the entire venture and was "in permanent session." Then we had about a dozen collaborators, the "inner circle," who kept in close touch with Dr. Kálmán, Dr. Varga, or the Silagis and established contacts, whenever necessary, with about forty further backers who were not involved in our day-to-day activities and not aware of every tactical move but were in general agreement with our program and ready to help us on occasion and upon request. There was a continuous flow of instructions, proposals, informations between the "nucleus," the "inner circle," and the backers. Once in a while a stimulus went out to the more or less passive sympathizers, too, and we also received interesting suggestions from our readers and friends.

While all our printed publications and part of the mimeographed material we had issued have survived, all our files are gone. After more than four decades, I cannot list from memory more than the names of ten founding members of the "inner circle" and of a handful of "backers." And I cannot always recall whether one or the other joined us before or after the publication of the first *Yellow Paper.*

Collaborators of the "inner circle," then, were Imre Adler, Pál Füredi, Dr. Ella Heller, Dr. György Heller, Dr. György Kreilisheim, Zoltán Mitzger, Dr. Endre Molnár, Dr. Julia Molnár, László Sonnenfeld, and István Vázsonyi.

Adler, Füredi, and Mitzger were office clerks; the Hellers and Julia Molnár were physicians; Dr. Kreilisheim was a graduate in law and a historian; Dr. Endre Molnár was a statistician; Sonnenfeld was a salesman; and Vázsonyi, the one ex-*Betari* (not related to the similarly named politician) had been a manager of an insurance company and was now a master-weaver.

In the fall of 1941, there was a valuable addition to our "inner circle." Francis Ofner (b. 1913), former national leader of the *Betar* of Yugoslavia, moved to Budapest after the Hungarian army invaded the Bácska (Bačka) district, and he became a devoted collaborator.

From among our Jewish backers, I may single out Dr. Gyula J. Pikler, Hugó Kelen, Dr. Béla Berend, and Dr. Rudolf Kasztner. Dr. Pikler (1864-1952), an eminent scholar, physician, statistician, and champion of social reform in the spirit of Henry George, rendered us valuable service by giving advice, information, and letters of introduction to potential gentile backers. Kelen (1888-1956), a renowned composer, became a fervent propagandist of our basic ideas and won sympathizers over to our cause; his most remarkable recruit would have been the author Károly Pap (1897-1944), a man of genius, whom we dodged, notwithstanding his prominence, in view of the extravagant proposals he would have wished to put in practice with our help (for instance an unauthorized mass demonstration for peace under Zionist banners along Budapest's main avenue, Andrássy Street). To our contact with Dr. Berend, then chief rabbi of the provincial city of Szigetvár, and to our relationship with Dr. Kasztner (1906-1957) I shall revert later.

From among our gentile friends, I may list Dr. Miklós Fehér, Dr. Gyula Ortutay, Theodora Puskás, and János Makkai. Dr. Fehér was a research fellow at the Anthropological Institute of Budapest University; he furnished me with important source material during my work on the book *The Personality of the Jewish People*. Dr. Ortutay, ethnographer and radio editor, offered us his assistance but our activities were cut short before we could have availed ourselves of his help. Miss Puskás, a daughter of the celebrated Hungarian collaborator of Thomas Alva Edison, brought us information of more or less influential Magyars who ostensibly conformed to the pro-German stance of the regime but inwardly loathed the Nazis. It was only after the war that I learned that she had worked for the British intelligence service all the time. The role of János Makkai will be dealt with in detail below.

Our team had no salaried employees. The expenses were covered first by the initiators alone, later a few better-off members of the "inner circle" also contributed to the costs. It was fortunate that I worked with a news agency, where I was in charge of the early-morning shift. My workday began at 6 A.M. and ended around 10 A.M., so that practically all day I was at the disposal of the JWC. I did a lot of canvassing, and when I had gotten an appointment with a gentile official or otherwise important person, I experimented with the shock treatment we had devised for our prospective Magyar partners.

The treatment had two phases. First I conveyed to my contact the information that we did not consider ourselves, and did not even long to be, Magyars; and then I reassured him that we held it perfectly legitimate that he was an anti-Semite—as long as this did not degenerate into hostility, since the feeling of aversion was mutual. Thus I was, almost in the twinkling of an eye, on an equal footing with my host. As a rule, the technique worked.

Next, I explained that we, Jewish nationalists, and they, Magyar patriots, had certain vital interests in common. Our objective was to live in freedom and dignity in our own state, and we were sure that the Jewish state would be reestablished in Palestine after the war. We therefore were determined to leave Hungary for the Holy Land. The Magyars also wanted, no matter whether on their own will or under German pressure, to see us leave the country. But while mass emigration would have to wait until after the war, Hitler *now* headed toward the destruction of the Jews. We were determined to survive Hitler; but it was to the interest of Hungary, too, that we survive. It was obvious that the Nazis would be defeated. Should the Magyars become accomplices of Hitler in the destruction of Jewry, they would have to face terrible punishment at the avenging hand of the victorious Allies. Therefore it was an all-important Magyar interest to shield us from the murderous assault of the Germans and their Hungarian followers. Of course we were fully aware that under existing political and military conditions, it would have been suicidal for a Budapest regime to openly side with the Jews. However, by leaning on our ideology, the Hungarian government could credibly simulate determined anti-Judaism while temporizing and using the time to help us to prepare for our eventual orderly mass-exodus.

Naturally we were looking for ways to profess and propagate this in print. We planned to present our arguments in a format that imitated the diplomatic documents, published by governments. We decided that our manifestos be gotten up as Jewish Yellow Papers, issued in the name of the JWC. I drafted the texts, we meticulously weighed every word, and my wife proved the critic and editor with the unfailing flair for the most forceful and cogent phrasing.

Not all we had put into spoken words could be printed. It was our axiom that Hitler would lose. While in Nazi Germany a whispered allu-

sion to that effect could entail capital punishment, in Hungary one certainly did not run a comparable risk, yet one could not dream of legally
publishing anything of that sort. In Budapest, everything intended for
publication was to be submitted to the office of a "Press Attorney," who
returned the manuscript rubber-stamped either "Multipliable without
cuts" or "Multipliable with the cuts indicated" or "Not cleared. Not
multipliable." It would have been quixotic to submit to the Press Attorney,
Dr. Tibor Lee, a dictum like "Hitler is doomed, and America will have
the final say after the war." With some artfulness, however, we eventually
got round the obstacle We included the crucial thesis in the Second
Jewish Yellow Paper; we placed the message into three different paragraphs
in the shape of the following seemingly incidental remarks:

> After the end of the present war, the victors certainly will help
> the Jewish people to obtain its new state. In this respect there is no
> difference of opinion between Berlin and Washington.
>
> The destination of the [postwar] exodus cannot be anymore a
> country with a gentile majority but only a Jewish state, and . . .in
> this regard the Germans and the Americans are in agreement.
>
> In the Anglo-Saxon countries, Jewish and non-Jewish public opinion
> alike regard Jewry as a nation and hold the Jewish assimilationists
> of Hungary in sovereign contempt. The White House also shares the
> view that Jewish overpopulation in Central and Eastern Europe is
> beyond all bearing, and it does not hide this belief. It has repeatedly
> been emphasized by the White House that it considers the establishing
> of the Jewish State one of the important objectives of the coming
> peace conference.

These statements struck the reader of 1941 as foolhardy (if he was on
our side) or as criminally outrageous (if he was pro-German). After all,
they clearly signaled disbelief in Germany's final victory and observed
casually, as a matter of course, that the United States would be the decisive force in the end. This was something one might have talked about
privately but did not put, at least not "legally," in print in Hungary in
those days.

The First Yellow Paper

While the intimation of our firm belief in Hitler's defeat was reserved for our second manifesto, the first Jewish Yellow Paper concentrated upon timeless matters of principle. Its manuscript was duly submitted to the Press Attorney, and when I went to fetch it, it was returned with the stamp "Not cleared. Not multipliable." (For the benefit of the Magyar speaking reader, I am quoting the savory original wording of the formula: "Nem engedélyezem! Nem sokszorosítható!") This we had anticipated and planned to try to obtain redress with the help of a prominent politician and deputy of the ruling party, János Makkai (b. 1905), political writer, author of books, and editor-in-chief of the daily *Esti Újság* (Evening News), an organ of the government.

Makkai had been the *rapporteur* of the Second Anti-Jewish Bill, but soon after its promulgation he himself co-authored a pertinent commentary generally appreciated as a guide to loopholes. And a little later we found out that whatever had prompted Makkai to become instrumental in the preparation of the law, he was no anti-Semite, not even a "peacetimer," and he was staunchly pro-British and pro-American (although his newspaper did not deviate from the official Hitler-oriented line). I do not remember the source of our information, but it proved correct. I had been the last correspondent for Hungary of the London *Daily Herald,* I introduced myself to Makkai in that capacity, and he was immediately ready to see me. He was not simply sympathetic, but outright enthusiastic. He pocketed the censored and banned manuscript, and presented it to Prime Minister László Bárdossy (1890-1946) who studied the manuscript, found it interesting, and worth a try; the gist of his conclusion was, "let us see how it will strike the Jewish public." Then Bárdossy did something that was, judging from the reaction at the Press Attorney's office, unprecedented: he had the Press Section of the Ministry of Foreign Affairs (Bárdossy was also Foreign Minister at the time) put another stamp, with a later date, next to the one of the Press Attorney, saying, "Multipliable without cuts." Thus the original ban was overruled.

The first Jewish Yellow Paper came out in July 1941 as a quarto-size pamphlet of eight pages, in strong yellow paper boards with the emblem of the JWC, the star of David and the tables of the Law combined, on the cover. It was dispatched to a carefully selected group of several hundred leading gentile personalities. (A copy went to Colonel Brunswick, "courier" of the Regent; we knew that it was his job to do all reading for his master, and while we had no illusions as to the mental capacities of Horthy, we thought that his "ghost-reader" should be informed.) A few extreme rightists only, whom we considered less infatuated, were on the mailing list but not one member of the assimilationist Israelite establishment. Samu Stern's bureau had to order the pack of Yellow Papers they wanted to get from our agent, Sándor Gondos, and pay for it. The colophon ran thus:

> The first Jewish Yellow Paper has been compiled by D. Sabbatai on behalf of the Jewish Work Collective. The Jewish Work Collective is a community of ideas. Its members serve the good cause of the Jewish people selflessly and anonymously with their literary activities.

In a sort of preamble I had this to say:

> The Jewish Work Collective, a voluntary cooperative of independent Jews from Hungary, has investigated the question of whether Hungary's Jewry is bound to share the fate of the Jews of Austria (and will of necessity perish in the course of a continuous series of personal tragedies) or whether there is a chance to escape that destiny.
> An intensive, thorough, and definitive scrutiny of the question has lead to this conclusion: Hungary's Jews can avoid destruction if they awake to the consciousness of how they ought to proceed and if they act accordingly—today; tomorrow it may be too late.
> The first Jewish Yellow Paper will expand that conclusion.

> In the Yellow Paper, we state facts with scientific exactitude; we draw the consequences of the facts unemotionally, yet with unsparing consistency; and we put our conclusions in a shape that will, by force of the unvarnished truth, be binding on every thinking and honest Jew and non-Jew alike.
> The Yellow Paper is not intended for those perfidious non-Jews, who yesterday correctly stated that the Jews cannot be assimilated

and then applauded to, or even found insufficient, two Hungarian
anti-Jewish laws; but today dare to address reproaches to the Tran-
sylvanian and Bácska Jews because, under Romanian and Serbian
rule, they told the truth: that a Jew is no Magyar (albeit no Romanian
or Serb either) but—a Jew. And the Yellow Paper is not intended for
the irredeemable Jews, who still believe themselves to be Hungarian.

The text of the first Yellow Paper consisted of nine short passages. First,
the "Jewish question" was analyzed. It was argued that the essence of the
problem lay in the fact that the Hungarian body politic as well as the
populace felt burdensome, and wished to end, the cohabitation with the
Jews, who would have liked to be absorbed by the Magyar majority but
were unable to do so for historical, economic, biological, and psychological reasons. It was a dangerous illusion that after the war, the Jews
would be able to regain their former status; the Jews had been forced out
of what the gentile considered profitable economic positions and professions and their 7 percent minority would under no circumstances be able
to retrieve what had been lost to the 93 percent majority of the inhabitants
of Hungary.

Then the text stressed that Hungarian Jewry was in fact a national
minority, even though their greater part did not profess it, and that to admit this would not only not be detrimental to the Jewish position but would
actually have been the unique basis for improving Magyar-Jewish relations
and the situation of Jewry. However, under the given conditions, our national minority should not fight for the restoration of its once equal status.
On the contrary, now it was in our own interest to cooperate in terminat-
ing the Hungarian-Jewish coexistence. "Emigration is the only effective
means to achieve [the Magyar-Jewish divorce]. It stands to reason that it
cannot be carried out overnight. Therefore the Jews in Hungary should
aspire to a bearable *modus vivendi* with the Magyars until the advent
of the days of the exodus."

The final sections of the first Yellow Paper dealt with the necessity
of preparing the Jews for an orderly emigration, with the creation of a
Jewish National Body, and with the forthcoming Third Anti-Jewish
Law.

We needed publicity, and we received it. If we can for once trust
a notorious Budapest Jewish weekly, "the contents (of the Yellow Paper)

elicited full understanding and appreciation in the press of the extreme rightist parties."[9] I have a memory of the very first gentile reaction to the first *Yellow Paper*, a report as foolish as it was spiteful, published by the Arrow-Cross (*Nyilas*) daily *Pesti Újság* (News of Pest). And *Esti Újság* brought a reserved, but benevolent commentary; when I visited János Makkai to present him a copy of the publication that had materialized with his help, he called in an editor, László Béry, and gave him relevant instructions.

The remains of the liberal press and *Pester Lloyd*, the German Language daily of the government, were silent. *Pester Lloyd* was still produced by Jews; there were not enough qualified German-speaking editors and reporters among the Magyar gentiles, and potential aspirants from Germany had no chance because of their lack of Hungarian. These Jews mostly agreed with the Israelite leadership, and the philo-Semitic editors of the liberal papers also believed in the wisdom of the assimilationist establishment. Only once was there an attempt to take up the topic of the JWC in *Magyar Nemzet* (Hungarian Nation), the best Hungarian daily, and an organ of the Magyar opposition to Hitler.

The chief editor of the paper, Gyula Hegedüs, succeeded in finding out who D. Sabbatai was; and a young reporter of *Magyar Nemzet* called on me. He began with a few naïve questions, I did not answer them but attacked him with a passionately severe lecture in the vein of our "shock therapy" and took him to task over why his paper was in league with Samu Stern and his like. The visitor was taken aback; he had obviously never heard such a tone before, went to pieces, and began to confess. First of all, he admitted that he was Jewish, despite his appearance. His assignment, he told me, was to unmask us as paid agents of Greek shipping companies interested in the transport of emigrants. Hegedüs had received the information from the Pest congregation and had been persuaded to do the muckraking. The reporter apologized and vowed to open the eyes of his editor-in-chief to the truth. *Magyar Nemzet* never did publish the truth, but at least it refrained from printing anything against the JWC.

Indignant protests were voiced by Jewish papers issued by Jewish officialdom; that much we noticed, but did not yet know of the discreet diplomacy of the assimilationists. They were quick to react, albeit in an underhanded way. Later they rendered an account of their clandestine counterattack in the "Report of the Board of the Israelite Congregation of Pest on Its Activities in the Year 1941." (*A Pesti Izraelita Hitközség elöljáróságának jelentése az 1941-ik évben kifejtett müködéséröl*), published in 1942. A separate passage on page 17 bears the title "Against the so-called Jewish Yellow Paper" from which here I quote only the relation of how the official Israelite leadership reacted to the appearance of our first manifesto:

> The legal representative bodies of Hungarian Jewry did not wish to honor that pamphlet with an answer in the limelight of publicity [in July 1941] and limited themselves to no more than addressing a petition to the Royal Hungarian Government, in which they stated that 'the Hungarian Jews do not identify themselves with, and are alien from, the contents of that pamphlet, and no matter to which denominational branch or organization they belong, they condemn it unequivocally and most resolutely, and they repudiate most severely the surmise that Hungarian Jewry, sharing the common fate within the Hungarian Fatherland since centuries and fully merged with the Magyar nation in language, soul, culture, and sentiment—should declare itself a separate nationality.'

All that in a single sentence—it sounds as awkward in Hungarian as it does in my translation; but I could not convey the unctuousness of the original.

Widening the Basis

While our canvassing efforts continued and preparations for the second Yellow Paper were in progress, four more projects were in the making. First of all, we wanted to issue, as a sequel to the vest-pocket size Spinoza Booklets, a serial of larger books, manuals of genuine Judaism, essays in "Judeology"; the term I have tried to render thus was *zsidóságtudomány*, the accepted Magyar version of the German *Wissenschaft des Judentums*. I had been working on a study of the unique nature of the Jewish collectivity for a couple of years and although I was far from finishing it, I compiled an interim digest of my findings, and we decided that it would be published under the title *The Personality of the Jewish People* as the opening volume of the planned serial. By the time I was called up for forced labor at the end of May 1942 and the JWC suspended its activities, the volume had gotten to the printing office; the book then was put on the market later in the year as a posthumous child of the group.

The second volume of the series should have been an essay on the nation-bound essence of Judaism. We wanted to show the misled Neolog masses that although a Jewish nationalist might be a nonbeliever, traditionally religious Jews who took the *Shulkhan Arukh* seriously (and the Neolog leaders and rabbis always professed to stand firmly on the basis of the *Shulkhan Arukh*), must be conscious of the ethnocentric fundamentals of their faith.

After the publication of the first Yellow Paper Dr. Béla Berend wrote us from Szigetvár via the Gondos bookshop, indicating his enthusiastic assent and offering his services. We were pleased to have a rabbi among our backers, and we asked him whether he would write such an essay for us. Dr. Berend visited us in Budapest in the fall of 1941, his answer was positive, and he delivered the manuscript in due time. Unfortunately the de facto dissolution of the JWC meant the death of the serial project, and Dr. Berend's manuscript, that would have well served the purpose, remained unpublished.[10]

The serial "Essays in Judeology" was conceived as an undisguised enterprise of the JWC; three further projects were to be presented as independent, neutral ventures.

When the Jewish Public Opinion Research Station began to distribute its recruiting leaflet, it was kept secret that Dr. György Heller, who figured as the initiator, and Dr. György Kreilisheim, who actually ran the institution, belonged to our "inner circle." In general, our model was the Gallup institute, but we did not have the means for copying its working system. Instead, we tried to recruit a team of correspondents whose composition would mirror the vocational and age structure of Neolog Jewry.

In January 1942, when the number of our voluntary collaborators amounted to about 200, we started dispatching the questionnaires by mail; but we continued our efforts to recruit more correspondents. Among the papers of her late husband, Dr. Martha Kreilisheim salvaged copies of the recruiting leaflet, of four questionnaires (issued in the first four months of the year), of two information sheets (with the evaluation of the answers given to the second and the third questionnaire) and a pamphlet with the report of a lecture on Jewish public opinion research delivered by Dr. Kreilisheim before the Society of the Friends of Jewish Culture in Budapest on May 19, 1942.

The other projects did not materialize. We did prepatory work for a correspondence course in Jewish culture (Jewish history; Zionist history; history of the Jewish literature, art, and music; problems and objectives of a Jewish "sociotherapy"; and Hebrew). Detailed drafts—including forecasts of costs—dating from August 1941, have turned up from among the posthumous papers of Dr. Kreilisheim.

We also prepared a puppet show. By it we hoped to reach the smaller children and to educate them in the national spirit. Two jobless schoolmasters would have presented themselves to the headmasters of the Jewish schools and to the teachers of religion in non-Jewish institutions as "Bible Puppeteers" (*Bibliás Bábosok*) and offer to perform biblical plays (Samson's story, David and Goliath, the Book of Esther, the Maccabees). The simple technical equipment (two curtains for a doorway and half a dozen hand-puppets) was immediately available, and it would not have been difficult to win access to Jewish classes since the connection of the puppeteers with the JWC was to be concealed.

Neither the correspondence course nor the puppetry operation got beyond the planning stage.

The Second Yellow Paper

I nursed the relations with Makkai during the months following the publication of the first Yellow Paper and he was startled when I brought up the fate of the deported Jews. About 20,000 who could not produce enough documents to prove their Hungarian citizenship to the satisfaction of the authorities, who bore them no good will of course, were expelled to the Nazi-occupied Polish territories. I was under the impression that the expulsion had been sanctioned by Bárdossy but he was shocked when he learned that the deported Jews had been brutally murdered by the Germans. Makkai and I agreed that the next Yellow Paper should induce its recipients to commit themselves to accepting our formula: emigration of nearly all Jews from Hungary, but—in the vital self-interest of the Magyars—only after orderly preparation and only after the end of the war.

The text of the Second Jewish Yellow Paper was ready in November 1941. I submitted it to censorship, and the Press Attorney, Dr. Lee, mindful of the Prime Minister's intervention in July, quickly granted the clearance with a few minor face-saving cuts (which could, by the way, easily be circumvented by means of a simple trick, thanks to the office's inadequate control procedure).

The preamble ran thus:

In its first Yellow Paper, the JWC, a voluntary cooperative of independent Jews from Hungary, exposed the incontestable axioms of the solution of Hungary's Jewish problem. It analyzed, with scholarly objectivity, and avoiding every display of sentiment, mainly those aspects of the problem that were related to minority rights.

The second Yellow Paper clarifies the questions of principle raised by the exodus of the Jews. The second Yellow Paper shows that the subsistence and the exacerbation of the Jewish question are inescapable facts of social life and that nothing but the exodus can thoroughly solve the problem in accordance with both the vital interests of Jewry and the needs of the Hungarians.

The first half of the manifesto presented variations of the theme of Jabotinsky's important discernment of the anti-Semitism of "things" in contrast to the anti-Semitism of "men."[11]   After that, I explained that a more or less homogeneous ethnic majority would instinctively tend toward eliminating a dissimilar minority unwilling to, or—as in the case of the Jews—incapable of, being absorbed; and that anti-Semitism was, however regrettable, a psychological outgrowth of the tendency for which I now used the term "a-Semitism," originally coined by Magyar right-wingers who somehow wanted to shun the inhuman, "dirty," implications of being anti-Semitic. Here I repeated in print what we had so often stressed orally: anti-Semitism was a variety of a more comprehensive phenomenon—namely xenophobia, and "of course xenophobia is mutual: a Jew with an intact mind does not like the gentiles more than the gentiles like him."

Then I went on to elaborate that under the given historical circumstances, there was no alternative to "a-Semitism," but that "once we disregard the possibility of the barbarous annihilation of the minority", there were only two courses for its implementation: elimination within a legal framework and elimination by revolutionary violence. It was here that the assertion of the certainty of the rebirth of the Jewish State after the war and the intimations as to the Nazi defeat were inserted.

These were the pivotal statements of the document:

It could prove catastrophic to keep on with the self-deceit, the ostrich policy, the assimilationist verbiage vis-à-vis the non-Jewish public, and the allegedly diplomatic restraint. Hungarian Jewry could perish if it refuses to face reality.

The only rational, useful, and radical solution is the *exodus* of the Jews.

There is only one field where the Jews can work unhampered—today and in the future, even in case of a further severe deterioration of their situation; there is only one field where the Jews will not evoke misgivings or envy; one field whose cultivation may prove life-saving and within limits also possessions-saving: the field of preparing for the exodus.

A true [gentile] friend of the Jews should also accept a-Semitism, even though he may deplore the departure of Jewry; because insistence on withholding the Jews could ultimately lead to the destruction of Hungarian Jewry—before the end of the war.

It is in the interest of the Hungarians that the efforts to bring forth the expatriation of the Jews should not degenerate into revolutionary anti-Semitism.

Only unimpassioned a-Semitism suits the needs of the Magyar. It is a *sine-qua-non* of the implementation of a-Semitism that values not be destroyed, Hungary's economy not be damaged, and the Jewish economic potential be utilized for the sake of the exodus in the common interest of Jews and Magyars. A-Semitic measures must, also in wartime and to the very last, remain rational, lest they be exploited against Hungary in the atmosphere that will prevail after the war.

This was the most outspoken published version of our warning and threat of postwar punishment. In the original manuscript, I had said "changed atmosphere." Dr. Lee deleted the attribute, but bravely let the sentence stand, and although we did not risk restoring the cut in that case, we were satisfied that the message was clear just the same.

In the concluding passage, we reacted to the Prime Minister's suggestion that one should watch the response of the Jewish populace to our initiative. We declared that it was none of the business of the assimilationist leaders of the Israelite *religious* organizations to meddle in the *political* affairs of Jewry; the Magyar authorities should find out for themselves the true opinion of the Jewish public.

> The solution of the Jewish question is worth a plebiscite. Submit the question first to the non-Jewish population whether they want the Jewish population of the country to emigrate, up to a certain age-limit, to the new Jewish State, after the end of the war. And when this referendum will be carried out and it has become clear that an over-whelming majority cast a yes vote, put the same question to the secret vote of the Jewish inhabitants.
>
> It is beyond the shadow of a doubt that the great masses of the Jews will vote for truth and for life.

The second Yellow Paper was, unlike the first, quickly "honored with an answer in the limelight of publicity" by the assimilationist leadership. The "Report of the Board of the Israelite Congregation of Pest," quoted before, had this to say:

> At the beginning of 1942, the first Yellow Paper was succeeded by a second one in which its authors already pressed—again through the intermediary of the extremist press—for effective preparations of the exodus, or rather emigration, of the Jews of Hungary. Thereupon we renewed, this time publicly at the general assembly of our congregation held in February [1942] and in the name of the lawful representative organs of Magyar Jewry, our protest against, and our indignation about, that new unwarranted pamphlet. We once more declared that the alleged [*sic*] grouping that called itself 'Jewish Work

Collective' was absolutely unknown to the officialdom of Magyar
Jewry and to all elements of the Hungarian Jewish community, and
[both] Israelite central offices most sharply rejected the recent manifestation of the grouping that could not be anything but an instrument of aspirations directed against the vital interests of Hungarian
Jewry. The lawful representative organs of Magyar Jewry . . . also express their conviction that the irresponsible pamphlet, which pro-
voked the indignation of the entire Hungarian Jewish community,
will not succeed in misleading the clear-headed Hungarian public, the
less so since Magyar Jewry firmly sticks to its supreme endeavor to
proving, by devoted work and affection, its allegiance to this fatherland for which it is, even amidst ordeals, for good or ill, ready to
make every sacrifice.

The general assembly at issue took place on February 3, 1942. When
the second Yellow Paper was drafted we had known of the tragedy of the
20,000 expellees; so did the assimilationist leadership. But when the ful-
mination quoted in the *Report* was read by Samu Stern in the ceremonial
hall of the Pest congregation, he and his colleagues had already learned
what had happened since January 21 in the city of Újvidék (Novi Sad):
Hungarian Soldiers and gendarmes had massacred, with Nazi thorough-
ness, about 3,300 men, women, and children, Jews and Serbs; it is true
that the perpetrators of the crime acted without the knowledge of the
Regent and the government, and the Budapest authorities put an end to
the carnage. Still it is noteworthy that it was the Jewish Yellow Papers
Samu Stern solemnly protested against and not the Újvidék atrocities.

But it was Jenő Lévai's weekly that put the finishing touch to Stern's
invective. *Képes Családi Lapok* (Illustrated Family Magazine) not only reported extensively on the general assembly in its issue of February 8, but
appended to it an article by a Tibor Bencze. Its headline was "Protest by
the Zionist Association Against the Sordid Intrigues of the Men of the
Yellow Papers," followed by the subtitle "Incitement to Emigration, with
no Unselfish Purpose." The subtitle was a broad hint: "incitement to
emigration" was a legal term, defining a criminal offense listed in the Hungarian penal code. The "protest" attributed to unnamed spokesmen of the
Zionists was pure invention. Apart from this, the scurrilous piece of writ-

ing was packed with abuse, fabrications, and sheer nonsense. It was obvious that the author had never read the Yellow Papers but had been briefed, and told what to say, by one of Samu Stern's men, and denouncing "incitement to emigration" was what mattered. The author asserted to be under the impression that the group behind the Yellow Papers was "out for a good stroke of business by exploiting the emigration of hundreds of thousands of Jews. By the way, one of the visible members, indeed the head of the so-called Jewish Work Collective, has already gained practical experience in that line of business, since, as we have found out, *he had enabled "innumerable jobless Jews to emigrate to Palestine."* (My italics.) Here was an oblique reference to Dr. Kálmán; the statement, intended as an exposure, was supplemented by the libellous innuendo that Dr. Kálmán had acted "not on an altruistic basis."

This was possibly the most staggering manifestation ever of the mental and moral degeneracy of the assimilationist establishment. The utmost accusation they could think of *in February 1942* was the assertion that a person had been instrumental in the emigration to Palestine of "innumerable" (*számtalan*) unemployed Jews.

Reaching for Allies

Canvassing was carried on all the time. I can recall only a fragment of the story. I have only incomplete memories of the many conversations I led with gentile politicians, civil servants, journalists, and VIPs and also with Jews whom we deemed potential backers or who approached us after learning of the Yellow Papers. Immediately after the war I made only few notes of what I had experienced in 1941 and 1942. Now, after more than forty years, I can remember only a fraction of what I have not set down in writing, although much has been evoked by the printed and written traces of our activities I chanced to ferret out in the course of the preparation of this memoir. But I have not tried to fill up the gaps by reconstructing or interpolating.

We made great efforts to meet the Minister of the Interior, Ferenc Keresztes-Fischer (1881-1948), a professed anti-Nazi (arrested by the Gestapo in March 1944 and taken to the Flossenbürg concentration camp), but János Makkai tried in vain to persuade him to receive me. The "legal

representatives of Hungarian Jewry," Samu Stern and the others, were the
people who would obtain sympathetic hearing in the Ministry of the Interior. Although certainly not fond of Jews, Keresztes-Fischer unswervingly
condemned anti-Jewish excesses but obviously preferred humble to proud
Jews. He probably did not like what we expounded in the Yellow Papers,
but on the other hand he did not put obstacles in our way either, however
hard the "legal representatives" pressed for sanctions against us.

Unforgotten is my visit to Mihály Kolosváry-Borcsa (1896-1946), president of the Chamber of the Press, arbiter of all journalists in the country,
to whom I was introduced by Makkai. The Press Czar received me so courte-
ously as if he had thought I was an ambassador of the Elders of Zion; maybe
he suspected something of the kind. He made me feel that he sincerely
regretted the hardship and suffering caused by the Magyar-Jewish divorce,
and he seemed to fully agree when I warned him that after Hitler's inevitable defeat Hungary would have to pay a terrible price should she become
part of the murderous crimes of the Nazis. Kolosváry-Borcsa insisted that
I feel free to call on him again should we think that he could do anything
for us. He later foresook the lesson, became involved in the murderous
crimes in 1944, and he indeed paid a terrible price. He was hanged as a war
criminal in 1946.

I cannot say when, exactly, I saw Kolosváry-Borcsa; the dating of my
audiences with Archduke Joseph Francis of Habsburg was easier; they took
place about the time of the pogrom of Újvidék, of which I was promptly
informed by Francis Ofner who still had his direct lines of communication
with the Bácska. And it was from me that the Archduke first heard the
ghastly news the Budapest authorities had tried to withhold.

Joseph Francis was a man with intellectual ambitions, but his talents
remained underdeveloped because he never had to struggle: everything was
presented to him on a silver-platter. As a teenager he had wanted to become a painter. Later he toyed with poetry and authored a tragedy, *Columbus*. Eventually he turned to nuclear physics and experimented in a
laboratory put at his disposal by the industrial tycoon Leopold [Lipót]
Ascher, a Jew. Joseph Francis had no feeling for politics. In 1918 he
swore allegiance to the new Hungarian Republic that had dethroned the
House of Habsburg (and he imitated Philippe Egalité by dropping the
dynastical name and assuming instead the Magyar "Alcsúti"). Under Hor-

thy, he again enjoyed princely privileges. After Horthy's forced abdication and the takeover by the Arrow-Cross mob in October 1944 he swore allegiance to them. But his was an essentially apolitical mind, and he was well-meaning and guileless.

He was one of the recipients of our Yellow Papers, and he sent his literary adviser, the Jewish journalist Béla Kornitzer, to Dr. Kálmán to gather additional information. Kornitzer was told that we would gladly brief His Royal Highness, and I was granted an audience. It was to last half an hour. He was punctual to a second and dismissed me after exactly thirty minutes, but I was asked to come again. The Archduke wanted to be instructed in Jewish history and Zionism, seemed to be thrilled by the for him astonishingly new idea of rebuilding the Jewish State and displayed interest in the question of whether there was a chance for a Jewish monarchy. He was very upset about the Újvidék atrocities. On the day after my second audience he was to attend a reception at one of the foreign legations, and he was determined to inform diplomats of neutral countries of the outrageous event. The extremely benevolent Habsburg would probably have proved a useful patron had the days of the JWC not been numbered.

Among the Jews with whom we talked about our purpose there were hardly any Zionists—at least any organized Zionists. Not that we would deliberately hàve kept away from them; the noncommunication came about naturally for a tangle of reasons. First of all, since 1935 a kind of alienation had prevailed between Dr. Kálmán and myself on the one hand and the leaders of the Magyar Zionist Association (*Magyar Cionista Szövetség*) on the other. That had nothing to do with the JWC. In 1935, Jabotinsky's following seceded from the World Zionist Organization and formed the New Zionist Organization, a terrible crime in the eyes of the WZO command in London. The Revisionists and the *Betar* group of Hungary wished to stay on within the framework of the Magyar Zionist Association, a legally independent Hungarian society, and the majority of the Association leadership would have liked to arrange for some *modus vivendi,* but the WZO center forced them to expel us. We knew perfectly well how reluctantly they obeyed, and they assured us of their personal respect, but for all that a heavy shadow hung over our relationship. Then there was discord in connection with *Aliya Bet,* vehemently condemned by the WZO at the time, and this made the shadow even heavier. Finally, we felt that there would have been no point in recruiting a person who, while possibly sharing already some of our basic convictions, had pledged himself or herself to serve within, and follow the directives of, one of the Zionist parties whose leadership in London or Tel Aviv was unconcerned with the special Hungarian Jewish situation.

On the part of the more or less amenable Jews we more often encountered attention than sympathy. But attention we did receive. The attitude we usually met with was that of a benevolent spectator watching a tightrope act: the onlooker crossed his fingers yet would not have dreamt of climbing on the rope himself. Such was the stance, to quote a typical case, of Aladár Komlós, the reputed writer. He took a warm interest in our pursuit and was acquainted with the Silagis. His wife, the actress Erzsi Palotai, even envisaged a recital of Jewish poetry under the auspices of the JWC. Her husband applauded the idea but never thought of joining the acrobat on the rope.

A Jewish backer who did show sympathy and even became more active than some men of the "inner circle," although there was no question of his "joining" us or assuming "membership" in the JWC, was Dr. Rudolf (Rezső) Kasztner (1906-1957). The explanation of that paradox lies partly in the lack of any formalized framework or clearly delineated rules in our group—whose operations developed miles away from the field of Zionist partisan politics—and partly in Kasztner's grasp of the situation: although he was a committed adherent of the Zionist labor movement, he fully realized that it was a policy of Jewish national unity that now was urgently needed, something Zionist Labor could not offer.

Kasztner had moved to Budapest after Hitler pressured Romania into returning the northern half of Transylvania to Hungary in August 1940. He immediately established close contacts to the "legal representatives" of Jewry on the strength of family relations and was also admitted into the leadership of the Magyar Zionist Association on the strength of his former role in the Zionist Labor Party of Romania. But it was Jewish national consciousness that determined his attitudes. In Bucharest he had been the secretary of the parliamentary faction of the Jewish Party, the political arm of the Jewish national minority, and it was there that his political realism had its roots. For him it was self-evident that Jews were not Magyars, that Jewry was a people; and he was as keenly aware of the deadly menace as we or maybe more so since he had witnessed what had been done lately to Jews in Romania.

When he came across the first Yellow Paper he contacted us. For some time our relationship had been limited to almost conspirational visits in my home. For the JWC, absolute discretion was a matter of course; and Kasztner told us that we had articulated his innermost convictions but for the time being, he would keep our unity of thought to himself. He did not question the correctness of our outlook but he had—at least at the outset—doubts about our bellicose tactics. He trusted that in view of the oncoming cataclysm it would be feasible to bring forth all-Jewish unity in Hungary by mere persuasion.

Kasztner indeed succeeded in bringing about a conference of prominent Jews, among them personages who had been more or less influential in Hungarian political parties, in December 1941, but his hopes were disappointed. The Magyar-Jewish personalities did not agree among themselves and those who played a role also in the congregations dismissed Kasztner's warnings as panic-mongering. His suggestion of forming some kind of emergency body was rejected. Kasztner now must have realized that not only was our strategy right but our tactics might be justified as well. And he began campaigning, without our knowledge, on our behalf.

One day in February 1942 (some time after the congregational general assembly of that month) Kasztner surprised me with news that Sándor Eppler (whom both Kasztner and I took to be the grey eminence behind Samu Stern) would like D. Sabbatai to come and see him in his office. I answered that if Eppler wanted to talk to me he could come to my home. Kasztner went off with the message and came back a little later with a compromise offer. He asked me if I would be prepared to meet Eppler in a neutral zone, at his own place, the Corso boarding-house at 12, Váci Street. I agreed and we soon had our meeting.

We were seated at a long table, Eppler on one end and I on the other. Of course Kasztner was there, but I have no memories as to the other participants. Eppler asked short questions and I gave detailed answers. Now I deplore that my notes jotted down after the war are so sketchy and mostly confined to the anecdotic, such as the telephone episode: a few minutes after our dialogue had begun, a young man rushed into the room shouting excitedly: "There is an urgent call for Mr. Secretary General!" Eppler, not interested, waved his hand and dismissed the anxious messenger: "Tell them it's all right." It was clear that he had arranged for a mock phone call in order to have a pretext for leaving swiftly should he decide that there was no point in wasting his time. But he did stay, and at the end of the long conference his attitude was so positive that I almost suspected an artifice. Eppler declared that although he was far from sharing all our views he acknowledged the legitimacy of our aspirations, he was interested in Jewish public opinion research, and was ready to talk things over with Dr. Kreilisheim. He agreed to look for ways and means to further our Research Station, whose links with the JWC were to be kept secret also for the future. Moreover, Eppler promised to induce Samu Stern to see us.

It soon turned out that my skepticism concerning the secretary general was unfounded. He received Dr. Kreilisheim (whose still extant notes show that his visit took place shortly before March 12, 1942), promised to dispatch a circular letter to all Neolog congregations in support of Jewish public opinion research, and discussed with his visitor ways for further promoting the project. And a short time later we received the invitation to meet Stern in Eppler's office.

Dr. Varga and I went there, and it was a strange experience to watch Eppler going out of his way in order to sell us to the president. He tried to bring it home to Stern that it was a hard fact that in the territories Hungary had lost to its neighbors in 1919, and now partly restored, many co-religionists had been considering themselves members of the Jewish national minority for two decades; and besides, in difficult times it might prove useful to have more irons in the fire (one potential "iron" being, of course, the JWC). It was a likewise strange experience to realize that far from being the grey eminence, Eppler's stance was that of a submissive employee. The president snubbed him, then turned to us and assured us that he would always fight our aspirations.

So we won a new insight in the workings of the assimilationist leadership. But we also realized how sincere Eppler had been in his efforts to help us. He intimated that he was not very impressed by Stern's obduracy and did not give up the hope that one day the president would mellow—at least a little.

Dr. Kasztner had one more surprise in store for us. He brought us another invitation, this time on behalf of leaders of the Hungarian Zionist Association. We were asked to come to Ottó Komoly's home. We were somewhat puzzled because we knew of a recent quarrel between Kasztner and his peers in the Zionist establishment. Kasztner was as worried of rescue operations as we were in view of the increasing flow of Jewish refugees illegally entering Hungary. The Zionist fund-raisers had collected significant amounts they now were unable to transfer. Kasztner wanted to borrow the money to the benefit of the refugees but the administrators of the funds were adamant in their refusal. We first were reluctant; we did not see the point of such a get-together. But Kasztner insisted; he said it was imperative for us and for the Zionist Association to be on speaking terms. So we yielded. Ottó Komoly was a genial host, the atmosphere was friendly, the majority of those present were sympathetic to our ideas and prone to admit that, in principle, we were right. Yet they shrunk back from our "radicalism." The meeting proved unproductive. Ottó Komoly alone seemed to have second thoughts on the reticence of his colleagues; there must have been some prior understanding between Kasztner and him. When Komoly saw us off he asked us to remain in contact with him.

The Last Yellow Paper

On March 7, 1942, László Bárdossy resigned as Prime Minister; he had fallen out with Horthy. Two days later Miklós Kállay was appointed to succeed Bárdossy. We had been speedily preparing a third Yellow Paper and did not know yet that the change at the helm of the government had cut the ground from under our feet. The Press Attorney certainly did, because he returned the manuscript with a total ban. János Makkai told me that the wind changed. Still he arranged for me a visit with Dr. Domokos Torma, a high-ranking officer at the Prime Ministry's Press Office, but it was of no avail.

We were not in the least inclined to give up. We issued our third Yellow Paper in spite of the ban: we had recourse to a trick. We issued *typed*—not *printed*—copies, and we pretended that there were no more than a dozen copies. Typescripts did not yet require approval from the Press Attorney, and then there was a rule that a dozen identical texts, even though printed, could be distributed without permission. The latter rule was established to the benefit of theatrical companies and applied primarily to scripts of plays. We referred to it without actually complying; the note-paper size typed copies received a yellow hard cover with the usual wording of the title-page of our manifestos, supplemented with the note: "Produced in 12 copies for Hungary's leading personalities."[12] In effect we prepared typescripts with four carbon copies and produced, all-in-all, over fifty of the third Yellow Paper. We skimmed our master list and mailed the document to the select. Nobody ever questioned the truth of the pretended circulation figure.

I have no memories of the response to the last Yellow Paper but I know that we still busied ourselves with our various projects and attached some hope to our newly won backer, Sándor Eppler, who displayed keen interest in the public opinion project and induced Jenő Kolb, founder and chairman of a "Society of Friends of Jewish Culture," that he invite Dr. Kreilisheim for a lecture on May 19, 1942.

It was a blow when Eppler died on May 16. Still we remained active in the vain hope that we would be able to carry on. Dr. Kreilisheim read his paper as planned, and the four-page report we had printed of the lecture and of the ensuing discussion shows that the JWC was still functioning as if nothing had happened. The leaflet records eight contributions to the discussion, three from collaborators of our "inner circle" (Sonnenfeld, Dr. Endre Molnár, and Dr. Varga) who had offered expedient cues for Dr. Kreilishem. (Three contributions came from participants who after 1945 or rather 1956, attained high honors in Hungary's academic life: Dr. István Hahn, in 1942 rabbi of a provincial Neolog congregation and author of a history of the Maccabees, after 1956 one of the foremost classical scholars of the country; Miklós Szabolcsi, in 1942 a young student, after 1956 an influential Magyar literary historian, and Dr. Imre Hirschler, in 1942 a modest doctor and after the war a prominent medical authority.)

We expected to encounter increased difficulties now that Kállay was Prime Minister but we were under the illusion that we would be able to pursue some of our plans nonetheless. We were mistaken. To quote a grim Budapest wisecrack: we were already dead, only we have not yet noticed it.

Kállay tried his hand at establishing clandestine links with the Allies, but at the same time he aimed at securing calm on the Jewish home front. He was at the service of Samu Stern and the other Jewish tycoons, but he also did his best (or worst) to placate the Germans and the domestic Nazis, the Arrow-Cross mob, by letting the army draft tens of thousands of Jewish men—not only those of military age—for labor service that differed in every respect, but in name, from the institution of 1940. In reality, the labor companies now were mobile concentration camps deployed on the Eastern Front. I received my summons on the day after Dr. Kreilisheim's lecture and was to join my unit on May 26. By the end of June, all younger male collaborators of our "inner circle" had been called up. Few survived; after the war it became a sad certainty that Dr. György Heller, Dr. Kreilisheim, Mitzger, Sonnenfeld, and Vázsonyi had perished.

The JWC had never been formally inaugurated, and it was not closed down formally either. After the belated publication of my book, *The Personality of the Jewish People,* arranged practically by my wife alone, the JWC silently disappeared from the public eye. Dr. Kálmán's energies were taxed to the utmost, first by assisting *Aliya Bet* and then by helping "foreign" Jewish refugees living in the underground, until his departure from Budapest with the "Kasztner group" on June 30, 1944. Dr. Varga temporarily withdrew from Jewish political activities.[13]

Dr. Béla Dénes, an old friend of mine, *Ikhud-Mapai* leader, and defendant in the infamous Budapest anti-Zionist show trial of 1949, assured me in 1946 that Dr. Kasztner and Komoly had drawn inspiration from the words and deeds of the JWC during their campaign for the creation of an emergency council—the *Va'ad Ezra u've'Hazalah;* the Relief and Rescue Committee—which at long last materialized in January 1943, with Komoly as president and Kasztner as his deputy. Perhaps. I could not check on this. But even if our effort would have been utterly abortive, I do believe that the try was worthy.

NOTES

1. *D'var ha-Shavau* (The Week's Word), Tel Aviv, February 6, 1981.
2. Nathaniel Katzburg, "Zionist Reactions to Hungarian Anti-Jewish Legislation 1939-1942" in *Yad Vashem Studies,* Vol. XVI. Jerusalem: Yad Vashem, 1984, pp. 151-176.
3. Ibid., p. 175.
4. *Das Jüdische Volk* (The Jewish People), Berlin, February 25, 1938.

5.   The gentleman whom I did not name in my report was Dr. Hugó Csergő (1877-1944), chief notary of the Pest congregation, ghostwriter of Samu Stern's speeches and articles.

6.   Aron Grünhut, *Katastrophenzeit des Slowakischen Judentums* (The Catastrophe Epoch of Slovak Jewry), Tel Aviv: The Author, 1972, pp. 79 ff.

7.   *Nyugat* (Occident), Budapest, vol. 28, no. 7, July 1935, p. 41.

8.   Ibid., p. 39.

9.   *Képes Családi Lapok* (Illustrated Family Magazine), Budapest, February 8, 1942. I shall come back later to the source of this quotation from a contribution characteristic of Jenő Lévai's Jewish weekly.

10.   Allegations concerning further contacts between the JWC and Dr. Berend or assignments given to him on the line of the JWC are devoid of any foundation.

11.   Cf. V. Jabotinsky, *The Jewish War Front,* London, 1940, pp. 55-56.

12.   All this I relate from memory since I have not had the third Yellow Paper in my hands since its publication. Dr. Kálmán had unearthed a copy after the war and delivered it to the Israeli Legation in Budapest before his *aliya.* It was understood that the Legation would forward it to me through Mr. Moshe Alon, then Press Attaché of the Israeli Consulate in Vienna where I lived until 1951. However, the document got lost and all my efforts to recover it have been in vain.

13.   Dr. Imre Varga and his wife, an Irish Catholic, were close friends of the Ortutays. It was Dr. Gyula Ortutay who in 1946 informed me of the circumstances of Dr. Varga's tragic end. The source of this information was Mrs. Varga who died about a year after her husband's death. According to Dr. Ortutay, Dr. Varga called on Samu Stern, then president of the Jewish Council (*Zsidó Tanács*) in Budapest about the middle of June 1944. He tried to persuade Stern of the necessity of armed Jewish resistance and explained the detailed plan of a guerrilla campaign, including the pinpointed employment of poison and bacteria, "weapons" within the reach of a determined physician. Stern reacted by telling Varga that he would immediately inform the Gestapo, because a person with such ideas endangered the existence of the entire Jewish community and must be

rendered innocuous. Varga was sure that Stern meant it and committed suicide.

In a memoir of undeniable merit, *Hogyan történt?* (How Did It Happen?) by Ernő Munkácsi (Budapest: Renaissance, 1947, p. 118 f.), there is a report of the Varga-Stern clash, but it strikes me as an embroidered story based on hearsay; some of its elements seem to be improbable.

The essence of the Munkácsi report is "an emotional and very impassioned speech" by Dr. Varga, "a young physician." Munkácsi says that Stern answered "in a calm and matter-of-fact tone" and declared that Jewish resistance not only was hopeless but would also immensely endanger all the Jews; he ended by stating the "the (Jewish) Council has fulfilled, and will fulfill, its duty" and then "rushed out of the hall." And "next day word got around that Dr. Varga had committed suicide in despair since his speech did not have the necessary response and results."

I doubt if any eyewitness would ever have called the 47-year-old Dr. Varga "a young physician." The longish portion of the "emotional and very impassioned" oratory does not make an impression of authenticity either, although Munkácsi has placed it between inverted commas, as if it were a verbatim quotation. It could hardly have been taken down in shorthand—or was it a prepared, and read, statement whose draft was in Munkácsi's hands? It reminds me rather of the rhetoric Thucydides used to put into the mouth of his heroes; but while Thucydides' fiction has psychological weight, the allegedly verbatim Varga quote has none. If anybody was unlikely to deliver emotional and impassioned speeches, it was Varga, a tight-lipped, laconic, extremely reserved man of action. And I cannot believe that Dr. Varga, who personally was exempt from all anti-Jewish discrimination, would have killed himself over mere disappointment; it was something different to be denounced to the Gestapo.

FIVE MONTHS

Fülöp Freudiger

The history of that year of horror, 1944, has already been recorded many times, both by professional writers (Jenő Lévai) and people who had been active in public life, like president Samu Stern, Ernő Munkácsi and others. I should not like to go over the same story in different words, but I would rather describe episodes from my personal experience and events in which I personally participated. Some of these were known to a few people only, and I believe them to be of interest to all who feel deeply over the fate of Hungarian Jewry, as they lead to a better understanding and evaluation of what has happened, and of what has failed to happen.

In 1954, I was summoned by Judge Halevy to testify at the Grünwald-Kasztner trial. I also served as a witness at the Eichmann trial in Jerusalem, as well as at the trials of the SS officers Hermann Krumey and Otto Hunsche in Frankfurt and Franz Novak in Vienna. In my testimonies I related most of these episodes and events which I intend to sum up here. I will describe everything as I knew it, then and there; what I have heard or read in the later years does not belong here. As I did not have a diary, it is possible that some of the dates that I quote are not precise to within a day or two, but on the whole, they are accurate.

I would have liked to entirely avoid any evaluation of the people together with whom I worked or criticism of their activities, but this is inevitable in an attempt to draw a clear and lucid picture.

* * * * *

Sunday, March 19, at dawn, German troops crossed the western border
of Hungary and with them came the *Sondereinsatzkommondo* No. IV of
the SS whose task was to carry out the "Final Solution of the Jewish Problem" in Hungary.

They had been well informed and well prepared. Already at 5:00 p.m.
of the same day I was met by a military car with a machine-gun in front of
the building of the Budapest Orthodox Jewish Congregation (35 Dób
Street) whose president I was at the time. A sergeant of the SS entered
the Congregation office and delivered an order for the leaders and Rabbis
of the Congregation to appear at the office of the Neolog Congregation
(12 Síp Street) at 10:30 the following morning.

Out of the seven members of the Orthodox Presidium, two of us came
the next day as ordered: Dr. Emil Deutsch and myself. The leadership of
the Neolog Congregation (who got the same order) was more or less completely represented. Three officers, a civilian and a female stenographer
arrived at the appointed hour. A soldier with a machine-gun pointing at
us stood facing the conference table. The officers took their seats on one
side of the table, all of us sat on the other side. I sat at one end near Dr.
Károly Wilhelm. The officer who sat facing the President, *Hofrat* Samuel
Stern, began with these words: "From now on all the affairs of the Jews in
Hungary are under the jurisdiction of the *Sondereinsatzkommando* of the
SS." He went on to speak about the maintenance of order etc. and demanded that a "profile" of all the institutions of the Budapest Jews be
sent to him. He wanted an exact list with the names of the leaders of
these institutions etc. for the next day, at the Hotel Astoria. As we were
in the dark concerning the identity of the officers, I ventured to ask: "To
whom?" "To me, *Obersturmbannführer* Krumey," was the answer. "Yes,
Mr. Krumayer," said President Stern. "Not Krumayer, K-R-U-M-E-Y!";
whereupon I inquired again as to who the other officers were. Krumey
introduced them: *Hauptsturmführer* Otto Hunsche and Dieter Wisliceny.

He wanted a larger meeting with the heads of all the institutions and organizations to be called for the following afternoon (Tuesday) and with this they marched off.

When we got up, I told Dr. Wilhelm that I had something very urgent to tell him. I had worked together with Dr. Wilhelm for five years and I knew him as an extremely capable man, whose advice was very much appreciated by President Stern. Both of us were members of the "Office for Aid of the Hungarian Jews" (*Magyar Izraeliták Pártfogó Irodája*) which had started its activities in 1939 in an effort to counteract, as far as possible, the effects of the anti-Jewish laws, which had become progressively more and more severe. The Executive Committee numbered 12 members: five were Neolog, four Orthodox, one of the status quo congregations, and two of the Zionist organization. This was, for the first time since their separation in 1868, that members of Orthodox Jewry built up a common organization with the Neologs. This organization, generally known as MIPI (Hungarian initials) had a budget of several million *Pengős*. Up until the Hungarian declaration of war against the USA, the American Joint Distribution Committee—the Joint—covered half of this; but afterwards we had to provide the whole amount.

"What is the matter with you? Why are you so agitated?" Dr. Wilhelm asked me. "One of the officers is Wisliceny; we have to establish contact with him at any price!" I replied.

As I had complete confidence in Dr. Wilhelm, I told him that it was Wisliceny who in 1942 carried out the deportation of 60,000 Slovakian Jews. As early as 1941, the concentration of Jews in the labor camps began. Expenses were covered by the Jewish Council aided by the Joint; but they also approached us. Being the son-in-law of the Chief Rabbi of Pressburg, Rabbi Akiba Schreiber, and having learned in the *Yeshiva* there, many of the leaders were my personal acquaintances, and, accordingly, they made special claims to my helping them, what I did, wherever and as much as I could.

By the autumn of 1942, 57,000 Jews had already been deported. Hlinka demanded of Wisliceny, on behalf of the Slovakian Government, that all Jews, about 90,000, be deported. Gisella Fleischmann and Rabbi M. B. Weissmandl sent a messenger to Budapest, first of all to Samuel Kahan-Frankl, the President of the National Organization of the Orthodox Jews

(*Magyarországi Orthodox Zsidó Központi Iroda*). The message stated that Wisliceny, whom they had already contacted previously through Ign. Steiner, would refrain, for the sum of 30,000 dollars, from deporting Jews above the number of 60,000 that he was committed to by the orders he got. This meant that for $30,000 the deportation of 30,000 Jews could be prevented! They even hoped that the 3,000 whose deportation was pending, could be rescued. The official national organizations, the Orthodox, as well as the Neolog and the Zionist, were ready to help and they had the money too, but not one of them did dare to carry through such a transaction which, in every aspect was against the law. Joseph Blum, who, before he came to Budapest, had been, for a long time, the representative of the Joint in Slovakia, was quite desperate that there seemed no prospect for complying with the supplication of Rabbi Weissmandl and Mrs. Fleischmann, and, as a last resort, came to me urging me to find a solution. Upon his undertaking to guarantee in the name of the Joint, the repayment of the sum after the war, I managed to procure 80,000 Swiss Francs from my friend Julius Link and my brother-in-law, Leopold Blau. 80,000 Swiss Francs were according to the official rate equal to $20,000, but since at this time the free-market-rate of the dollar in Switzerland was about 2.60, there was the possibility to convert them into the $30,000 they had asked for. This was in the first week of Spetember 1942, and until he got the money a few weeks later, Wisliceny deported the 3,000, but otherwise he kept the agreement and there were no more deportations. (The remainder of Slovakian Jewry was deported in February 1945, in retaliation for the fighting of the partisans in which Jews were also involved; this was not done by Wisliceny. 8,000 [approx.] managed, in 1942 to cross to Hungary where they lived with false, or bought, papers as Hungarian Jews.) Dr. Wilhelm knew the fate of the Slovakian Jews, except for the role of Wisliceny and the story of the 30,000 dollars of which I now informed him. He agreed with me about contacting Wisliceny, but we found, at that time, no solution how to do this. In the end, it was far easier than we thought.

Already, by Monday morning, every Jew found at a railway station was arrested and sent to the Kistarcsa detention camp. Going by train was forbidden and rigidly controlled. My brother-in-law, Leopold Blau, was arrested at the Western Station (*Nyugati Pályaudvar*) of Budapest while escorting a Slovakian family to their train. (No harm came to these people as they had Christian papers.) At night hostages were taken with the active cooperation of the Hungarian police; about 400 were detained at the National Rabbinical Seminary *(Országos Rabbiképző Intézet)* which was taken over by the SS. This was continued on Tuesday. In the morning they came to our factory to arrest my cousin, Denys de Freudiger, but as he was absent, they arrested my brother Samuel. I was in the manufacturing hall and when some of the Polish refugees who were working for us heard what was going on, they grabbed me on the spot and hid me under a pile of goods. After the police had departed, taking my brother with them, our porter handed me a note written by him which read: "I am being taken to the Rabbinical Seminary. You have to come there too by four o'clock, otherwise I don't know what will happen to me." My wife had come to the factory just in time to see my brother taken away in a police van, whereupon both of us went to the Congregation Office to speak with President Stern. I told him what had happened and asked what could be done to help my brother; Stern told me bluntly that several hundred prominent Jews were arrested as well, and for the present, nothing can be done. "If so, then I will go to the Astoria," I told him, upon which he inquired whether I had lost my mind. Nevertheless, my wife and I went to the hotel. My wife remained outside so that she would know if anything happened to me and I entered the hotel. The SS sentry let me pass when I told him I wanted to speak with Wisliceny.

Wisliceny was sitting in the hall with a beer in front of him. I approached saying: "I should like to speak to Herr Baron." He was not titled, but in Bratislava he was called thus, which he knew. He gave me a sharp look. "Didn't I see you yesterday?" he demanded. "Yes, yesterday at the meeting in the Congregation Office. I am Philipp de Freudiger, president of the Orthodox Community. "What do you want?" "I want to notify the Herr Baron that I shall not be able to attend the meeting this afternoon. I have to go to the Rabbinical Seminary," and I showed him my brother's note. He read the note and said: "Nonsense, I am the commander there in the Seminary; nothing will happen to him. You are coming to the meeting and report to me afterwards."

The meeting was held in the Síp St. building and opened by Hermann A. Krumey, but he left early. To an audience of 60 people or more Wisliceny repeated that, apart from certain restrictions, nothing would happen, provided that order was maintained, which was the task of the Jewish leaders, etc. At the end of the meeting, my cousin Denys, who as president of the Orthodox hospital also attended, and I reported to him and he ordered us to be at the Seminary the next morning.

When we came there at 10 o'clock he was sitting in the entrance-hall with some N.C.O.s. "You probably want to speak to your brother?" I assented, and he sent a sergeant to fetch him. My brother and I exchanged a few words; he asked for *T'fillin* and I told him that I hope to get him free. When he was again led away, Wisliceny called us and asked: "To whom is the money from abroad being sent?" Denys wanted to reply, but I intervened quickly inquiring in a surprised manner: "What money?" "Quit pretending, I know everything." Wisliceny said and added, "Send me corroboration that your brother belongs to the leadership of the community and I shall send him home." This he actually did as promised.

The story of the "money from abroad" was as follows: When a steadily increasing number of refugees came from Slovakia to Budapest, a few eager members of our community got together to organize some help for them. A committee, later known as our *Vaad Hatzala* (Rescue Committee) was formed by Dr. Adolf Deutsch (later a member of the First and Second *Knesset*), my brother-in-law Leopold (to everyone Lipi) Blau, Kövessi, Schonberger, Sussman, Joseph Frank and the brothers Leo and Hermann Stern. They asked me to take over the leadership of the Committee. In Hungary, aiding illegals was a serious crime, punishable by administrative internment, that is, without trial, and therefore, it was a question whether it was not too dangerous for me as President of the community to participate. I, however, relied on the saying of our sages that "agents of a *Mitzvah* come to no harm," and there is no greater *mitzvah* than rescuing human beings.

We helped the refugees to procure Hungarian or Christian papers, to find homes for them and distribute bread and breadcards to them, as bread was rationed during the war. Hermann Stern, the secretary of our congregation, excelled in procuring these breadcards. A large number of the refugees were Orthodox but we distributed them to everyone who asked for them. The *Mizrachi* organization also extended help to many people, but insisted that they register as party members. The work was successful, and some 8,000 refugees were more or less provided for.

Months later, refugees came from Poland, mainly from the Bochnia ghetto, near Krakow and near the Slovakian border. They brought with them forged identity cards where they figured as Christians, and on the strength of these, I could arrange with the KEOKH (*Külföldieket Ellenőrző Országos Központi Hatoság:* National Central Alien Control Office) temporary resident permits for them because Poles, provided that they were not Jews, received the right of asylum in Hungary.

In several cases, we ourselves, sent guides to help the refugees cross the Carpathian Mountains, but it wasn't easy to find enough suitable people; they were few. In connection with this, we came to know of the existence of another *Vaad Hatzala* working for the same aims and my brother-in-law considered it wise to coordinate the work. I agreed, and one evening he brought along Joel Brand, with whom he had become acquainted while doing this work.

Brand was a rather short, stocky man; a man of action and an idealist. He was of Hungarian origin, but was reared and lived in Frankfurt and spoke mainly German. We discussed the possibility of collaboration, but finally Brand said that this depended ultimately on Dr. Rezső (Rudolph) Kasztner. Up until then I didn't know Dr. Kasztner, and gathered from Brand that upon the re-annexation of Northern Transylvania to Hungary, Kasztner had left Kolozsvár (Cluj) for Budapest, where he, like a few others, attempted to keep up his leading position in the Zionist organization. That wasn't easy under the old Hungarian establishment and everybody was satisfied when Dr. Kasztner undertook the *Hazala* work, which was too dangerous for most.

I met Dr. Kasztner at Leo Stern's, because I wanted a member of our committee to be present. Before concluding the agreement, Dr. Kasztner asked: "How much money would the Orthodox give for the joint work?" I told him openly that the raising of funds was a steady worry for us, as we couldn't give receipts owing to the illegal character of our work, and also because of the anti-Jewish laws becoming progressively more severe, our contributors had less and less "free money;" he on the other hand, was receiving money from abroad, so why demand from us as well? "Because the money I receive is from my party, the *MAPAI* (The Labor Party of Palestine) and so it is right that the other partner should contribute as well." I didn't promise any definite sum or percentage, but that we would continue our efforts of raising whatever we could. Two years later I found out that this was not the case at all!!! The money which Dr. Kasztner got came from *Eretz* (Palestine), from a non-partisan general collection by the whole *Yishuv*. The delegation stationed in Kushta (Istanbul) was composed of all parties; Dr. Kasztner however, who was a member of MAPAI, a rather minor party in Hungary at that time, made from this "MAPAI money" in order to profit his party. He was a party man through and through. Conducting *Hatzala* on a party basis was alien to us, and we ourselves had abandoned the separation principle of the Orthodoxy in view of the sacredness of this work. Apart from this, our collaboration proceeded successfully and up to 1944 about 2,000 Polish refugees came to Budapest, and part of them also went to the larger provincial towns.

So Wisliceny knew about the money from Istanbul, but wanted to hear from me about the recipients!

I went to 12 Síp Street where President Stern received us with the news that a "Central Council for the Jews of Hungary" had been nominated by Krumey in lieu of the various congregations and offices. It was made up of the following leaders: from the Neolog side, President Stern, Dr. Ernő Boda, Dr. Ernő Pető and Dr. Wilhelm; from the Orthodox, Kahan-Frankl and myself, and from the Zionists, Dr. Nisson Kahan. I asked Stern, our newly appointed president to sign the document concerning my brother, but he didn't want to sign; so Kahan-Frankl did and my brother was released that afternoon.

The Central Council consisted of the same members who had worked together for five years in the Executive Committee of MIPI; it was located in Sip Street. The office building, synagogue and school of the Orthodox congregation were requisitoned by the SS immediately on Monday. The Council, they felt that Stern would rather listen to me, a non-Zionist. Thus, they got the Information Department, which became well-known as "Partere No. 3," and the Department for the Provinces. Contact with the of one department or two. Although Nisson Kahan was a member of the Council, they felt that Stern would rather listen to me, a non-Zionist. Thus, they got the Information Department, which became well-known as "Partere No. 3," and the Department for the Provinces. Contact with the country was very bad because from the very beginning travelling was forbidden to Jews, the mail was censored, and was forwarded only by Christian messengers, if reliable ones were found. I thought that if anybody was able to establish some sort of contact it would be the Zionists, and therefore I pleaded for these two departments.

Over the next few days I had to go several times to the Majestic Hotel on the Swabian Hill (Svábhegy) of Buda where the *Sondereinsatzkommando* were installed; among other things to ask permission to take the Holy Scrolls from the synagogue, and, at this occasion I met an officer whom I hadn't seen till then. As I later learned, this was Adolf Eichmann. when I wanted to contact Wisliceny, I heard that he wasn't in. The next Wednesday when I came in the morning to the Council, I found a telephone order there from Wisliceny that "Freudiger, Dr. Nisson Kahan, and the Baroness Edith Weiss should come to the Rabbinical Seminiary." Dr. Kahan and I were there, but the Baroness was nowhere to be found; so finally, the two of us went to Wisliceny and explained to him that we two came alone because we couldn't locate her. He exchanged a few words with us and then sent Dr. Kahan to the lobby and told him to wait there. I remained alone in the room with him. He told me to be seated, locked the door, and then handed me a letter with the words "read this." It was a letter written in Hebrew by Rabbi Weissmandl, and it opened with bitter laments that it was now apparently the turn of Hungarian Jewry to suffer the same fate as the rest of the Jews in German-dominated Europe, may the Almighty have mercy on us all. He then proceeded to recommend that we continue negotiations about the "Europa Plan," even though it now concerned only Hungarian Jewry. He wrote that we could trust Wisliceny.

The Europa Plan was an offer made at one time by the Council in Bratislava, according to which they undertook to pay two million dollars if the Germans would refrain from deporting European Jewry to Poland. The offer was made to Wisliceny and forwarded by him to Himmler, who didn't comment on it. Meanwhile the Jews of Greece, Belgium, and Holland were deported, and so the two million dollars would be solely for Hungarian Jews.

"Have you read it?" "Yes, *Herr Hauptsturmführer.*" He took the letter, tore it up and threw the pieces into the burning stove. "Till then—the money coming—we need it" "We or I?" I inquired. "That is no affair of yours" Wisliceny said. "You shall hear from me" and with this he dismissed me.

I hurried downstairs to Dr. Kahan who was glad to see me in one piece and we went to Síp Street. There I brought the Council up to date. Apparently, Wisliceny had gone to Bratislava to be informed as to whom to contact, and accordingly, he wanted one personality from each of the Orthodox, Neolog, and Zionist organizations and brought a letter from Weissmandl to inform us. At any rate, it was now up to us to do what we could.

Several days passed without hearing anything further from Wisliceny. I didn't understand why, until I heard from a friend, Bandi Diamant, that Kasztner-Brand were negotiating with the SS. A certain Mr. Schmidt, who posed as the Director of the "Danube Steamship Co." (an Austrian firm, which was also based in Hungary) but was the leader of the counterespionage of the *Wehrmacht* in Hungary for several years, and Józsi Wininger, who did courier services for him, mostly to and from Istanbul and occasionally brought money from there for Kasztner, had been asked by him to arrange a contact with Krumey for them. Diamant learned all this from a female dancer of the Arizona, who was on good terms with Wininger. Kasztner was ready to pay 20,000 dollars for the contact alone, and unwittingly counteracted Wisliceny's endeavors.

The Economic Department of the SS, under *Obersturmbannführer* Kurt Becher, especially interested in procuring goods necessary to the Germans, began negotiating with the owners of the Weiss-Manfred Works, the greatest factory complex in Hungary, located on the Danube island of Csepel. This was done on the initiative of Schmidt and the bargain was concluded: Against the transfer of all the factories, 36 members of the Baron Weiss family (Baroness Edith included; this is why we couldn't locate her) were flown to Portugal.

Wisliceny had forwarded the Europa Plan to Eichmann, seeking his consent to continue the negotiations with me, but Eichmann got furious and called him an ass who let himself be a dupe of this scoundrel Freudiger, who offered two million dollars for all the Jews of Hungary, while Becher got X-times that for just 36! On the recommendation of Schmidt he decided positively concerning the contact between Krumey and Kasztner-Brand. This took place at the end of March.

On one of the very first days in April, upon entering President Stern's room, before the daily session of the Council, I found Dr. Boda, Dr.

Pető, and Dr. Wilhelm there with the President in a heated debate with Dr. Kasztner and Brand. "It's good that you are here as you know these gentlemen," Stern said to me. "They claim that they have come from Krumey who is demanding 200,000 dollars and they are requesting the Council to raise this money. What is your opinion?" Kasztner had told me nothing up till then about his negotiations with Krumey, but I presumed that 200,000 dollars might be the first installment of the two million, and expressed the opinion that the money should be raised and given. Stern told Kasztner-Brand that he will give his answer after the meeting. After they left, Wilhelm asked me, "Are you really of the opinion that we should hand over 200,000 dollars to these men? Have you seen the smaller one, even his eyes are not straight!" (Brand's eyes were in fact not quite symmetrical.) I set his mind at rest concerning Brand's reliability and at the meeting I pleaded for the raising of the requested sum, on the ground that it could only help. Kahan-Frankl and Dr. Nisson Kahan shared my opinion and it was accepted, with the additional clause that I be personally responsible for the whole affair and that I was to hand the money only to Krumey in person. This was conveyed as an answer to Kasztner-Brand, and also, that the collecting of such a sum would take some time. Stern immediately began with the work, demanding large sums from the rich and I started careful arrangements for the purchase of dollars. I couldn't manage to procure more than 80,000, whereupon Krumey was ready to accept also *Pengős* at a rate of 35 per dollar.

On April 12th Brand informed me that Krumey demanded the money for the next day. We were still half a million *Pengő* short. (None of the sums received by Kasztner from *Eretz* were used for this purpose.) It was a difficult problem how to raise this sum in one day. Kahan-Frankl lent 100,000 *Pengős* from the money of the *Orthodox Landeskanzlei* (Orthodox Treasury), and since the 14th and 15th were the 7th and 8th days of Passover, and the 16th a Sunday, and so our factory would be closed for three days, I lent the missing 400,000 *Pengős*. As our factory was working for the military too, it was exempt from the monetary restrictions applying to Jews and we had this sum, in cash, there. Later on, both of us got the lent sums back by successive installments.

Brand came to my private office to fetch the two suitcases in which the dollars and *Pengős* were packed; Joseph Blum of the Joint happened to be with me. According to the decision of the Council I had to hand the money to Krumey personally, so we discussed the possibility of accompanying Brand to Krumey; we couldn't know, however, how the latter might react. So Brand went to Krumey and told him that the money had been raised by the Council and was at present in the care of Freudiger who was awaiting his orders. Soon the telephone rang in my office and Krumey —whose voice I recognized—told me to give Brand the money, it's alright. I was assured that Krumey got the whole sum; the 20,000 that Schmidt-Wininger received was not deducted; that was paid from the money Kasztner had at his disposal.

The *Sondereinsatzkommando IV/B* (Eichmann's *Kommando*) was stationed at the Majestic Hotel and in a few adjacent villas. The Council had several younger officials who acted as sort of "liason-officers" between the Swabian Hill and the Council, as there were always things to arrange. But for any special request, I had to go there personally, sometimes getting results, more often, not. All the anti-Jewish regulations were published in the Hungarian Official Gazette, Hungary not being "occupied" by the Germans and having remained "independent." In spite of this we had to deal almost exclusively with the SS. Whenever we turned to the Ministry of the Interior—where a special "Jewish Department" had been created under Councillor Zsigmond Székely-Molnár—the answer we got was always "Do as you were ordered."

The members of the Council received "immunity cards" signed by Krumey. Dr. Kasztner, Brand, and his wife, Hansi, as well as several of their group also received such cards. The Becher department also arranged for such cards for a number of people against a lot of money, goods, and foreign currency. Kasztner, and some of the others included, were also exempt from the compulsory wearing of the "Yellow Star"; the members of the Council got no such exemption. Stern wanted me to take this up with Krumey, but I declined, as in my opinion, this would unnecessarily annoy the thousands of Jews who came daily to Síp Street wearing the badge. My brother Samuel and myself refrained from removing our beards upon the entry of the Germans, unlike all Orthodox members. This may have been a gesture of spite, but in the end, it helped me in our subsequent escape. The red beard and the yellow star went very well together.

Besides the Jewish Department of the Ministry, a new State Security Service was created too, which was called, quite proudly, "the Hungarian Gestapo." The chief of it was Péter Hain, who was for a decade the security officer for Miklós Horthy and was working secretly for the Germans for years. His helpers were Detective Inspector Ödön Martinides, who was the originator of the "repatriation" of some 20,000 Jews to Galicia, and their subsequent murder in 1941, and Inspector László Koltay. Koltay had his office in the Majestic also, and the Council got orders from him too. He was always rude, even when sober, and used with special liking the expression "hang and shoot" in dealing with the Council.

In the first days of April, Budapest got its first heavy air-raid. The American planes came by day, the Russians at night. Several houses were damaged and had to be evacuated. On April 5th Koltay demanded from the Council 500 apartments for Christians who had lost their shelter because of the bombers working on behalf of the Jews. As the raids continued, he demanded 500 again and again; the Council had to organize a housing office to deal with this matter.

Though the negotiations concerning the Europa Plan etc. were not in my hands, I went to Wisliceny almost daily, pleading first of all for the release of the people interned in Kistarcsa. Officially this detention camp was under the jurisdiction of the Ministry of the Interior, but there our interventions were to no avail, under the pretext that the inmates had been arrested according to the order of the SS, at the railway stations and while travelling. After several entreaties I attained the release of a score on April 4, and a week later several hundred. My brother-in-law had been released too. Then all the men under the age of 16 and over 60, as well as women under 18 and over 50 (or 55) were released and the others transported "to work." The selection was rather lax; I personally knew quite a number who had been released although they were between 16 and 60. It seemed, therefore, quite plausible that people fit for work were actually taken for that purpose. At that time we knew nothing at all about Auschwitz.

Still, the last week of March the leaders of the *Mizrachi*, Mr. M. Salamon and E. Frankl, both belonging to the Orthodox congregation, came to me and asked me to try to get Krumey to make possible the transport of 700 children and youngsters to *Eretz Israel*, as this transport was ready for shipment in Constanţa, several days after March 19th, the Romanian permission secured, and only the entry of the Germans prevented it. I went to Krumey with this request and did my best to persuade him. He was not

uninterested, but said, "The object is too small." Later on he came back
to this during the negotiations with Kasztner-Brand.

In spite of the prohibition on travelling, we once got a special permit to
gather the heads of the provincial communities for a discussion. President
Stern reviewed the events from March 20 onwards, and we heard what the
situation was in the provinces. The general opinion was to try as far as
possible, to come to terms with the SS Commandos in every town, as
nothing could be expected from Hungarian authorities. Only a very few
were skeptical concerning "coming to terms" with the SS and just one
single member (from Munkács) was absolutely opposed to it. He demanded a passive resistance, a non-cooperation; this was, however, decisively
overruled.

On a Sunday morning, April 16th, Dr. Imre Reiner who headed the
Judicial Department of the Council, received me in great agitation. He had
received news from Nyíregyháza, where his parents and other members of
his family were living, that during the night the Jews had been notified
that they were to leave their flats within a few hours and be concentrated
in a few streets. They were allowed just one suitcase per person and were
to leave everything else behind in the flats. "Go to Krumey and try to do
something against this," he begged me. "You'd better go yourself, doctor,"
I said, "since it was you who got the news, you can better explain what
it is all about." He didn't want to do that and so finally both of us went
together to the Swabian Hill. Krumey was not in his room and as we were
waiting in the anteroom Eichmann passed by. "What are the handsome
ones doing here?" he addressed us. "Waiting for *Obersturmbannführer*
Krumey," I replied. "What do you want of him?" whereupon Dr. Reiner
told him in a few, but very agitated words of the news he got. "Come in
here," Eichmann said and led us to his office where a large map of Hungary adorned the wall. "I have ordered the concentration of the Jews in
the area of the Eighth Army Corps." With a broad gesture, he indicated the
northeastern part of Hungary. "This is border territory; over these mountains are the Russians and unreliable elements cannot be allowed to move
about freely, that is clear. It concerns 310,000 Jews." "Nyíregyháza is
border territory? It is 300 kilometers from the border," I asked. "This
you should ask your Hungarians, why it nevertheless belongs to the border
corps. It is up to you to guard against epidemics, the rest will be alright."

(Eichmann feared epidemics, as in a former case, one had nearly ruined his career.) Dr. Reiner asked him how it was possible to ensure hygiene when the space allocated was one square meter per person. "Shut up with this *Greulpropaganda!*" Eichmann shouted, "Where did you get this from?" "Because my 90-year-old parents were herded in this manner." Meanwhile Krumey too had come into the office and Eichmann turned to him: "Have the first-degree relatives of Council members brought to Budapest." "What are 'first-degree relatives'?" I asked. "Don't you know this either? Father, mother, children and spouse." "And brothers and sisters?" I asked. "They are second-degree." said Krumey. "Na, well," said Eichmann, "let them come too," whereupon Krumey told us to submit a list of the names and addresses of family members and with that we left for Síp Street.

Queries addressed by the Council to the Ministry of the Interior on this matter remained unanswered. The list for Krumey was not big, and in the end, Kahan-Frankl's mother and sister in Máramarossziget and Dr. Wilhelm's two sisters in Kassa were not sent to Budapest. Stern didn't want Dr. Reiner to put his family on the list, arguing that Dr. Reiner, as well as some other people, such as Dr. Adolf Deutsch were only assigned to the Council, but were not official members of it. Dr. Reiner, however, didn't give in referring to the fact that Eichmann had told him personally to have them brought and that was good enough.

It soon became evident that Eichmann had not told us the truth, or at least not the whole truth, as a few days later the concentration in other parts of the country began too. On April 26, directives were issued by the Ministry, decreeing that Jews were not allowed to dwell in places with less than 10,000 inhabitants and were to be transferred to the nearest large town. There they were herded together in empty brick factories or other similar bigger compounds. The Jews of the larger towns were mostly herded together in the houses of a few streets, which were afterwards boarded in and a completely closed ghetto was created. The whole ghettoization was carried out in a few days, even before April 26.

The Council was at a loss as to how to deal with this situation. Krumey reminded us of our talk with Eichmann, pretending that the general ghettoization was a Hungarian decree. We demanded a meeting with Secretary of State László Endre, the infamous "Jew eater," as the Jewish Depart-

ment in the Ministry of the Interior was under his authority. Endre post-
poned this meeting for several days, but finally set a date. When the whole
Council arrived at the given hour, we saw Endre coming toward us on the
staircase with hat and gloves. In passing, he told us that his secretary, Albert Takács, would receive us. This was a calculated humiliation for the
Council, but we could do nothing but talk to Takács.

To President Stern's complaints, Takács countered that all of this was
not true in relation to the facts; people were not mishandled, were
settled decently, had more than adequate bedding and had victuals for two
weeks on them—he himself, had made sure of all this. "And what will
they have after two weeks?" I asked. Takács looked at me rather angrily
and didn't answer. After a few more banal sentences we were dismissed.
On our way downstairs I said to Stern: "And after two weeks comes the
deportation." "How can you say such things?" "Takács has not answered
my question concerning the supply of victuals after the two weeks, because this will not be necessary after two weeks."

As it turned out, I wasn't entirely right; the ghettos lasted longer than
two weeks, but nevertheless they were the first stage of the deportation.
For a genuine Hungarian Jew such a thing was simply unthinkable! True,
about 20,000 Jews had been sent to Poland in 1941, but this was a limited
action of the Central Alien Control Office against Jews who were not
citizens. Also the order for "repatriation" issued by Secretary of State
Ámon Pásztoy (former Chief of the Office) instigated by Chief Inspector
Ödön Martinides, utilizing the opportunity of the vacation of the Minister
of the Interior Ferenc Keresztes-Fischer, had been immediately recalled by
the Minister on the day of his return. Hence deportation from the country
was out of the question. Therefore, most of my colleagues considered my
fears grossly exaggerated.

My differing opinion had its special reasons. For the last two years I
was in almost daily contact with "my" Polish refugees. I had constantly
to arrange for the prolongation of the permit of residence of one or the
other of these "Christian" Poles. More than 20 of them worked in our
factory; many came to see me at home, etc. On the days immediately
following March 19, they came to me careworn and alarmed about their
fate. True, they had Christian papers, but "the German knows everything." Part of them wanted to flee immediately and advised me to do

the same. One of the cleverest of them, Leiser Landau, told me: "*Rashe-kol* (President) don't believe anything the Germans say! They will promise much and keep little. If you can, give them money, valuables, maybe you will be able to get something in return. And give them coffee, they go crazy for coffee." Again and again they said that it would come to a deportation. At first I didn't believe them, but when you hear the same thing over and over again it sinks in.

I was also in frequent contact with Rabbi Michael Dov Weissmandl whose letters were brought to me mostly by the courier of the Hungarian legation in Bratislava and in these letters he revealed the deportation of the Slovakian Jews before my eyes. Several days before the beginning of the ghettoization I received a letter from him asking us to urgently take into our heart the fate of "our 310,000 brethren in PKR." As all his letters were written in Hebrew, I broke my head for hours what the three Hebrew letters *Peh-Kuf-Resh* could possibly mean. Next day, with the help of Dr. Reiner, the puzzle was solved: they were the initials of Pod-Kar-patska-Russ, as they called in the Slovakian Republic the northeastern part of the territory which was returned to Hungary (Carpatho-Ruthenia). The number corresponded to that of Eichmann.

The situation in the ghettos was not uniform; it depended on local police and gendarmerie. In the larger towns an SS officer was also in command. It varied from bad to worse. The whole thing was carried out in a rush. People showing the least resistance were beaten up and threatened with shooting. There was neither the time nor the possibility for organized resistance. The ghettos were sealed and guarded heavily. Escape, even with outside help, didn't succeed. The shock caused by the sudden ghettoization brought an apathy to many; one didn't think of what would happen tomorrow, all one wanted was to live through today, however it was. A small part of the Slovakian refugees—mostly who had Christian papers—crossed back to Slovakia. Although they thus managed to escape the fate of Hungarian Jewry, the same fate overtook them half a year later in Slovakia. The path of the would-be refugees led to Romania. Romania was also under German influence, but after the partial deportation of the Jews to Transnistria, Marshal Ion Antonescu managed to get a relative normalization of the situation. Possibilities of escape—before the ghettoization—were unsafe and risky. One day someone succeeded and the next day another was captured and arrested at the very same place, and brought later on to the nearest ghetto. Gendarmes or SS men, who for lots of money, were to get people over the border, took the money and delivered their clients to the police instead. I personally knew of many such cases, which by far exceeded those where the flight was successful.

In the second week of the ghettoization, a delegation from the local council of Miskolc came to visit the Central Council, by special permit. They reported that two streets had been taken away from the ghetto territory and the Jews there were herded into even narrower quarters; they asked for help to get back the two streets. Kahan-Frankl was the "member on duty" (it was an afternoon, after office hours) and explained to them, in his refined, diplomatic manner, that the SS left the ghettoization to the Hungarians and that there was not a chance to get the Ministry of the Interior to act in any way in opposition to the local authorities. I happened to be present also, and when the members of the delegation pressed on and on, and one of them demanded in desperation, "What shall we do? It cannot possibly go on like this!" I burst out, "Break through the wooden walls and take the two streets back." "This is madness," Löw, the Director of the Congregation told me appalled. "We came to get your help and not crazy advice." "A year and a half ago you also said to me 'madness' when I demanded 100,000 *Pengő* from the Congregation of Miskolc for the Aid Organization. Where is your men's money today?! If you break down the boards, maybe they will shoot, but possibly return the streets—otherwise certainly not. There isn't a difference, in the end there will be the deportation." I said this in great agitation, but Löw remained by the "madness" and they willy-nilly put up with having two less streets.

The negotiations of Kasztner-Brand with Krumey assumed concrete forms after the delivery of the 200,000 dollars and had been taken over by Eichmann. Kasztner asked as a first step, to permit *Aliya* (emigration) to *Eretz Israel* for the 700, mostly in possession of, or waiting for, a Palestine Certificate. Eichmann declared an *Aliyah* inadmissible with regard to the Mufti of Jerusalem, who was, for the time being, in Berlin and had offered his friendship to the Nazis. At the same time a new plan emerged: to let the whole Hungarian Jewry emigrate against adequate delivery of goods to be determined. Though it seemd to be a new form of the Europa Plan it is not plausible that its originator had been Eichmann. The Economic Department of the SS with Becher at its helm, belonging directly under the *Reichsführungsamt* of Himmler, made every effort to secure delivery of certain goods of which Germany was in dire need, owing to the heavy bombardments of their industrial centers. Owing to this pressure, Eichmann was ready to offer "blood for goods" and later on even exclaimed, "I'll give you 100 Jews for every LKW!" (lorry).

The emigration of the 700 was finally promised in the form of a "Spanish Transport." Eichmann said that he was willing to transport them to the Spanish frontier, with the destination to be South America. "And what the ship will do on the high seas is not my business," that is, even if it turned toward Palestine he was covered in regard to the Mufti.

Although the final destination of this eventual transport was more than doubtful, it was drawn up by Kasztner as an *Aliya* and accordingly belonged to the Zionist organization. At a whole night session they distributed the places among the several factions and it was also agreed to allocate, for "Freudiger and his people," 20 places. Two or three days later Kasztner and Brand came to me and informed me about the entire activity, including the resolution to give me 20 places, which I categorically refused. I told them that it wasn't an *Aliya* but a "Spanish Transport," the permission for it induced by the 200,000 dollars collected by the Council, so the distribution of the places would have to be done by the Council as well. Apart from this, they should have taken into consideration that the Orthodox Jews constituted half of the Jewish population in the whole country, and in Budapest alone, more than 10 percent; for such a ridiculous allocation I was not ready to participate, and they had to assume the whole responsibility. The next day I was informed by them that, according to a new resolution, there was to be at my disposition 20 places more for Orthodox Jews from the country and 20 more for our refugees, and besides this sixty, "Freudiger and his family" are ex-quota. Our *Hatzala* Committee resolved to accept this proposition, *faute-de-mieux*.

During the second week of May I received news from Rabbi Weissmandl to the effect that an agreement had been reached between the Slovakian and Hungarian railway authorities concerning the transit of 310,000 people to Nazi-occupied Poland. That meant that the deportation was about to begin! A heated debate took place in the Council about the reliability of this information. After considerable efforts, Dr. Pető managed to talk to Minister of Finance Lajos Reményi-Schneller in his private flat. The Minister had, in previous times, been a member of the

Board of Directors of a bank together with Dr. Pető. The Minister stated firmly that there was no question whatsoever of the deportation of the Jews. Even if Jews were being concentrated in special areas, and if Jews capable of labor would eventually be taken to work, this would only happen within the borders of the country! Meanwhile my brother Samuel tried to find out from a former Chief Inspector of the Railway Directorate whether the news of Rabbi Weissmandl was correct. This Chief Inspector was Jewish and as a result of the anti-Jewish edicts was pensioned prematurely but still had access to his former colleagues. On May 14, he informed us that the previous week a high ranking delegation had been in Bratislava for negotiations with the Slovakian management, but he couldn't find out about what. On the 15th I put this information before the Council and insisted that Weissmandl was right, no matter what Reményi-Schneller had stated. President Stern wanted to make inquiries at the Jewish Department of the Ministry. Dr. Pető made a call to the Ministry, asking for Zsigmond Székely-Molnár and was told by his secretary that Székely-Molnár was not in his office but went to the Railway Management. We couldn't hear what was said on the phone but saw Dr. Pető suddenly turn ashen, and in his agitation, could hardly replace the receiver. "It seems that Weissmandl's letter is true" he said—and so it was! Next day the deportation started in Munkács . . . .

It took some time for the news to reach us, mainly through some well-meaning Christians. The transfer from the ghettos to the wagons was carried out by the Hungarian gendarmarie with inhuman brutality. At the slightest resistance people were beaten, whipped, bayonetted, even shot. All their belongings were taken, a bodily search was carried out on many, and women were undressed for this purpose. The sick, the recently operated, mothers after childbirth with the babies, the deranged, all were herded into the wagons, 70-80 persons per wagon, which had a capacity for only 36. (The legend on these freight cars was generally known: "36 persons or 6 horses.") A deportation train consisted of 45 wagons; 3,200 to 3,500 Jews in all.

The conduct of the gendarmerie was the same in all places. In Nyíregyháza, Alexander (Sándor) Németi, President of the Orthodox Congregation, was beaten to a pulp because he protested against the transport and —at the third phase of the deportation—the President of the Orthodox Congregation of Debrecen, Eugene (Jenő) Bernfeld, was shot on the spot while arguing that there was an order to send him to Budapest—and that was true. People had become anyway broken and spiritless through the weeks they had spent in the ghettos or crammed into empty brick factories. "Happen what may, it cannot possibly be worse than it's now," they thought. (No one had an idea about Auschwitz at that time.) Thus no largescale resistance was ever thought of; also the men between 18 and 50 had mostly been away in the labor service companies and absent.

At the beginning of May, a meeting took place near Lake Balaton between Endre and Eichmann with his staff to discuss the technicalities of the deportation which at this time was agreed for the 310,000. Wisliceny suggested sending a train with 3200 people per day, as he had done it in Slovakia. For Endre this was not sufficient; he demanded 6 trains daily with 20,000 Jews in all. The department of transportation of the SS was under *Hauptsturmführer* Novak, consisting of 220 men. Wisliceny explained to Endre that this was just enough to load one train a day, escort it to Auschwitz and bring it back. "I will give you 5,000 gendarmes if necessary, but I want 20,000 a day. I want to finish the whole thing in a fortnight," said Endre, and in the end Eichmann decided that four trains would roll daily. The meeting ended with a wild drinking bout.

All this Wisliceny—who had to leave Budapest at Eichmann's order at the end of April to be the commander of the deportation detachment—told me when I managed to reach him in his Swabian Hill villa on his return around the 10th of June, after completion of the deportation of the 310,000. "The Hungarians really seem to be the offspring of the Huns," he said, relating to the gendarmes who did the loading, "we would never have succeeded in this way without them."

On May 14, Dr. Kasztner wanted to tell us something urgently. Leopold Blau, Julius Link and I met him in my office and he told us that Eichmann decided to send Joel Brand to Istanbul where he should arrange the delivery of 10,000 trucks and he was ready to give 100 Jews for every truck, i.e., one million Jews.

We were quite nonplussed and beyond ourselves at this news. "How can you imagine that the Allies will give, or even allow, the delivery of 10,000 trucks to the Germans? That is absolutely impossible!," I told Kasztner. "The President of the Orthodox Congregation is not a Zionist and doesn't know what the Zionists can attain through their men in Istanbul, from Henry Morgenthau and others," he answered me. "I am no Zionist and so

I do know what they cannot attain." Link interposed: "Brand is not the appropriate person for such a mission. To attain something from the Americans someone with an official standing and a name should go, like President Stern, Budai-Goldberger, or Freudiger, but not Brand." "Why don't you go? That would be better by far," asked Blau.

Though Brand had our full esteem for his *Hatzala* activities, Dr. Kasztner was a person of quite another caliber, with considerable qualities and special aptness for political activities. Always ready to take upon himself any danger, he had dictatorial inclinations and was a party politician by all means. A man of large conceptions, but a bohemian without any interest for, and understanding of, affairs involving economics or administration, of distressing unpunctuality concerning appointments or terms.

Kasztner admitted that they did not have the possibility to choose or propose the envoy; Eichmann decided that Brand should go and so Brand had to go. He asked me to arrange with President Stern to give Brand a letter of accreditation. When I spoke to Stern about this, he agreed to give Brand such a letter in the name of the Central Council, but insisted that it should be signed by me too.

To my question why he didn't keep the Council or at least us three informed about the negotiations with Krumey, or Eichmann respectively, taking this turn, he gave evasive answers; at any case the fact couldn't be changed any more, we had to accept it.

The Brand mission is too well known that it should be necessary to relate about it here; it is only the final episode which may be of interest.

July 19-20, Wisliceny was in Bratislava; it was two months already after the journey of Brand, who didn't return; he was arrested and held by the British. Nevertheless, the negotiations with the SS went on and Kasztner tried to assert that the goods agreed upon were coming and quite unexpectedly there was an announcement on the English radio about the mission of Brand, concluding that although it was asserted that the lorrys wouldn't be used on the western front, His Majesty's Government had to take into consideration its eastern ally too and could not but refuse it. Hearing this, Wisliceny said that all further negotiations seemed to have no sense any more, but Rabbi Weissmandl found his way promptly and interpreted the announcement as a proof of the success of Brand arguing that, after two months of silence, the British did now find it necessary to inform everyone concerned by an official radio-announcement, because they intended to accede to the request secretly. Wisliceny accepted this more or less and I shall come back to this later on.

As soon as the Council learned about the beginning of the deportation, I went to Krumey asking him for particulars and was told by him that they were taken for work, as the German men being in the army, there was in Germany an acute shortage of workers. "Children and old people for work?," whereupon Krumey tried to explain to me, that psychologically it had a conducive effect to the working capacity of the men if they were together with their families. "Where did the trains go?" "To Waldsee." The next day I was again at Krumey and told him that I had a very detailed map of Germany, but couldn't find Waldsee; where is it? "Waldsee is in Thüringen and from there they are distributed to several places," and that was that, I had no possibility to continue the questioning.

After approximately two weeks, Krumey sent with one of his liaison-officials a package with several hundred postcards written by the deported Jews, with the order to forward them to the addressees. The cards were all dated from Waldsee and consisted of more or less the same message: I am well, going to work, what's news from home, etc., and signature. We didn't believe in Krumey's information about Waldsee, but reading these cards, involuntarily one thought: maybe . . . .

After Koltay had exacted some 2,000 flats and many of these remained empty, as there were not so many Christians made homeless by the air raids, he conceived a new claim and sent a list of 224 persons, ordering the Council to call in these men to the Rabbinical Seminary—which was now in the hands of the Hungarian Gestapo—for the next morning, with 50 kg. baggage.

This order caused a prolonged debate in the Council. The first reaction was to refuse it, but later on the opinion prevailed that Koltay could take all the persons easily with his policemen to the Seminary and it was only his sadism that he wanted the Council to do it. On the other hand, it was surely more humane if the concerned were informed by a messenger of the Council and not taken away immediately by a rude cop. I hoped also that upon receiving the summons to be next morning at the Seminary there might be many a one who wouldn't turn up, disappearing somewhere

instead. Unfortunately, this was not the case, and only a very few chose
this way.

The first list was a mixed one of better-known personalities, and afterwards he sent several other ones, which were specialized; one contained
newspapermen and authors, two or three, lawyers. From the Seminary,
they came to an internment camp on the Csepel Isle, to Horthy-Liget, and
most of them were in the end deported.

On the first list of lawyers, I found the name of my own lawyer, Dr.
Dach, and though it was a grave risk, I could not but warn him. I went in
the evening to him and told his wife that it might be prudent if her husband wouldn't sleep at home that night. She understood immediately why
I came to see them (he fainted meanwhile) and complying with my advice,
he immediately after I left them contacted his cousin who was a physician working in the largest mental hospital and arranged for his immediate
acceptance there. He remained there a few weeks, and when he returned,
the lists were not timely any more.

On the next list I saw the names of several lawyers known to me, but
didn't venture to do something, as at the previous occasion I had a narrow escape and if I got caught I endangered the whole Council. But when
I came from the Council to my office and found there one of the lawyers,
Dr. Frank, sitting with our director, Edmond (Ödön) Stern, I couldn't
resist and made a sign to Mr. Stern that I wanted to speak to him. I told
him to hint cautiously to Dr. Frank about the coming night, which he did
and I saw Dr. Frank leaving shortly afterwards. To my greatest astonish-
ment, half an hour later, his father-in-law, a well-known pediatrician,
came to me in great excitement and told me that his son-in-law wanted
to disappear from home, owing to the information he got from here, but
he could not allow this because with his disappearance he would endanger
his wife and child who would be at home and might be taken instead of
him. A man when he is called, has to go and not run away, etc. I was quite
perplexed and told him bluntly that being an associate professor did not
give him the right to prevent his son-in-law from saving himself and it was
less than probable that Mr. Koltay would check the lists whether one person was missing and call his wife instead, but if he did fear it, then the wife
should disappear together with her husband. All this couldn't convince him,
and when he left angrily, I was really afraid that now it would crash.

A few weeks later, I learned that Dr. Frank remained at home and put huge plaster casts on both his legs and when the messenger of the Council came, he showed him that he couldn't obey the order as both his legs were broken, which was duly reported by the messenger. He had to play this act for a few weeks, and in the meantime, this action of Koltay petered out.

The first phase of the deportations lasted till the 6th of June; in three weeks more than 300,000 Jews were deported. After an interval of several days, the second phase started: the eastern and southeastern parts of Hungary, which were at the beginning of the war taken from Romania and reunited with Hungary. Afterwards came the pure-Hungarian territories, with centers first Debrecen, then Szeged, Komárom, including the environs of Budapest, and as last one, Szombathely, with the whole West-Hungary. All this was finished on July 7th. On June 28th, 1600 gendarmes, who had been working for the deportation-commando, came to Budapest; but in the meantime, it was the turn of West-Hungary.

Based on Eichmann's decision to allow the transfer of family members of the Council to Budapest, Kasztner asked permission to bring 300 people from the ghetto of his town, Kolozsvár (Cluj), to Budapest. At first, Eichmann didn't want to hear about such a large number, but in the course of the negotiations for the delivery of goods, Kasztner managed to obtain his consent and was taken by Wisliceny into the ghetto there to arrange the transfer. I learned about the whole thing one morning while going to the Majestic to ask something from Krumey. I met there Ernő Szilágyi, the leader of the *Hashomer-Hatzair* and a prominent member of the Zionist executive, who seemed happy to see me there. He told me that Kasztner and Hansi, the wife of Joel Brand, who had taken over the work of her husband after he had gone to Istanbul, had been detained the day before and nobody knew by whom and where they were and therefore he had to present to Krumey the "list of 300." He was very astonished to hear that I didn't know anything about the list and told me the whole story, asserting that he took it for granted that Kasztner kept us well-informed, and begged me to hand over the list to Krumey as he didn't know him personally. He asked me also whether I was not interested to include some persons onto the list, he was ready to change it accordingly. I told him that it wasn't a private affair of mine, I had to con-

sult my *Vaad-Hatzala* or maybe the Council, but in any case, our stand-
point was to ask for the Rabbi and president of the Congregation; moreover, I had heard that the Rabbi of Szatmár, Joel Teitelbaum, had been
caught a few days earlier attempting to flee to Romania and had been put
into the Kolozsvár ghetto and if he and his fellow-Zionists would in-
sert such a man into their list, that would be a correct thing to do. In
any case, I was ready to go to Krumey whenever he wanted it, even with
him together. The next day we went to Krumey with the list that I didn't
check; but when the transport was brought to Budapest, I saw that Szilágyi did everything I had spoken about the day before at the Majestic.

Kasztner and Hansi Brand returned after a few days, at Krumey's intervention. It was the Hungarians who wanted to elicit from them their connections with the SS; they were questioned for hours and even maltreated.
When everything was arranged, Kasztner asked from President Stern a
place for the 300, which would serve as an internment camp of the Council under protection by the SS. This became known as the Columbus-camp,
situated in the former Institute for the Blind and Deaf on Columbus
Street.

I received quite regularly mail from Bratislava, mainly from Rabbi Weissmandl and also from Nicholas (Miklós) Sternfeld, a friend of mine who
worked for the *Hatzala* there. In the beginning of June, about the 8th
or 10th, the courier of the Hungarian Embassy who arrived from Bratislava with the evening express train, brought me a bulky package containing many letters and even passports from South American states to
convey them to the addressees, who were unfortunately all deported already. I found also a report of several pages of the statement of two Jews
who had miraculously succeeded in escaping from Auschwitz, and now
described with all the details what was going on in Auschwitz, the particulars about the gas-chambers, giving a minute list of when and how many
people were gassed—Jews, gypsies, etc., 1,750,000 in all—ending that the
gas chambers had now been put in good repair for the awaited Hungarian
Jews.

Having read the protocol to this end I got a shock; I sat stunned for
hours until at last my wife helped me up. The next morning, I took this
protocol to the Council and showed it to a few of the members who were
all desperate to learn that all declarations and assurances of the Ministry

and the SS were deceit and falsehood. We decided—unofficially—to spread this protocol and bring it to the knowledge of the more-or-less humane personalities of Hungarian society, politicians, etc. That took some time, but it had its results. M.P.'s, bishops, even Horthy (through his son) got it, and the passivity with which the actions of Endre-Eichmann had up until then been viewed, began to become less and less. Dr. György Polgár, the leader of the MIPI, had a great share in the distribution of the Protocol, and the manager of the Palestine Office, Nicholas (Moshe, Miklós) Krauss, who was in contact with the Legation of Switzerland and with a certain division of the Ministry of Foreign Affairs, succeeded on June 19th to send it to Switzerland too.

The copying of the Protocol and the preliminary work I organized with a few young officials of the Council, with the consent of Stern, Kahan-Frankl, Pető, Wilhelm, but rather secretly; for the work within the Council had already been for weeks not as it had been in the beginning. On the 8th of May, the original Council nominated by the *Sondereinsatzkommando* had been dissolved by the Ministry of the Interior and a new one nominated quite officially. From the first one remained the above-mentioned four and I, and, as new members, were nominated Lajos Stöckler, Dr. József Nagy, Dr. Béla Berend and János Gábor (up till then, our liaison-official), and later on, even a member for the converted: Dr. Sándor Török. The relation to the new members was not the same and with a certain caution. That this precaution was not out of place I learned after quite a short time. Dr. Emil Bärtl, former secretary of the Upper House, had now been assigned to work in the Jewish Department with Zoltán Bosnyák. He was on very good relations with my brother Samuel and asked quasi for his and my assent to accept this assignment, wanting it for an alibi for himself, promising that he would inform us about everything. We heard then from him that they were informed in the Department about what was going on at the sessions of the Council, telling us even how they got this information. From this time on it was arranged gradually that at the meetings of the Council in the forenoons the administrative and similar matters would be handled; all serious and important ones would be discussed by the four of us in the afternoon, privately. Later on, I didn't even participate at the official sessions, as my presence was not needed for the matters discussed there and I had many other things to do.

The Protocol made a tremendous impression on everyone, and under its influence, three young officials of the Council, Miss Erzsébet Eppler, László Pető and György Gergely, came to me one evening to discuss the possibility of organizing some kind of resistance. I told them straightaway that, though I appreciated that they had come to my lodging quite privately, I didn't think that I was capable of such work; they could get two things from me: alibi and money. I was ready to take full responsibility for them, vis-a-vis President Stern, and I had money at my disposal which had no connection with the Council. I advised them to speak with Szilágyi, who had very good contacts with the Social Democrats; maybe the workers could be attracted to this idea. A few days later, I heard from them that Szilágyi did his best to bring the Social Democrats to some action, but without success; the motivation was that their leading personality, Árpád Szakasits, had been arrested and the workers were intimidated. Our trio tried other ways, too, but had to give up in the end.

The money I had promised, if necessary, was based on the information we had received in April already from the HIJEFS (*Hilfsverein für jüdische Flüchtlinge im Auslände;* Society for the Aid of Refugees Abroad)—an organization set up by a few Swiss Orthodox Jews, like Mr. Yitzhak Sternbuch from Montreux (his wife Recha was well-known for her activity on behalf of the *Hatzala*-work), Messrs. Rand, Rubinfeld, etc.—that one million Swiss francs were at our disposal for *Hatzala* purposes, naming Julius Link as their trustee. We were of the opinion that a resistance work belonged to the conception of *Hatzala.*

At about the middle of June, skimming through a pack of Waldsee cards, sent by Krumey for distribution to the addressees—most of them deported already—I found one with the date erased by india rubber and Waldsee written thereon. As customary with textile manufacturers, I had a thread counter with magnifying glass in my pocket and with the help of it I could make out the letters "witz" engraved by the hard pencil into the card and quite readable even after erased. The next morning, I went to Krumey and told him that Waldsee was in reality Auschwitz, where the Jews were annihilated. "That isn't true, how can you assert such a thing?" said Krumey to me. "Please, *Herr Obersturmbannführer,* look for yourself," I said and gave him the card and the magnifying glass. Krumey viewed the rectified date and then said to me, "Freudiger, I know you for a clever man; you shouldn't see everything!" Though said in quite a calm voice, the threat was obvious, but to my luck it had no consequences.

One week later—about the 25th of June—I too received such a Waldsee card, written by Joseph and Samuel Stern, the brothers of our manager, Mr. Edmond Stern. They wanted in the first days of June to arrange an escape to Romania with wives and children, but the SS man who should have brought them there in his truck, against a huge sum, instead took them to the next deportation center. From the deportation wagon, they tossed a picture postcard of two of their children with an S.O.S. message for me; the card was found by someone humane and deliverd to my address. Now they wrote me from Auschwitz and signed the standard message: Joseph *R'evim* (Hebrew for hungry) and Samuel *Blimalbish* (without clothing). I didn't show Krumey this card, remembering his former threat and the Waldsee-fiction having been dropped in the meantime.

At the beginning of June, the ghettoization of Budapest had been enacted; the execution thereof enjoined the Council. There prevailed, generally, the idea that the Allied bombers did not raid the parts of the city where Jews resided, and it was therefore inopportune to make the greatest part of the town *Judenrein* by concentrating the Jews in a ghetto; it was decided to create "Jewish Houses" spread about the whole city. These houses would be for Jews only; the Christians residing there had to vacate their lodgings and change to the lodgings vacated by the Jews. The Council drew up a plan to lodge the approximately 200,000 Jews in 3,500 houses, within six weeks. Endre wrote on the document: "2,500 houses, two days." With great effort, the Council attained to increase the houses to 2,700 and a few days more for the execution, which took place between the 16th and 21st of June. The "Jewish Houses" had a large yellow star on their street doors, which had to be closed except during the few hours when it was permitted for Jews to move in the streets.

Before the second phase of the deportations began on June 10, Wisliceny came for a few days to Budapest, and he did so between the other phases too, which lasted only four to five days. I strived at every such occasion to seize him and pleaded again and again to send from the ghettos to the Columbus Camp as many as possible. In some places I gave him a list of names, in some places I asked generally. He never answered my entreaties, but from Nagyvárad, Debrecen, Sopron, Pápa, Székesfehérvár, and formerly from Kassa and Nyíregyháza, he sent me approximately 80 persons, who were all rescued, thank God.

Calling on Wisliceny at his lodgings, I remembered the advice my Polish refugees gave me, and as he didn't smoke, I used to bring him bonbons. It was only that these boxes of sweets contained not only bonbons, but pieces of our family jewels, too; a string of pearls, a brooch of diamonds, a.s.o., a gold watch, and when I had no more jewels, then 50,000 *pengő* once and again. I gave him the little package when leaving, not mentioning its contents, that it shouldn't look like a *quid pro quo*. Wisliceny accepted it likewise; only once he told me at the next encounter, "the bonbons were good." My Poles were right, it was worthwhile.

Dr. Kasztner succeeded in getting the permission to include the 300 men he brought from Kolozsvár into the "Transport to Spain"—or *Aliya* to Palestine, as he called it—and 100 persons more, against payment of 10 million *pengős:* all in all 1,200 persons. Dr. Kasztner, together with the leaders of the Zionist parties, began with the organization of the transport in the offices of Síp Street 12. An enormous rush began; having the character of an *Aliya*, it caused a competition beyond all limits. Heart-rending scenes took place there; a howling, screaming, pushing crowd, filled up the corridors leading to "Room 18," where the commission was sitting. Several members of this commission, Dr. Ottó Komoly, president of the Zionist Organization, Ernő Szilágyi, Sándor Offenbach, etc., made superhuman efforts, worked day and night to compile the list of the participants.

The work of our commission was easier by far. We had only 60 places at our disposal and these also for certain categories, divided by three. From the 100 places, which cost 100,000 *pengős* each, Dr. Kasztner was ready to give us as many as we wanted for our people who had the possibility and were willing to pay this sum. Children under 12 were not taken into account and their age was not examined minutely and this was also an alleviation.

Although according to the arrangement with Kasztner "Freudiger and his family" were ex-quota, it was against the principles of my brother-in-law, Leopold Blau, in the moment when there was the possibility to get places for money, and so he did not accept them, but paid for two places for himself and my sister. I for myself hesitated, then, on June 16, Dr. Tatușescu, a lawyer from Bucharest, called on me and brought me a letter from my friend Eugene (Jenő) Meisner (his wife was our cousin) telling me that he was sending Dr. Tatuşescu to see in what way he could help us. Dr. Tatuşescu had the best relations in Bucharest; in 1942-1943, he was very helpful in getting the permissions for the transit of the children-transports to Palestine and he worked also for the Joint there. He called on me at the offices of the Council and the next day we met at home; Joseph Blum from the Joint was also present. After discussing several possibilities, we agreed that he should try to obtain 500 entry-permits, having heard at my last meeting with Wisliceny that Romanian and Finnish Jews might be repatriated into their homeland, which was also under German control. Blum assured the lawyer that his fees and expenses would be paid for by the Joint and Tatuşescu promised to return as soon as possible; but we didn't hear from him after then and didn't know what to expect.

I saw that all Zionist leaders, except Dr. Komoly and Kasztner, registered, and most of the notables of the Neolog community, too, and they all took it for granted that I too would go with the transport, so I told Dr. Kasztner on the 25th of June to put me and my family on the list. I had to decide, as the departure was planned for the end of that week. All the participants, especially the refugees and all those whose papers were not in order were accommodated in the Columbus Camp and, when this was filled up, in an auxiliary camp in the Ménesi Road, also under SS guard, which meant an absolute protection against the Hungarians.

On the afternoon of the 28th, I received a message that Wisliceny wanted to see me in the evening at his *pied-à-terre* in town. That was a vacated Jewish flat, which he used when he felt bored at the Swabian Hill and wanted some distraction. When I went to him he told me straighaway that I could not go with the transport, that my name was cancelled from the list. The decision to go with the transport had been a difficult one for me, but now I was exasperated because of the refusal. My protests and supplications were without avail; Wisliceny told me that Eichmann did not allow Council members to depart and that was that. "Put your whole clan onto the transport and you with your wife and children remain," he told me. In my excitement I told him that if he prevented me and my little family to save ourselves, he was responsible for our lives. "Alright, I will take care of you," he answered.

So I had to remain in Budapest, and my mother, my brother Samuel and his wife and my cousin David—they all were now living in my mother's flat, in the same house as I—decided that they would remain, too. All the people admitted to the transport were ordered to be in the Columbus Camp on the 29th or in the Ménesi Camp respectively and spend the night there, as the boarding of the wagons had been stipulated for the next forenoon. But the next forenoon there was an air raid alarm, and so the transportation of the people from the Columbus Camp toward the railway station began only at noon. Later on an SS sergeant escorted the people from the Ménesi Road, six to seven hundred men, of which approximately 500 had to be transferred to the Columbus Camp and 200 or so to the station; but he came first to the station. Arriving there, not only the 200 who were admitted to the transport, but all, remained there and, after some difficulty, could board the wagons. (There were some people among those already placed in the wagons who protested against placing 10 to 15 more people in each wagon!) A week before it had almost come to fist fights for a place in this transport and in the end several hundred people went with it who never hoped to be admitted. . . . All in all, 1706 people went with this transport, which didn't go to the Spanish frontier as promised, but which after much excitement and perils arrived in Bergen-Belsen. They had to endure much suffering there, but 300 of them were sent to Switzerland at the end of August, and the remaining 1,400 at the beginning of December. Three people died (normally) and four babies were born in Bergen-Belsen.

When the second phase of the deportations (Transylvania) started, Dr. Kasztner pleaded with Eichmann to halt the deportations, arguing that there should be Jews to barter when Brand returned from his mission. Eichmann didn't accept this; he said that instead the thumb screw had to be applied, otherwise International Jewry would not be willing to deliver the wanted goods. He was nevertheless ready "to put some 15,000 Jews on ice" in any case, and to send them to Strasshof in Austria. So it came that five transports from Debrecen, Szeged, Békéscsaba, were sent to Strasshof and nearly all of the people in these returned, thank God, except the few who died or were killed by accidents or bombings. These transports were already in Strasshof and that was also the reason why the SS commander did not allow the 1,700 to be brought there till the continuation of their dispatch to the West could be arranged and in the meantime they were sent to Bergen-Belsen.

As a partial payment for this transport, the Economic Department of the SS, under *Obersturmbannführer* Kurt Becher, received cash, foreign exchange money, 18 kilograms gold and 180 carat diamonds. They claimed 1,000 to 2,000 dollars per person and wanted the remainder in goods; an integral part of these was the delivery of thirty tractors. These were purchased in Switzerland and Kasztner gave instructions to open the necessary accreditations. It was urgent, as after the delivery of the tractors, negotiations for a second transport could have begun. Dr. Kasztner asked Saly Mayer in St. Gallen, plenipotentiary representative of the Joint in Europe, to give two million Swiss francs to a trustee in order to pay for the purchases against this sum. But quite shortly the answer from Mr. Mayer arrived that Kasztner had no more funds at his disposal and it was only after a substantial delay that we were informed that there was money available, but that it was not permitted to be used for the purchase of goods.

In view of the precarious situation of the transport, the fate of which might have been connected with the delivery of goods, particularly the delivery of the tractors, these were accredited from private means (Julius Link). When Saly Mayer gained intelligence about this, he threatened to suspend all payments in the event that the tractors would actually be delivered. Kasztner had to find all kinds of subterfuges, and as the hope of Brand's return had to be abandoned by this time, he tried to persuade Becher than one of his staff should travel with him to Switzerland to have a parley there with Jewish representatives about the bargin: Jews against goods.

The political situation in Hungary slowly began to become unfavorable toward the Germans. The successful invasion in Normandy, the great losses of the Hungarians in the Ukraine, the frequent and regularly-repeated air raids and the more and more numerous call-ups were conducive to an anti-German mood. The official propaganda lost much of its validity; the Auschwitz Protocols gained credence. The King of Sweden sent a letter to Horthy in which, appealing to the chivalrous spirit of an Austro-Hungarian Admiral, he demanded discontinuation of the deportations. The Swiss Ambassador Maximilain Jäger delivered an ultimatum from President

Roosevelt on June 27th in which the immediate halting of the deportations was demanded, for otherwise Hungary would be treated as no other
civilized nation had ever been treated. The Hungarian government did not
respond to this ultimatum which expired on June 29th, and on July 2nd
Budapest experienced an exceptionally heavy air raid by American bombers; this time not against factories on the outskirts of town, but against the
city proper. There were hundreds of casualties, and unfortunately, the
buildings where the American citizens were interned were also hit and
ninety-five people were killed.

The government did not, but Horthy responded to Jäger and declared
that after the 7th of July there would be no more deportations. In fact,
the deportations of the Jews of Western Hungary (the last phase) was
terminated on July 7th; there only remained Jews in Budapest and in the
internment camps of Kistarcsa and Sárvár.

During the air raid of July 2, our house was also hit by a bomb and
my cousin Denys (David), who did not go down to the shelter in the
basement but remained in my mother's flat, was torn to pieces. The house
had to be evacuated and we moved to the old-age home of the Orthodox
Congregation which was at the foot of the Swabian Hill.

According to the plan the deportation-commando should have removed
its seat to Budapest on July 7. Budapest was surrounded by troops of
gendarmes; abut 1,600 had been brought to Budapest on June 27-28 and
billetted. During several days it was said: now our deportation would begin!
But the till then smoothly running deportation apparatus suddenly began
to stagnate. Horthy took a firm position against further deportations, according to the answer he gave. At a cabinet meeting, without Endre and
Baky, it was decided accordingly.

Endre and Baky wanted to carry out a *putsch,* based on the gendarmerie, allegedly devoted to Baky, and with the help of Eichmann.
But the opposite side was not idle either. General Károly Lázár, commander of Horthy's bodyguards, with the cooperation of other high-
ranking officers of the army, ordered an air raid alarm to be sounded,
which lasted for several hours. During this time, tanks and armored vehicles
took position at strategically important points of the town. Baky was
taken into custody at his lodging; Endre suddenly made a journey to
Germany. Upon the insistence of the Germans, both of them remained in

their official positions, but the Jewish affairs were taken away from them and given to the charge of Gendarmerie Colonel Ferenczy.

Ferenczy had been the commander of the 5,000 gendarmes that Endre put at Eichmann's disposal to assist with the execution of the deportation which they carried out with the greatest brutality. Ferenczy too excelled in baiting Jews, but entered immediately into a changed course and went over to the new line of the government. Both the gendarmerie and the police, which up till then had been under the control of the Ministry of the Interior, were transferred to the Defense Ministry and Minister Lajos Csatay was not a friend to the Germans!

An embittered struggle began between the Germans and the Hungarian side. For Eichmann the deportation of Budapest's Jews became a question of prestige and had to be carried out at any price. He pushed the matter to a trial of strength. On July 14, *Hauptsturmführer* Novak presented himself with his SS men at the internment camp in Kistarcsa and put 1,500 Jews into wagons to send them via Budapest-Hatvan to Auschwitz.

We had some inkling that something might happen in Kistarcsa, as the commander of the camp, Police-Major István Vasdényei, one of the few right-minded police officers, asked through Dr. Ernő Bródy, a Council official, on the 12th of July for "dry provision" for 1,500 persons and we guessed that this was in connection with the transport. The moment the Council had been informed of what had happened in Kistarcsa, it made the greatest effort to reach Horthy and when he heard through his son that in spite of his decision a deportation train was rolling off, he sent his adjutant to the shunting station with the order to stop the train there or to prevent its leaving the country. The adjutant succeeded and the train was sent back to Kistarcsa.

Great exultation prevailed at the Council. It was the first time that we succeeded in obstructing a deportation and in saving 1,500 Jews! Alas, the joy did not last long.

On the morning of the 19th we received an order from *Hauptsturmführer* Hunsche that the whole Council had to report immediately at the Majestic. We all went there together and, upon the request of President Stern, I went to Hunsche to report that we had arrived and also told him that Dr. Kasztner had again disappeared and asked for help in locating him. When Hunsche heard that one member, Dr. Béla Berend, was not present

—he was not at the office when we got the order—he demanded, first of
all, that he be brought there, too. In the meantime, we had to wait. Berend
arrived at about 11 o'clock; Hunsche said a few words to us and let us wait
again. Stern and a few others began to get nervous about the rather enig-
matic situation. I tried to ease their minds by telling them that if Eichmann had wanted to arrest us, it would not have been necessary to put on
this act since he could have had his SS men take each one of us from our
homes at night. I told them that Hunsche's intentions would be revealed
in due course.

At about noon, I went to Hunsche again and told him that President
Stern did not feel well; we had had nothing to eat or drink. He sent for
a cup of coffee and a slice of bread with butter for President Stern; the
others did not get anything.

At about 3:00 p.m., he took us into his office and gave us a lecture
—with several interruptions of half to three quarters of an hour apiece—on
how the lives of the Jews should be organized in the future. This sounded
most peculiar, as there were no more Jews in Hungary except in Budapest,
and after awhile Stern asked him if and when the Jews would return that
his teaching might be realized. Hunsche did not answer but continued with
his performance. After 6 o'clock I called his attention to the fact that members of the Council were only allowed on the streets until 8 p.m. and
it would take a while for us to get to our homes. "Don't be troubled by
this. You will be accompanied by my men; each one of you" was his
response, and then he returned to his tale. Shortly afterwards, his telephone rang; he answered it, but went immediately into the adjoining office and spoke from there. We heard only when he said, "Then everything
is settled, O.K." and returning to us he said, without finishing the last
sentence that the telephone call had interrupted, "You can go now;
there is enough time till 8."

I was the first one to arrive home, the old-age home was the nearest
to the Swabian Hill, so I phoned the Council office immediately where
they were glad that we were safe, but I was told that Novak had come
to Kistarcsa again during the day, this time with trucks, and had loaded
the Jews on them and had headed directly to the Slovakian frontier
where the Jews were put into wagons and sent to Auschwitz. Novak and
his helpmate Lemmke locked Vasdényei in his office, disconnected his

telephone and demanded that the 1,500 people who had been returned the last time be loaded onto the trucks. Vasdényei had in the meantime sent 280 of these to Sárvár, so Novak demanded that 280 others be loaded to complete the 1,500, and it was only after a protracted argument with Vasdényei that Novak consented to take only 1,220.

Now it was clear. The Council was ordered to report to Hunsche and was held incommunicado for as long as it took Hunsche to receive the news that Novak and his transport were over the frontier, in order to prevent any possibility of intervention against the deportation. The next day, when I went to see Wisliceny, I met Hunsche at the Majestic. He asked me smiling: "Is Stern calmer now or is he still nervous?" "We are all nervous now" I answered.

The week before, on July 10, I went to Wisliceny at his lodgings to find out what the plans for Budapest were. He told me that no decision had been made yet and told me by the way that while he had been in Greece deporting the Jews there, every time a prominent Jew came up he produced a Spanish passport and claimed that as a citizen of Spain he was not deportable. Wisliceny immediately changed the subject. I understood this as a wink from him to me, but did not know what to do about it. The next day Dr. Tatusescu arrived. It had been impossible to get permission for the 500 that we had suggested because 130 Romanian Jews had been registered all-in-all, but he brought instructions for the Consul-General Daianu to put at his disposal 130 certificates of repatriation, according the above number, without controlling the identity of the persons. It was also necessary to arrange things with the Hungarian police (the KEOKH) and Moshe Krauss, an old acquaintance of Tatuşescu, took it upon himself to arrange for this. Dr. Tatuşescu received instructions from Eugene Meisner to bring our family and the families of his cousins, Abeles and Diamant. He also brought a letter from Dr. Ernest (Ernő) Marton to Moshe Krauss in which he suggested putting up a commission for the distribution of the other 120 places or so, consisting of President Stern, Kasztner, Krauss, and myself. Stern declared that he wasn't interested in the whole thing and didn't want to participate; Krauss had objections against Kasztner, and a few days later Kasztner disappeared anyway, so only two of us remained of the original four. We agreed that instead of having discussions about the distribution, each of us will distribute together with his collaborators, about 65 places, having consented to deduct all three families from my share.

I, for myself, had not yet made up my mind to leave Budapest, but, upon insistence from my family and bearing in mind Wisliceny's hint, I decided to have the papers prepared, in any case, for us too.

In this changed atmosphere of the first days of July, the long-continued toils of Moshe Krauss showed results. As representative of the Jewish Agency and director of the Palestine Office, he had good contacts with the relevant departments of the Ministry of Foreign Affairs and of the Swiss Consulate. He persuaded Consul Charles Lutz, who was in charge of the interests of Palestinian citizens (the British having been under the protection of the Swiss Legation since the outbreak of the war), to recognize not only those who possessed a Palestinian Immigration Certificate as Palestinian citizens, but even those who had applied for one expressing his intention to become a citizen. Consul Lutz accepted this and tried to help whenever possible.

Krauss attained through Lutz that the Swiss Embassy take an interest in a large-scale project to render possible the emigration of 4,000 Jews to Palestine via Romania and Turkey, for the present. Ambassador Jäger and Lutz took up the negotiations with the Hungarian and the German authorities. As a consequence of Horthy's mid-July declaration that provided the assistance of neutral states Hungary was willing to foster the emigration of the Jews, the Hungarian ministries showed the greatest compliance. Even Premier Döme Sztójay promised to do his best to obtain the permission from the Germans.

Several conferences had been held in the chambers of the Ministry of Foreign Affairs with the participation of Lutz, Krauss, the delegate of the German Legation Veesenmayer, Captain Horst Grell, Colonel Ferenczy, his adjutant Leó Lullay, etc. Ferenczy furthered this action with all his might. It had been decided that at first a group of 2,200 persons should be made up. They were to receive a Swiss collective-passport and travel under the protection of the International Red Cross, accompanied by the functionaries of the Red Cross and the Swiss Legation. Ferenczy promised to send an adequate force of gendarmes with the transport to ward-off any eventual foul trick of the SS at the last moment. The negotiations with the Romanian railway management were on the brink of concluding. A special envoy of the Red Cross, Mr. Robert Schirmer, was expected in Budapest for the above matter.

The representatives of Sweden decided, quite independently from this action, to rescue 2,000 Jews who had relatives or some other connections to Sweden. Raoul Wallenberg, who later met a tragic fate under the Russians to the great regret of everyone, came to see us at the Council. He arranged passports or documentation for these Jews stating that they were under Swedish protection and their names were put down for immigration to Sweden.

Krauss established his office at the later widely-known "Glass House" which served as an auxiliary building of the Swiss Embassy and was put under the Swiss flag. This house belonged to the Weiss Brothers, the greatest distributors of plate glass; two of them had emigrated to Palestine and Krauss had obtained permission to use the building for his rescue work. In this Glass House and in the many other "Swiss Houses" and "Swedish Houses" that were created later many hundreds of Jews found their haven until the liberation of Budapest.

On the counterside the action of Dr. Kasztner which was based on co-operation with the real forces of Hungary—the SS—came to a halt. The first transport of 1,700 men was still sitting in Bergen-Belsen and nobody knew for sure if and when they might reach neutral grounds. Becher demanded the promised goods, especially the tractors, and in the meantime a preliminary check, to see the status of the "account." This was not a simple matter, as all these affairs had been arranged by Kasztner in a rather bohemian way. At last he had to find some solution, and he commissioned Ing. Andreas (Bandi) Biss, Brand's cousin, to care for financial matters, and Biss tried hard to reach some lucidity and order.

Kasztner had been attacked by several persons at the entrance to his house, on the 17th or 18th of July. He was kidnapped despite his resistance. He had been detained several times before, but the SS always managed to free him. This time, however, they were unable to find any trace of him, though they tried their best.

Friday, July 21st, early in the morning, I was ordered by Wisliceny to go to his lodging. He told me the already-related episode about his meeting Rabbi Weissmandl in Bratislava and the BBC radio broadcast and that Rabbi Weissmandl used as proof of his interpretation that: "Freudiger

has 250 trucks (LKW's) at his disposal, already." Wisliceny asked if this
was so, and though it was the first time that I had heard anything about
this matter and had not one truck at my disposal, I answered affirmatively.
Wisliceny said, "I have reported to Eichmann and you will be called to
him; confirm it to him." I responded, "Well, I will go to him now." He
said, "No. He mustn't know that I have spoken to you. Go back to the
Council and wait for the call." So I returned to the city, although Wisliceny's quarters were only ten minutes from the Majestic.

Arriving at the Council, I was greeted by a great hello. Eichmann had
already called twice and had become very enraged, threatening the telephone operator with detention, if he could not locate me within an hour.
On the spot I returned to the Swabian Hill and reported directly to Eichmann. "I have information that you have 250 trucks at your disposal
for us," were his first words. "Yes, *Herr Obersturmbannführer,* I do."
"Go to Becher to arrange their delivery. See to it that he is satisfied and
you will be satisifed, too." I was rather astonished by Eichmann's words,
as he had never spoken this way to me before. I clicked my heels and
turned to go, when I suddenly remembered that Becher was not in Budapest. He had left for Berlin several days before to discuss the fate of Budapest's Jews. The day before, on July 20, there had been an attempt on
Hitler's life, and all traffic had been halted for the time being. So I told
Eichmann that as far as I knew Becher was not in his office, and I asked
him if I should not report to *Hauptsturmführer* Grüson instead. Eichmann
replied, "Wait till Becher is back again. If he isn't in his office by Tuesday,
report to me," and with this I went away.

It was about 2 p.m. when I arrived at the Council, where Dr. Wilhelm
and Dr. Pető were waiting for me. I asked Julius Link and Offenbach to
join us and we discussed what should and could be done. In Link's opinion, 250 good, second-hand trucks should be bought in Switzerland, and
he thought they could be purchased for a half-million Swiss francs or even
less. To avoid differences with Saly Mayer, as had occurred with the tractors, the trucks should be bought through the HIJEFS, bypassing the
Joint.

The next morning, Alexander (Sándor) Abeles—a friend and a member
of the family on the Tatuşescu list who was staying, in the meantime, at
the Columbus Camp—told me that during the night there had been a session of the remaining members of the Kasztner committee and that it had

been decided that it was inadmissible that "the negotiations with Becher be allowed to pass into the hands of Freudiger" and that it should be by any means worked out that Biss go to Becher. I could not believe that people with whom we had worked in best understanding would take such action and I told Abeles that he wanted to induce me into deciding to leave with him to Bucharest, but he asserted that this was the naked truth and chided me for not being able to imagine what politics can produce. It was a Saturday and, as nothing urgent was scheduled for the Council, I stayed at home. During the morning, Ottó Komoly, Hansi Brand and Offenbach came to see me at the old-age home. I immediately knew the intention of their visit; Sándor Abeles had been right! It was quite obvious that they found it rather difficult to put forward what they had to say, and they beat around the bush for a quarter of an hour or so. In the end I came to their assistance by saying that my task was not an easy one since I had never negotiated with Becher up until now, and so we decided that on Monday or Tuesday I would go together with Biss to Becher. After they departed, quite satisfied, I told my wife, "You have won. I, too, will go to Bucharest." Until then I had only wanted to send the family, something to which my wife did not consent.

But, our going to Becher together never came to be, as the next day, Sunday, Kasztner reappeared. He had been detained near Budapest—where remained unknown—and had been interrogated several times regarding his foreign relations—allegedly by people closely connected with Endre and Baky; he didn't know for certain. I gladly consented that Kasztner continue the negotiations with Becher, as he had been doing this since the beginning. I went to Wisliceny on Monday, to report my meeting with Eichmann (of which he already knew) and to report the return of Kasztner who would go to Becher regarding the 250 truck affair. Wisliceny found nothing against this, and when I got ready to leave he told me in his casual way, "Freudiger, you should go away now." He did not tell me anything more, but this warning was enough to strengthen my decision to leave.

During my testimony at the Eichmann Trial, Justice Benjamin Halevi gave me to read aloud a document written by Wisliceny in his death cell on March 25, 1947, brought to the trial by Ing. Steiner from Bratislava. This document contained polemics on Kasztner's report on the activities of his *Vaad Hatzala* and his relations with the SS, submitted by him to the first Zionist Congress after the war. Among other things, Wisliceny described how Endre had accused me before Eichmann of being the head of a Jewish conspiracy based on information he received from inner circles, and he demanded from Eichmann to attend to my "disappearance." Eichmann agreed, and it was decided that I would "depart" at the end of August, either separately or with the first deportation train, along with my family. Wisliceny came to know about this and advised me to flee.

The uncertainty about the fate of Budapest continued. Eichmann was categorically in favor of the immediate deportation, and in the meantime, his men overwhelmed the guards at the internment camp at Sárvár and the several hundred inmates were sent beyond the frontier in trucks. Becher did not share this opinion; he needed goods and was eager to squeeze out whatever he could. He resumed negotiations with Kasztner, intimating to him his readiness to come to terms about the head quota; the main point being the earliest beginning of the deliveries. Knowing that Kasztner was dependent on the consent of Saly Mayer (Joint), he deliberated on making a journey with Kasztner to Switzerland, to negotiate directly with Mayer and possibly with other representatives of "International Jewry," too. Kasztner stipulated that the 1,700 people sitting in Bergen-Belsen first be forwarded to a neutral land, possibly Switzerland. Eichmann agreed, as a gesture of goodwill, to send 500 of these to Switzerland; they could be selected in Budapest. Kasztner accepted this for the time being, but persisted with his demand that the remaining 1,200 should shortly be sent also.

One afternoon, to demonstrate his power, Eichmann ordered scores of armored cars, carriers with machine guns and SS men in full armament, to drive along the circular main roads of the town. This demonstration made a certain impression.

The preparations for Krauss's "collective passport" were in full swing. Thousands of candidates wanted to register, and even though it was not as bad as it was for the "Spanish Transport" in June, there was a mad rush on Krauss and his staff who worked in the "Glass House." We agreed with Krauss upon registering 10 percent of the 2,200 places through the Orthodox committee (according to the ratio of the two congregations in Budapest). Besides this, Gyula Link gave the greatest possible publicity to aiding everyone who needed money to flee independently, but there were almost no takers. To be registered for an official collective pass was what many strived for, but to take the risks of a clandestine border crossing upon oneself was quite another matter.

A few of us had already tried to bring Kasztner and Krauss together on a common platform. Apart from his personal animosity, Kasztner showed a firm disinclination to this as he thought it unimaginable that the SS would tolerate several thousand Jews to leave the country without a ransom when the SS intended to use them as barter for a large-scale export business. On the other hand, Krauss found it ridiculous to solicit the SS's sanction or even pay them for it, while the Hungarian government, the Swiss, the Red Cross, and so on, wanted to carry out this transport, and even the German Legation had given its assent. After much cajoling and pressure, we succeeded in drawing Kasztner's *Vaada* into common work with Krauss on this planned transport.

The collective passport was completed; two huge volumes with the pictures of 2,200 people. This time, due attention was paid not to include non-Jews, as had been the case with the Bergen-Belsen transport, when a number of converted Jews were sent with it (mostly people included in the 300 from Kolozsvár), which aroused angry feelings in many. It was provided with the Hungarian exit permit; the approval of the Germans should have been given by Grell on behalf of Veesenmayer on August 2, but it had not materialized. It was stressed by the Germans that everything had been agreed upon, and that only some formalities were delaying the fixing of the visa.

The Swedes, too, had completed their list. 640 people should have travelled first, to Sweden via Germany. The Swedes' request for an exit permit and permission for a transit through Germany had been received with much courtesy, but the railway lines in Germany were so overloaded that it was impossible to fit in non-military transports; perhaps in the near future.

The playing together of the SS and the diplomatic representatives was quite clear. Either the SS would be paid what it had demanded for all the Jews, or not one would leave Hungary! To promise what was necessary in order not to give umbrage to the more and more important neutral states, and then to protract and obstruct the execution—that was their formula. Lutz and Krauss could not but seek an intervention of the Hungarians with Veesenmayer. They did not succeed since a crisis was approaching the government. Prime Minister Sztójay was ill; several ministers had been de-missioned. Though Miklós Bonczos replaced Jaross, one could never tell if another Nazi servant would not be placed at the helm again, during the following days.

For Eichmann, the deportation of Budapest's Jews became an obsession. He threatened that if the government upheld Horthy's anti-deportation point of view, he would, in spite of it, deport all Jews within three days. This was not an empty threat, as the whole deportation commando, which had been billetted in Keszthely for more than a month, had been ordered to Budapest. Horthy allegedly gave in to Veesenmayer's pressure, as far as consenting to the deportation of certain categories of Jews, especially those who held no Hungarian citizenship.

The situation was more than tense. People kept on asking when the deportation would begin; this was the first question I was asked by officials every morning when I came to the Council. Even if the man-on-the-street, or rather, of the Jew-houses, remained passive and ready to accept whatever fate was in store for him, there was also a growing number who tried to counteract eventual deportation by leaving the houses and going into bunkers or by providing fake identity papers as Christians. The Zionist youth, from *Hashomer Hatzair* to *Mizrachi, chalutzim* or students, all began to organize themselves for this purpose, waiting for what the next day might bring.

But within Eichmann's three days, telegraphic instructions from Himmler to Winkelmann suddenly arrived, warning not to use pressure to arrive at the deportation of Budapest, if political difficulties would grow out of it. Eichmann was taken aback and wanted these instructions to remain concealed, but we learned about them through Wisliceny. Ferenczy's role was not clear. On one side it was said that his aide, Lullay, had already chosen the concentration camp sites; on the other side, he had reported what had happened until then, including Auschwitz, to the Minister of the Interior Bonczos, in such a way that this had induced the Minister to make up his mind quite decidedly against any renewal of deportation. On August 9, President Stern held a conference with Ferenczy and Lullay, Dr. Wilhelm, Kasztner, and Krauss. Ferenczy asserted that if Horthy declared being against the deportations once and for all, he would, with his 19,000 well-armed gendarmes, prevent Eichmann from executing his threats.

Himmler's instructions had been brought to Horthy's knowledge through his son—as requested by Ottó Komoly—with the result that he was again adamantly against any kind of deportation. So, the fear of the imminent beginning of the deportations subsided for the time being.

I did not participate in Stern's conference, having been occupied with the preparations for our flight, during these last days. We had to fake Romanian birth certificates, on whose basis we would be registered at the KEOKH as Romanians with right of repatriation. The Romanian Consulate was helpful (for 25,000 Swiss francs) and we received from them all the necessary forms, even official rubber stamps, and Alexander Diamant arranged everything for the three families. The certificates were naturally not for our real family names, which were too well-known in Budapest as not Romanian. We registered at the KEOKH under the name "Freund." My brother and I shaved off our beards to change our looks; however, when we went to the KEOKH to sign the protocol, the department chief, Police-Major Nándor Batizfalvy recognized me but did not react. He, on the contrary, told me before I signed with the unfamiliar name, "Be careful of the signature." Afterwards he told Krauss, who had arranged the whole matter at the KEOKH, "It is terrible how worn out Mr. Freudiger looks!"

In the meantime it turned out that the Consulate had no repatriation certificates at all and Tatuşescu went to Bucharest for a new supply. On the night of his journey, the Ministry of the Interior was bombed by Russian planes and totally burned out; Tatuşescu had to return empty-handed. Finally it was arranged with Daianu to get passports valid for one journey only and having not enough passports either, one passport for each head of family, with all other members listed therein as children, without regard to their age or real status. It looked rather quaint, children of 40 years or more and husband and wife as brother and sister, but there was no better solution. To each passport we got a *Passierschein* (permit) from the "Exit Authority" of the *Wehrmacht*, the German Military.

Dr. Kasztner, having been informed after his return about the action with Dr. Tatuşescu, remonstrated vehemently against the agreement of

Krauss with me and was again at loggerheads with him. Based on the letter of Dr. Marton, he demanded to participate at the distribution of the places. The first transport was compiled already; 30 persons, including Gyula Link and his wife and six persons who didn't belong to the families, all on account of my 65 and it was out of the question to make any changes in it. Of the members of the Council, only Dr. Wilhelm accepted my offer to arrange passports for them, and so we got one for him and his daughter. I gave my place in charge of Dr. Reiner and asked him to care for the remaining 27 of my half; at the same time I tried my best to settle the controversy between Kasztner and Krauss, but with not much success. The departure of our group was fixed for August 10, with the direct train Budapest-Bucharest.

I spoke with Wisliceny on the 9th and he told me that as it looked, Eichmann would not be able to carry out his plan, nevertheless, it was time that I "slink off." I told him about our departure planned for the next day and we agreed upon going to his lodgings the next morning. I went there together with Dr. Reiner and asked Wisliceny to accept Reiner as my deputy and to continue with the information and so on, through him, which Wisliceny promised to do. I told him also that from then on Dr. Reiner would dispose with our connections abroad and he could rely on him in everything.

After Dr. Reiner left, I asked Wisliceny to give our transport an escort, and told him that I felt rather uneasy because so many knew about my impending flight and that public life brings not only friends. Wisliceny answered that he only had one absolutely reliable man, *Scharführer* Naumann, and he was not available, but that I need not be anxious and should some hindrance whatsoever come up, he would take care of it.

"Maybe you should come with us," I said half-seriously.

"It wouldn't be a bad thing, but there is a kinship liability in our case; my mother and brother would be detained and maybe executed, if I slink off. No, it wouldn't work," he answered.

"You think that this war will end in victory?" I asked.

"Nonsense! This war was lost long ago," was his reply.

"Then why do you continue? What do you hope for?" I asked him.

"That England shall get the intelligence at last and go with us against the Russians," he said.

"England with Germany, maybe; England with Hitler, never!" I said.
"Hitler or not, not that is decisive," and with this he wished me good
luck and sent me away.

From the Swabian Hill I went to the Council. "You are going away
now, when everything seems to come straight?" President Stern asked me,
"but you always had your special things." "You are a banker, Mr. President,"
I said, "and the saying goes that in order to make a profit on the stock exchange one has to buy low and sell high. May the Almighty grant that it
should be really high this time." I asked him to co-opt Dr. Reiner to the
Council in my place, took leave from Dr. Wilhelm, Boda, Pető and from the
three young officials who were connected with me, and my mission at
the Council came to an end. I took off my yellow star, hailed a taxi
(with the star, this was forbidden), and rode to the railway station where
my family was anxiously waiting. From now on I was the Romanian Jew,
Philipp Freund.

Our train's departure was scheduled for 2:30 p.m. When I joined my
family at about 2:00 p.m., they already knew that there was a delay because the train had to wait for two coaches to arrive from Berlin which
had been greatly detoured since the normal route had been bombed
and heavily damaged at Almásfüzitő the night before. We waited three
gruesome hours in fear of having our identity recognized by someone
who might know one from our group, but at long last the train started.
Batizfalvy sent an escort for the official "repatriation transport," detective Cingléry. I had known him for more than twenty years, but I hoped
that he would be unable to recognize me without a beard. Every kilo-
meter we were further from Budapest, we felt more at ease, until we
approached the border. It was about 11:00 p.m. and pitch dark, in compliance with the anti-air raid regulations, when I heard Cingléry ask my
wife at the door of our compartment, "Mrs. Freudiger, where is your husband sitting?" She hesitated, but he reassured her that he only wanted to
say goodbye. When she pointed me out in the dark, he wished me good
luck and begged me not to forget all the services I had received from him
for two decades, when everything would be back to normal. Shortly afterwards we arrived at the border town, Lökösháza. Cingléry reported the
repatriation transport to the border police, and as all of us had exit permits, we passed the border without any difficulty. Then all of a sudden

the customs control wanted to retain us until the next morning, arguing that they could not check our luggage in the dark by the light of flashlights alone. We were desperate, but they remained adamant. After much bargaining, it was agreed that one small handbag containing bare necessities would be screened for each member of the transport and that the rest of the baggage would be unloaded and remain there. We gave them all the keys to our luggage and several thousand *pengős,* and they promised to forward them to Bucharest after they were searched. We were relieved and happy to be allowed to continue our journey, even though we never expected to see our belongings again; we felt we had acquired our freedom. It was a great surprise when the railway manager in Bucharest informed us a week later that the baggage had arrived. Quite a lot of things were missing, no one knew if it had been confiscated by the Hungarians or stolen by the Romanians, but we felt lucky to get anything we could.

The morning after my flight, Dr. János Gábor reported it to the *Sondereinsatzkommando* and Eichmann went into such a fury that he detained him on the spot and ordered the whole Council arrested for complicity. After a day or two, the members were released, but Eichmann sent a message to Manfred von Killinger, the German Ambassador in Bucharest, that the Jew Freudiger had fled to Romania and was most likely staying in Bucharest; he was to be located and returned to Budapest at any price. Killinger had no time to execute this order, as two weeks later Romania surrendered to the Russians, and on August 28 Killinger committed suicide.

The first night in Bucharest we were visited at the hotel by the men of the *Siguranţa* (Security Service) and were told not to leave the hotel. Our friends, Meisner, and so on, arranged for residence permits at the *Siguranţa* the next day. Few questions were asked; it was only a question of money, how much. I reported to Dr. Wilhelm Fildermann, the leader of Romanian Jewry and representative of the Joint, the next day, and repaid him for the sum he had given to Dr. Tatuşescu on our behalf and thanked him for his help. He was so impressed with what I told him about the tragedy of the Hungarian Jews, that he asked me to write the whole story for the Joint and him. So, we three, Link, Diamant and I, drew up the document (Alexander Diamant was the composer), which later became known as the "Bucharest Report." We had to be rather cautious in this report, since the SS was still in Budapest and the war was still going on. We wanted the report to be confidential, so we only made seven copies; two for Fildermann, two for Dr. Marton and three for ourselves. But—as I later learned—Dr. Marton, the newspaperman, could not resist reproducing it and circulating among his friends, and so it was sent to Switzerland, too, and translated into English.

We remained in Bucharest until October 1945, under the Russians, who occupied Romania in September 1944.

EPILOGUE

In the years following the Holocaust, I was reproached on several occasions for the alleged shortcomings of the Central Council of Hungarian Jews (*Magyar Zsidók Központi Tanácsa*). Specifically, I was asked why the Council failed to:

1. Inform the Jews about their impending fate;
2. Induce the Jews to flee for their lives; and
3. Organize any resistance against the deportations.

During his visit to Jerusalem in 1950, Dr. Károly Wilhelm informed me that shortly after the liberation in 1945, the Chamber of Lawyers (*Ügyvédi Kamara*) initiated disciplinary proceedings against the three lawyer-members of the Council: Dr. Wilhelm, Dr. Pető and Dr. Bóda. After a thorough inquiry, which lasted for several days, all three were cleared of all charges. The Chamber concluded that the Council had done all it could under the given circumstances. The Chamber's decision speaks for itself; I shall nevertheless try to answer the above questions to the best of my knowledge and conscience.

1. The Council did not know about the deportations until the day that they began! As late as the day before the beginning of the deportations, Lajos Reményi-Schneller, Minister of Finance, emphatically denied such a possibility. When, after two weeks or so, we became convinced that the trains were going to Auschwitz and not to Waldsee, as we had been informed by Hermann Krumey, we still did not know what Auschwitz really meant. By the time we learned the truth about Auschwitz, the first phase of the deportations, involving some 310,000 Jews, was already over. The Jews in the provinces were put into almost hermetically-closed ghettos.

The Jews of Budapest knew the same facts as the Council; nothing was concealed from them.

In addition, I must also note that travel was forbidden from the first day of the occupation, personal contacts were reduced to a minimum, and the information media were strictly controlled.

2. You cannot induce someone to flee who is not ready to take the risks of escape! These risks were considerable, as were the uncertainties of being a refugee in a foreign country. But those who had the courage and found a way to flee during the weeks preceding the ghettoization (or later from Budapest) did escape, and some of them—unfortunately, only a smaller part—managed to find a safe haven.

During the three weeks from July 15 to August 9, 1944, when the threat of deportation hung over Budapest, Gyula Link gave the widest possible publicity to the possibility of flight and offered money (from the HIJEFS funds) to those who might need it, but there were no more than two or three takers. As an example: I was berated here in Israel by a member of my former Congregation for having told him to try to escape, instead of giving him what he requested: a certificate stating—falsely—that he was an employee of the Council. He did not want to flee; what he wanted was to remain in Budapest with more safety.

3. To organize an effective resistance—if indeed such a thing is possible—takes time; the great speed of events made it *a priori* impossible in this case.

To resist the ferocious gendarmes about to drag one from the ghetto into a freight car, whether individually or on an organized basis, was an impossibility and equivalent to suicide. The ablebodied men, i.e., most men between the ages of 18 and 50, were not there, since they were serving in labor service companies at this time. For effective resistance, we should have resisted entering the ghettos, but no one knew about their planned creation. The ghettoization began within four weeks of the appearance of the SS, and was completed in one week. It was another four weeks until the deportations started.

The situation was not the same as in Poland, where the Jews lived in the ghettos for one to two years or even longer. During this time, they were able to adapt to life there, with all its difficulties, and to create organizations, both overt and underground, that finally led to the uprising in Warsaw.

An American Jew reading about the gallant fighters of the Warsaw Ghetto, or the Israeli *sabra* who cannot understand the situation and mentality of the Jews in Europe, feels a great pride about the uprising. This is a very positive feeling, but what was really achieved by the uprising? We must answer: NOTHING! Those who fought were killed, and the others were sent to their death. The few who escaped and joined the partisans could have done so just the same without the uprising.

The remainder of Slovak Jewry, some 13,500 persons, were sent to Auschwitz and other camps between October 1944 and March 1945, as retaliation for taking part, to some extent, in the partisans' fight; at this time, the Russian Army was on the other side of the Carpathian Mountains, in no hurry to come to their aid.

As all this shows, resistance or uprising against a superior armed adversary does not pay and it is questionable whether resistance should have been organized or furthered, even had it been possible. The negotiations with the SS and payments to them, accomplished the following: 1,700 persons went to Bergen-Belsen and from there on to Switzerland; 16,000 were sent to Strasshof rather than to Auschwitz, and remained alive; and, starting on the third week of deportation, several hundred people were sent to Budapest and placed under the protection of the Council, in addition to the 360 from Kolozsvár. (Over 80 persons from eight different towns were sent to Budapest by Wisliceny in response to my personal entreaties.) The negotiations and payments also contributed to the fact that if Brand had returned from Istanbul with a successful deal of some kind, the picture would have been far better and hundreds of thousands would have been rescued.

Negotiations and payments are surely less glorious than uprising and fighting, but they may possibly bring better results. I imagine that this is not a popular opinion, but our sages said that to rescue one living soul is equivalent to building a whole world, and this is surely more important than popularity; so I hope that the Almighty will judge our actions of 1944 accordingly.

Jerusalem, November 21, 1972

LETTER FROM
FÜLÖP FREUDIGER TO REZSŐ KASZTNER[1]

August 20, 1944

Dear Rezső,

When I said good-bye to you I told you that I will inform you in an exhaustive letter about all the things I didn't have an opportunity to tell you about, and now that I begin to write this letter an old affair comes to mind. It may have been a year and a half ago, I don't remember exactly, that one fine day I received a thick registered letter in which a gentleman then unknown to me sent me the minutes of a meeting where an honor committee of a labor service company determines that a particular individual performed selfless work on behalf of his comrades and that all other allegations should be viewed as libel. I found it a little strange to see "the maiden proving her innocence" and put the letter aside with a smile. It seems, however, that thereby I committed a crime for which "midoh kneged midoh"[2] I must atone, and I now must write an exculpating letter to the same gentleman. I assume this punishment with Joszi,[3] especially since, as we agreed, you will read this letter with the same friendship, developed between us during long months of cooperation, that I have shown to you during all this time.

289

Now let us turn to the subject. In chronological order, the matter began around the middle of June when W.[4] told me I should determine what I could do myself for my departure and what I would need his assistance for. [Understand this to mean my incorporation into the repatriation of foreign Jews.[5]] Then I asked Moshe[6] whether he could get two passports. This did not work out, but the question came up of a Swiss *Schutzpass* and, with my customary sincerity, I of course told him what it was all about, just as I always told you of my conversations with W., in which, however, you showed no particular interest because you did not want to leave. By chance, at the same time, around June 20, there arrived Dr. Tatu,[7] who had been sent directly to me by Bubi Meisner[8] to see how he could be of assistance to us. Dr. Tatu then came to see me together with Blum[9] and a gentleman from here named Nadler[10] who was with us at the time; in the course of the conversation I remembered W.'s proposition and we entrusted him with this task. Moshe knew this gentleman from before, so that we continued our negotiations with him as well. The material part of the affair was negotiated by Blum who gave him a letter for Fildermann,[11] so that this project would no longer be a family matter but rather one contemplated on a broader base, a Joint public project. In the meantime Blum left and Dr. Tatu arrived late, only around July 20. Here Dr. Ernő M.[12] got involved in addition to Fildermann and he represented the first Zionist coloration since neither Fildermann nor Nadler nor the other gentlemen involved here were in any way Zionists; they did not want then and do not want now to make it into a Zionist affair, but only to save specifically their own acquaintances or people of their community. Tatu brought me a letter from Nadler and one from Marton. The latter wrote that you, Ottó,[13] Moshe and President Samu[14] should be involved in the selection of the people. Moshe, who was already involved, did not think this would be right exactly because of the relation between you and him, which since then has pained me even more and caused me even more aggravation but which unfortunately I could not help. Since Moshe was needed for handling the Hungarian[15] and also because we had worked together up to that time, I was compelled to give in. After all, this was not really a Zionist matter and Moshe represented the Zionist interest very well. Moreover, this matter did not interest you personally and you were somewhat less involved. All of this put me in the painful but necessary position of having to handle the Tatu matter without you. To be absolutely frank, on Tammuz 17,[16] when I told you about the arg. teudot[17] (which you also rejected), you told me: "You don't think that you will be leaving?.," a statement that made me think; and I was not particularly excited at the thought that Mrs. Joel[18] should learn of my decision in advance. I continued to work hard to bring you together with Moshe and make peace, because even if you as a Zionist did not have much interest in the affair, I was personally unhappy that I wasn't going to be handling it with you. The failure was definitely not because of me; you may remember our conversation of August 7 in Gyula's[19] office when both you and Ottó noticed how depressed I was. Now at least you know why!

Summarizing the facts: I can understand that you said good-bye with "a bitter taste," but believe me, I also was very much pained because I had to exclude you, for reasons beyond my control, and I want to hope that this sincere statement will give you satisfaction. After all, in the course of the friendly relationship that was established between us two during the past months there was more than one occurrence that caused "a bitter taste" for me too, but I always swallowed hard and considered the case closed. Here I am not even thinking of such things as when you were arrested on Whitsunday and I went here, there, and everywhere clutching at every straw, and then it did not occur to you for three days after you were freed to even telephone; this was settled by my recognizing that one cannot be angry with you. Rather, I think of when one nice morning I met you by chance on the Hill[20] and asked you what the file in your hands was, and you then told me that it was the list of those to be brought back from Kolozs[21] about which I had known nothing until then, so that unless I had accidentally found out about it this would have been a 100 percent Zionist affair, which however. . . . I further think of when most recently W. brought the assignment that during your absence I should take over the negotiations about the 250 LKW,[22] and when I immediately informed Ottó, etc. found that according to a party decisin Mrs. F.[23] should be "involved" because Rezső could only be replaced by someone from the party! And when a few days later you were able to be active again, you went to B.[24] without me although we had an agreed-on rendez-vous. I could continue with the list but the two just mentioned brought to mind my resolve to leave, which had not been firm before. Believe me, I did not bring up these matters with pleasure and I do it only to point out that those who are interested in being viewed with indulgence should also be indulgent toward others and, just as despite the hurts, I kept an honest friendship towards you, you also must understand what happened—and "tout comprendre, c'est tout pardonner." I hope that with this the misunderstanding is over, isn't that right, Rezső?!

Returning to the Tatu case, here they don't want to turn it into a Zionist thing even now; please tell Perec[25] that that kind of letter was out of place. Fildermann and Ernő are working on behalf of 300 additional people. Ernő will write, and Tatu will do it in person.

What's new otherwise? What are the news on the first transport? What is with the Sally[26] travel? What is with the big transports? I would be obliged if you would write or write through friends about everything that has happened since.

Further travel, for the time being, is very uncertain; the situation changes from day to day. I await your kind reply as early as possible and remain, with kind regards,

(signed) Philo

1. This letter by Freudiger, a leading member of the Jewish Council of Budapest, was written to Kasztner, the *de facto* head of the Relief and Rescue Committee (*Va'ad Ezra ve'Hatzala*—Vaada), shortly after his arrival in Bucharest on August 10, 1944. It aims to explain the circumstances of his departure, which became the source of a great controversy both during and after the war. For further details see Freudiger's "Five Months" in this volume.

2. "Measure for measure."

3. Unidentified.

4. Dieter Wisliceny, a leading member of the Eichmann-*Sonderkommando* in Hungary.

5. Reference is to the negotiations relating to the possible repatriation from Hungary of approximately 150 Jews possessing Romanian citizenship.

6. Moshe (Miklós) Krausz, the head of the Palestine Office (*Palesztina Hivatal*) of Budapest, an opponent of Kasztner.

7. Tatuşescu was a Romanian diplomat used by the Jewish leaders of Romania as a courier against compensation.

8. A relative of the Freudigers then living in Bucharest.

9. József Blum, the former representative of the American Joint Distribution Committee (Joint) in Budapest.

10. A leading figure of the Jewish community in Bucharest.

11. William Fildermann was the head of the Jewish Community of Romania.

12. Ernő Marton, a leading Zionist figure in Transylvania and founder and editor-in-chief of the *Uj Kelet* (New East) of Kolozsvár (Cluj), had escaped to Bucharest early in May 1944.

13. Reference is to Ottó Komoly, the head of the then outlawed Hungarian Zionist League (*Magyar Cionista Szövetség*) and the *de jure* head of the Vaada.

14. Samu Stern, the President of the Jewish Council of Budapest.

15. Meaning the negotiations with the Hungarian authorities for the repatriation of the Romanian Jews. Moshe Krausz had good contacts with the National Central Alien Control Office (*Külföldieket Ellenőrző Országos Központi Hivatal*–KEOKH) in Budapest.

16. The seventh day of the month of Tamusz, a day of fasting.

17. Reference is to emigration certificates.

18. Hansi Brand, the wife of Joel Brand.

19. Gyula (Julius) Link, a relative of the Freudigers, who also escaped on August 9, 1944.

20. The Swabian Hill (*Svábhegy*) in Buda where the German and Hungarian police and security units involved in the Final Solution had their headquarters.

21. The list of the 388 Jews to be removed from the ghetto of Kolozsvár.

22. Reference is to the 250 trucks the Jewish leaders claimed were then available for transfer to the Germans. For further details, see Ran-

dolph L. Braham, *The Politics of Genocide. The Holocaust in Hungary.* New York: Columbia University Press, 1981, pp. 957-959.

23. Unidentified.

24. SS-*Obersturmbannführer* Kurt Becher.

25. Peretz Révész, a refugee from Slovakia, who played a leading role in the *Halutz* resistance.

26. Saly Mayer, the representative of the Joint in Switzerland, was one of the most controversial Jewish leaders in the free world during the Nazi era. The question pertains to Kasztner's planned visit to Switzerland with Kurt Becher. The objective of the planned trip was to obtain funds from Saly Mayer to induce the Germans to allow the 1684 "prominent" Jews, who were taken out of Hungary in the so-called Kasztner transport, to leave Bergen-Belsen for Switzerland. For details on this issue, see *The Politics of Genocide,* op. cit., pp. 951ff.

THE RED CROSS HOME OF THE JEWISH ORPHANAGE FOR BOYS IN BUDAPEST

Otto Roboz

It is well known that on March 20, 1944, the day after the occupation began, the Germans ordered the heads of all the Jewish institutions in Budapest to attend a meeting convoked in the great all of the religious community. As director of the Orphanage for Boys I went there with Aladar Vadász, a member fo the Orphanage Board. I was surprised to hear *Obersturmbannführer* Hermann Krumey (Eichmann's deputy, who appeared with military escort) call the pale Samu Stern, who sat next to him on the podium, "Herr Hofrat." Without blinking an eye, Krumey announced: "Nobody will meet with harm because of his Jewishness. Of course, if anyone is guilty he will be punished."

In two days an order concerning the fate of the orphanage arrived from the authorities. "The Germans needed the buildings," so every Jewish institution dedicated to the welfare of children had to cease operations; the Germans were taking over the buildings. All the children under state care in the Orphanage for Girls, the Institution for the Deaf and Dumb, and the Institution for the Blind would be transferred to the Orphanage for Boys. No objections could be raised. Each of my colleagues at the

295

orphanage understood the gravity of the situation. We tried to make room for every child. The home for apprentices adjoining the Orphanage for Boys was evacuated to make room for the residents of the Orphanage for Girls.

Incidentally the Germans never did make use of the evacuated buildings; they stood empty until the end of the war.

The blind children posed a problem. Their attendants did not stay with them. The director, Dezso Kanizsai, an excellent special educator, called on me on March 24 to warm me that the very sensitive blind children would not be able to fit in with the rest of the children and so he preferred to return them to their parents' care. Unfortunately, no one imagined that the fate of the children sent from Budapest to the countryside would be sealed sooner.

The fact that the Hungarian and German authorities did not close down the Orphanage for Boys deceived many people. The chief officers of the Jewish religious community, Secretary General Ernő Munkácsi and Chief Counselor Hugó Csergő, who occupied the same posts in the Jewish Council established by the authorities, asked that I accommodate them, together with their families, in the building of the Orphanage for Boys. The Csergős moved into my director's apartment, where others had also taken refuge. Soon there were 40 of us in the apartment. Mrs. Lajos Hegedus, our matron, vacated her apartment for Ernő Munkácsi. At the same time, she received shelter in the room of another employee of ours. The presence of the Jewish Council's top executives did not make things easier for the Orphanage. However, it did contribute to the misconception that the facility would enjoy special protection.

Mrs. Hegedüs helped us feed every hungry mouth. We shared our meager rations so that no one would go hungry. Mrs. Ignaz Friedmann, the president of the ladies' association that supported the Orphanage for Girls, called on me at the end of March and, deeply moved, thanked me for ensuring that the children of both the Orphanage for Girls and the Orphanage for Boys received equal treatment. Her gratitude surprised me; to me this was only obvious. Speaking for myself and all of my colleagues, I assured her that we thought it only natural that, at least, we persecuted Jews should not discriminate against each other. In addition, Olga Falus, the director of the Orphanage for Girls, who was also an outstanding teacher, helped us in caring for the children. Mrs. Friedmann left promising that she would see to it that whatever food she could get would reach our matron Mrs. Hegedüs. She fulfilled this promise.

Although the authorities allowed the Orphanage for Boys to keep functioning, week by week it became harder and harder to run. The sign "Jewish Orphanage for Boys" hanging on the gate was enough to provoke irresponsible elements to throw bricks and stones more and more often at the windows that faced the street. These early attacks did not claim any victims. The Germans then gave us a placard that was supposed to offer some vague protection, but instead it called attention to the fact that the building was Jewish.

After such preliminaries and on hearing the news of the first deportations from the countryside about the middle of May, a brave and far-seeing member of the resistance movement, Pál Árkos, called on me. He, too, was in his thirties, and he, as well as Aladár Vadász and I, had once been a pupil at the Orphanage for Boys.

Árkos was the first to suggest that we put up a sign that did not emphasize the Jewishness of the institution. After discussions lasting far into the night, we came up with "Children's Home" or "Red Cross Home for Children." Vadász observed shrewdly that we should forget about placing the building under the protection of the Hungarian Red Cross because at that time we could not even approach the Hungarian Red Cross.

Árkos prepared the sign, and we hung it up on the gate, but it was torn down in a few days. In fact, this provided absolutely no protection from either the Hungarian authorities or the Germans.

After the deportations had moved from the border regions into the interior of the country, it was impossible not to realize with a shock that the Germans' true purpose in crowding the children into one place was to make it easier to deport them once the deportations began in Budapest.

As the only possibility of protecting ourselves, we hit on the idea—and Ottó Komoly, president of the Hungarian Zionist Alliance helped us with this—of putting on the gates of the Orphanage for Boys a sign bearing the name of a neutral country or an international organization which it was hoped the Germans would respect. Much later, Komoly brought the good news that the International Red Cross, headquartered in Switzerland, would appoint him chief of the children's department of the International

Red Cross; thus, we would call the orphanage the "International Red Cross Home for Children." Later, the Swiss consul, Charles Lutz, and the representative of the International Red Cross in Hungary, Friedrich Born, would help us in all this.

Meanwhile weeks and months passed amid much agitation. Many times crowds to be deported were herded past the Orphanage for Boys on their way to the Eastern Train Station (*Keleti Pályaudvar*). More than once Ferenc Lebovitz, one of our teachers, together with his colleagues managed to save some small children who were passed over the fence by their parents. More and more children asked for and received asylum; the number of adults grew as well.

Since there was no more room in the dormitories on the third floor, some of the children had to sleep in the basement dining-hall. One night in early June a bomb was thrown in from the street, causing the death of a very young child.

Also at the end of June, Munkácsi asked me to stand duty one night in his stead at the Jewish Council. He told me I could look through the papers in his office, but if I wanted to sleep that night, I was to leave the so-called Auschwitz Protocols alone.[1]

That night in Munkácsi's office, I of course read the "Auschwitz Protocols" first and then the piles of letters from Jews in the countryside. Béla Bernstein, Chief Rabbi of Nyíregyháza, among others, wrote that the Jews of the region were being herded into Kisvárda, where they were left without food and water and subjected to the cruelest tortures. There was no doubt that the week following the writing of that letter the same fate befell Chief Rabbi Bernstein, as well as the other Jews from Szabolcs County and the members of the local Jewish Council.

On July 9, Raoul Wallenberg arrived in Budapest. By the time he arrived, the fate of the rural Jews was sealed—the Jews of Hungary, with the notable exception of those of Budapest, were all deported. The deportation of the Jews of Budapest was only a matter of time. As it turned out later, Wallenberg had brought more than six hundred Swedish passports, primarily for those who had blood ties or business relations with Swedes, as well as for a few well-known individuals. Wallenberg also brought a personal letter to Regent Horthy from the Swedish King, Gustav V, asking him to put a stop to the cruelty, deportations, and murders perpetrated against the Jews.

Wallenberg inquired after the children's fate first when he visited the Jewish Council. That was why Samu Stern, president of the Council, asked me to meet with Wallenberg at his apartment. Stern did not feel that it would be a good idea to have the confidential conversation in the Council's building on Síp Street. My first talk with Wallenberg took place on July 19 in the company of Vadász. Only Stern was missing from the discussions. His housekeeper was waiting with this message: the president had been ordered to German headquarters, but he promised to be back by 10 o'clock in the morning. He wanted to be with us when we talked with Wallenberg. (As it turned out later, Samu Stern, along with the other members of the Jewish Council, had been kept by the Germans until late at night so as to prevent the Council from intervening in the deportation of the inmates of the work camp in Kistarcsa.)[2]

Wallenberg arrived at exactly 10 o'clock. His youth surprised me, his modesty even more. After waiting for a half-hour, Wallenberg asked us to begin discussing the fate of the children; we could inform Stern later about our talk. We told Wallenberg what had happened until then. We told him how all the children were housed under one roof in the orphanage at Vilma Kiralynő Road 25-27, where more and more children were being given asylum.

Wallenberg listened to our account with great interest. At this, our first meeting, he revealed his plans at length and in great detail. They surprised both of us. Wallenberg intended to organize a train "under the Swedish flag" that would take not only the children of the Jewish Orphanage for Boys but also thousands of other children to Sweden.

This, however, never happened. The plan was fantastic and, of course, impractical. But perhaps this illustrates most characteristically how naive Wallenberg was when he first arrived in Budapest and how little he understood the obstacles in his path. It was under the growing danger that he grew into the uncompromising hero who saved tens of thousands of Budapest Jews.

I would not be saying much if I said that Wallenberg did more for the Jews of Hungary than all the other Swedes put together. During the long years of Jewish persecution in Germany, no more than one thousand German Jews were granted emigration visas to Sweden. This number rose to 3,000 with the Jews of Austria and Czechoslovakia, but you do not have to be an outstanding mathematician to realize that this was half a thousandth percent of the six million who perished.

Neither the government nor the Jews of Sweden rose to the occasion; in addition to the excuse of "unemployment," they clung to the pretext that allowing Jewish refugees into Sweden would give rise to anti-Semitism. Sweden did not let in a single Jews from the Baltic states or Poland. Virtually all the Baltic and Polish Jews perished. Later, however, about 900 Norwegian Jews—and about 5,400 Danish Jews in October 1943—received asylum. They were Scandinavians and, as brother nationalities, could cross the Swedish border.

In order to render the work of the Orphanage for Boys more difficult, the defense authorities decided that "the building would have to make room for a company of labor servicemen in the basement of the building," thereby reducing the children's opportunities for bathing and limiting their space in the bomb shelters. All of these were "orders" from which there could be no appeal. The labor servicemen—they were persecuted, too—surrounded as they were by woebegone faces, tried to behave with modesty.

Among those who took refuge in the orphanage was the teacher József Csillag, later killed, who brough with him his wife and modest furniture. Csillag was a sad and disappointed man. His only son had died at the age of ten. His bitterness was intensified by the fact that when the post of director of education and school principal of the orphanage became vacant, he, as the oldest teacher, should have been appointed to this position by the president, but wasn't.

In August a police squad appeared at the orphanage. They lined everyone up, but since the squad was from the 7th District Police Station where we had a lot of old acquaintances, the old people, the sick, and the small children were allowed to stay in their rooms. The others they took with them. The police were ordered there on the personal initiative of a low-ranking police officer. At my request his superior countermanded the order, and in a few hours, the police brought the group back unharmed.

Until August the Orphanage for Boys was able to continue its work only at its center on Vilma Királynő Road. At this time German formations began evacuating the buildings they had taken over, including the annex of the Orphanage at Nos. 5-7 Mihály Munkácsy Street in the 6th

District of the city. At one time this house had been part of the orphanage. Later it became a high school for girls. When the latter moved to its
new home in the early 1930s, the building was converted into a tene-
ment house whose rental income helped support the orphanage. This
building was among the first to be occupied by the Germans. When, however, they abandoned the building in August, we asked the 6th District
Board that it be given back to the orphanage. Beginning in September,
800 children and 400 adults were packed into the two buildings.

Our colleague Friedrich volunteered to take over the duties of caretaker of the building on Mihály Munkácsy Street. Ernő Lakatos and
Ferenc Lebovitz saw to the children's welfare. Dezső Beck, our board
member, moved into the Orphanage for Boys and helped us a great deal
with our work. Generally, everyone who had any connection with the
institution tried to carry out volunteer work in addition to his regular
duties. Our director of education, Mór Léderer, assumed the role of
liaison officer in our collaboration with Wallenberg, Léderer, who had
taught religion in a German school, spoke excellent German and so was
quite fitted for this job. Wonderfully, the children themselves took part in
the work. A 12-year-old boy bravely made the rounds of the dark courtyard every night checking for light filtering out. In our case, any flicker of
light could have led to an accustion that we were aiding and abetting the
enemy.

In September we sensed a certain thawing in the political atmosphere.
We prepared for the High Holy Days in an optimistic mood. More and
more friends of the orphanage appeared to pray in our synagogue. This
meant financial aid for the children's provisions. The *shammes* (sexton)
of the prayer house had even dusted the pews when the morning before
the festival the sirens unexpectedly began to scream. Naturally, everyone
marched down to his shelter. Soon afterwards a bone-shaking explosion
shook the building: a bomb had fallen on the orphanage and had pene-
trated through one of the wings of the building all the way to the basement. The eve of *Rosh Hashana,* the galleries beneath the open roof of
the synagogue stood out against the sky. There was only one victim of
the air raid—one of the men from the labor service company. The company was soon ordered to leave the building.

When we dug ourselves out from beneath the rubble, we had to re-
organize our rescue work. We had to transfer several children to the

building on Mihály Munkácsy Street, where we also made room for newly arrived adult refugees.

A smaller work-camp detail that had "illegally" rallied around Attila Juhász, a humanitarian army captain. Since they had nowhere to go, we made room for them in the Orphanage for Boys. We showed the authorities that, since the labor servicemen had been taken away, we now had room for a group of Jewish labor-camp inmates.

Some of these inmates helped the orphanage in its work. István Pelcz and György Veres, for example, made outstanding contributions. Pelcz regularly went with the older students to buy bread. Once Arrow Cross gunmen pursued him. Pelcz ran with a swiftness that would have put an Olympic champion to shame and leaped over the orphanage fence, where his pursuers stopped short. Forty years later all this may not seem very important, but in those days every slice of bread counted, and every attack averted meant life, a life saved. We even made room for the next-of-kin of the labor servicemen who were quartered with us, and during the second half of October, when the scramble for Swiss, Swedish, and Red Cross papers began, I managed, by taking great pains, to get papers for them, too. Zionist youth also gave us a lot of valuable help in obtaining papers.

Conditions got a lot worse. At one time Árkos warned me that these trips were perilous and it was possible that one day I simply might not return. But Árkos did more than just warn me. Within a week he had perfect identification papers made out for me in the name of Ottó Rácz, Protestant factory worker. To this day I don't know whether it was recklessness or naivete that kept me going on my trips on foot between the two buildings. At that time I did not yet know that these papers would later, indirectly with Wallenberg's help, save children when the Arrow Cross attacked the orphanage.

Less significant events, as well as tragic ones, took place every day in the building on Munkácsy Street. One morning at dawn, our volunteer caretaker, Friedrich called me over saying that the night before, the Arrow Cross had searched for a lawyer in the building, and, though he had tried to deny that there was even a single lawyer there, they took away Béla Bolgár, the husband of one of our teachers. Another time Friedrich called me asking me to restore order in the dining-hall, for one of the adults had stood in line three times for lunch before all the children could be fed once. Most of the adults respected the children's privileges, and I extracted a promise from the unnamed adult with the big appetite never again to take the children's portion.

Although a sign stamped with the seal of the International Red Cross hung over the gates of both buildings—it did outstanding service in protecting us from the Germans—not a single Red Cross member took part in the work of the establishment. Some of the self-sacrificing employees and refugees of the Orphanages for Boys and Girls formed this "Red Cross." We found this to be quite natural; not even the Swiss consul or the Hungarian representative of the International Red Cross had planned it otherwise. Both Komoly and I were grateful to them for allowing us to use their name. Komoly had no time for the Orphanage for Boys, for he was busy setting up more and more small-scale but successful so-called International Red Cross Homes for Children, as well s working to save the Jews in general. The Orphanage for Boys did not ask for more than an "International Red Cross" inscription. The establishment itself worked well and was well organized.

Many people, however, who were not involved in these events, have imagined that the International Red Cross Home for Children was something other than what it was, and the tendentious writings that appeared after the war and the romanticized books published later have even misled historians. The fact is that, following the example of the Orphanage for Boys, more than a dozen smaller but successful homes for children were established under the aegis of the International Red Cross. Brave young men established these homes with the tireless aid of Komoly. The Germans, strangely enough, respected the sign. They must have known that they would soon lose the war.

On December 24 Arrow Cross military gunmen attacked the buildings housing the children of the Orphanage for Boys. Led by a man named Kocsis, they appeared at the home on Munkácsy Street. They ordered everyone without exception—even the babies—to assemble in the courtyard so that their identity papers could be checked. Instead of checking papers they took everyone's modest possessions and ordered everyone to line up. Friedrich, the home's caretaker, immediately called our center on Vilma Királynő Road. I called Wallenberg right away because he was the only one from when we could expect any help. There was no answer.

Friedrich's second call shocked us. Kocsis had ordered his men to shoot dead anyone who stayed inside or who put up any "resistance." In despair, my colleague Léderer and I took turns dialing Wallenberg's secret number, but to no avail. We had only minutes to act. One of us had to reach Wallenberg to prevent a massacre.

There was no other solution but for me to go out and brave the streets patrolled by the Arrow Cross militiamen. I had to catch the streetcar on Damjanich Street and get to the Swedish Embassy. At the stop on the corner of Damjanich and Bajza Streets another would-be passneger and I realized with a shock that the streetcars were not operating. On the sidewalk opposite us, an Arrow Cross gun with a rifle headed for me.

"Papers."

I handed him the Christian papers that Árkos had given me; he examined everything and finding them in order, went off looking for another victim.

"What did the wretch want?" I heard a familiar voice behind me. It was Uncle Spacsek, a one-legged veteran of the First World War who in better times, as a street vendor, had sold candy to the children of the orphanage. He was brandishing a massive crutch, and I felt that he would have easily knocked down the Arrow Cross gunman with it had he reached for his gun. I stook there petrified. Suddenly I saw a man of about 30 carrying a small Christmas tree across the street. Good ideas always come to one during the most trying of times. I stopped him and asked him to give me the Christmas tree; I would gladly pay him for his trouble. Perhaps he had witnessed my identity check or perhaps he was a Jew himself or perhaps it was just the Christmas spirit that took him:

"Just pay me its price," he said, and, with the tree on my shoulder, I walked down Damjanich Street.

A friend of mine, a doctor, lived there. I rang his doorbell and asked him if I could use his phone to call Wallenberg's secretary. The secretary assured me that she knew at which home Wallenberg had been staying for the past two days and would immediately relay the message to him. Almost an hour had gone after Friedrich's first call, but I had no doubt that Wallenberg would act in minutes. And that was exactly what happened.

My report to the People's Court referred to that trip of mine and Wallenberg's intervention immediately afterwards. "We have reason to believe that the massacre was prevented by the intervention of the Swedish Embassy."[3]

Meanwhile the Arrow Cross members made good their threat in the building on Munkácsy Street and used their weapons. They killed Endre Tibor Lohr, a three-year-old child, Iván Vámos, a baby of a year and a half, together with his mother, Mrs. Sándor Vámos, our 30-year-old nurse. They also shot Mrs. József Kraus and Mrs. József Stern, respectively 78 and 68-year-old sick women.

They lined up the children from the orphanage, but sent 15-year-old Lajos Kohn, who was so crippled that he could not keep up with the procession, back into the building. As he limped toward the building, they shot him in the back.

The procession was driven through the city to the Radetzky Barracks on Margit Avenue, where they confiscated the remaining papers and possessions, saying: "You won't need anything anymore." At that moment, wearing civilian clothes and an Arrow Cross armband, a high-ranking officer arrived whom Wallenberg's ultimatum had reached. He ordered Kocsis: "Don't commit any massacre here, but escort the group to the ghetto on Síp Street."

A squad of Arrow Cross men led by a certain Szabó arrived at our home on Vilma Királynő Road. They lined people up with the same brutality as they had in the Munkácsy Street home, but no blood was shed in the building. The group was marched to the Radetzky Barracks, but orders from Wallenberg's man reached the squad just as they arrived in the barracks courtyard, and the group was sent back to Budapest.

In this case, too, the order was to take them back to Síp Street. But since the Arrow Cross man who have the order lisped, it was thought that he had said Sziv Street rather than Síp Street. There they found two empty buildings from which the Jewish residents had been taken earlier. Those brought there were chased into the buildings at 33 and 46 Szív Street.

The trials of the children and their escorts who were driven into the building at 46 Sziv Street were not yet over. The 27-year-old janitor, Vince Szakács, rushed into the Arrow Cross Party headquarters complaining that the children, playing in the courtyard, had broken his broom. Three Arrow Cross soldiers arrived and shot a 9-year-old orphan girl, Rose Albert, and 16-year-old Tibor Schwartz.

They they lined up the children—including many of nursery school age—and their attendants. No one was allowed to take his things. The group was driven toward Váci Street. A rocket flare threw the Arrow Cross gunmen into confusion, whereupon 30 children managed to escape. By dawn most of them had staggered back to the Orphanage for Boys.

Three of them, however, did not return. They had been allowed to enter a building at 41 Petneházy Street, where the janitor István Illés, denounced them. The Arrow Cross men took the children to the Danube, where they killed Lajos Marmelstein, eight years old, and Lászlo Neumann, 14 years old. The third, Izsák Katz, managed to jump into the river and escape before being shot.

Those who had not escaped in the confusion caused by the flare marched on toward the Danube. Here three children and one teacher were chosen to "tidy up the huts next to the banks to prepare their quarters for the night." Then they killed József Csillag, a 50-year-old teacher, Gábor Schwartz, 17 years old, and Thomas Moses, 16 years old. One of the three children, Gábor Révész, seeing his companions pushed into the Danube and shot at, ran and jumped into the icy river from another section of the quay. He swam to the steps of the Parliament, where he managed to reach the banks. (Today he lives in Sidney, Australia.)

The leaders of the smaller band of children took them from the banks of the Danube back to Sziv Street. The next morning the larger group was taken by the Arrow Cross to the orphanage building on Vilma Királynő Road. The Arrow Cross soldiers asked me for papers certifying that they had handed over only 70 children, because, as they said, they had been ordered to kill the others.

All this happened on Christmas Eve.

The leaders of the children who were taken to Sziv Street were so frightened by the excitement of the night that they dared not leave the house. I called the Jewish Council and asked them to get a police escort to return the children to the orphanage. Frigyes Görög answered the phone. His answer was depressing but objective. "We have reached such a low point," he said, "that only individual action can help." Since we had been taking "individual action" for months, I asked Attila Juhász for two soldiers. One of them was Pelcz, who pulled on a military fatigue-jacket. They were the "official" escort that returned the children and adults to the orphanage.

The Christmas massacre claimed 13 lives. They were the ones missing from the 1,200 who had escaped. My only brother, Károly Roboz, was also missing. The Arrow Cross had taken him to Sopron, where he was killed.

Work multiplied for our matron, Mrs. Hegedüs, because we had to feed the children in the ghettos, in addition to our own children, from our scant supplies. Our cantor, Miklós Hartmann, who worked in the ghetto bakery, tried to provide larger slices of bread to every child in the ghetto. In addition, a 12-year-old orphan, pushing a small hand-cart, regularly took food from the orphanage to his fellows. Among the Arrow Cross guards at the gates to the ghetto, this child met an acquaintance who pillaged the contents of the little cart. Still, the child could enter and leave the ghetto unharmed. Lebovitz and Lakatos stood imperturbably at the children's side, protecting and consoling them.

Mrs. Hegedüs was killed at the end of the siege. She was standing by the window looking onto the courtyard of our school principal's apartment when a stray machinegun bullet hit her in the head. It was as if fate were saying to her: "You have done your duty." Principal Léderer was luckier, because another bullet hit the wardrobe in his room and pierced the shoulder of his coat hanging there.

More than forty years have passed. It has become increasingly clear since then that we Jews can rely only on ourselves. This is proved by two thousand years of history and the events of 1944.

It is taking nothing away from Wallenberg's outstanding achievement to say that the children were *the real heroes.* All of them, boys and girls, behaved better than many of the adults in the house of cards that those buildings were. In spite of the fact that they were adolescents, an age when every child is hungry, they never complained about the lack of food. True heroes were the two boys Gábor Révész and Izsák Katz. When the Arrow Cross attempted to shoot them, they jumped into the icy Danube, and swimming with its current, managed to escape the volley of machinegun fire. And the 12-year-old orphan who took food from the orphanage to his fellows, he was a real hero, too, an example of the Jewish will to live.

I have been asked recently whether I was angry or bitter because it wasn't the Germans but the Hungarian Arrow Cross Party that attacked the orphans. No, I said. I felt only a deep sadness which has grown after 40 years. I think of the crutches of the First World War veteran. I have the painful thought that if just one percent of the population—a hundred thousand people in a nation of ten million—had followed Uncle Spacsek's example, perhaps all the murders could have been prevented.

NOTES

1.   These Protocols were based on the reports of two escapees from Auschwitz. For details, see Randolph L. Braham, *The Politics of Genocide. The Holocaust in Hungary.* New York: Columbia University Press, 1981, pp. 707-716.

2.   Kistarcsa is a small town, about 15 miles northeast of Budapest, where the Hungarian military had been interning Jews since 1942. Thousands and thousands were sent from there to die in forced-labor service camps. It is from this camp, too, that the first transports were taken to Auschwitz late in April 1944.

3.   Béla Vihar, *comp. Sárga könyv. Adatok a magyar zsidóság háborús szenvedéseiből, 1941-1945.* (Yellow Book. Data on the Wartime Suffering of Hungarian Jewry, 1941-1945). Budapest: Hechaluc Kiadás, 1945, p. 175.

DEPOSITIONS

DEPOSITION OF LÁSZLÓ FERENCZY *

I. In my previous testimony I already noted that I was entrusted with the supervision of the provincial ghettos. With regard to this point, I declare that throughout my official provincial activities nobody ever tried to establish contact with me either in writing or by telephone or in person or through someone else. I would have had definite knowledge if someone had turned to some other authority in matters of the ghettos or deportations because I would definitely have found out about it. The Jewish

---

* The leader of the Hungarian dejewifying unit, Gendarmerie Lt.-Col. László Ferenczy was in charge of the ghettoization and deportation of the provincial Jews. Convicted of war crimes, Ferenczy was executed in the spring of 1946. He prepared this deposition (No. 5356/1946) on April 19, 1946, for the Criminal Division of the Budapest Headquarters of the Hungarian State Police, when the Hungarian authorities were considering the possible prosecution of the members of the Jewish Council and of the Relief and Rescue Committee (*Va'ad Ezra ve'Hatzala*) of Budapest.

Source: Hungarian National Archives (*Magyar Országos Levéltár*), Budapest, Berend Trial File No. NB 2600/1946, pp. 105-107.

Council definitely had to know about the "consequences" of the deportations (Auschwitz). Thus, had they been on top of their mission, had they indeed intended to do something to postpone the deportations, then they definitely would have had to establish contact with me. This, however, did not take place. If they had taken any steps at the beginning of the provincial deportations for their prevention, we would definitely have met. On the occasion of my first appearance before the Regent, which as I already testified was thanks to Ernő Pető's intervention, I called the Regent's attention to the events of Auschwitz, showed the Regent the documents I took along, some of which I had received from the Council; he then became inclined to take steps to prevent the deportations from Pest. If this revelation had taken place in time, which in view of Pető's first-rate connections with the Regent could easily have been arranged, it is absolutely certain that the Regent could have stopped the provincial deportations just as he did those of Budapest. All of the Council's activities in this connection were restricted merely to saving the rich. I got definite information on this during my provincial supervisory work because my plain-clothes investigators were present in all the locations where ghettos were established, and I received reports from several places to the effect that the rich people were being taken out of the ghettos; it even happened that these were not even taken into the ghetto but were allowed to go to Budapest. German authorities went to all of the places with prepared lists so that this is the only way it was possible for some to be exempted from ghettoization beforehand. For example, when the ghettoization was completed in Gendarmerie District VIII we proceeded to the area of Gendarmerie District IX. Before we even got there the Germans had already removed the rich people from there also. On one occasion I raised this issue with Wisliceny, who served on the part of the German authorities as *Hauptsturmführer* Eichmann's deputy in setting up the provincial ghettos and the deportations. He informed me that they removed these wealthy Jews on the basis of a previously prepared list. It was my impression that this list could have been put together only through the Council, as I later corroborated in connection with the Kasztner case. In the course of subsequent events I also noted that the leadership of the Jewish Council, Stern, Wilhelm and Pető, maintained the closest cooperation with the Germans. This is also how they were able to acquire the exemption certificates known as *Immunitäts Ausweis* (Immunity Certificate). To me, for example, they never turned on behalf of any poor Jew.

II. Several times it happened that Kasztner came to me, either with the three Council members or just some of them. Thus Kasztner's relations with Stern, Pető and Wilhelm became clear to me. To prove this I relate a strange case. On one occasion Kasztner declared that he would go to Switzerland for the transfer into Switzerland of the wealthy Jews taken to Germany by the Germans. For about two weeks I did not see him. At this time I was in the Ministry of Foreign Affairs, where I raised this Kasztner issue. As to whom I talked to there, I can no longer recall definitely today; it must have been some Ministerial Counselor. In response to my account he brought out a completely fresh document which the Swiss Consulate had sent to the Foreign Minister. In this document I read the following, with my own eyes: On instructions from its own government, the Consulate stated that Samu Stern,[1] Kasztner and three other individuals all known to me, five people in all, crossed the Swiss border without an entry permit although they had the necessary German transit visa as well as passports. It demanded that similar occurrences should cease. The identified individuals were arrested by the local police and removed across the border. This document can definitely be found either in the Hungarian Ministry of Foreign Affairs or in the Consulate. According to Kasztner's statement, the purpose of the trip was to transfer the rich exempted Jews from Germany to Switzerland and for its effectuation the Swiss Zionists were ready to give a carload of nickel, a carload of chromium, a carload . . . (illegible) for each carload of Jews . . . (illegible). I am not sure whether it succeeded, but I have definite information that a train left the country's borders on July 7 at Hegyeshalom. Entrainment for this transport took place around June 28 at the Rákos rail yard. As I investigated it, this train idled around for about a week. I found out from someone in the Council, Kasztner or one of the three, that they had paid 15 million *Pengős* to the Germans for this July 7 transport. Thus, if each person paid 50,000 then 3,000 people might have left the country on that train. According to my recollection, I still saw Kasztner at the beginning of September, but after that he completely disappeared from my view.

III. On the Council's, i.e., Ernő Pető's, relations with the Regent I can reveal the following: when I stated that I would like an audience with the Regent, it was Pető himself who offered to make this possible. Pető also informed me of the day and the hour when we should go to young Horthy to discuss the meeting with the Regent. I went to see him at the stated time. In the course of my conversations with Miklós Horthy Jr. I discovered that he knew the Petős for a long time. I believe that he was a witness at his daughter's wedding. Accordingly, he maintained an old relationship with the Pető family. He then took me to his father, bypassing the Cabinet Office and his aides-de-camp. Thus the whole thing was more in the nature of a conversation than of an audience. From this one can also see what a first-class and old, intimate relationship existed between Pető and the Horthys. They could have used this relationship in the prevention of the provincial deportations as well. However, the Council was under the impression, which the Germans told them several times, that only the provincial, i.e., the unassimilated, Jews would be deported and not those of Pest.

IV. I already stated, at my request, the Council brought a batch of notes to my office via Berend.[2] These notes contained the demands of the Germans starting on March 19. Some of the requests were surprising. For example, I definitely recollect that they fulfilled, among other things, a demand for shirt fabric by name. I also remember a request for silverware, money, and better known paintings. They released all this on personal request. Among those who made requests was Wisliceny. Thereupon I issued instructions that they must refuse any further demands of the Germans by referring to me. I know that such a rejection did not result in ill consequences for the Council. On one occasion the Germans phoned me for the satisfaction of such a request but I refused permission referring to higher orders. With this, the matter was closed. If after this measure of mine the Council nevertheless issued such items for the Germans, this could have happened only of their own will and surely for their own interest, because by then they could have refused by referring to me.

V. Around October 20, Ernő Pető came to see me. Then the issue was raised that, according to the Minister of the Interior, Wilhelm and Pető and perhaps also Stern could not be in the Council. I advised them to hide.

Pető told me that he felt secure in my proximity. Since he had an old good acquaintance in the building where I lived, he wanted to move there. I told him that as far as I was concerned he could come but that I didn't want ot know where he lived because if someone asked me where he was I wanted to say frankly that I knew nothing about him. He then moved there. On a number of occasions I met him on the staircase and we passed each other like strangers.

I gave this testimony voluntarily without any coercion and corroborate this with my signature.

László Ferenczy

Minutes taken by
(illegible signature)

NOTES

1. Samu Stern was not among those who negotiated with Saly Mayer and others on a bridge linking Austria and Switzerland between Höchst and St. Margrethen. During the first meeting, on August 21, 1944, Kasztner was accompanied by Wilhelm Billitz, one of the directors of the Weiss-Manfred Works. The SS delegation was composed of Kurt Becher and his aide Max Grüson. This meeting was followed by several others, both "legal" and "illegal," but Stern was not present at any. For further details, see Randolph L. Braham, *The Politics of Genocide. The Holocaust in Hungary.* New York: Columbia University Press, 1981, pp. 957-964.

2. Reference is to Dr. Béla Berend, the controversial member of the Jewish Council of Budapest. For details, see ibid., pp. 452-462.

DEPOSITION OF SHULEM OFFENBACH*

I have known Rezső Kasztner since the beginning of the 1940s, when he was involved in collecting contributions for the Pro-Palestine League (*Pro-Palesztina Szövetség*). I began to play an active role in Jewish public life in 1943 as controller for the campaign to aid Polish refugees. As I recall, funds came from abroad, illegally of course, to Brand and in this way the Polish Committee (*Lengyel Comité*) received money from Brand; I supervised the Committee's accounts.

---

* A leading member of the *Va'ad Ezra ve'Hatzala* (Relief and Rescue Committee) of Budapest, Shulem Offenbach was born in Lodz on March 18, 1899. He was one of the *Vaada* and Jewish Council members the Hungarian authorities planned to indict after the war for alleged collaboration with the Germans. Offenbach prepared and signed his statement before the Budapest Headquarters of the Hungarian State Police (*Magyar Államrendőrség Budapesti Főkapitánysága*) on July 20, 1946.

Source: Hungarian National Archives (*Magyar Országos Levéltár*), Budapest, Berend Trial File No. NB 2600/1946, pp. 277-280.

After the Germans' entry I heard that Jenő Brand[1] and Rezső Kasztner were organizing a transport going to Palestine. I looked up Kasztner and told him that I wanted myself and my family to get into the transport. I got a promise to this effect. Brand left for Turkey, because his negotiations with the Germans had led to the possibility of emigration of all of the Jews of Hungary against the delivery of a countervalue from abroad. Brand left to arrange for the deliveries and to acquire the Americans' consent. At the time of his departure, Brand asked me to take over the management of finances in his group. I accepted. From abroad, various monies came flowing in, for example, from Switzerland and Turkey, partly from the Joint and partly from various Zionist organizations. At the beginning these funds were used for various rescues of Jews—men were smuggled in from Slovakia and Poland—to help the Slovak and Polish refugees here. In May 1944, I was just paying a visit at Mrs. Brand's apartment at 15 Semsey Andor Street—this was after Brand's departure—when Péter Hain's men came into the apartment and arrested all of us. Beside me and my wife, they took Mrs. Brand and Kasztner and his wife to Swabian Hill (*Svábhegy*).[2] We were there about four days when they brought in László Szántó,[3] his wife and his father-in-law. The Germans aksed to have us transferred to them; then they let us all go free. I found out that they had picked us up because they had gotten a hold of the printer who produced false papers for Mrs. Brand and actually they wanted to pick up Mrs. Brand. They also went to my apartment to search it and left only the furniture behind. They took away my diamonds that I had stitched into one of my jackets, so the only thing left was what I had hid elsewhere before this time. The Germans freed us because they did not want a suspension of the negotiations with Mrs. Brand. Péter Hain's men also took along the public funds at Semsey Andor Street.

The first transport left on June 30, 1944. We collected the offered valuables in the last seconds of the few days before departure. It was very dangerous in those days to deal with Jewish valuables and therefore we tried to effectuate the collections as quickly as possible. There was no possibility of preparing an accounting. I evaluated the valuables roughly and threw them into a briefcase. The jewelry was immediately forwarded to Swabian Hill because we feared a repetition of the Semsey Andor Street event. Three or four days after the departure of the transport, Kasztner sent me to Swabian Hill in the company of a jeweller named Lóránt to make an inventory of the valuables that had been taken there. We worked on this for three days. We evaluated and inventorized the valuables in several suitcases. I saw at that time that others were also involved in collecting valuables, since there was much more there than what I had collected. We handed over the inventory to Andor Biss, who had joined our work not long before then, and it was he who settled the accounting with the Germans. This accounting document must be in Switzerland.

After the departure of the first transport we began to organize a second transport. We established a financial committee which negotiated with people who appeared about the amount that could be offered by the various people. I led the committee and took over the valuables that were offered. After a few weeks I saw that the departure date of the second transport was not sure, so I terminated the committee's work and we began to return the amounts paid in up to that time. To the best of my knowledge we returned their valuables to everyone. While there were some whose valuables were no longer available, since the Germans consistently demanded things, I came to an agreement with these people; there were a few whose property could only be returned after liberation.

Funds continued to arrive in the old manner. At this time we spent these funds on the most varied activities. We constantly had to pay off the Germans. We had to supply the camp at Columbus Street. The supplying and feeding of the Strasshof camp consumed a lot of money. We took people out of internment camps and provincial ghettos. We rescued people into Romania and Yugoslavia. All of this consumed money. We constantly helped the Slovak and Polish refugees. The number of people in the camp declined starting in August, but after the *Nyilas* acquired power the number of camp inmates grew again to almost 3,000. Already in September, at the request of the Hungarians, all of the camps were transferred from the protection of the German command to Hungarian jurisdiction. At this time Ottó Komoly negotiated with the International Red Cross and the camp came under its jurisdiction. Komoly opened a Red Cross office at 4 Mérleg Street and thereafter our campaign was conducted as Section A of the International Red Cross. I managed financial matters even after this. Aside from 170,000 *Pengős* we did not receive any funds from the Red Cross; we supported our institutions from our own funds. Our major task was the rescuing of children. We established chidren's homes. In addition, we supplied the brick factory[4] with food and freed people from jail, moving freight cars and internment camps. We continued to help refugees. Toward the end of December I became sick and therefore went to Buda; I only came back after the liberation, in the middle of March.

I have never taken for my own use any of the funds that I managed, and I have never asked or accepted any money for helping someone. I must note that at Mérlag Street we also dealt with the issuance of protective papers. Since there were not enough of these, we had a considerable quantity of false ones printed and had false stamps made. We distributed these protective papers by the thousands to whoever appeared. We never sold them for money; in fact, when I found out that one of the inhabitants of the Columbus Street camp was selling protective papers I spoke to Ottó Komoly and this woman, who worked in the Baross Street office of the Red Cross, was immediately dismissed from the office. It is true that from the end of November I lived in the Pannonia Hotel, but this was necessary because by that time I was very ill and I was in bed there.

When I got involved in the Kasztner campaign I had a property of $30,000 in various kinds of foreign exchange and jewelry. When the Hungarian authorities arrested and robbed me, they took along only the diamonds stitched into one of my jackets. When valuables were taken to the Germans as payment for the transport I also contributed; I gave gold and a diamond ring. When the Hungarians took me from Semsey Andor Street, they took along the valuables I kept there—gold, foreign currency, and a diamond ring. After my car was stolen from in front of the Pannonia Hotel early in November, I bought a new one for nine gold Napoleons from an official of the Swiss Legation named Iritz. But this car also was taken away. Of course I had many personal expenses during this time, but at liberation I was left with approximately $10,000 to 12,000 worth of property from my valuables hidden in several places. In August 1945 several of us got together and founded the Industrial and Economic Corporation (*Ipari és Közgazdasági r.t.*). To this I contributed approximately $10,000, and since the enterprise was founded I have been its director. Before this, in April, the Joint appointed me to the leadership of its office in Hungary. Since I had differences of opinion with Wiermann, and moreover was not happy with doing Joint work, I left this work in September or October 1945.

Before I went to Buda I went to my friend János Pfeiffer, who at the time lived on Stefania Road, and asked to leave a small chest with him for a few days until I would return. Unfortunately, as I already mentioned, I only returned from Buda months later, in March 1945. At that time Pfeiffer stated that he took the chest to their factory, but that it was robbed and the chest was also taken away. The chest contained my papers and personal valuables. It did not have a single penny in cash. The public funds amounting to approximately $14,000 were hidden at 33 Francia Road. They remained there and after liberation Biss gave a full accounting of them.

I have nothing else to state. I made this statement voluntarily without any coercion, and after rereading it corroborate it with my signature.

(Signed) Shulem Offenbach

NOTES

1. Better known as Joel Brand.
2. It was in the Swabian Hill of Buda that the German and Hungarian dejewification units and security services had their headquarters.
3. László Szántó was a friend and associate of Joel and Hansi Brand. Mrs. László Szántó, neé Gebriella Kertész, signed a particularly accusatory deposition for the Political Police Division of the Budapest Headquarters of the Hungarian State Police on July 19, 1946 (No. 5356/1946), when the Hungarian authorities were planning to indict Rezső Kasztner and his colleagues, including Offenbach, for alleged collaboration. Her statement contains particularly harsh condemnatory observations about Joel and

Hansi Brand, Rezső Kasztner, and Mr. and Mrs. Andor (Andreas) Biss based mostly on circumstantial evidence. For its text, see Hungarian National Archives, Budapest, Berend Trial File NB 2600/1946, pp. 85-88.

4.   Reference is to the brickyard at Óbuda.

DEPOSITION OF LAJOS STÖCKLER *

After the legal warning, the witness states the following:

I became actively involved in Jewish public life on July 26, 1944. It was then that they appointed me to the third Jewish Council. I debated thoroughly whether to assume this assignment, because I viewed the Council's activities up to that time with concern. Even before the German occupation I had been asked several times to assume some function in the life of the Community, which however I did not accept becuase I did not see any possibility of achieving any substantial changes in the existing order.

---

* A lace manufacturer, Lajos Stöckler was born in Budapest on January 24, 1897. He was appointed to the Jewish Council of Budapest on August 26, 1944, and emerged as one of its controversial figures. During the *Nyilas* era, he served as the Council's head. He made this deposition before the Political Criminal Division of the Hungarian State Police of Budapest (No. 5356/1946) on May 14, 1946, when the Hungarian authorities were considering the indictment of the members of the Jewish Council and of the Relief and Rescue Committee (*Va'ad Ezra ve'Hatzala*) of Budapest

In my view, the broad strata and groups of Jewry should have been included in the direction of Jewish life. However, the electoral law of the time was not suitable for this, not being sufficiently democratic. The leadership that came into being under such conditions did not represent the Jewish masses. The leadership at the time consisted of the representatives of big capital; they directed the Jewish collective. This was the situation during the German occupation as well. In my judgment, because of its attitude this leadership was unsuited to adequately represent the interests of the broad masses during a period of crisis, in view of its lack of contact with them.

To the question of what needed to be and could have been done on behalf of provincial Jewry to make them as safe as possible from deportation, I answer as follows: What happened to Jewry abroad was so well known that it could not have been unknown to the Jewish leaders. The systematic destruction of Jewry in the neighboring countries, and not last Hitler's plan regarding Jewry, clearly showed the coming fate of European Jewry. It is my conviction that the first obligation of the then Jewish leadership should have been to warn of the danger, despite the instructions of the Germans or their calming declarations that were made with the intention to mislead. If this had happened, the life of many Jews who came to be deported would have been saved. The constant reassuring news influenced Jewish public opinion to remain in place, that there was no special danger.

---

for collaboration. After the war, Stöckler also served as the head of the Jewish Community of Pest and of the Central Office of Hungarian Jewry. For further details, see Randolph L. Braham, *The Politics of Genocide. The Holocaust in Hungary.* New York: Columbia University Press, 1981. For his own account, see his "Gettó előtt–gettó alatt" (Before the Ghetto –During the Ghetto). *Új Élet* (New Life), Budapest, January 22, 30; February 6, 13, 20; March 6; April 17, 1947.

Source: Hungarian National Archives (*Magyar Országos Levéltár*), Budapest, Berend Trial File No. NB 2600/1946, pp. 111-114.

That I judged the political leadership of Jewry to be unsuitable induced me to get involved in Jewish public life on July 26, 1944. During the first period I wanted to get acquainted with the Council's work, i.e., I wanted to be convinced to what extent the accusations of the public opinion at the time were well-founded. With regard to Pest, one of the most important measures of the Council was relocation. At that time very serious accusations were voiced in this connection, namely that certain influential Jews allowed their own views to prevail in both the designation and selection of the buildings. Thus, in the first place questions were raised why Samu Stern, the then leader of the Council, was exempted from relocation and could remain in his apartment in the house he owned, and why his son-in-law could remain there also. This substantiated the assumption of Jewish public opinion that the anti-Jewish measures were not applied uniformly. This reinforced in me also the assumption that the Jewish leaders were in a more advantageous position than the masses represented by them.

To the question of whether I knew Rezső Kasztner, I can answer that on one occasion, as I entered the room of President Samu Stern, I found Kasztner, Wilhelm and Stern there. It was then that he told us about his arrest by the Gendarmerie. Later I found that it was Kasztner who managed matters relocating to the Columbus Street camp. It was also he who arranged that the inhabitants of this camp should get first to Germany and then to Switzerland. Among his closest collaborators were Offenbach, Joel Brand, and Brand's wife. About Brand I learned subsequently that he had been sent to Istanbul.

With respect to the exemption certificates, I can state that they were very important during that particular period. There was a great scramble for them. People who previously had not played any role in Jewish public life also received them. Since the exemption certificates started to be issued before my appointment, I cannot make any detailed comments about them.

The head of the Housing Office was Rezső Müller. He carried out the instructions of the authorities relating to housing with punctilious precision.

He organized a special apparatus for this purpose. Moreover, he was the responsible head for the entire administration. Responding to the question that was asked, I state that I have heard talk that women could approach Ernő Szalkai, who worked in the Housing Office, only by way of the bed. I have no knowledge whether any disciplinary action was initiated against him for this.

On the question of the exemptions by the Regent, I confess that I reacted with the greatest revolsion when the Council's three leading members —Stern, Pető, and Wilhelm—appeared at Síp Street as the first ones without their star, ahead of everyone else. I am convinced that those who were themselves in a more advantageous position and were exempted from the measures that affected the community were not able to represent that community from whose burdens they extricated themselves through the exemption by the Regent. The three leading Council members received this exemption ahead of everyone else at a time when the decree on the subject had not even appeared yet. What I said here does not represent my own opinion alone, because I spoke about this to many of my friends and acquaintances and their opinion, like that of Pest's Jewry, coincided with mine. Moreover, I have stated on several occasions that I do not hold those Council members suitable for the management of the affairs of the community who acquired protective papers for themselves and their families from the Legations, thus securing their own and their families' persons. To my knowledge the three leading Council members were in possession of exemption papers.

Twenty-five labor servicemen from the clothes-gathering company, among whom György, the son of Károly Wilhelm, who was the unit's organizer, were assigned to Division T of the International Red Cross. After the assignment György Wilhelm looked me up, then already in my function as leader of the Council, in the presence of his father and Council member Dr. István Földes, and submitted a request that the Council contribute 200,000 *Pengős* to the maintenance of his unit. Both I and Dr. István Földes rejected the request most resolutely and they no longer came to us with such requests.

The situation changed after October 15. The composition of the Council disintegrated. We were together for the last time at Ferenczy's about October 21. Then one day Gendarmerie Captain Lullay appeared at our headquarters and informed us that Ferenczy wanted to eliminate Wilhelm and Pető. Then, on Ferenczy's instructions, we had to establish a new Council, in which we requested that the three leading Council members be kept. Ferenczy was not in favor of this and following a conversation with Stern he accepted that the latter should remain in the Council. After that I myself and the other Council members also appeared several times before Ferenczy. He never asked about Wilhelm and Stern. Ferenczy did not investigate their whereabouts at the Síp Street headquarters either. Today, of course, I find it strange that Pető hid in the same house where Ferenczy lived.

On one occasion there appeared an exempted Jewish reserve officer from the Felvidék named Elek and reported to Samu Stern that he had intervened for the removal of Ferenczy. I also was present during this report. Samu Stern forbade this in the sharpest tones and stated that he insisted on Ferenczy and would not allow any intervention opposing this.

I cannot provide technical details relating to the departure of Fülöp Freudiger and his partners. However, I do know that Freudiger went to the railway station in the Council's car. To my knowledge he also said goodbye to the leading Council members. It was for this and not for the postponment of the deportations that the three Council members and Dr. János Gábor were held for a few days.

Dr. László Pető, Ernő Pető's son, was a member of the liaison group with the authorities. He used to go up to Swabian Hill to the German command. Later he got to the Swedish Legation together with Mrs. Windholz, his immediate coworker. At the time the possible deportation from Pest was an everyday topic.

Dr. György Gergely was also a member of the liaison group with the authorities. He prepared the secret instructions. He was the Council's man who knew everything.

Responding to the question of who was responsible for the Council's activities, I say it was Samu Stern, Dr. Károly Wilhelm and Dr. Ernő Pető, because during my tenure they did not report about their secret negotiations and did not include others in their prior negotiations. At the time I protested several times about this, as proved by the appended documents. I have nothing else to state. I gave this deposition voluntarily without any coercion and after reading it I approve it with my signature.

Taken by: Police Lieutenant First Detective Pál Purjesz

(signed) Lajos Stöckler

CONTRIBUTORS

John S. Conway is Professor of History at the University of British Columbia, Vancouver, Canada. He is the author of *The Nazi Persecution of the Churches, 1933-1945* (London, 1969), which also appeared in French, German, and Spanish editions. In more recent years he had contributed numerous articles to scholarly journals on the subject of the Holocaust, and in particular on the role of the Christian churches during this period.

Yehuda Don is Professor of Economics at Bar-Ilan University, Ramat Gan, Israel, where he is also Director of the Institute for the Study of the Economy of Jewish Communities. He is the author of several works, including *Industrialization in the Cooperative Agricultural Settlements (Moshavim)* (1976) and *Industrialization of Underdeveloped Regions in North-Eastern Brazil* (1979), and of numerous articles on economics, economic development, and Hungarian Jewry.

Fülöp Freudiger, also known as Philipp de Freudiger, was a manufacterer and President of the Orthodox Jewish Community of Pest. He was a member of the Central Jewish Council (*Központi Zsidó Tanács*) from March 20, 1944, through August 9, 1944, when he escaped to Romania. He settled in Israel where he died on March 15, 1976 at age 75.

Victor Karady is a sociologist and social historian associated with the *Centre National de la Récherche Scientifique,* Paris. He is also a lecturer at the *École des Hautes Études en Sciences Sociales.* He is the author of numerous studies which appeared in such prestigious journals as the *Actes de la Recherche en Sciences Sociales.* He served for many years as a member of the editorial board of the *Révue Française de Sociologie.*

327

Otto Roboz, a resident of Washington, D.C., is a specialist in economics and finance. In Hungary, he served as Director of the Jewish Orphanage for Boys of Budapest. During the Holocaust year of 1944-45, he was instrumental in saving at the Orphanage hundreds of Jewish children and adults, acting in cooperation with the International Red Cross.

Denis Silagi is a historian and journalist associated with the Voice of America Bureau in Munich. He is the author of numerous works, including *Der geheime Mitarbeiterkreis Kaiser Leopolds II* (Munich, 1960), *Jakobiner in der Habsburger-Monarchie* (Vienna, 1962), *Ungarn: Geschichte und Gegenwart* (Hannover, 1962), and *Der grösste Ungar: Graf Stephan Széchenyi* (Vienna, 1967). He contributed a large number of articles to such prestigious journals as *Die psychoanalytische Bewegung* (Vienna), *Schola et Vita* (Milan), *Der Monat* (Berlin), *Südostforschungen* (Munich), and *Mitteilungen des österreichischen Staatsarchivs* (Vienna). He also collaborated on the *Biographisches Lexikon zur Geschichte Südosteuropas* (Munich, 1971-81) and on *Handbuch der Europäischen Geschichte,* Vol. VII (Stuttgart, 1979).

Péter Várdy is a Lecturer in Philosophy at the Technische Hogeschool Twente in Enschede, The Netherlands. His publications deal with social-philosophical issues, including those pertaining to Hungarian-Jewish reality and the philosophy of science. His most recent study on Hungarian Jewry appeared in *Zsidóság az 1945 utáni Magyarországon* (Jewry in the Post-1945 Hungary; Paris, 1984).